AFTER BLANCHOT
LITERATURE, CRITICISM, PHILOSOPHY

Edited by
Leslie Hill
Brian Nelson
Dimitris Vardoulakis

Newark: University of Delaware Press

Monash Romance Studies

General Editor: Brian Nelson

Monash Romance Studies is a series of refereed scholarly publications devoted to the study of any aspect of French, Italian and Spanish literature, language, culture and civilization. It will publish books and collections of essays on specific themes, and is open to scholars associated with academic institutions other than Monash.

Proposals for the series should be addressed to the general editor, from whom details of volumes previously published in the series are available:

Professor Brian Nelson
School of Languages, Cultures and Linguistics
Building 11
Monash University
Melbourne Vic. 3800
Australia.
Email: brian.nelson@arts.monash.edu.au

© Monash Romance Studies 2005

First American edition published 2005
Associated University Presses
2010 Eastpark Blvd
Cranbury, NJ 08512

ISBN   0 87413 946 5

Cataloguing-in-Publication Data is on file with the Library of Congress

Typeset in Ehrhardt.
Design and layout: Caren Florance,
          *Letter*PRESS Design+Layout, Canberra
          letpress@webone.com.au
          +61 2 6242 5948

AFTER BLANCHOT
LITERATURE, CRITICISM, PHILOSOPHY

TABLE OF CONTENTS

ABBREVIATIONS

A   *L'Amitié*. Paris: Gallimard, 1971.

Ab   *Aminadab*. Paris: Gallimard, 1942.

AC   *Après-coup, précédé par le ressassement éternel*. Paris: Minuit, 1983.

AO   *L'Attente l'oubli*. Paris: Gallimard, 1962.

AM   *L'Arrêt de mort*. Paris: Gallimard, 1948.

AMV *Au moment voulu*. Paris: Gallimard, 1951.

AwO *Awaiting Oblivion*. Trans. John Gregg. Lincoln: University of Nebraska Press, 1997.

BC   *The Book to Come*. Trans. Charlotte Mandell, Stanford, Stanford University Press, 2003.

BR   *The Blanchot Reader*. Ed. Michael Holland. Oxford: Blackwell, 1995.

CI   *La Communauté inavouable*. Paris: Minuit, 1983.

DH   *Le Dernier Homme*. Paris: Gallimard, 1957.

DS   *Death Sentence*. Trans. Lydia Davis. Barrytown, N.Y.: Station Hill, 1978. = *SHR*: 129–87.

ED   *L'Écriture du désastre*. Paris: Gallimard, 1980.

EI   *L'Entretien infini*. Paris: Gallimard, 1969.

EL   *L'Espace littéraire*. Paris: Gallimard, 1955.

F   *Friendship*. Trans. Elizabeth Rottenberg. Stanford: Stanford University Press, 1997.

FJ   *La Folie du jour*. Paris: Gallimard, 2002.

Fp   *Faux Pas*. Paris: Gallimard, 1943.

FP   *Faux Pas*. Trans. Charlotte Mandell. Stanford University Press: Stanford, 2001.

IC   *The Infinite Conversation*. Trans. Susan Hanson. Minneapolis: University of Minnesota Press, 1992.

ID   *The Instant of My Death / Demeure: Fiction and Testimony (Blanchot / Derrida)*. Trans. Elizabeth Rottenberg. Stanford: Stanford University Press, 2000.

LS   *Lautréamont et Sade*. Revised edition. Paris: Minuit, 1963.

LV   *Le Livre à venir*. Paris: Gallimard, 1959.

MD   *The Madness of the Day*. Trans. Lydia Davis. Barrytown, N.Y.: Station Hill, 1981. = *SHR*: 189–99.

MH   *The Most High*. Trans. Allan Stoekl. Lincoln: University of Nebraska Press, 1996.

PD   *Le Pas au-delà*. Paris: Gallimard, 1973.

PF   *La Part du feu*. Paris: Gallimard, 1949.

RE   *Le Ressassement éternel*. Paris: Minuit, 1951.

SHR *The Station Hill Blanchot Reader: Fiction and Literary Essays*. Ed. George Quasha. Barrytown, N.Y.: Station Hill, 1999.

SL   *The Space of Literature*. Trans. Ann Smock. Lincoln and London: University of Nebraska Press, 1982.

SNB *The Step Not Beyond*. Trans. Lycette Nelson. Albany. New York: SUNY, 1982.

TH   *Le Très-Haut*. Paris: Gallimard, 1948.

TO1 *Thomas l'obscur*. Paris: Gallimard, 1941 (first edition).

UC   *The Unavowable Community*. Trans. Pierre Joris. Barrytown, N.Y.: Station Hill, 1988.

VC   *Vicious Circles: Two Fictions and "After the Fact"*. Trans. Paul Auster. Barrytown, N.Y.: Station Hill, 1985. = *SHR*: 3–50, 487–95.

WD   *The Writing of the Disaster*. Trans. Ann Smock. Lincoln: University of Nebraska Press, 1986.

WF   *The Work of Fire*. Trans. Charlotte Mandell. Stanford: Stanford University Press, 1995.

WTC *When the Time Comes*. Trans. Lydia Davis. Barrytown, N.Y.: Station Hill, 1977. = *SHR*: 201–60.

AFTER BLANCHOT

Leslie Hill

THERE IS LITTLE DOUBT TODAY THAT MAURICE BLANCHOT (1907–2003) IS one of the most distinctive, significant, and profoundly influential voices in the whole twentieth century, a writer whose work breaks new ground in its account of the philosophical implications of the thing called literature (if it may be thought to exist at all), and provides powerful new insight into the demands, challenges, and future possibilities of literature and literary criticism. Blanchot's written output is itself imposing. It includes works of fiction, book reviews, literary and philosophical essays, and a host of circumstantial political interventions of different kinds. In the original French, Blanchot's complete works add up to more than three dozen volumes, each one of which provides compelling testimony to the breathtaking range, boldness, and untiring persistence of Blanchot's writing, its extraordinary sensitivity to singularity and nuance, and the depth and complexity of its engagement with some of the most pressing literary, philosophical, and ethico-political issues of recent times.[1] Over the last ten years, the vast majority of Blanchot's texts have become available in translation; and, as the essays in this volume show, it has now at last become possible for the wider English-speaking audience to explore Blanchot's thinking and writing at length and in detail.

It is sometimes said, with a mixture of irony and admiration, that the work of most major philosophers or thinkers can be summed up in one single central intuition, thought, or concept, with everything else being no more than the specification, elaboration, and refinement of that inaugural idea. So it is perhaps that one might read Heidegger exclusively in terms of the ontico-ontological difference, or Levinas with an emphasis placed solely on the transcendence of the Other; and so too one might begin to approach Blanchot. But there would be one crucial and essential difference, which is that Blanchot never has only one idea, but always two, and that these two are never reducible to attributes of the one. For if Blanchot is a thinker of extreme possibility, of the literary work as a reaching to the limit, an exhaustion of the possible, of totalisation, force, and decision, he is also, simultaneously, and with even greater intensity, the thinker of impossibility, of worklessness, radical weakness, undecidability, and otherness, of writing therefore as an ever futural response to what is unthinkable within the horizon of the present, the same, the familiar, the already known.

Whence one of Blanchot's most resonant watchwords, found in *The Infinite Conversation*, and informing his own work as a thinker, critic, writer of fiction, political commentator also, which speaks of the perpetually recurrent, twofold task of "naming the possible, responding to the impossible" (*IC* 48/*EI* 68). This commitment to doubleness on Blanchot's part, to that which is more than One, or otherwise than One, as each of the essays in this volume repeatedly demonstrates, does not however lead Blanchot in the direction of dialectical thought; but nor does it imply a simple repudiation of the dialectic, which, by a gesture of opposition, would merely confirm the original power of dialectical thought as a thought of original power. It takes Blanchot instead down the path towards a very different way of thinking, no longer dominated by the self-identical concept, but attentive to the fragile singularity that paradoxically precedes and outlasts the concept, and to the oscillating movement of a syntax of the always other word, of what, using a modest, retiring term, Blanchot in the late 1950s and early 1960s began to call the neuter, *le neutre*, and which opens in his work onto a thought of difference without identity, otherness without positionality, writing as both inscription and withdrawal, affirmation and suspension. In numerous different guises, and not always named as such, indeed always resisting what Derrida once referred to as the "as-such-ness" of the "as such," as Christophe Bident shows in his invaluable survey of some of Blanchot's conceptual vocabulary, the thought of the neuter runs through all of Blanchot's thinking – both as a possible concept and yet as a name for something other than a concept.

Blanchot's affirmation of abyssal ambiguity or duplicity, to that which is fundamental yet absolutely without foundation, finds one of its most insistent emblems in a thinking of death: of that dying which, on the one hand, is necessarily only ever mine, and is my ultimate possibility, dominating and enabling all the other forms of meaningful action or interaction in which I might engage in my lifetime – but which also, on the other hand, is never mine and cannot be experienced by me "as such," is impossible for me to accomplish as an act or action (since what disappears in dying is precisely agency itself), and is therefore unavailable to me, beyond my competence or power, even though it may constitute the limit of my existence and therefore determine my own possibility as the one who I am (or what I may think I am). In Blanchot (and this explains the writer's abiding interest in the Heidegger of *Being and Time* as well as his unyielding critical detachment from Heidegger, as several of the essays included here remind us) the awareness that death is the ultimate horizon, the possibility of my impossibility, as Heidegger famously puts it, is constantly doubled, ghosted, crossed, undermined, put into doubt by another, equally compelling realisation, which Blanchot shares with Emmanuel Levinas, which is that death is also the impossibility of that possibility. Impossibility, here, is not marginal contingency, a simple accident belonging on the fringes of worldly experience, but a trait that is constitutive of all thinking in general, at whose centre it persistently remains. From this insight, which, as Kevin Hart shows in a fascinating inquiry into Blanchot's understanding of the sacred, informs much of the writer's relationship not only to the philosophical tradition but also to theological debate and religious mysticism, there derive numerous other significant implications for the nature and reach of literature "as such" (if indeed the term may be retained) and the scope and limits of ontology, ethics, and politics, concerns that, in several different ways, as the contributions of Christopher Fynsk, Hector Kollias, and Alain Toumayan enable us to see more clearly, gave rise to a series of faithful, mutually admiring, yet never complacent, sometimes uncompromising exchanges with Levinas, whom Blanchot first met as a fellow student in Strasbourg in 1925 or 1926 and who remained a life-long friend and privileged interlocutor.

The breadth of Blanchot's achievement is also exceptional. First, he is the author of some of the most innovative, powerful, and challenging fictional texts of the twentieth century, which include not only three substantial novels, *Thomas the Obscure* (*Thomas l'obscur*, 1941), *Aminadab* (*Aminadab*, 1942), and *The Most High* (*Le Très-Haut*, 1948), but also a sequence of shorter first-person narratives, or *récits*, as they are more often known, notably *Death Sentence* (*L'Arrêt de mort*, 1948), *The Madness of the Day* (*La Folie du jour*, 1973, first published in 1949 as "Un récit," "A Story"), the much shortened, revised version of *Thomas the Obscure* (*Thomas l'obscur*, 1950), the two early stories brought together as *Le Ressassement éternel* (1951) and later republished with an important retrospective postface under the title *Vicious Circles, followed by "After the Fact"* (*Après coup, précédé par Le Ressassement éternel*, 1983), *When The Time Comes* (*Au moment voulu*, 1951), *The One Who Was Standing Apart From Me* (*Celui qui ne m'accompagnait pas*, 1953), and *The Last*

Man (*Le Dernier Homme*, 1957), not to mention a series of further, unclassifiable works, composed entirely of short fragmentary texts, which participate to some extent in the fictional mode, but only in so far as they problematise, outstrip, and transform it, and draw literary discourse towards something unprecedented, impossible to qualify, external to itself, and entirely distinctive: *Awaiting Oblivion* (*L'Attente L'Oubli*, 1962), *The Step Not Beyond* (*Le Pas au-delà*, 1973), and *The Writing of the Disaster* (*L'Écriture du désastre*, 1980).

At the same time, Blanchot's work as a literary critic, cultural commentator, and philosophical writer is scarcely less impressive, including as it does a further dozen books, such as *Faux Pas* (*Faux Pas*, 1943), *The Work of Fire* (*La Part du feu*, 1949), *Lautréamont and Sade* (*Lautréamont et Sade*, 1949, revised 1963), *The Space of Literature* (*L'Espace littéraire*, 1955), *The Book To Come* (*Le Livre à venir*, 1959), *The Infinite Conversation* (*L'Entretien infini*, 1969), *Friendship* (*L'Amitié*, 1971), and several others, the vast majority of which were based on the regular review articles and essays that, modestly at first, then with an ever increasing sense of purpose, Blanchot wrote from 1941 for a range of different newspapers or periodicals, of which the two most important were probably *Critique*, founded shortly after the war by Georges Bataille, to which between 1946 and 1952 Blanchot contributed a series of decisive articles (including, perhaps most famously, the essay "Literature and the Right to Death" that concludes *The Work of Fire* and is at the centre of discussion in several of the essays in this volume), and *La Nouvelle Revue française*, edited from 1953 till his death in 1968 by Jean Paulhan, in which Blanchot published the bulk of his literary critical work during what was to be a prodigiously prolific decade-and-a-half, ending in May 1968. And there were other newspapers and journals, too, both before and after, all offering Blanchot the possibility of making an incisive intervention into contemporary literary, philosophical, and political debates: the *Journal des débats*, *L'Arche*, *Les Temps modernes*, *La Quinzaine littéraire*, *Le Nouvel Observateur*, *L'Éphémère*, *Le Nouveau Commerce*, many others too.

Responding regularly to the journalistic demands of these periodicals, sometimes weekly, but more often on a month-by-month basis, and at times within constraints imposed by the editors with whom he worked or by the publishing cycle itself, Blanchot was nevertheless able, in his articles, not only decisively to transform contemporary understanding of such important literary figures as Sade, Hölderlin, Baudelaire, Mallarmé, Rilke, and Kafka, but also to set the agenda for reception of the work of several more recent contemporaries, many of whom – in no short measure as a result of Blanchot's own intervention – are now universally acknowledged as key reference points in the history of modern and contemporary writing, including such names as Bataille, Pierre Klossowski, Michel Leiris, René Char, Henri Michaux, Samuel Beckett, Marguerite Duras, Louis-René des Forêts, Paul Celan, others too numerous to mention. Michel Foucault was hardly exaggerating when he declared in 1967, as Christophe Bident recalls in this book, that "it was Blanchot who made all discourse upon literature possible," which is also no doubt why Blanchot was such a significant presence, too, for other leading figures in the recent history of literary criticism or theory, like Roland Barthes, as Bident himself goes on to show, or Paul De Man, as Hector Kollias suggests, both of whom were similarly employed, during the same period as Blanchot, in redefining the tasks facing literary criticism today.

Though the majority of Blanchot's essays are literary in focus, often using this or that recent publication as a springboard for further reflection or analysis, there is nothing narrow about this relative concentration on the literary. Literature, writing, for Blanchot, raise some of the most important and urgent questions for thought itself, and this is why, in writing about so-called literary texts and about the institution called literature, Blanchot was also powerfully engaged in a wide-ranging and probing intellectual debate with philosophy and philosophers, from Hegel to Kierkegaard, Nietzsche, Heidegger, Sartre, Levinas, Derrida, Nancy, and others. Yet while Blanchot in all his essays is always cogently mindful of the philosophical horizon of thought, he addresses philosophy from a singular, eccentric place, a place that is not properly within philosophy, nor indeed outside philosophy (since to claim to have done with philosophy, as Levinas was wont to argue, and Blanchot quick to agree, is all the more surely to remain enclosed within it), but which, like "literature" itself, is simultaneously internal and external to philosophy: internal in the sense that literature is after all philosophy's creation, but external in so far as what goes under the name of literature is nevertheless unnamable "as such," and silently resistant to philosophy's imperious pretence to tell the truth about "literature" – about that which, by never coinciding with itself, Blanchot argues, cannot be deemed either truthful or untruthful at all, since it is always something else, something other, something neuter, neither this thing nor that thing, nor even any thing at all, but only ever a disappearing trace, nomadic, disobedient, contestatory.

During his lifetime, Blanchot steadfastly refused to be photographed in public and to be exposed to media attention. But this did not mean Blanchot cast himself in the guise of the retiring aesthete. On the contrary, Blanchot began his writing career in 1932 as a journalist and political commentator for one of France's longest-established conservative evening newspapers, the *Journal des débats*, and soon advanced to the position of editor on the paper, a role in which he continued until the summer of 1940; while during the period from 1932 to 1937, some nine months before the Munich crisis that was to make war in Europe an inevitability, he contributed, more spasmodically, not to say ferociously, as the political climate steadily worsened, to a series of short-lived but often violently polemical revolutionary nationalist publications, engaged in what Blanchot himself, before the decade was out, was to acknowledge as a deeply flawed, unstable, ambiguous, and ultimately unsustainable politico-cultural project of radical national renewal. In subsequent years, indeed already during the bleak years of France's Occupation and at any event once war was over, though politics remained his passion, as Blanchot once put it, the ideological purpose, nature, and extent of his political involvements were markedly different.

Indeed, when in 1958 Blanchot returned to the political fray, after a period of withdrawal from day-to-day politics, he did so as a committed member of the non-communist, anti-militaristic, anti-colonialist, internationalist left, in the company of such new-found political friends as Dionys Mascolo, whose lengthy, anti-Stalinist treatise *Communism* (*Le Communisme*, 1953) Blanchot had warmly reviewed when it was first published (*F* 93–7/*A*109–14), and Robert Antelme, best known for his concentration camp memoir, *The Human Race* (*L'Espèce humaine*, 1947 and 1957), which had a profound influence on Blanchot's post-war thinking about politics and ethics, as Christopher Fynsk shows in a finely articulated reading of Blanchot's 1962 essay on Antelme from *The Infinite Conversation*. Alongside Mascolo and Antelme, and together with other political friends such as the writer Marguerite Duras and the novelist and poet Louis-René des Forêts, Blanchot played a not insignificant role in supporting resistance to Charles de Gaulle's return to power in 1958, in challenging the legitimacy of France's continuing colonial presence in Algeria in 1960 and 1961, and in the events of May '68 in Paris, with the writer playing a leading part in the discussions of the Writers-Students Action Committee (the *Comité d'action écrivains-étudiants*) that met throughout the summer of 1968 and sought to translate into words – many of which turned out to be Blanchot's – the surprising radicality of the social and political upheavals of that year. And though Blanchot withdrew once more from active politics after 1970, politics remained a compelling concern of his, and led for instance to the publication, some thirteen years later, of what has rightly been seen as Blanchot's political testament, *The Unavowable Community* (*La Communauté inavouable*, 1983).[2]

But though Blanchot in his writing is crucially aware of context and circumstance and deeply sensitive to the necessary differences between literary, critical, philosophical or political discourse, the fact remains that the various threads running through his work are not easily to be disentangled, for necessary rather than contingent reasons. Writing for Blanchot is profoundly disrespectful of all authority, all dogmatic, or pre-emptive distinctions between literature, politics, philosophy. "This is why," Blanchot explained in 1958, in an essay collected in *The Book to Come*, glossing a remark made by Dionys Mascolo, "speaking of politics, it is always of something else that the writer speaks: of ethics; speaking of ethics, it is ontology; of ontology, poetry; speaking finally of literature, 'his single passion,' it is to return to politics, 'his single passion'" (*BC* 248–9/*LV* 338). In this way, Blanchot's fictional works, for instance, though they address them in very different ways, cannot simply be divorced from his philosophical, literary critical, or political concerns. And these too impinge in important ways on his fiction. As Michael Holland argues in his detailed discussion of the shifting editorial frame within which Blanchot's two pre-war stories, "The Idyll" and "The Last Word," have been presented at different times, Blanchot's narratives not only contain a sustained reflection on the history and politics of the recent past, but also develop a complex critical relationship with a number of canonic literary works, ranging from the novels of Dostoevsky, for instance, as Holland points out, to the less well-known but also highly influential writings of the novelist Jean Paul, as Dimitris Vardoulakis shows in a suggestive and original exploration of Blanchot's relationship with German Romanticism. Robert Savage too, in his persuasive account of the relationship between Blanchot's *The Most-High*, Heidegger's essays on Hölderlin, with which Blanchot was deeply familiar, and Hölderlin's own translations from the Greek of Pindar, shows the extent of Blanchot's engagement with literary and philosophical issues, as does Chris Danta in a fascinating investigation of the treatment of the biblical story of Abraham in Kierkegaard, Kafka, and Blanchot.

Among these literary and philosophical contexts that extend the boundaries of Blanchot's fiction, undermining the simple opposition between the literary and critical, are not only the works of others, including such authors as Melville and James, Kafka and Broch, as Caroline Scheaffer-Jones demonstrates in a wide-ranging discussion of the artwork and worklessness in Blanchot's thinking, but classical myth too, particularly the story of Orpheus, which is an important crux for Blanchot's own writing, as several of the papers collected here indicate. Yet if Blanchot's work as a whole offers a sustained meditation on the Orpheus story, as Sheaffer-Jones goes on to argue, it is not because Blanchot wishes to resurrect myth as a model for the artwork as a form of resurrection, which is a dangerous, if seductive enterprise at the best of times. It is rather because the story of Orpheus itself secretly displays at its core a relation or non-relation to death or dying which is not a dialectical overcoming of death, but an affirmative exposure to the otherness of the other, to that which, as I suggest in my own chapter, necessarily resists all moral or moralistic evaluation grounded in dogmatic identification.

As is apparent from each of the essays collected, the contexts of Blanchot's writing are many and various. Just as Blanchot engages in detail with some of the most prominent thinkers and writers of the twentieth century, including Heidegger, Levinas, Sartre, Benjamin, Bataille, Foucault, and others, so his work resonates in different ways too with the work of other important and influential thinkers, such as Barthes, as Christophe Bident shows, or Deleuze, as Eleanor Kaufman goes on to suggest, adopting a rather different perspective, in her thought-provoking essay on Blanchot's "Midnight," or with other, sometimes lesser known authors in the English-speaking world, such as the Italian poet Giorgio Caproni, whose proximity to Blanchot is the subject of Paolo Bartoloni's perceptive exploration of the two writers' work. And it is important too not to neglect Blanchot's considerable significance as an inspiration for many contemporary practising artists, including not only writers and thinkers, but also, as Elizabeth Presa's remarkable contribution testifies, those active in the visual arts, in sculpture, film-making, theatre, dance, and so on. Here too there is impressive and enduring evidence of the influence of Blanchot's work.

But although Blanchot's significance as a writer and thinker is hard to underestimate, it is nevertheless only in relatively recent years that, thanks to the philosophical work of Jacques Derrida, Philippe Lacoue-Labarthe, and Jean-Luc Nancy, and to the remarkable biographical and bibliographical research of Christophe Bident, Michael Holland, and others, that Blanchot's work has become properly accessible in all its historical complexity, singularity, and urgency. The essays in this volume

– bringing together established critics of Blanchot's work and several younger researchers also, some of whom are approaching Blanchot for the first time – are themselves ample proof of the ever wider audience that Blanchot's writings have begun to find, not only in France, but also internationally, and the book as a whole represents an important new phase in critical reception of Blanchot's work. The idea of a collection of essays on Blanchot was forged at the conference "Blanchot, the Obscure" – indeed, some of the essays collected here were first delivered as papers at the conference, held on 19–20 August 2004 in Melbourne. This international conference on Blanchot's work was organized by the journal *Colloquy* under the auspices of the Centre for Comparative Literature and Cultural Studies, the School of Languages, Cultures and Linguistics,[3] and the School of Literary, Visual and Performance Studies at Monash University, and with the support of the Alliance française in Melbourne, and thanks are due not only to these bodies for supporting that original initiative, but also to the many individuals, in Melbourne or elsewhere, in August 2004 and since, who by their efforts have helped to make this volume of essays possible. For my part, I should like to take this opportunity to thank in particular my two co-editors, Brian Nelson and Dimitris Vardoulakis, for their dedication, their unflagging belief in this project, and their matchless efficiency.

Blanchot's virtually last book, *The Instant of My Death* (*L'Instant de ma mort*, 1994), which was to be followed only by slim volumes reprinting texts already published earlier, recalled one of the important turning points in Blanchot's life, his near execution by a firing squad in the tumultuous days immediately preceding France's Liberation in 1944. This foretaste, experience, or non-experience, or experience of non-experience of dying, with its echoes of both Orpheus and Dostoevsky, to mention no more than these, was evidently to mark Blanchot for the rest of his life, and his thinking of death as both possibility and impossibility no doubt owes much to what occurred (or failed to occur) in July 1944. It is now known, of course, that Blanchot was to survive this first confrontation with death for some sixty years more. But sadly, Blanchot died on 20 February 2003. To write about Blanchot's work today, then, and to write about the relationship between literature, criticism, and philosophy in Blanchot's work, is to have to do so after Blanchot. In some ways, perhaps, it was always thus, and Blanchot, more than most, was acutely aware of the extent to which no author can ever claim proprietorial control over his or her words; in that sense every writer, at the very instant he or she is writing, is always already dead, dying.

Nevertheless, 20 February 2003 definitively changed the literary, philosophical, critical, and intellectual landscape.

What, then, does it mean: to come after Blanchot?

Three things, at least. First, it is to recognise that it is no longer possible to continue to believe in an essentialist determination of literary discourse, or any theory of literature premised on an answer – no matter what kind – to the question: "what is literature?," or any account of aesthetic experience based on an encounter between subject and object, or any philosophy of the artwork founded on truth, irrespective of whether truth is defined as some kind of adequation between text and world, or as a more fundamental or originary alethic disclosure. All this has disappeared; and there is no way back.

There remains, secondly, the question of history. In purely chronological terms, we who read this volume, or who may have contributed to it, or not contributed to it, all come after Blanchot. So what is Blanchot's legacy, what is it that he bequeaths to us, his readers? As so often, Blanchot himself provided an answer in advance. Invited in 1975 to lend his support, in the form of unpublished or other material, to a special issue of the journal *Gramma* to be devoted to his work, Blanchot declined, courteously but firmly, explaining his reluctance to be seen to authorise that project, and thus limit its freedom and independence, with the following words: "My absence [i.e. from the issue]," he wrote, "is a necessary step rather than any decision on my part. I would like nobody to be surprised nor disappointed by it. Publishing is always more difficult. Publishing on the basis of my name [*éditer sur mon nom*] is impossible." Blanchot, then, steadfastly refused to endorse or underwrite the prestige or power associated with the name of the author. And in this exchange with Christian Limousin, he reminded his correspondent of the strange status of names in general. For any name, however irreplaceably singular it may be, is always already preceded, limited, challenged even, by the abiding anonymity of the person, animal, or thing it claims to name. Each and every name, in this sense, is necessarily always already impersonal, anonymous, other. Who, or what, is named by the name "Blanchot" cannot be decided in advance of reading, and reading itself can never be final or brought to any conclusion. It is endless, and always belongs to the future. Blanchot "after Blanchot," then, can best be understood literally, that is to say, in the sense of that which is "according to Blanchot," "d'après Blanchot," as one might say in French – and that which is "according to Blanchot," is nothing other than the infinite process of reading and rereading Blanchot: without end. This is one of the realisations that, each in his or her own way, all the contributors to this volume have had to confront. Indeed, while each of the papers presented here explicitly or implicitly pays tribute to Blanchot, without whom it would not exist, each one can but recognise that there is still no end in sight. Everything has yet to be done. A bewildering number of intertexts are still to be unearthed; the full import of Blanchot's intervention into philosophy is still to be measured; a way of addressing his fictional texts has still to be found; the history of Blanchot's political involvements still requires its theoretical articulation; and we still need to discover how to address the clarity and obscurity, the simplicity and transparency of Blanchot's infinitely variable prose; not to mention everything else…

Here, a third meaning to the phrase "after Blanchot" comes into view. For if we come after Blanchot, it is surely because Blanchot is still before us, still in front, still in the future, still to come. These were of course already the late Jacques Derrida's words in 1976, words he signed again in 1986, and signed for a third time in 2003: "If there were, which I do not believe, some pertinence in complimenting Blanchot for the fact, if it didn't amount to an abusive attribution of mastery, and if *The Step Not Beyond* didn't make the very metaphor itself obsolete in advance, I would say that never so much as today have I pictured him so far ahead of us. Waiting for us, still to come, still to be read and re-read by the very readers who have been doing so ever since they first learned to read and thanks to him."[4]

ENDNOTES

[1] For more details concerning Blanchot's extensive bibliography, English-speaking readers may consult the almost complete list of publications provided in my *Blanchot: Extreme Contemporary* (London: Routledge, 1997), 274–98. Readers of French also have access to the more extensive listing given by Christophe Bident in his biographical essay, which, it is hoped, will soon be available in English translation, *Maurice Blanchot: partenaire invisible* (Seyssel: Champ Vallon, 1998), 586–613. A further, more recent list of publications by Blanchot in French, which is constantly being updated, is available too on the Espace Blanchot website (www.blanchot.fr), where information relating to all aspects of Blanchot's work is also to be found. Plans for the publication of Blanchot's complete works in French, the need for which was powerfully articulated by Jacques Derrida in the closing session of the March 2003 Paris conference on Blanchot, organised by Christophe Bident and Pierre Vilar, are currently in limbo. Some time before his death, after several rounds of negotiation, Blanchot agreed with Christophe Bident upon a plan for an edition of his complete works. The edition was to comprise twelve volumes, beginning with the 1941 text

of *Thomas l'obscur* (which Blanchot was otherwise unwilling to see reprinted) and concluding with *L'Instant de ma mort*. Blanchot's desire was for the edition to be published by Gallimard in a format closely resembling that adopted for Georges Bataille's complete works with the same publisher; and there were to have been two general prefaces, by Jacques Derrida and by Louis-René des Forêts (both of whom have since died). The proposal was duly presented to Antoine Gallimard by Derrida and Monique Antelme, acting on Blanchot's behalf, in 2000. The publisher, however, was unwilling to proceed for editorial and commercial reasons, arguing that an edition of Blanchot's complete works was unnecessary, since many of the individual texts were still available in standard editions, and expressing the view that a complete edition of Blanchot's works would enjoy only very limited sales. Readers will make of these arguments what they will; at the time of writing there seems however little prospect of any change to the publisher's decision. (I am grateful to Christophe Bident for supplying this information.)

[2] For a fuller account of Blanchot's political and intellectual itinerary, see my *Blanchot: Extreme Contemporary*, 1–52.

[3] The proceedings of the conference have been published as a special edition of *Colloquy* journal, titled "Blanchot, the Obscure" and edited by Rhonda Khatab, Carlo Salzani, Sabina Sestigiani and Dimitris Vardoulakis. See *Colloquy: text theory critique*, 10 (November 2005), http://www.arts.monash.edu.au/others/colloquy/issue10/index.htm.

[4] Jacques Derrida, "Pas", *Gramma*, 3/4 (1976), 150; *Parages* (Paris: Galilée, 1986), 55; *Parages*, revised edition (Paris: Galilée, 2003), 51.

THE MOVEMENTS OF THE NEUTER

Christophe Bident
trans. *Michael FitzGerald and Leslie Hill*

NEITHER THE ONE NOR THE OTHER, NEITHER CLEAR NOR OBSCURE, THE neuter [*le neutre*] – from the Latin *ne-uter*, neither this nor that – is a crucial term in Blanchot's creative conceptual achievement. If the work of a philosopher, as Deleuze puts it, consists in creating concepts – true ones – then the neuter, along with two or three other words, such as friendship, disaster, community, might be enough to make it possible for us to treat Blanchot as a philosopher. At the same time, however, we should realise that Blanchot did not in truth define the neuter as a concept; it might therefore be asked, with some justification, whether 'the neuter' in Blanchot – to use Deleuze's useful distinction – is not more of a percept than a concept. For if the neuter is irreducible to the clear or the obscure, it is in the first instance because it is also irreducible to itself: broadly undefined, it does not present itself as a concept which is clear, or that clarifies, or that serves as a source of clarification, or one that is operative or operational; migrating restlessly from literature to philosophy, from philosophy to literature, it is ultimately perhaps neither a concept nor a percept: *neither* the one *nor* the other.

The *neuter*, of course, is not a word invented by Blanchot. It is one of those concepts that do not rely on an act of lexical creation, and yet whose articulation within language and discourse makes it possible to open new fields, new spaces, new horizons of thought. Even the substantivisation of the adjective, as found in Blanchot, is nothing new. The neuter is as old as the obscure, and Blanchot reminds us that "the choice of the singular neuter [*neutre*]" in the language of Heraclitus is one of the key factors contributing to that "enigmatic power which is its own" ("Heraclitus" [1960] *IC 86*). Yet perhaps it is only with Blanchot, at least within so-called Western culture, that the neuter becomes a concept. It was for a long time more a scientific function, or a grammatical or philosophical category. In mathematics, we speak of a "neutral element"; in chemistry, of a "neutral medium"; in physics of a "neutral body" or "particle"; while in biology an unsexed individual is termed "neuter." In grammar, we speak of the Latin neuter, or the Indo-European neuter – though the category is not universal across all languages, and is not present in the same manner in French and in English. The neuter can also be a philosophical category, especially in the moral and legal field, particularly in the area of international law; and undergoes numerous changes with the invention of phenomenology, whose many variations and transformations, from Hegel to Heidegger, from Levinas to Derrida, play a considerable role in the thought of Blanchot, as a kind of background against which the perceptual and conceptual creation of the neuter stands out.

We ought to situate the neuter in this way on at least three different planes: that of Blanchot's literary, critical and philosophical work, where the term emerges little by little; that of the history of grammar and philosophy, as well as semiology and psychoanalysis, where the emergence of Blanchot's neuter itself emerges amidst gains and losses, and much debate; and finally, on the level of aesthetics, for the neuter, in subterranean, or submerged ways, is arguably one of the major focal points of all twentieth-century art, in painting, dance, theatre, and mime (a few names will suffice: those of Kandinsky, Klee, Schlemmer, Wigman, Lecoq, Grotowski, or Decroux).

There is of course also a fourth plane, that of politics, which is not easy to grasp and which potentially, for mythological or ideological reasons, can give rise to serious misunderstanding. The neuter, in common parlance, may take on a moral and political meaning, and does so with pejorative connotations. "Neutral" is a word used for standing aside, remaining aloof and uninvolved, and keeping a distance, not through sagacity but lethargy – and one can see the effects of such a misunderstanding if we recall the hasty impatience of those readings, or non-readings, that have attacked Blanchot both for his changing political views and for his withdrawal from the gaze of the media. It therefore bears some repeating, I think, that Blanchot's neuter, like that of Barthes, is an active notion. We will need of course to specify how and why, in what specific ways, this particular use of the neuter breaks with the pejorative usage I have just evoked. But I would like to show that if the neuter is so clearly characteristic of the work of numerous artists and thinkers in the twentieth century, this was never in any moral or political sense, but rather, let's say, for historical reasons: for it seems to me that the neuter appeared, in each case, according to each of the perspectives I have mentioned, as the concept or percept most amenable to rethinking an emergence of being, of the body, or the face, within a space criss-crossed by negations imposed with a kind of totalitarian brutality with the express purpose of excluding any possibility of dialectical reversal. It is perhaps for this reason that I referred to an emergence, rather than, say, a blossoming of the neuter. And it is here, lastly, that a fifth plane may be distinguished, one which would envisage the positioning of the neuter in relation to nihilism and the negative.

The ground to be covered is nothing short of immense, and I shall limit myself here to tracing out the first of the planes I mentioned: the emergence of the neuter within the texts of Blanchot. At the same time, however, I will endeavour to put this particular line of inquiry into relation with the others, so as not to fall into the trap of simply providing a descriptive inventory.

We can approach this first set of concerns by following several genealogical, i.e. differential and genetic, threads, which, according to case and to particular texts, combine or prolong each other, intersect, cross, diverge, or weave together. I believe I can distinguish three such threads in the work of Blanchot.

First thread: the emergence of the neuter at the heart of the field of the obscure, the night, the "density of the void" and "murmur of the silence" that Emmanuel Levinas attributes to the *il y a*, the "there is."[1] This is a movement whose trajectory is clearly in evidence in Blanchot from the 1930s to the early 1940s, but which also extends throughout the rest of the writer's work. Blanchot's neuter can be attributed in part to a set of specific biographical, intellectual and historical circumstances: Blanchot's time as a student at the University of Strasbourg, his meeting with Levinas, his acquaintance with phenomenology, based on first-hand knowledge of the German texts, his reading of Sartre, and his friendship with Georges Bataille. The word neuter itself, however, does not occur often in Blanchot's political writings, though it is used there in extreme ways, reflecting various subtle and sometimes violent ideological shifts. Let me single out one particularly astonishing example, in a front-page article written by Blanchot for the *Journal des débats* in July 1932, on the relationship between writers and politics. Already in this piece, Blanchot is very close to rejecting a straightforwardly moral approach to the interest or disinterestedness of writers, in favour of a theory arguing for their active neutrality. Readers may remember the debate, which took place some fifteen years later, after the war, between Blanchot and Sartre about commitment – or the impossibility of commitment – in literature.

Let me quote the closing lines of Blanchot's 1932 article which run as follows:

> Those who defend the mind [*l'esprit*] by restoring principles, are on the side of those who defend the land in humble, everyday struggle. They make it possible to envisage a healthy politics. They are the ones who prepare us for action, in which they too can take part and become personally involved. They appear neutral [*neutres*]. But, as Vigny says in *Stello* and as M. Daniel Rops reminds us: "The neutrality of the solitary thinker is an armed neutrality, which, when needed, comes alive."[2]

But the principal traits of what later will become *the* neuter are only implicit here, or virtual, present only in the negative, like the memory of texts still to come. The word itself therefore does not appear as such, but Blanchot's texts contain several clues as to what is to come. Already, then, the literary trace of the word, present as an absence, in the *negative*, so to speak, is opposed to the *negative* usage of the word in contemporary journalism. Here, if we could, we might reinvent, on the evidence of much subsequent mutual commentary and quotation, those *imaginary dialogues* that surely took place at the time between Blanchot and Levinas, first in Strasbourg, when Levinas returned from the confrontation between Heidegger and Cassirer in Davos; and then in Paris, when Levinas published his "Reflections on the Philosophy of Hitlerism." A considerable part of Blanchot's work was sketched out and decided during these years as a result of the critical admiration, which he shared with his friend Levinas, for the philosophies of Husserl and Heidegger. What drew both thinkers into the field of phenomenology, and to its margins perhaps, was the description of such paradoxical manifestations of consciousness as sleep, dreams, insomnia: what Eugen Fink, Husserl's assistant at the time, describes as a kind of "non-knowledge of the being of a being [*non-savoir de l'être de l'étant*]."[3] It is worth noting the term "non-knowledge," for Fink's text dates from 1939, the year immediately preceding the meeting between Blanchot and Bataille, and we know how important the term "non-savoir" or *non-knowledge* was to be in the exchanges between Bataille and Blanchot, in much the same way that the *il y a* was in the dialogue between Blanchot and Levinas. In Bataille, Blanchot and Levinas, reflecting the deep affinity in thought between them (which it fell to Bataille to evoke, in a famous article of 1947–8 on existentialism), we can see at least three ways in which Heideggerian phenomenology begins to tremble.[4]

What, then, do the *il y a* and *non-knowledge* have in common, in their very indeterminacy? First, their verbal or grammatical impersonality, not to say neutrality; and, second, their atopia, in other words, their neutrality in terms of semiological category. It is not hard to understand, even in a rough-and-ready way, the fundamental role that these two notions, coined by his two older friends, might have played in the elaboration of Blanchot's neuter (and, though there is no place to do so here, we should also say something about Blanchot's evident fascination with Sartrean *nausea* during this same period).[5] Levinas and Bataille later in turn acknowledge Blanchot: the first, by conceding to the neuter the power to help uproot Heideggerian ontology;[6] and the second, by underlining the infinite movement to which the neuter condemns the formalisation of experience. The neuter, then, comes to be grasped in relation to the *il y a*, just as the *il y a* had been grasped in relation to Being; and equally in relation to *non-knowledge*, just as *non-knowledge* had been grasped in relation to knowledge. From this point on, are we still within the bounds of phenomenology? Can we still appeal to the interiority of experience? And are we still in a relation of subject to object, origin to finality? We are more nearly at the very limits of ontology and ethics, faith and atheism, confession and atheology, expression and intransitivity, philosophy and literature – where such notions tremble, are suspended, and deprive us of all property or propriety.

Let us move on quickly. Blanchot for his part never concedes to Levinas the movement of hypostasis which is meant to silence the *il y a*. As for Bataille, can we ever really be certain that Blanchot persuaded him that the experience of 'non-knowledge' might have the status of ethical and aesthetic authority? One might say that the neuter is a kind of non-hypostasised *il y a*, insofar as the *il y a*, according to Levinas, could be said not to lead to God, but "to the absence of God, the absence of any being."[7] It might be argued similarly that the neuter is the written form of *non-knowledge*, unreconciled in its very reconciliation, something which is emphasised by the experience described in Bataille's diary entry for 16 October 1939, which he presents, it may be noted, as not being written, but which he certainly describes in the singular and by recourse to the neuter: "I had to stop writing. I went to sit, as I often do, by the open window. No sooner was I seated than I fell into some kind of trance [*extase*]. This time, unlike the night before, when I was full of painful uncertainty, I was in no doubt that this kind of state is more intense than erotic pleasure. I can see nothing: *it* [*cela*] cannot be seen or felt. *It* [*cela*] that makes it dreary and burdensome not to die. [...] Only fright [*l'effroi*]

can totally measure *what's there [ce qui est là]*."[8] "*It*," "*what's there*," as
Bataille insists on each occasion by his use of italics, is also reminiscent
of "the NOTHING [*le RIEN*]," which he also sometimes writes in
capitals, introducing yet another variation on the neuter. I should also
recall here, albeit in passing, alongside this scene from Bataille, the
notorious and presumably autobiographical passage from *The Writing
of the Disaster*, that ecstatic moment through the broken window pane
experienced by the child of seven or eight: "*What happens then: the
sky, the* same *sky, suddenly open, absolutely black and absolutely empty,
revealing (as though the pane had broken) such an absence that all has since
always and forevermore been lost therein – so lost that therein is affirmed and
dissolved the vertiginous knowledge that nothing is what there is [que rien est
ce qu'il y a], and first of all nothing beyond*" (*WD* 72). I won't press the
point. But let me cite instead these words of Levinas, once more, on the
genealogy of the thought of the *il y a*: "My thinking on this point," says
Levinas, "has its origin in childhood memories. You sleep on your own,
the grown-ups get on with their lives, while the child is aware of the
'buzzing' silence of the bedroom.'"[9]

It is in the impersonality and atopia of the *non-knowledge* of the *il y a*,
if I may put it this way, that what later comes to be called and authorised
as the neuter begins to be experienced. And it is in the darkness of
the bedroom at night that, pending the emergence of the concept, the
percept is welcomed and unfolds, albeit a percept that is at the limit
of perception (remember Bataille's words: "*that* is neither visible nor
sensible"). In his first published piece of literary criticism, on *Ce qui
était perdu* by François Mauriac, Blanchot had taken an interest in "an
obscure presence": terrifying, impenetrable, ineffable, and unnamable.
"For each of the characters in the novel," he wrote, "amidst the shadows,
there is an obscure, concealed but perceptible presence, which gets in
everybody's way, one after the other. They do not all recognise this
ineffable power, and are unable to find a name for it, but we can hear the
terrible shock it inflicts on these mediocre or monstrous souls."[10] The
year is 1931; Blanchot was barely 24. The night-time struggle against
death of Irene, Mauriac's heroine, already anticipates the death throes
of Anne in *Thomas the Obscure*, that first novel which Blanchot started
writing the following year, in 1932, publishing a first version of it in 1941,
where the adjective neuter makes an early appearance. In the "dangerous
impasses" and metamorphoses of the advancing night, Thomas remains
the only one to be light, buoyant, pure, transparent, indifferent. "The
rays of life had never penetrated a more neutral [*neutre*], less vulnerable

body. Thomas walked alongside the dead, gazing at them with the indifference of a stretcher bearer in time of plague, and while the porous Anne, having failed in her own case to avoid death's contagion, was succumbing beneath the weight of passion, he was passing through the fervour of night unharmed and unaware" (*TO1 113*).

Another thread has therefore appeared, one which will continue to weave its way through many more of Blanchot's texts. Where it takes us is to the perceptual and conceptual elaboration of a poetics of the neuter. In a way, it is the same thread, tightened, strengthened, reinforced, and powerfully so, though for a long time it was to remain invisible. But in the course of 171 newspaper articles written between 1941 and 1944 it slowly became the *guiding thread* or editorial line of Blanchot's conception of fiction. It gave rise to what soon became one of the two most significant bodies of literary criticism in French in the twentieth century: the other, still finding its own voice at the time, listened closely and took note. But when in 1953 Roland Barthes published *Writing Degree Zero*, Blanchot's neutral writing occupied within it a place that was paradoxical in more ways than one.[11] The critical work of the author of *The Work of Fire* was cited and commented on twice, once in relation to its account of impersonality in Kafka's stories and the opposition between first person and third (37),[12] and then in response to Blanchot's texts on Mallarmé: "it is common knowledge," Barthes wrote, in parentheses, towards the end of his exposition, "how much this hypothesis of Mallarmé as a murderer of language owes to Maurice Blanchot" (76). But what is even more remarkable than this recognition of his debt to Blanchot is the way in which Barthes invokes the neuter only then to replace it with the image of the zero degree. In many ways, Barthes's zero degree is merely a linguistic variation on the neuter, as Barthes himself points out: "it is well known," he says, "how certain linguists presuppose the existence of a third term, called a neutral [*neutre*] term, or zero element, standing between the two terms of a polar opposition (such as singular and plural, the preterite and the present tense)" (76). But if ultimately, as far as the title of his book is concerned, Barthes opts for the scientific term (which played a key role in establishing Barthes's reputation), even while maintaining a clear preference within the body of his text for the word neuter or *neutre* (at least this is what the statistics suggest),[13] then this was because Barthes was able in that way to assert his own originality, his own commitment to an historical, ideological and semiological reading of literature, style and writing, influenced by Russian formalism and by Marxism. What Barthes saw in neutral writing was "the very movement of negation, and the inability of bringing it to a close within duration" (5). On each occasion, not only in Blanchot, but also in Jean Cayrol or Albert Camus, this failure of the negative — writing's burden — makes it possible for Barthes to position the writer as someone who turns his back both on the neo-classicist and bourgeois ideology of Literature (with a capital letter) and on its broad continuation in communist writing: "in this way," he says, "thought maintains its responsibility without being covered over by the subsidiary implication of its formal properties in a History that is not its own" (77). One can sense here how far a reading of this kind is indebted to the idea of committed non-commitment [*dégagement engagé*] with which, four years earlier, Blanchot had concluded *The Work of Fire*. But it would be too much to claim that Barthes was moving here towards a radical anti-Sartrean, pro-Blanchotian position. The reality is more complex. For if Barthes pays tribute to Blanchot, it was only, as we have seen, in relation to his critical works. When Barthes goes on to analyse "blank writing [*l'écriture blanche*]," "neutral writing," even "the degree zero of writing" in any detail (which he hardly does at all in reality), it is not to Blanchot or Cayrol that he turns, but Camus: the Camus of *The Outsider*. It is hard to imagine of course that Barthes had not read Blanchot's own article on *The Outsider*, collected in *Faux Pas*, together with the writer's other less well-known review of Cayrol's *Lazare parmi nous* in *L'Observateur* in 1950. But as far as the particular writing that provides him with the title of his book is concerned, but to which, oddly, he devotes only a few short pages, barely the length of a chapter in fact (entitled "Writing and Silence"), Barthes finally concludes that it ends in aporia: for while it may vanquish Literature, it ultimately reverts to a kind of neo-classicism, with "the writer, acquiring the status of a 'classic,' becoming a pale imitation of his own initial creation, with the result that society turns his writing into a mere mannerism and is thereby able to rid itself of him by imprisoning him within his own formal myths" (78). There is here, I think, a clue to Barthes's long-standing ambiguous attitude to Blanchot, which is made up both of fascination and of distance. I shall return to this, in much the same way that Barthes himself returns to address the neuter some twenty-four years later.

But let me come back to Blanchot, and to this second thread to which I have been referring: the perceptual and conceptual elaboration of a poetics of the neuter. There is another text which, though Barthes says nothing at all about it at the time (he was hardly alone in this), nevertheless perhaps made an impression on him. This is Blanchot's story *The Madness of the Day*, which first appeared in 1949 in the periodical *Empédocle* under the title "*Un récit[?]*," sometimes with and sometimes without the question mark, depending on the page. Blanchot's text, of course, might be thought to correspond rather well, even better at any event than *Thomas the Obscure*, to a notion of "blank [or white] writing." Black and white, obscure and blank, are strange words here, each of them being displaced into a form of alterity by which it is not so much commuted into its opposite, but rather effaced, taking on a neutrality that may be defined perhaps first of all as a poetics of space and colour.

Here we would have to – will have to – read or reread Kandinsky's or Klee's much earlier texts on colour, or even the beginnings of Jacques Lecoq's exploration, during the post-war years, of the white or neutral mask ("Movement work based on the neuter [*à partir du neutre*]," writes Lecoq, "provides a series of fulcrum points that will be essential for acting, which comes later").[14] I just want to suggest here, very much in passing, these convergent interests on the part of various contemporaries. If I am allowing myself this, it is also to get a sense of everything in Blanchot's *récits* and articles from the 1950s that was of such tremendous interest to a number of other creators of still embryonic percepts and concepts: I am referring to Derrida, Deleuze, Foucault, Beckett, René Char, Jacques Dupin, Marguerite Duras, Jean-Luc Godard, Claude Régy, and others. What artists and thinkers such as these each found in Blanchot's texts was a precise description and tireless articulation of the inner secrets of their own work. Blanchot's essays and *récits* in this context belong together. That is how the thread I was mentioning earlier gets stronger: it becomes double, and on each occasion can be read in relation either to literature or to criticism, in respect of the space of literature or art, or on the level of philosophy. Central to this whole very strange thread is the concept or percept of the neuter. In the *récits*, which slowly become stripped of proper names, Blanchot describes the nameless movement by which each singular ordeal is dissolved into an indefinite experience; while in the critical texts he attempts to isolate the share of the neuter particular to each singular creation, by way of a transformation of the direct discourse of the essayist into the free indirect discourse of the writer, in which what is said about the work belongs neither to the author nor to the critic, neither the one nor the other, nor even the work itself, but to every work, in a transformation marked by a fatal but unquestionably ethical delicacy in the sense that it preserves the essential movement of creation, which is neutral, therefore, since it is rooted neither in the one nor the other, even as each time it seeks a path, its own path, that is proper to it. The neuter might be said, therefore, to correspond somehow to a capacity to slip into the other's *impersonality*, or, alternatively, to reflect a desire to put to the test the paradox of one's *own* impersonality.

    A moment ago I wrote: the share of *the* neuter. Yes, because *the* neuter in Blanchot here becomes a noun, a substantive, albeit a substantive without substance, constantly transforming itself or being transformed, passing through – rather than closing off or giving rise to – a plurality of singular writings: the function of the first substantivisation of *the* neuter in a critical text by Blanchot is to mark a desubjectivation of novelistic narration of this kind (I am referring here to the uncollected article, "L'étrange et l'étranger", from October 1958).[15] Having made a notable appearance as an adjective in a crucial text, "The Essential Solitude," both the first chapter of *The Space of Literature* and the first essay published in the first issue of *La Nouvelle Nouvelle Revue française* in 1953, the year of publication of *Writing Degree Zero*; having also provided in that selfsame article the grammatical genre for such leitmotifs as the impersonal [*l'impersonnel*], the interminable [*l'interminable*] or the unceasing [*l'incessant*], and later the surviving [*le survivant*], the unworked [*le désœuvré*], the idle [*l'inoccupé*] and the inert [*l'inerte*]; having in addition infiltrated the heterological theory of the image presented in several separate texts, articles and *récits*, thereby reactivating, as Georges Didi-Huberman has recently argued, the trembling, the flickering, the potential dispersion, and the dissembling resemblance of each and every image, experienced in everything from the negative of a die or photo-negative to the positive of a cast or a print;[16] having, in all these ways, actualised its potency, the neuter now takes pride of place in Blanchot's critical masterpiece, *The Infinite Conversation*, with the word itself from now on sporting a capital letter, as Blanchot's major concept and contribution to thinking. All of which presupposes a radicalisation, not to say revolution, in discourse upon literature, and this is no doubt why Foucault was able to claim that "it was Blanchot who made all discourse upon literature possible."[17] For his part, Blanchot accepts that Freud, Sartre, and Heidegger had begun to effect that revolution or at least approach it. With those exceptions, "by an admittedly gross simplification, it might be possible to see in the entire history of philosophy the attempt either to acclimatise or to domesticate the neuter by putting in its place the law of the impersonal and the reign of the universal, or an effort to challenge it by asserting the ethical primacy of the Subject-Ego, the mystical aspiration to the singular Unique" ("René Char and the Thought of the Neutral" [1963] *IC 299, trans. modified*). And even in the case of Heidegger, Blanchot retorts, "aren't we dealing with a half-hearted excuse for the Neuter [*un Neutre un peu honteux*]?"[18] And if I might be allowed, for my part, in what is no doubt another gross simplification, to sum up in a word the many remarks that develop this observation and serve to enounce and denounce the reasons for which it is impossible to provide a strict definition of the neuter, replacing a comprehensive definition with an understanding of an area that is impossible to define, I would say, using a neo-Derridian neologism, that the neuter is the *absance of sense* [*l'absance du sens*]. This is how the neuter matters to sense, is decisive for it, refers it back to its essence and its origin, the conditions of both its validity and performance. The examples are familiar ones: psychoanalysis, which provides an exemplary model of the material actualisation of such *absance*; phenomenology, which has changed the course of philosophy, without however reaching the limit of its endeavours; lastly, and above all, literature. This is why the elaboration of a discourse on the neuter can only be in the form of a poetics; and also why the neuter is the strict complement of the negative in the on-going struggle against all forms of nihilism: according to the articulation that recurs in several texts on Bataille as well as several letters addressed to him, the negative names the possible, the neuter answers to the impossible. The one transforms values, the other suspends them, knowing full well that nihilism can also lurk beneath the affirmation of those very values to which it gives its power, and through which it ultimately produces sense. No ontological, ethical or linguistic discourse would be feasible without the *absance of sense* that the neuter manifests, and of which it is the sole manifestation. *Absance* is what Blanchot later begins to call *interruption*. If there is a historicity of the neuter, it can only be read by way of a poetics of interruption, the many different variations on which are to be found as much in psychoanalytic discourse (Freud) as in novelistic dialogue (Duras), theatrical aesthetics (Brecht), or poetic writing (Mallarmé).

The neuter, then, is irreducible to all forms of sublimation. What it does is to keep at bay the restless wanderings of the negative – those guilty, shameful, even voyeuristic effects Blanchot reads in Bataille, Kafka or Duras, or the murderous, nihilistic, or sadistic ones he recognises in Antelme's descriptions of the world of the camps. It shows that to escape destruction as well as guilt is on each occasion both a miracle and a necessity.

Faced with these wanderings of the negative, writing neither blackens nor whitens nor neutralises anything. It presents, articulates, stages. Most importantly (and I shall return to this) it does not *reveal*. It inquires into the conditions that make it possible. *How is literature possible?* This is the question which Blanchot endeavours to address from the early 1940s onwards, and which becomes all the more insistent, for reasons one can imagine, in the aftermath of war. At stake here was a call to the reader to take up a different position, an active, joyful one, as Roland Barthes describes it soon after the publication of *The Infinite Conversation*: in "writerly" [*scriptible*] texts the reader turns into a writer. The reader no longer receives passively, so to speak, a text addressed to him: he occupies the place of a third person, this third person that Blanchot, with the writer in mind, calls an invisible partner or *"partenaire invisible,"* using a reversible formula since this invisible partner or *"invisible partenaire,"* as Blanchot calls him elsewhere, in what is the *only* other occurrence of the expression in his work, also names the lack proper to all language, the appeal to a metalanguage that might supply the measure of all *absance*, that interruption which requires a third, rather than another, in order to manifest itself, between the "hole-word" [*"mot-trou"*] and the "word too many" [*"mot de trop"*], which is the neutral foundation of language held in common ("Wittgenstein's Problem" [1963] *IC* 460 n.).

What happens, then, when we come to read a text as a third person? It is this that continually fascinated Blanchot in the work of Marguerite Duras, in both *The Ravishing of Lol V. Stein*, to which the following passage refers, and *The Malady of Death*, for which it might equally have been written: "the need (the eternal human wish) to place in another's charge, to live once again in another, in a third person, this dual relationship, both fascinated and indifferent, and irreducible to all mediation, which should therefore be viewed as a neutral relation, even if it implies the infinite void of desire" ("The Narrative Voice" [1964] *IC* 462 n.). And it is this same third person, not without an element of voyeurism, that gives Blanchot's own narratives their particular orientation. Blanchot says as much in what was to remain for a long time his last, very last *récit*, "The Infinite Conversation," published under this title in *La Nouvelle Revue française*, and then, shorn of its title, at the beginning of the volume of essays which henceforth bore its name: "*They take their seats, separated by a table, turned not towards one another, but opening, around the table that separates them, an interval large enough for another person to consider himself as their true interlocutor, the one for whom they would speak if they addressed themselves to him*" (*IC* xiii–xiv).

To place the reader in the position of a third person, then: like a voyeur of the scenes of desire separating the narrator from Claudia and Judith, in *When the Time Comes*; like a voyeur or blind participant [*non-voyant*] in the ghostly scenes separating the writer from his partner, invisible but sensed behind the glass, in *The One Who Was Standing Apart From Me*; like a witness to the jealous scenes separating the narrator from a female friend and the person called, as the title puts it, *The Last Man*; like a witness, too, to the scenes of language which, between a man and a woman, mark the possibility or impossibility of speech, conversation, approach, address, attention, in *Awaiting Oblivion*. A neutral power traverses the physicality of these exchanges, in a process that is endlessly interrupted and endlessly recommenced: an intimate touch, or a touch at a distance, a movement of attraction, identification, courtesy, retreat without return, repulsion, hesitation, indecision, with incidental gestures, incisive, definitive, derisory ones, and suspect memories, insistent spectres, opaque transmissions, scratched transparencies, moments of pure astonishment, yawning gulfs, lethargy, and pursuit.

To place the reader in the position of a third, then; but, as we have said, as an active third, not called upon to fill out the story, but rather to measure the possible recognition of any story, through a poetics of ellipsis, interruption, fragmentation, uncertainty, paradox, incompletion, lack, interrupted development, disconnected continuity, infinite commentary, ghostly spacing, and silent oralisation. This is the narrative poetics that, in the end, it is urgent for us to read and, put simply, to take seriously. But this is of course an immense task, some of the implications of which I have tried to measure elsewhere, in another essay, on the basis of a modest reading of the opening sentence of *When the Time Comes*.

From among these many implications, let me just emphasise one: the historical impact of a poetics of the neuter. For how does a poetics of this sort acquire such extreme potency of sensible abstraction [*abstraction sensible*] by endeavouring to gauge what can happen, at the selfsame time, to the philosophy of history – or, at the very least, a philosophy concerned with history and held within its horizon?

In order to begin answering these questions, let me say that if Blanchot's fictional and theoretical work employs itself, time and time again, in crossing and recrossing this poetic line, it is because Blanchot was constantly in quest of the foundations of an ethics. He spent at least

thirty years thinking through the implications of this question. From
Faux Pas (1943) to *The Step Not Beyond* (1973), the poetics of the
neuter is directed towards the attempt to rediscover a just relationship
with the world. What first of all needed to happen was little short of a
veritable Copernican revolution: the move from a classical conception of
literature as *revelation* to a modern conception of writing as *contestation*;
this was what was at stake in the debate with Bataille. Next came the
distance necessary for an autobiographical account of the path travelled
by Blanchot, found in the opening pages of *The Step Not Beyond*, where,
several years after abandoning narrative writing except in the form of
fragments, the writer points to the political and philosophical meaning
of his writing experience. In both cases, the neuter puts to the test the
conception and even the possibility of the *récit*, that is, of an *order of
discourse*. It is this third thread, the ethical thread, that I would like to
pursue now. Let me call it: the infinite movement of the recognition of
the neuter.

We know, then, from the 1940s onwards, that literature reveals nothing.
Or that such is not its essence. If it thereby secures a "right to death,"
it is because death, while being unrevealable [*irrévélable*], is nevertheless
recuperable [*relevable*], if only to the extent that it ceaselessly contests
the homogeneous consistency of language. Everything in the end, from
personal experience to historical reality, both meditated on at length and
even in silence, confirms Blanchot in this belief. Let us not be taken in,
he seems to say to us. It is not the task of the story of death that is *The
Madness of the Day*, or the story of disaster that is Robert Antelme's
The Human Race [*L'Espèce humaine*], to *reveal* death or disaster.[19] But by
their unflinching and unwavering gaze – all the more so since everything
about the experiences they recount leads one to flinch and avert one's
gaze – through both resistance and good fortune, the story of death
and of disaster both call out, in the limpidity of their unfolding and the
obscurity of their reading, for a movement of recognition without end.

Literature can thus turn language into "matter without contour,
content without form, a capricious and impersonal force that says
nothing, reveals nothing, and contents itself with declaring – through
its refusal to say anything – that it comes from the night and will return
to the night" ("Literature and the Right to Death" [1947–48] *WF 330*).
This failing or lack is also therefore a contentment, a contentment of the
neuter, through which, between its coming from the night and its return
to the obscure, appearance [*l'apparition*] – refinding such mythic images
as those of Orpheus or Lazarus, only then to abandon them because they

restrict the movement of writing too much – appearance, then, offers its unstable passage to the infinite gesture of recognition [*reconnaissance*]. But the recognition of what, in this lack and this contentment of the neuter? How to avoid the risk of another myth, a second myth, the myth of a neuter freed from a whole metaphysics of truth and secrecy? How to work towards a recognition in which nothing is revealed?

These are the questions that Blanchot considers, it seems to me, in silence and obliquely, during the long years that were to lead him back to politics, following his meeting with Robert Antelme, and make possible his first proper and incisive comments on the camps, his 1962 article on *The Human Race*, collected in *The Infinite Conversation* under that very title (translated into English as "Humankind"). This is his response: "to be other [*autrui*] for oneself" ("Humankind" [1962] *IC 135)*. It is an ethical and aesthetic response, for his formulation describes equally both a general attitude and a poetics – that of Antelme – governing even the mode of expression of a deceptively simple and transparent narrative. Blanchot does not analyse this poetics in his article. But everything in it accords with his formulation. "To be other for oneself" designates all the more brutally the position of the third, since what was at issue, for each and every individual, during the years spent in the camp, was the necessity of having to disregard the other. Here then is a book, *The Human Race*, of which each reader realises, as he or she opens it, that it is written after the camps, but where the reading of each page manages to call this knowledge into question. Its whole expressive and poetic strategy forces the reader, through its imagination and artifice, to place the origin of speech in the camps. What is most strikingly in evidence is its neutralisation of discursive utterance, which systematically substitutes a "here" for the "there" of the camps, merging together both speech-act and referent, allowing the use of the deictic to put us at the heart of the world being described. It is ultimately this poetics of the neuter which Antelme sets out to Dionys Mascolo, in a letter written four or five years after his return from the camp: "Dionys, I should like to say to you that I don't think of friendship as a positive thing, I mean as a value; much more than this, I think of it as a state, an identification, therefore as a multiplication of death, a multiplication of questioning, the most miraculously neutral place from which to perceive and feel the constant of the unknown, the place where difference in its most acute form only lives – as one might say at the 'end of history' – and only reaches its full potential at the very heart of what is most contrary to it – the proximity of death."[20] Friendship, this ethics of the third person, this oblique address to a witness to the othering [*altruisation*] of the subject, is experienced only in this "most miraculously neutral place," in the "proximity of death" and the virtuality of the "end of history." And in the circumstances, what it makes possible, in the strange flatness of a writing that is by turns gentle and violent, linear and discontinuous, is the experience or ordeal of "an identification," "a multiplication of death, a multiplication of questioning." And this is indeed the direction in which Antelme's poetics takes us.

Numerous parallels could be drawn between the work of Antelme and that of Blanchot, which in purely quantitative terms are so very different. Antelme's growing influence on Blanchot in the immediate postwar period, and even more so after their meeting in 1958, is clearly apparent. What interests Blanchot is the ethical dimension of that poetics. There is little doubt that he drew deep sustenance from it, which is why, from the opposite perspective, we can understand Antelme's remark that, though he wrote no other book than the story of his experiences in the camp, he would only be able to write other narratives if they resembled Blanchot's *récits*.[21] Let me briefly take another example, that of *Awaiting Oblivion*, published the same year as the article on *The Human Race*. This text pushes back ever further the limits of Blanchot's paring down of narrative – while showing the richness of this reduction. Writing plays at revealing nothing, turns incessantly around its secret, this obscure object of all narration, present here as a point of suffering or enjoyment; it dislocates origins, voices, orders of utterance – and, therefore, disorients space-time. This is neutral writing, then, passing between two people, a man and a woman, and a writing whose movements are withdrawn in its infinitely attentive approach and resonate in a paradoxical excess of indiscretion with regard to the most intimate exhaustion of the other; a writing whose movements circle without interruption, or by dint of numerous interruptions, multiplying many different angles and returning to them; a writing whose movements circle around origins, tremors, the conditions of speech, speech which only ever refers back to other forms of speaking, endlessly evoking in that way the recognition of its possibility, the possibility of its recognition. Might such a writing have been possible without the poetics of Antelme? For it is a poetics for which Levinas, without realising it, supplies one of his most potent formulas when he speaks of the task of philosophy as being "indiscretion with respect to the unspeakable [*l'indicible*]."[22]

In this way, then, at the beginning of *The Step Not Beyond*, where the shifts between different forms of language, the complexity of their arrangement and distribution, without it being clear where their origin lies, or for whom they are intended, reach a point of greatest intensity, Blanchot is able to recognise how far his "initial words written facing the sky" manifested a "power of uprooting, of destruction or change," "a possibility of radical transformation . . . even for a single individual – the possibility, that is, of his or her abolition as a personal existence." Blanchot is alluding here of course to the opening sentence of *Thomas the Obscure*: "Thomas sat down and looked at the sea," from which, significantly, he extracts only the first and last words, and commutes the former into a neutral pronoun: "*il – la mer*," he writes, marks, and eliminates. By that token, the relationship to being is what changes: "To write as the question of writing, a question that bears the writing that bears the question, no longer allows you this relation to being – understood primarily as tradition, order, certainty, truth, all forms of rootedness – that one day was given to you from the past of the world, like a dominion you were expected to run in order to strengthen your 'Ego,' albeit this was as if split in two, from that day when the sky opened upon its emptiness" (*SNB 1–2*). A return to the *il y a*, the *there is*, a demarcation of writing, the recognition of a new birth, through writing, *against* an ethical and political order of which it may be noted that, by way of a subtle shift in the listing, from "tradition" and "order" to "any form of rootedness," it may be taken to refer not only to all nationalistic philosophy as such, but more particularly to the philosophy of Heidegger.

So far, then, pursuing three separate but interwoven threads, I have sought to articulate the process by which Maurice Blanchot was able to distinguish and name the neuter, to write, extract, ex-scribe, and recognise it. It was this recognition that in its turn earned its author the recognition of other thinkers and other writers. In order to say more it would be necessary, for instance, to explore in some detail the relation between the neuter and the outside in, say, Foucault's "Thought of the Outside" in 1966, or between the neuter and force in Derrida's early texts, or between the neuter and exteriority in the work of Jean-Luc Nancy. Let me conclude here, however, by returning to another moment of recognition. For some four years after the publication of *The Step Not Beyond*, Roland Barthes gave a series of lectures, at the Collège de France, on the neuter. His main concern, as in the case of Blanchot, during the 1970s and towards the end of his work, was to survey, reconnoitre, recognise the neuter. This also implied a recognition of Blanchot, and of Blanchot's own texts on the neuter, which are cited at length as a source authority, and therefore a recognition of everything in Blanchot that Barthes himself, at the time of *Writing Degree Zero*, had failed to read.

Let me remind you of that early argument. Despite his admiration, Barthes came to the conclusion that neutral writing represented a form of aporia. The neuter, we may remember, was identified by Barthes with the zero degree. Yet the 1978 lecture series distinguishes between at least two different usages of the neuter: one, which is both political and grammatical, is linked to the zero degree, to the evasive rhetoric of the neither-nor, exemption, and annulment; and another, which is also political and grammatical, associated with the heteroclite (literally "that which tips from one side to the other"), the irregular, the unforeseeable, all that is disruptive.[23] In this way, the neuter has the capacity to throw into turmoil any principle of representation and systematisation. It is defined from the outset as that which unsettles and unbalances each and every paradigm. The political, historical, ethical, aesthetic implications of this are vast, and constantly intervene within the lecture course, which may be read as a kind of neutralisation machine, an active neutralisation serving to neutralise that reactive neutralisation carried out by all forms of power, whether belonging to "politics," the media, or ideology, what Barthes more generally calls the "ideosphere." Here, the meaning of Barthes's return to Blanchot – and recourse to Blanchot – can be readily understood, particularly when Barthes quotes as follows from *The Infinite Conversation*: "The exigency of the neuter [Blanchot writes] tends to suspend the attributive structure of language, this relation to being, whether implicit or explicit, which, in our language, is immediately posited once something is said."[24] This necessity for an ontological critique, which reaches the perception of the *absance of meaning*, which Barthes for his part calls "the exemption of meaning [*l'exemption de sens*]," radicalises "the exigency of the neuter" (in Blanchot's terms), the "desire for the neuter" (as Barthes puts it), and appeals to the one thing that might bear this exigency and answer this desire: which is writing. Some pages later, Barthes puts it thus: "Writing is precisely that discourse which decisively thwarts the arrogance of discourse." And he adds: "I do not have (or do not yet have) the conceptual means to theorise this position (which would presuppose a 'what is writing?')."[25] We should remember too that *Writing Degree Zero* presented itself, in the closing words of the introduction, as "an introduction to what could be called a History of Writing." We have thus moved from historical inquiry to ontological inquiry; from prolegomenon to critique, even deconstruction; from a reservation about neutral writing to the certainty of the neutral power of writing. For Blanchot, the work puts itself to one side of the madness of the day, plunges into the heart of the night and writes itself in this neutral time of insomnia, the other night; while for Barthes, it extends and maintains the infinitesimal and precious time through which we pass from the oblivion of sleep to the cares of the day, these few seconds which, reutilizing the same two adjectives, he names "blank, neutral waking," "a sort of groping between the body which is undying (or close to death) and that which is full of care."[26] Writing, Barthes suggests, is the active side of this exemption, suspension, and interruption of language, which it alone can manifest, better still than silence, which always risks entering into coalescence with a fresh paradigm. But this remains a suggestion. For is it indeed possible to theorize this activity of exemption? Is it possible to join together or conjoin these two *effects* of the neuter: activity and exemption? Barthes had been dubious to begin with, but from now on, modestly, he declares himself not to have the right "conceptual means" at his disposal. But is this really what is at issue here? Blanchot himself multiplies various propositions on the neuter without ever unifying, synthesising, or homogenising them. In both writers, then, the neuter is incapable of acceding to the status of a theoretical object. The one and the other alike evaluated it and above all practised it bodily and stylistically. In the case of Barthes, by way of a mastery of language that had nothing dogmatic about it, it was in the form of a reading of a heteroclite text in random sequence. In Blanchot, in the frantic persistence of a desire to write which in ever more complex forms questioned its own possibilities of manifestation. The neuter thus retains its questioning force. It opposes the forces of neutralisation imposed upon the body and speech by all agencies of power. It unravels all prevailing protocols of recognition. It questions the limitless desire, everywhere dominant today, to trace limits and establish identities and communities. It is easy to understand, therefore, what it is that prompted Jean-Luc Nancy to take up this question of the exemption of sense, under that very title, in a paper given at the Centre Roland-Barthes in Paris in 2002.[27] Faced with the vacancy of sense that characterises our epoch, and against the peremption of sense that nihilism, in its very haste, would like to settle once and for all, against the obligation of sense to which reactionary humanism, just as hastily, wishes to return, "an exemption of sense," writes Nancy, "designates a wanting to say [*un vouloir-dire*] in which the wanting merges with the saying and renounces wanting, with the result that sense absents itself [*le sens s'absente*] and makes sense beyond sense [*fait sens au-delà du sens*]. . . . Instead of rounding off its meaning [*signification*], it reiterates its own signifying [*signifiance*], which is where it finds pleasure [*jouissance*], pleasure whose sense [*sens*] becomes a 'vanishing point.'" "The goal," he adds, "if goal there is, is not to have done with sense. It is not even to agree with one another: it is to speak anew."[28]

Faced, then, with the vacancy of sense, against the peremption of sense, against the obligation of sense, Blanchot too gave himself over to the language of the neuter, along with numerous others thinkers, creators of percepts or concepts, who recognised themselves in it.

ENDNOTES

These "movements of the neuter" are taken from what is still for me work in progress and likely to remain so for several years to come. I should like to thank Brian Nelson, Kate Rigby, Dimitris Vardoulakis, and all the members of the editorial collective of Colloquy, for their kind invitation to allow me to begin airing these efforts publicly. I am also indebted, in particular, to Michael FitzGerald and Leslie Hill for translating these pages.

[1] Emmanuel Levinas, *Existence and Existents*, trans. A. Lingis (The Hague: Martinus Nijhoff, 1978), and in particular, for the passages indicated, 63–4.

[2] Maurice Blanchot, "Les Écrivains et la politique", *Journal des débats* (27 July 1932), 1.

[3] Eugen Fink, "Le Problème de la phénoménologie d'Edmond Husserl" [1939], in *De la phénoménologie* (Paris: Minuit, 1974), 203.

[4] "The thought of Levinas is no different, it seems to me, from that of Blanchot's and my own." Georges Bataille, "De l'existentialisme au primat de l'économie" [1947], *Œuvres complètes* (Paris: Gallimard, 1988), 11: 293 note. It is worth mentioning here what Blanchot wrote after Bataille's death, but which can be extended, I think, to include Levinas: "What therefore characterises this kind of dialogue is that it is not simply an exchange of words between two Selves [*deux Moi*], two humans existing in the first person, but that the Other [*l'Autre*] speaks there in the presence of speech which is his sole presence, a neutral speech that is infinite and without power, in which what is at stake is the unlimited of thought, in the safekeeping of forgetting" ("The Play of Thought" [1963] *IC* 216, trans. modified). Perhaps each of these dialogues would require a third member, both excluded and included.

[5] "Nausea is the distressing experience that reveals to him what it is to exist without being [*exister sans être*], the pathetic illumination which puts him in contact, in the midst of things that exist, not with those things, but their existence." It is

noticeable that Blanchot here is reading Sartre's experience in the singular neuter ("L'Ébauche d'un roman", *Aux écoutes*, 1054 [30 July 1938], 31/ "The Beginnings of a Novel", *BR* 34).

⁶ See in particular Levinas, "The Poet's Vision" [1956], *Proper Names*, trans. Michael B. Smith (Stanford: Stanford University Press, 1996).

⁷ Levinas, *Existence and Existents*, 61.

⁸ Bataille, *Guilty*, trans. Bruce Boone (Venice, San Francisco: The Lapis Press, 1988), 32; trans. modified. This earlier passage, dated 21 September 1939, is also worth citing: "In acute serenity, facing the dark starry sky, opposite the hill and dark trees, I rediscovered what makes my heart like a banked fire, covered in ash, but incandescent within: a feeling of a presence irreducible to any notion whatsoever, like the kind of earth-shattering silence that comes with ecstatic experience [*l'extase*]. I become a vast flight from myself, as if my life were ebbing away in slow rivers through the inky darkness of the night sky. At such times I am no longer myself, but what emerges from me reaches and encloses in its embrace a boundless presence, like a kind of loss of myself: and which is no longer *either myself or anyone else* but a prolonged kiss, in which we can no longer tell our lips apart, is bound up with this ecstasy, and is as obscure and as familiar to the universe as the movement of the earth across the ruined sky" (*Guilty*, 18; trans. modified, emphasis mine).

⁹ Levinas, *Ethics and Infinity* [1982], trans. R. Cohen (Pittsburgh: Duquesne University Press, 1985), 48.

¹⁰ Blanchot, "François Mauriac et ceux qui étaient perdus", *La Revue française*, 26 (28 June 1931), 611.

¹¹ Roland Barthes, *Writing Degree Zero* [1953], trans. A. Lavers and C. Smith (New York: Hill and Wang, 1977). The pagination for citations of *Degree Zero* will appear in the body of the text.

¹² The contrast is equally crucial in Deleuze, for instance, who writes that "literature begins only when a third person is born in us that strips us of the power to say 'I' (Blanchot's 'neuter')." Gilles Deleuze, *Essays Critical and Clinical*, trans. Daniel W. Smith and Michael A. Greco (London: Verso, 1998), 3.

¹³ In those passages dealing with contemporary writing, that is, Camus or Blanchot, I count ten occurrences of the word "*neutre*," as against four for the expression "zero degree." This explains the oddity of the initial reference (in the introduction) to "those neutral writings, described here as 'the zero degree of writing'" (5), since more often than not Barthes uses the same words.

¹⁴ Jacques Lecoq, *The Moving Body*, trans. David Bradby (London: Methuen, 2000), 38; trans. slightly modified.

¹⁵ "The time of the stranger is the reign of the *neutre*. We can see here why the novel no longer likes people who say 'I,' or plots that can be retold. It is because the novel belongs to the stranger" ("L'étrange et l'étranger", *Nouvelle Revue française*, 70 [October 1958], 682). We should also add that this first substantivisation is indebted to Levinas since, in the body of the article, it immediately follows a

footnote referring to an article by Levinas, published the previous year, analysing Heideggerian ontology in terms of the Neuter (681). But it also no doubt owes something to Barthes, since this first substantivisation, which takes up the terms of the discussion in "The Essential Solitude," is also accompanied by a note referring to a number of recent studies of the French *nouveau roman* in the journal *Arguments*, including a text by Barthes.

[16] Georges Didi-Huberman, "De ressemblance à ressemblance," in *Maurice Blanchot: récits critiques*, ed. Christophe Bident and Pierre Vilar (Tours: Farrago, 2003), 143–67.

[17] Michel Foucault, "On the Ways of Writing History," [1967] *Essential Works* (Harmondsworth: Penguin, 2000), 2: 287.

[18] Blanchot, "L'étrange et l'étranger", 681 n.

[19] Robert Antelme, *The Human Race*, trans. Jeffery Haight and Annie Mahler (Marlboro, VT: The Marlboro Press, 1992).

[20] Robert Antelme, letter dated 1949 or 1950, cited by Dionys Mascolo in *Autour d'un effort de mémoire* (Paris: Maurice Nadeau, 1987), 23–4.

[21] Antelme's remark is quoted by Dionys Mascolo in an interview: "If I wrote something," Antelme is reported as saying, "it could only be something which resembled the *récits* of Maurice Blanchot." See Dionys Mascolo, interview by Aliette Armel, *Le Magazine littéraire*, 278 (June 1990), 38.

[22] Levinas cited by Blanchot in *WD* 114.

[23] Roland Barthes, *Le Neutre: cours au Collège de France (1977–78)* (Paris: Seuil/ IMEC, 2002), 170–1.

[24] Barthes, *Le Neutre*, 76; *IC* 386.

[25] Barthes, *Le Neutre*, 206.

[26] Barthes, *Le Neutre*, 67.

[27] See Jean-Luc Nancy, *La Déclosion: déconstruction du christianisme I* (Paris: Galilée, 2005), 179–88.

[28] Nancy, *La Déclosion*, 186–7.

"THE PROFOUND *RESERVE*"

Kevin Hart

[1]

I TAKE MY TITLE FROM THE CONCLUDING PAGES OF MAURICE BLANCHOT'S "Les Caractères de l'œuvre d'art," the penultimate chapter of *L'Espace littéraire*. The expression occurs in one of those moments that Blanchot's readers – even many of those who admire him unreservedly – seem not to notice, times when he indicates the irreducible connection between art and the sacred. "Why is art so intimately allied with the sacred?," he asks (*SL* 233/*EL* 310). He begins his answer by translating "art" and "the sacred" into more general terms, as "that which shows itself and that which does not," and then posits a relation between them. Taken together, art and the sacred constitute, "the movement whereby disclosure and dissimulation change places without ceasing, appealing and reaching to each other where, nevertheless, they are realized only as the approach of the unreachable" (*SL* 233/*EL* 310–1). Here art is leagued with phenomena while the sacred is defined as that which resists being given as phenomenon, and then a relation is indicated that prevents us distinguishing between them with any assurance. Art and the sacred are "realized only as the approach of the unreachable," a proposition that denies any final concreteness to either art or the sacred and that alerts us to a relation, in which both subsist, that withholds itself from experience. It is in this strange movement that offers itself only in withdrawal, in the experience of non-experience, that art and the sacred find, Blanchot says, "the profound *reserve*" which the work of art needs (*SL* 233/*EL* 311).

That Blanchot does not believe in God is evident to even the most cursory reader of his works, and that he endorses a non-theological future and embraces "the renunciation of mystery, the ultimate insignificance of lightness" is well known.[1] If he is drawn to the writings of certain mystics, chiefly Meister Eckhart and St John of the Cross, it is because they anticipate the more severe rigors of inner experience, a ravaging of the self that erodes any confidence in deity or unity that a Christian might have. So it is quite unexpected to find Blanchot openly wondering what will become of art when everyone comes to agree with him that God is dead or, in the language of Hölderlin that he prefers, that the gods have departed. When there is a consensus that we are indeed without a deity, art will lose "the sense of what made it speak" and, far worse, "the intimacy of its reserve" will vanish (*SL* 233/*EL* 311). Neither can be replaced by an appeal to nature or what remains to be discovered in the world about us. Modernity has foreclosed on those alternatives, he thinks, and now we no longer even regret the passing of the divine. Yet, without the sacred, art will have no reserves on which to draw, and so what will become of it? The question is addressed in the final chapter of *L'Espace littéraire*, "L'Expérience originelle."

At first Blanchot puts a brave face on the apparent loss of the divine and its consequences for literature. "The time of art is the time before time," he observes, and adds: "The collective presence of the divine evokes this time by hiding it" (*SL* 246/*EL* 331). It is in our anguish over the uselessness of art, so evident now that it has no connection with God or the gods, that we realize how successfully the divine has concealed art. Yet the punctuality of this recognition is hollowed out by Blanchot's insistence that the poet's distress at the loss of the divine is lived "at every time" (*SL* 247/*EL* 332). The true poet, it would seem, is alerted to the absence of the divine by the act of writing itself: a claim that would have surprised Dante and Hopkins, among many other poets both earlier and later. Blanchot allows himself an opportunity partly to recover from their startled looks, however, for he consigns the divine, though not the sacred, to oblivion. The latter category, it seems, can be freed from the former. Indeed, no sooner has Blanchot released the time of art from the instant of creation than he begins to talk of the poet's "sacrifice" (*SL* 247/*EL* 332). As if that were not enough, he goes on to evoke in a phrase that might seem to come straight from the *Beiträge* that the poet's task is to maintain a space between "the gods who are no longer and who are not yet" (*SL* 247/*EL* 332–3).[2] It is a double absence that impinges on the writer, though not one from which the sacred has been calmly erased. Whether this "and" binds together the two absences, and bears testimony to the sacred light that emerges before the dawn, is a question "reserved in the work" and is said to be "prophetic" (*SL* 247/*EL* 333).

We do not usually consider a question to be prophetic, yet since for Blanchot prophetic speech bespeaks an endless wandering, it makes perfectly good sense in the context. A question does not conclude anything, and for Blanchot this particular question is entirely open and therefore unsettling. How could it be answered? To assign the conjunction "and" the role of binding the two absences would be to set the poet in the dimension of religion minimally understood as *re-ligare*, a tying together again. It would be a bare religion with no consolation coming from the past and only the slightest hope flowing from the future.[3] Attentive to the traces of the gods to come, the poet could speak only in the moment of losing the power to say "I" and becoming "no one." To write would be to sacrifice the self, and the poem would declare, "nothing has meaning yet" (*SL* 247n./*EL* 332n.). Such would be the scenario were the question to be answered positively. If answered in the negative, however, the poem would fail to hold open a space in which any gods could abide, now or at any time. The poem would bear witness to a perpetual interruption from the time before creation, an *"other* time" characterized by a ceaseless repetition of empty images ("Prophetic Speech" *BC* 81/*LV* 112). Yet, once again, the poet's individuality would be sacrificed in the act of composition, and the poem would be "sacred speech," a discourse presented without warrant for either its existence or meaning and that testifies to "the insecurity and grief of that which escapes every grasp and all ends" (*SL* 247n./*EL* 332n.). My sense is that for Blanchot the question is unable to be resolved in either direction; it marks a risk to be taken, not a possibility to be weighed. And even were it to be answered resolutely in the negative it would not thereby eliminate the words "sacrifice" and "sacred," for the poet sacrifices himself and his language and thereby generates an effect of the sacred. Perhaps the "profound *reserve*" is inexhaustible. Perhaps the very act of writing poetry generates the sense of the sacred that art needs, and does so, with varying confessional commitments, including atheism, in each and every age. Perhaps the absence of the gods cannot be fully regulated by art, not even by the art that seems to have disappeared wholly into a poem.

To read the concluding pages of *L'Espace littéraire* is to find oneself in a world at once timeless and historical, a world shared by Heraclitus and Heidegger, Hölderlin and Char, yet shaped for us, here and now, by the pain of living without the gods. *L'Espace littéraire* does not end with the meditation on the poet's "and," however. In fact, it can hardly be said to end at all: it finishes with four appendices, none of which is hardly less lyrical or critically astute than the chapters that precede it, one of them, "Les Deux Versions de l'imaginaire," being one of Blanchot's most disquieting essays. I want to suggest that this meditation on the imaginary opens onto a quite different world than the one in which most readers of *L'Espace littéraire* expect to find themselves, a distant world that seems to us to be defined by a response to the question of art and the sacred. I regard this lost world as a "profound *reserve*" of another sort entirely, yet it too is best approached by way of the image.

[2]

Among neoclassical critics and their heirs, the image abides in its distance from what is represented, and this distance is essential for recovering the meaning and truth of what it represents. We have seen that, for Blanchot, divinity conceals the time that is proper to art. In the same manner, a neoclassical understanding of the image occludes a fundamental relation, which he calls resemblance. He insists, on good phenomenological grounds, that an event or a thing resembles itself, by which he means that no sooner does a phenomenon give itself to experience than it is doubled, becoming both itself and its image.[4] This relation of resemblance cannot be grasped because it has always and already occurred, and, in consequence, it cannot reassure us with a meaning and a truth as the neoclassical notion of the image does. Not at all: resemblance undoes any sense that reality and representation name distinct orders of being because it indicates that the imaginary is within what is. What was thought to be a relation between identifiable items turns out to be a relation within being itself.

On this account, the image is ontologically troubling, to be sure, yet there is more to worry us than the fact that "the image [is] capable of negotiating nothingness," for there is also the eerie thought that it elicits "the gaze of nothingness upon us" ("The Museum, Art and Time" *F* 40/ *A* 50–1). To be transfixed by this dark gaze is to have entered the state of fascination, and to remain there would be to pass from "I" to "no one," from negativity to the neutral. It would be to lose one's grip on reality, to slip from a world of meaning to a non-world of non-meaning. All artists meet this dark gaze, Blanchot says, but unless they turn away, leaping back to a world that has been forged by the "labour of the negative," as Hegel puts it, they will never complete the work in hand. For Blanchot, the artwork abides in two dimensions, one marked by meaning and the other by a lack of meaning or, to put it another way, one characterized by the possible and the other by the impossible. To talk about art is to use two vocabularies at the one time, one oriented to dialectics and one responsive to the neutral (see *WD* 20/ *ED* 38).

We can bring these matters into focus more surely by recalling a section title of the essay "Kafka et l'exigence de l'œuvre," "L'Art et l'idolâtrie." Here Blanchot considers Felix Weltsch's proposal that Kafka found himself before the divine interdiction against images (Exod. 20:4), and observes that, if Weltsch is correct, Kafka was caught in a difficult situation. He would be a man "who must, on pain of death, exile himself from images and who, suddenly, discovers himself exiled in the imaginary without any dwelling place or subsistence except images and the space of images" (*SL* 82/*EL* 100). Perhaps Kafka attests the religious sense of the interdiction while also yielding to idolatry in art. It would be an unstable compromise, one that would set in motion an asceticism with respect to his writing: incompletion, unwillingness to publish, and doubts over his vocation as an author. Blanchot agrees with Kafka that art and religion are different, yet argues that "art is justified" because it seeks "to make manifest, through the image, the error of the imaginary, and eventually the ungraspable, forgotten truth which hides behind this error" (*SL* 83/ *EL* 101). Reached only by incessant contestation of received categories and values, this truth is what Blanchot will call the Outside, and for him it is the last vestige that we have of the sacred. It is the truth that remains when the sacred has been disengaged from the divine and all that attends it, especially unity (and hence the unity of truth). When concluding his reflections on Kafka and idolatry, he tells us that there exists for the writer neither this world nor one beyond but only "the outside, the glistening flow of the eternal outside" (*SL* 83/*EL* 101). This sentence separates Kafka and Blanchot, even as it seeks to join them. Kafka remains an iconoclast, even in the midst of his need to write. Blanchot, in figuring literature as that which places us before the gaze of the Outside, draws closer to the iconodoules, even while retaining an implacable atheism.

[3]

There are some writers who need to be placed in a long perspective before their work becomes clear to us. Blanchot is one of these: we see him only partially if we read him from the vantage point afforded to us by Heidegger, Nietzsche or even Hegel. He hints that Heraclitus is important to him, especially the obscure one who is folded into the lyrics of René Char, and this is surely so. Now and then we find writers who snap into focus better when we view them from a perspective whose co-ordinates they do not give. For Blanchot, Pascal might be one such vantage point. And sometimes a sharp focus is best achieved when the co-ordinates are not even indicated by the writer in question. I suggest that we can better understand Blanchot if we see him, even for a moment, in terms of arguments developed by the anti-iconoclasts in response to two bouts of iconoclasm, one in the eighth century and another in the ninth.[5] Let us therefore go back to the Byzantine Empire and to hostilities that had been sparked off by Emperor Leo III's edict of 726 and that concluded with the restoration of icons at the Feast of Orthodoxy under the Empress Theodora on the first Sunday of Lent in 843.[6] Leo's edict required that icons should be placed sufficiently high in churches so that they could not be touched. (At the same time, the image of Christ at the Chalce gate of the imperial palace in Constantinople was removed and replaced with a cross.) The Patriarch St Germanos opposed the Emperor at a *silentium* or council meeting on 17 January 730, and was accordingly deposed. The new Patriarch, Anastasius, signed the decree, thereby giving Leo ecclesial authority to order the destruction of religious images, including decorated altars and veils as well as relics and icons.[7] Thus started a furore now largely forgotten in the West, and one that Blanchot probably did not know in any detail.

Whenever the task is to make sense of "art and the sacred" it is tempting to return to the disputes between iconoclasts and anti-iconoclasts. There is much to learn there about everything that makes us uneasy about associating art and the sacred and equally much to learn about how to reduce, if not totally overcome, that unease. Yet we should be wary, not only because those passionate debates were deeply political as well as theological but also because they were not concerned with art as much as representation. People clashed over whether images had pedagogic value; they did not argue over aesthetics. What matters in an icon for its defenders is the dignity of the prototype, not the exactness of mimesis, the artistic value of the image or the imagination of the artist. The word "prototype" cannot be avoided for, as Origen argued, an icon has a prototype, and this distinguishes it from an idol (*Patrologia Graeca*, hereafter *PG*, 12, 353D–354A). There are icons because there are prototypes, and there are images of the invisible God because God has become incarnate. Such is St John of Damascus's view in his third defence of icons, a position he refines by conceding that images give us very faint knowledge of what by nature cannot be perceived.[8] They place us in the land of analogy where Denys the Areopagite had long before said we had to abide.[9]

Such a concession would not appease any iconoclast simply because he or she would never accept a distinction between icon and idol. Scripture offers irrefutable evidence for the iconoclast. Exod. 20: 4 is the chief exhibit, needless to say, but a range of others, including Ps. 97: 7 ("Confounded be all they that serve graven images") and Isa. 42: 8 ("I am the LORD: that is my name: and my glory will I not give to another, neither my praise to graven images"), could also be cited, along with a variety of texts from the New Testament.[10] Since Leontius wrote his defense of Christians against the Jews in the early seventh century (*PG* 93, 1597–1609), anti-iconoclasts, in turn, had quoted Exod. 25: 18–22, which tells how two gold cherubim are to be fashioned from gold and placed on either side of the ark. They also had at their disposal a range of other passages that seemed to indicate that God appeared in time and a place: Gen. 3: 8, Gen. 32: 24–30, Exod. 33: 23, and Isa. 6: 1. To rely wholly on Scripture would be ill advised for either party, and appeals to the Church Fathers were similarly available to both groups: the iconoclasts would cite Epiphanius of Salamis's *Panarion* while their opponents would quote Athanasius's third discourse against the Arians.[11] Were more authorities desired, the iconoclasts could find evidence in the Desert Fathers, up to and including John Cassian's tenth conference, while their opponents could appeal to St Cyril of Alexandria's letter to Acacius of Melitene or St Gregory of Nyssa's commentary on the Song of Songs.[12]

No wonder then that Constantine V, Leo III's son and co-emperor since 720, buttressed the iconoclast case by developing philosophical arguments. His case in the *Peusis*, as partly preserved in the Patriarch St Nikephoros's refutation of it (*PG* 100, esp. 301C), is that a true icon can represent the prototype if and only if it has the same nature as the prototype. Yet wood and gold do not participate in the divine nature, and accordingly no constructed thing can be a true icon. Consequently depictions of Christ cannot be icons. Only the Eucharist can be properly so called: the consecrated bread and wine share Christ's nature but do not evoke His physical image. It was Constantine who argued that while an image of Christ can circumscribe His human nature, nothing can circumscribe His divine nature, and who thereby brought christology to the fore in debates between iconoclasts and anti-iconoclasts. His phrasing remains in the *Horos*, the definition of "icon" that was adopted by the Iconoclast Council of Hiereia (754), known as the "headless" council because neither the Pope nor the eastern patriarchs attended. The same phrasing was firmly repudiated in the seventh action of Nicea II (787).

For an iconodoule, Constantine's argument misses the point entirely. To begin with, there has never been a question of an icon circumscribing the divine nature. Nor does an icon participate in the nature of what it represents. Rather, it is *like* its prototype, even when, for lack of a model or want of artistic skill, it does not resemble the person's face or gestures. (Miraculous icons, such as the Veronica, belong to another species.) The Eucharist is not an icon, the iconodoule will add, precisely because it is identical with its prototype. Accordingly, icons are not to be venerated or adored, only the person who is represented.[13] In the words of St Basil of Caesarea, which were much quoted (usually out of context) by the iconodoules, "the honor paid to the image passes on to the prototype."[14] In contemplative prayer we move from the visible to the invisible, from *aesthesis* to *theoria*.[15] Given that an icon is a material means to a spiritual end, it is indeed improper to revere its wood and paint; and an index of this is the requirement that damaged icons are to be destroyed. Consistent with this movement from the earthly to the heavenly is the view that icons exist in a hierarchy, beginning from below with the apostles, martyrs, saints and angels (who are to be venerated), rising to Our Lady (who is deserving of hyper-veneration), and with Christ (who calls for adoration) at the summit.

There can be no doubt that the definition of "icon" is at the base of the theological conflict between iconoclasts and anti-iconoclasts. Yet the dispute is all the more complex because the iconoclasts are not against all images. As we have seen, they regard the Eucharist as an icon. They have no objection to the cross, as long as it does not have the figure of the suffering Jesus, and they also speak of Scripture as an image. For iconoclasts and iconodoules alike, the Old Testament foreshadows truths to be revealed, while the New Testament is the image of those same truths. Iconoclasts maintain that the evangelists had written of Christ in words but that visual depictions of Christ's acts transgress the injunction not to represent God. The word of Scripture is living; the wood and gold of the icon are without life. Such is the point of the inscription of 814 that was set under the Cross erected by Leo V at the imperial palace where an icon of Christ had been venerated:

> The Emperor Leo and his son Constantine
> Thought it dishonour to the Christ divine
> That on the very Palace gate he stood
> A lifeless, speechless effigy of wood
> Thus what the book forbids they did replace
> With the believer's blessed sign of grace.[16]

In these workaday verses we see a critique of icons that in principle, if not always in fact, is motivated by an ethics as well as a theology of transcendence. Only if we imitate the acts of Christ and the great men and women whose stories are told in Scripture can we participate in the good.

Against this insistence on the speechlessness and deathlike quality of icons, the iconodoules replied that there is no difference between writing in words and writing in gold. "If the one is worthy of honor, the other is worthy of honor also," the Patriarch St Nikephoros argued, then added a pointed question, "why do you worship the book and spit upon the picture?"[17] He adduced ten arguments for the superiority of icons over the symbol of the cross, some of which are reflected in the seventh action of Nicea II (Henry Denzinger, *Enchiridion Symbolorum,* hereafter *D,* 302). That action turned on the distinction between *proskynesis* ("reverence") and *latreia* ("adoration"), first drawn in the late fifth century by Anastasius, Bishop of Theopolis. We venerate icons (relative worship) and we adore God (absolute worship): the distinction was clear and sharp.[18] Clarity was lost, however, when Adrian I sent a poor Latin translation of the acts of Nicea II to Charlemagne; and the Frankish bishops, unfamiliar with eastern liturgical practices, objected – not without justification – that *adoratio* translated *proskynesis* and, in consequence, insisted that icons are idols. St Nikephoros would have been horrified. For his part, he urged that iconoclasts were inconsistent: either they should reject the gospels or they should accept the gospels and the icons. The proposal was eventually endorsed in a canon of the eighth ecumenical council in 869–70 (*D,* 337). St Nikephoros would have been glad.

The anti-iconoclast case was not merely a logical one. It turned just as surely on the doubtful orthodoxy of the iconoclasts on the very sensitive point of the Incarnation. St John of Damascus begins by agreeing entirely with the iconoclast position. He freely admits that "God, who is without form or body, could never be depicted."[19] The new covenant has changed all that: Christ's Incarnation is the condition of possibility for making icons of the divine. The Incarnation has decisively reset the old distinction between life and death, including that between the living word of Scripture and the lifeless gold of the icon. "But now when God is seen in the flesh conversing with men, I make an image of the God whom I see. I do not worship matter; I worship the Creator of matter who became matter for my sake, who willed to take His abode in matter; who worked out my salvation through matter" (23). A distinction between the Father (unable to be represented) and the Son (able to be represented) can be found as far back as Justin Martyr's *Dialogue with Trypho.*[20] It is St John's conclusion that is new. In vigorously defending the invisibility of God, iconoclasts like Constantine risk deviating from the christology of Chalcedon (451). "Show his saving cross, the tomb, the resurrection, the ascension into the heavens," St John declares. "Use every kind of drawing, word or color. Fear not; have no anxiety; discern between the different kinds of worship ... For adoration is one thing, and that which is offered in order to honor something of great excellence is another."[21] Perhaps St John suspected that Constantine had Monophysite leanings as well as having been influenced by the Paulicians.[22]

Cross, tomb, resurrection, ascension: St John names the four last things of Jesus's earthly life, two before the sign of glory and two with or after it. St Theodore the Stoudite will argue strongly against the iconoclasts of his age that the resurrected Christ is circumscribed as He was before His torture, execution and death. In his *Seven Chapters against the Iconomachi* he tells us that "The representation of Christ is not in the likeness of a corruptible man, which is disapproved of by the apostles, but as He Himself had said earlier, it is in the likeness of the incorruptible man, but incorruptible precisely because He is not simply a man, but God who became man."[23] The icon does not simply represent Christ or the Virgin or a saint; it seeks to present a created being in whom the *imago dei* has been fully restored.[24] Thus the sense of alienation that anyone not brought up in the Orthodox tradition feels on first looking at an icon. We are confronted by a face that is both human and divine, or, with the saints, one that is human with the divine shining through it, or, in the case of the angels, created with the divine shining through it all the more brilliantly and freely.

It is St Theodore who, with the Patriarch St Nikephoros, is one of the most respected voices to resist the revival of iconoclasm in the ninth century. And it is St Theodore who develops a particularly striking argument against the iconoclasts.[25] St John of Damascus certainly knew his Aristotle, as his *Fons Scientiae* bears testimony, yet it is St Theodore and St Nikephoros who actually put the Philosopher's vocabulary to use in their defence of icons.[26] I quote from St Theodore's third refutation of the iconoclasts:

> The prototype and the image belong to the category of related things, like the double and the half. For the prototype always implies the image of which it is the prototype, and the double always implies the half in relation to which it is called double. For there would not be a prototype if there were no image; there would not even be any double, if some half were not understood. But since these things exist simultaneously, they are understood and subsist together. Therefore, since no time intervenes between them, the one does not have a common veneration from the other, but both have one and the same.[27]

The reasoning here loops through Aristotle's *Categories* 6b: since prototype and image are correlative, there cannot be one without the other. St Theodore does not deny the absolute priority of the prototype with respect to the image, but he does insist that the presentation of the prototype to thought cannot occur without reference to the image.[28] Or, to phrase it in the style of the christological debates that characterize the revival of iconoclasm, Christ is the prototype of His image. It follows that an icon is not a mimesis but an ontological relation. To pray before an icon of Christ is not to stand before Him as one being before another. Yet it is to expose oneself to the divine gaze.

[4]

Iconoclasts affirm a "profound *reserve*" in a prototype without visible image. The Father and the Son transcend the world so completely that their being is held aloft beyond all representations, and as a consequence a deep reserve is enjoined on us with respect to icons. And it could also be said that the anti-iconoclasts, especially those of the ninth century, are bound to a "profound *reserve*" in another way entirely. For them, especially in the formulation of St Theodore, the category of prototype and image bespeaks the source of all images: it is a reserve at the level of concept, not being, that generates images. With hindsight, and with its misleading assurances, we can see here something that would become more pronounced centuries later when Duns Scotus appeals to a neutral concept of being that includes both Creator and creation, namely, a category that envelops both God and image of God.

It is this second sense of the reserve that I wish to keep in play with respect to Blanchot, although there can be no question of altogether eliminating the first sense or of assimilating the neutrality of a category to his understanding of being.[29] Throughout, it needs to be kept in mind that Blanchot has little or no interest in the vitality of particular images. He is unlike the Romantics, for whom the image is linked to the symbol, and unlike Stephen Dedalus who, in *A Portrait of the Artist as a Young Man* (1914–15), was so concerned with the "esthetic image." Blanchot has no wish to distinguish images from discursiveness. Likeness does not interest him, ontology does. He prizes an attunement to the imaginary taken to be a profound reserve of empty images.

Blanchot makes no explicit remarks on icons, and certainly does not broach the theology of the icon, although we can catch something of his sense of their importance in his reading of André Malraux's appreciation of Byzantine art. Contemplating the "reliefs, mosaics, ikons" of the Orthodox tradition, Malraux observes that Christianity aimed to be the truth, not reality, and "if the true life was to be portrayed, it must break free from the real." It is easy to imagine Blanchot marking that line, and then reading on with special interest:

> The task of the Christian artist was to represent, not this world, but a world supernal [*l'Autre Monde*]; a scene was worthy of portrayal only insofar as it partook of that other world. Hence the gold backgrounds, which create neither a real surface nor real distance, but another universe; hence, too, a style of which we can make nothing so long as we read into it any attempt at realism; for it is always an effort towards transfiguration. A transfiguration not of the figures only; Byzantium aimed at expressing the whole world as a mystery.[30]

It is perhaps with this passage in mind that Blanchot reflects on a central issue to do with sacred and art that derives from his reading of the three volumes of *La Psychologie de l'art* (1947–50).

He does so in 1950, a year before "Les Deux Versions de l'imaginaire," although the essay in which this reflection takes place, "Le Musée, l'art et le temps," will not be collected until it appears in *L'Amitié* (1971). When we look around in the museum without walls we see "[w]hat we prefer," namely, "those works, which, like our own, are ignorant of appearance, do not submit to it, create a world that is other and whose power and victorious strangeness fascinate us," works "of Byzantine style," for example, which express a "rupture" with the world about us (*F* 23/*A* 33). When reading these words we find a path that leads back to early pieces such as "Le Roman pur" (1943) and "Mallarmé et l'art du roman" (1943), and we note an eerie affinity between Blanchot's early narratives, *Thomas l'obscur* (1941) and *Aminadab* (1942), and the icons. Both create alternate universes, one beneath the world and the other above it. In 1947 Blanchot had discerned an analogy between criticism and theology, one that did not satisfy him; yet, at a pinch, his theory of the new novel could be approached as a displaced theology of the icon.[31] The analogy limps in a particular way, for icons are deeply embedded in a richly elaborated world that is completely familiar to their votaries. Blanchot would say that this world is a misplaced concreteness – Christianity mistakes God for the Outside – and that his narratives present the unfamiliar as unfamiliar.

When we reflect on Byzantine art, Blanchot argues, we realize that the Orthodox artists have not been centrally involved in a search for form. Icons of Christ, Mary and the saints derive from values, not form, and specifically from "those values alien to the world,"

> those to which we owe all of our gods, those from above and those from below ... If art is defined and constituted by its distance in relation

to the world, by the *absence* of world, it is natural that everything that puts the world into question, what one calls, in a word – a word whose usage has become so unrigorous – transcendence; everything that surpasses, denies, destroys, threatens the body of relations that are stable, comfortable, reasonably established, and anxious to remain. (*F* 23/*A* 33)

Byzantine art is not a decadent, fallen style, of interest only to specialists in the history of art and the faithful who venerate icons. Not at all; for like Lascaux it leads to an essential meditation on art and the sacred. The Hegelianism is perhaps as much Blanchot's as Malraux's:

Gods thus become, in the greater part of the Museum, the surprising illusion that has permitted the artist, in consecrating himself to their cult, to consecrate art. Art is at this moment religion, that is to say, a stranger to itself, but this strangeness, being what tears it away from profane values, is also what brings it closest to its own truth without its knowledge, although this truth is not manifest. In this sense, one could say that gods were only the temporary substitutes, the sublime masks – but without beauty – of artistic power for as long as this power, through the dialectic of history and of metamorphoses, could not achieve, in the artist finally reduced to himself, the consciousness of its autonomy and solitude. The Pantocrator waiting for Picasso. (*F* 23–4/*A* 33)

Yet the icon makers, in seeking truth over reality, nonetheless miss the truth. For them, resemblance turns on presenting the *imago dei* in the resurrected Christ or the immaculate Virgin or the saint whose faith has been tested by martyrdom or persecution. The truth, as Blanchot sees it, is that resemblance is *itself* transcendence, and that it pivots on the corpse as guarantor of the image. Specifically, he has in mind the idealization that death confers on the dear departed (and certainly not the restoration of the divine image). The argument remains eschatological, but the end in question is one's deathbed and not the new heaven and new earth. Transcendence requires absence, not presence; it takes place "beneath the world," at the level of the transcendental, and does not take us to the heavens above the world. Once again, a long quotation is needed:

Resemblance is not a means of imitating life but of making it inaccessible, of establishing it in a double that is permanent and escapes from life. Living figures, men, are without resemblance. One must wait for the cadaverous appearance, the idealization by death and the eternalization of the end for a being to take on the great beauty that is its own resemblance, the truth of itself in a reflection. A

> portrait ... does not resemble because it makes itself similar to a face; rather, the resemblance only begins and only exists with the portrait and in it alone; resemblance is the work of the portrait, its glory or its disgrace; resemblance is tied to the condition of a work, expressing the fact that the face is not there, that it is absent, that is appears only from the absence that is precisely the resemblance. (*F* 32/*A* 42–3)

The lifelessness of the icons, which so disturbed Constantine and his followers, is precisely that which separates art and the sacred and allows art to come into its own. In doing so, it invites us to accept that it escapes being determined by the dialectic of history and opens onto the Outside.

For St Theodore, Christ already is His image. At the level of likeness, there is no distance between the reality and the image of the divine, and therefore iconoclasm is refuted. For Blanchot, a phenomenon, in presenting itself to consciousness, has already produced its image; the distance we presume between being and image is already within being. St Theodore affirms an absolute reality, God, and the strength of this reality shines through an icon in the gaze of Christ. Blanchot does not draw on Aristotle's *Categories*. His inspiration is Nietzschean – there is no "true world" behind the play of appearances – and accordingly he holds that there is no prototype. And his phrasing is phenomenological. He asks us to acknowledge that a phenomenon resembles itself, and on performing the reduction invites us to recognize that being is always and already hollowed out by its capacity to produces images. It is in writing, whether in ink or gold, that the "I" becomes fascinated by the dark gaze of the Outside, and must accept that there is no God. There are no bad icons for St Theodore and St Nikephoros, since all of them are correlative with their prototypes. And perhaps there are no bad stories, adds Blanchot, presumably because all of them can attune their writers to the Outside (see "The Narrative Voice (the 'he,' the neutral)" *IC* 380/*EI* 557). The icon does not represent but presents, say the anti-iconoclasts, and Blanchot adds that literature does exactly the same (see "Literature and the Right to Death" *WF* 328/*PF* 317). The analogy between the two arguments is far from exact. As already implied, the Outside does not have the ontological or even the ontic solidity of the prototype. It stands for the Sacred and functions as the Sacred, rather than actually being the Holy One. Besides, the iconodoules prize sight over hearing, while Blanchot comes to value hearing over sight. Yet there is enough common ground between the two arguments, over a millennium apart, to stimulate thought.

It is strange that iconodoules use an argument for revering images of the divine that can also be used, in quite another context, to buttress a sophisticated and consequent atheism. Rather than reflecting on the paucity of original arguments, or the power of context to inflect argumentation, I would like to show how the old battle between iconoclasts and anti-iconoclasts continues today in a covert manner. Jean-Luc Marion has impressively argued that metaphysics, from Plato until today, has remained iconoclastic in its response to the image, and that Nicea II has a contemporary relevance that we ignore at our peril. For Plato, of course, the image was utterly derivative and to be treated with suspicion. In Nietzsche's reversal of Platonism the image is detached from its original, and reality becomes a "world of images." Now, in a reality in which there is no prototype there can be no image either – *"with the real world we have also abolished the apparent world,"* Nietzsche declared[32] – and so the figure of man as spectator of images assumes great importance, and idolatry emerges with renewed vigour, this time as the self-idolatry of the human. Thus interpreted, the will to power becomes a virulent form of iconoclasm; and, thus diagnosed, our sorry postmodern state can be cured, as Nicea II indicated, only by the icon of Christ.[33] It is with this history of metaphysics in mind that I locate a more specific irruption of iconoclasm and anti-iconoclasm. I can best indicate what I have in mind by calling Levinas an iconoclast and, with far less confidence, Blanchot an anti-iconoclast.

[5]

In recognizing Blanchot as an anti-iconoclast of an atheistic kind I distinguish him to a limited extent from Nietzsche. Marion is correct to see the metaphysician of the will to power as an iconoclast. Yet Blanchot figures the poet, and Hölderlin above all, as uttering the sacred in the moment when he loses his "I." The sacred is presented in literature, in what he will come to call (without thereby eliminating the notion of literature) writing. Put differently, in risking the act of writing, understood as contestation of selfhood, truth and unity, an author exposes himself or herself to the dark gaze of the Outside, the radical anteriority of which invites us to use the adjective "sacred" when talking of it. Literature (or writing) cannot circumscribe the Outside – its anteriority forbids such a thing – but it remains the icon of the Outside.

I make that last remark with a profound reserve of my own, not least of all because there is a streak of idolatry in Blanchot. To place the divine under the authority of the sacred, as he does (following Heidegger), is to risk allowing the sacred to take on the role of an idol. At the same time, a strong movement of iconoclasm runs through Blanchot, beginning with his early recognition that "experience" and "contestation" name the one event, and going up to his general acceptance (and modification) of Levinas's ethics in *L'Entretien infini* and *L'Écriture du désastre*. Levinas's is an ethics that has been shaped by a Jewish iconoclasm that has been radically re-interpreted by reference to a God whose meaningfulness is given not in His act of being but in my being-for-the-other. That said, I can begin to justify my unusual way of regarding these two writers by offering a brief and partial reading of Levinas that is centred on "La Réalité et son ombre" (1948), an essay that is at once close to and distant from two texts that have already concerned us, Blanchot's "Les Deux Versions de l'imaginaire" (1951) and "Le Musée, l'art et le temps" (1950).

"La Réalité et son ombre" begins by contesting the dogma that art expresses the ineffable. All art worthy of the name, it is suggested, has embarked on a passage towards the ideal. Yet there is another manner in which art breaks with the world; there is "a disengagement *beneath*," an "interruption of time by a movement going beneath time."[34] This is the movement of "resemblance" (82), and it results in a "split in being" (85). Levinas speaks in almost the same words as Blanchot when he says: "Let us say that the thing is itself and its image" (82), and that art derives from a movement that "precedes ... the world of creation" (83). Differences between the two friends can be heard, though, when Levinas talks more insistently than Blanchot about the image as an idol, and that this recognition "leads us to the ontological signification of its unreality" (85). Like Constantine V, Levinas admits no distinction between idol and icon: all images are idols. Each of them abides in a frozen present, without a future; each is "life without life" (86), an inhuman interval that can never be completed.[35] Philosophy raises itself above art in criticizing idolatry, in freeing human beings from the immobility of the image and releasing us into the plethora of possibilities that are integral to each of us. Spiritual life is to be sought not in art but in criticism of the artistic image, a point that brings to mind the poem that Leo V set under the Cross erected at the imperial palace all those centuries ago. Indeed, Levinas does not hesitate to say that creation and revelation play no part in art, and to make a bold claim. "The prohibition of images," he says, "is truly the supreme commandment of monotheism" (89).

When making that remark Levinas is not proposing a dogmatic re-assertion of Exod. 20: 4 but attempting to give it phenomenological concreteness by way of what we now call "religion without religion." As Jacques Derrida puts it, the expression names a "nondogmatic doublet of dogma, a philosophical and metaphysical doublet" that figures the truths of religion as possibilities, not actualities.[36] It is a new species of iconoclasm, one in which Levinas has become an essential reference point and one to which Marion has subscribed, although doubtless in another style and with reservations.[37] In its general and modern form, religion without religion is an endorsement of the primacy of ethics, now widely understood as hyper-obligation, with a corresponding devaluation of the materiality of ritual and sacrament. The transcendence conventionally accorded to the deity is reset at the level of the other person and is thereby assimilated to a reinvigorated biblical humanism, a "humanism of the other man."[38] Ethics is not the corollary of the religious but is its medium; the sacred must be thoroughly secularized in order for us to have a proper relation with God, one that is without relation and certainly without any eroticism.[39] God is not erased, Levinas insists, but our access to Him is redirected by way of responsibility for the other person, which takes hold not in the present, or any present that has come or is to come, but in an immemorial past. I do not need to have entered into a contract with the other person in order to be responsible for him or her. In the words of rabbi Israel Salanter, which Levinas likes to quote, "the material needs of my neighbor are my spiritual needs."[40] Now these might be a few of my spiritual needs but they will never be all of them. Some spiritual needs can be satisfied only in prayer, and the person at prayer has already exceeded his or her being in the world and hence has a more complex relation with ethics than Levinas allows.[41] One difficulty with Levinas's philosophy of religion is that no one can pray to the God he has in mind – or, rather, prayer for Levinas can be no more than an attitude of radical receptivity to the other person. Another difficulty is how, or whether, his philosophy can be fitted to a theology without turning it into even more ethics. What, for Levinas, would be the non-ethical part of theology?

In Levinas's inflection of "religion without religion," what matters is not the divine prohibition of images in Exodus but its philosophical interpretation. Such is his contribution to what he regards as keeping idolatry at bay, namely endless exegesis of Torah.[42] Philosophical interpretation of Scripture, the translation of the Bible into Greek, would be a demythologizing in the interest of ethical meaning, not enlightened reason (as with Spinoza), and would accordingly mediate faith and reason.[43] The direction of this exegesis is made clear in a later essay,

"Interdit de la représentation et 'droits de l'homme'" (1981), in which we are invited to consider that "beneath the mistrust of images of being recommended by Jewish monotheism," there might be "a denunciation, in the structures of signifying and the meaningful, of a certain favoring of representation over other possible modes of thought."[44] The Greek notion of transcendence, considered as spatial elevation, gives rise to idolatry, Levinas maintains; and western philosophy, in its fashioning of ontology, is an elaborate secularization of this worship of images.[45] Even phenomenology, as projected from the *Logical Investigations* (1899–1901), is vulnerable to this criticism, since Husserl maintains there that intentional experience is either a mental representation or based on one.[46] The God of Levinas, like the God of Kant, does not offer Himself to experience. There can be no declaring "My Lord and my God," as Thomas did, to the resurrected Christ (John 20: 28).

We have to read phenomenology against itself, Levinas says, to show that "the activity of totalizing and totalitarian representation is already exceeded in its own intention."[47] That can be done by pointing out that "representation already finds itself placed within horizons that it somehow has not willed, but with which it cannot dispense" (121). In showing that meaningfulness, *Sinngebung*, need not be constituted epistemologically, in terms of representation, there arises the possibility of "an ethical Sinngebung" (121). That possibility is actualized in stripping "transcendence" of any spatial sense, which turns it into a deceitful immanence in any case, and refiguring it as an intention that cannot be filled because it has nothing at which to aim. Unable to be represented because He comes to us from an immemorial past, God can never be brought into a correlation with a human gaze. The *imago dei* passes through the other person's face, and is encountered there, in an experience without experience, in the mode of command. Here as elsewhere, Levinas avoids phenomenality in favor of intentional analysis. He bypasses, for instance, all talk of the divine glory abiding in the Tabernacle (Exod. 35–40) and shows no interest in the theology of the *Shekhinah*. His philosophy ignores the religious motivations of iconoclasm and seizes on its ethical implications. To object to him that icons are not art in any straightforward sense of the word would get one nowhere. They are images, and can contribute to life only to the extent that they call their ontological status into question.

When Levinas considers Blanchot's *L'Espace littéraire*, he notes that his friend "abstains from ethical preoccupations, at least in explicit form," yet he praises him for exposing himself to the movement of disengagement that passes beneath the world.[48] The neutral that Blanchot follows in his exploration of the Outside is mobile and plural, unlike the Scotist neutrality of Being that preoccupied Heidegger.[49] I quote Levinas: "Art, according to Blanchot, far from elucidating the world, exposes the desolate, lightless substratum underlying it, and restores to our sojourn its exotic essence – and, to the wonders of our architecture, their function of makeshift desert shelters" (137). Art is "a black light, a night coming from below – a light that undoes the world, leading it back to its origin, to the over and over again, the murmur, ceaseless lapping of waves, a 'deep past, never long enough ago'" (137). Unlike other artists, Blanchot does not mistake the shadow for the prey but broods upon the link between the two and thereby generates a critique of art in the very elaboration of an artwork.

In subsequent reflections on his friend, Levinas is less struck by the fulfillment of the "literary absolute" in Blanchot's *récits* than by the implicit form of Blanchot's ethics.[50] We are told that in *L'Attente l'oubli* (1962) Blanchot "preserves that movement that is located between seeing and saying, that language of pure transcendence without correlation."[51] It is here – in a work of art, of all places – that we find an instance of noesis without noema, Saying without the Said, and an overflow of "prophetic meaning" (185 n. 4). What Levinas values in his friend's writing is its prizing of the other person's transcendence, and what he passes over is that writing's attunement to the Outside. Doubtless he would have been struck by the attempt, in *L'Entretien infini*, to figure the Outside in terms of the human relation and thereby to regard it as the medium in which ethics can take place: "I have in this relation with man a relation with what is radically out of my reach; and this relation measures the very extent of the Outside" ("The Relation of the Third Kind: *Man without horizon*" *IC* 69/*EI* 98). The strangeness of this relation was once called "religion," Blanchot thinks, and then it was hailed as art; it is his proposal that what enables art also fosters ethics and, with it, a communism beyond communism, or what he likes to call the "unavowable community."[52] Be that as it may, it is Blanchot the iconoclast, not the anti-iconoclast, who chiefly interests Levinas. Yet one of the things that helps to make Blanchot so intriguing is that his commitment to contestation enables his writing to become a site where iconoclasm and anti-iconoclasm cross one another while remaining in the service of atheism.

54   *Kevin Hart*

ENDNOTES

[1] See *OW* 43/*CQ* 83; and, "Atheism and Writing, Humanism and the Cry" *IC* 262/*EI* 392.

[2] See Martin Heidegger, *Contributions to Philosophy (From Enowning)*, trans. Parvis Emad and Kenneth Maly (Bloomington: Indiana University Press), vii.

[3] For this sense of "religion," see Blanchot's remarks on Levinas in *WD* 64/*ED* 106–7.

[4] In his account of the image Blanchot focuses on the cadaver resembling itself. See "The Two Versions of the Imaginary" (*SL* 254–63/*EL* 341–55). Also see the comments of one of the partners in a dialogue, "Speaking is not Seeing" (*IC* 30/*EI* 42); and "The Experience of Proust" (*BC* 14/*LV* 23).

[5] It is not suggested that iconoclasm was a new phenomenon in the eighth century. The Synod of Elvira, c. 306, condemned images in churches, and of course there are biblical injunctions against images.

[6] The date of 726 is not without controversy. See M. V. Anastos, "Leo III's Edict against the images in the year 726–7 and Italo-Byzantine Relations between 726 and 730", *Polychordia: Festschrift Franz Dölger zum 75*, 3 vols (Amsterdam: A. M. Hakkert, 1966–68), 3: 5–41. It is likely that Leo's edict was the consequence of his interpreting a volcanic irruption in the Aegean Sea as a sign of divine displeasure at icon worship.

[7] See St Nikephoros Patriarch of Constantinople, *Short History*, trans. Cyril Mango (Washington, DC: Dumbarton Oaks Research Library and Collection, 1990), §§ 59–60.

[8] See St John of Damascus, *On the Divine Images*, trans. David Anderson (Crestwood, NY: St Vladimir's Seminary Press, 1980), 77. In the formula of Marie-José Mondzain, "L'essence de l'image n'est pas la visibilité, c'est son économie et elle seule qui est visible en son iconicité," *Image, Icône, Économie: Les sources Byzantines de l'imaginaire contemporain* (Paris: Seuil, 1996), 110.

[9] See Denys the Areopagite, *The Celestial Hierarchy*, in Pseduo-Dionysius, *The Complete Works*, trans. Colm Luibheid, The Classics of Western Spirituality (Mahwah, NJ: Paulist Press, 1987), 124A.

[10] The main texts are as follows: John 1: 18, John 4: 24, John 20: 29, Rom. 1: 23, 25, Rom. 10: 17, 2 Cor. 5: 7 and 2 Cor. 5: 16.

[11] See Frank Williams, trans., *The Panarion of Epiphanius of Salamis*, 2 vols (Leiden: E. J. Brill, 1987–1994), 2: 427–29, 518–19; and John Henry Newman, trans., *Select Treatises of St Athanasius in Controversy with the Arians* (Oxford: James Parker and Co. and Rivingtons, 1877).

[12] See John Cassian, *Conferences*, trans. and pref. Colm Luibheid, intro. Owen Chadwick (New York: Paulist Press, 1985), 128; Cyril of Alexandria, *Select Letters*, ed. and trans. Lionel R. Wickham (Oxford: Clarendon, 1983), 34–61; and Saint

Gregory of Nyssa, *Commentary on the Song of Songs*, trans. Casimir McCambley, pref. Panagiotes Chrestou (Brookline, MA: Hellenic College Press, 1987), *passim* but esp. 115.

[13] See St John of Damascus, *On the Divine Images*, 73–4; and St Theodore the Studite, *On the Holy Icons*, trans. Catharine Roth (Crestwood, NY: St Vladimir's Seminary Press, 1981), 107, 108.

[14] St Basil, "De Spiritu Sancto", *Basil: Letters and Select Works*, Nicene and Post-Nicene Fathers, vol. 8, 28. See Theodore, *On the Holy Icons*, 59. Basil was quoted out of context even in the seventh action of Nicea II.

[15] See Denys the Areopagite, *The Ecclesiastical Hierarchy*, 373A.

[16] Cyril Mango, trans., in *Iconoclasm: Papers Given at the Ninth Spring Symposium of Byzantine Studies*, ed. Anthony Bryer and Judith Herrin (Birmingham: Centre for Byzantine Studies, 1977), 185. The icon was destroyed by Leo III and replaced by a cross sometime after 726, restored by Irene after 787, replaced by a second cross by Leo V in 814, and finally restored by Theodora after 843.

[17] Quoted by Jaroslav Pelikan, *The Christian Tradition: A History of the Development of Doctrine*, 5 vols, II: *The Spirit of Eastern Christendom (600–1700)* (Chicago: University of Chicago Press, 1974), 131.

[18] St Thomas Aquinas preserves the teaching in *Summa Theologiæ* 2a2æ 94, 2 ad 1. Also see *Summa Theologiæ* 2a2æ 103, 3 for the distinction between latria and dulia.

[19] St John of Damascus, *On the Divine Images*, 23.

[20] See Justin Martyr, *Dialogue with Trypho*, trans. Thomas B. Falls, rev. Thomas Press Halton, ed. Michael Slusser (Washington, DC: Catholic University of America Press, 2003), ch. cxxvii.

[21] St John of Damascus, *On the Divine Images*, 18–9.

[22] On this question, see Sebastian Brock, "Iconoclasm and the Monophysites", *Iconoclasm*, 53–8.

[23] I quote from Leonid Ouspensky, *Theology of the Icon*, 2 vols, trans. Anthony Gythiel and Elizabeth Meyendorff (Crestwood, NY: St Vladimir's Seminar Press, 1992), 1: 161.

[24] See on this theme Kenneth Parry, *Depicting the Word: Byzantine Iconophile Thought of the Eighth and Ninth Centuries* (Leiden: E. J. Brill, 1996), ch. 10. Also see Ambrosios Giakalis's discussion of appeals to the resurrection, stemming from Origen, as an argument against icons in his *Images of the Divine: The Theology of Icons at the Seventh Ecumenical Council*, foreword Henry Chadwick (Leiden: E. J. Brill, 1994), 71.

[25] Not all readers of St Theodore affirm his originality. Roman Cholij, for one, maintains that there is no evidence "of any original *creative* thinking" in the saint's anti-iconoclast writings. See his *Theodore the Stoudite: The Ordering of Holiness* (Oxford: Oxford University Press, 2002), 25. For Miguel Tamen, on the other hand, St Theodore's solution to the problem posed by the iconoclasts is "brilliant." See his *Friends of Interpretable Objects* (Cambridge: Harvard University Press, 2001), 21.

[26] See, for instance, St Theodore, *On the Holy Icons*, 23.

[27] St Theodore, *On the Holy Icons*, 110.

[28] St Nikephoros says much the same thing. See Giakalis, *Images of the Divine*, 91–2. Theodor Damian quotes Dumitru Staniloae's objection that St Theodore's ontology of the image is flawed because the prototype must precede the image. I do not believe that St Theodore denies this thesis; his point is confined to the sphere of economy and does not extend to the sphere of theology. See Damian, *Theological and Spiritual Dimensions of Icons According to St Theodore of Studion* (Lewiston: Edwin Mellen, 2002), 214.

[29] For a discussion of this last point, see the introduction to my *The Dark Gaze: Maurice Blanchot and the Sacred* (Chicago: University of Chicago Press, 2004).

[30] André Malraux, *The Voices of Silence*, trans. Stuart Gilbert (Frogmore, St Albans: Paladin, 1974), 212.

[31] See Blanchot, "Le Roman, œuvre de mauvaise foi", *Les Temps modernes*, 19 (1947), 1304.

[32] Friedrich Nietzsche, "How the 'Real World' at last Became a Myth", *Twilight of the Idols/The Anti-Christ*, trans. R. J. Hollingdale (Harmonsworth: Penguin, 1968), 41.

[33] See Jean-Luc Marion, "The Prototype and the Image", *The Crossing of the Visible*, trans. James K. A. Smith (Stanford: Stanford University Press, 2004), 80–3. I leave aside in this essay Marion's inflection of the distinction between idol and icon in his own work except to name two remarkable books in which the distinction is discussed at length: *The Idol and Distance: Five Studies*, trans. and intro. Thomas A. Carlson (New York: Fordham University Press, 2001) and *Being Given: Toward a Phenomenology of Givenness*, trans. Jeffrey L. Kosky (Stanford: Stanford University Press, 2002).

[34] Emmanuel Levinas, "Reality and Its Shadow", *Unforeseen History*, trans. Nidra Poller (Urbana: University of Illinois Press, 2004), 78.

[35] It should be noted that Levinas rescinds from his total rejection of art. In a interview given in 1988 he observes: "This possibility for the human of signifying in its uniqueness, in the humility of its nakedness and mortality, the Lordship of its recall – word of God – of my responsibility for it, and my chosenness *qua* unique to this responsibility, can come from a bare arm sculpted by Rodin." "The Other, Utopia, and Justice", *Entre Nous: On Thinking-of-the-Other*, trans. Michael B. Smith and Barbara Harshav (New York: Columbia University Press, 1998), 231–2. Also see my comments on Levinas's ambivalent relation to literature in the entry on Levinas in *The Edinburgh Encyclopaedia of Modern Criticism and Theory*, gen. ed. Julian Wolfreys (Edinburgh: Edinburgh University Press, 2002), 218–25.

[36] Jacques Derrida, *The Gift of Death*, trans. David Wills (Chicago: University of Chicago Press, 1995), 49.

[37] See Marion, "Metaphysics and Phenomenology: A Summary for Theologians", *The Postmodern God: A Theological Reader*, ed. Graham Ward (Oxford: Basil

Blackwell, 1997), 296 n. 27. Marion's agreement with Derrida makes sense only if we understand "revelation" (with a lower-case "r") to mean *Offenbarkeit*, revealability. That this is plausible was indicated by Marion in his remarks at a conference, "In Excess: Jean-Luc Marion and the Horizon of Modern Theology", held at the University of Notre Dame, May 9–11, 2004.

[38] See Levinas, *Humanism of the Other*, trans. Nidra Poller (Urbana: University of Illinois Press, 2003).

[39] See Levinas, "The Will of God and the Power of Humanity", *New Talmudic Readings*, trans. Richard A. Cohen (Pittsburgh: Duquesne University Press, 1999), 66; and *God, Death, and Time*, trans. Bettina Bergo (Stanford: Stanford University Press, 2000), 163.

[40] Quoted by Levinas in "Judaism and Revolution", *Nine Talmudic Readings*, trans. and intro. Annette Aronowicz (Bloomington: Indiana University Press, 1990), 99. Also see Levinas, "A Religion for Adults", *Difficult Freedom: Essays on Judaism*, trans. Seán Hand (Baltimore: The Johns Hopkins University Press, 1990), 17.

[41] On this theme, see Jean-Yves Lacoste, *Expérience et Absolu: Questions disputées sur l'humanité de l'homme* (Paris: Presses Universitaires de France, 1994), I, D, §28.

[42] See Levinas, "Contempt for the Torah as Idolatry", *In the Time of the Nations*, trans. Michael B. Smith (Bloomington: Indiana University Press, 1994), 58. Also see his "The Strings and the Wood: On the Jewish Reading of the Bible", *Outside the Subject*, trans. Michael B. Smith (Stanford: Stanford University Press, 1994), 128–9.

[43] See the interview with Levinas, "On Jewish Philosophy", *In the Time of the Nations*, 170.

[44] Levinas, "The Prohibition against Representation", *Alterity and Transcendence*, trans. Michael B. Smith (London: Athlone, 1999), 122.

[45] See Levinas, *God, Death, and Time*, 164, 166.

[46] See Edmund Husserl, *Logical Investigations*, 2 vols, trans. J. N. Findlay (London: Routledge and Kegan Paul, 1970), 2: 743.

[47] Levinas, "The Ruin of Representation", *Discovering Existence with Husserl*, trans. Richard A. Cohen and Michael B. Smith (Evanston: Northwestern University Press, 1998), 121.

[48] Levinas, "The Poet's Vision", *Proper Names*, trans. Michael B. Smith (Stanford: Stanford University Press, 1996), 137.

[49] See Levinas, *Totality and Infinity: An Essay on Exteriority*, trans. Alphonso Lingis (The Hague: Martinus Nijhoff, 1979), 298–9.

[50] See Philippe Lacoue-Labarthe and Jean-Luc Nancy, *The Literary Absolute: The Theory of Literature in German Romanticism*, trans. Philip Bernard and Cheryl Lester (Albany: SUNY, 1988).

[51] Levinas, "The Servant and her Master", *Proper Names*, 148.

[52] See "On One Approach to Communism" *F* 97/*A* 113–4; also see *UC*.

"AFFIRMATION WITHOUT PRECEDENT"
Maurice Blanchot and Criticism Today

Leslie Hill

> *There can be no understanding without prejudgement, and it would be contrary to the very sense of understanding to make it artificially free of all "prejudice." However, by that very token, it is essential to remain constantly vigilant and, while scrutinising a text, allow oneself to be scrutinised by it in turn.*
>
> Maurice Blanchot[1]

"QU'EN EST-IL DE LA CRITIQUE?" "HOW DO THINGS STAND WITH LITERARY criticism?" This was the title, with echoes of both Mallarmé and Heidegger, under which, in Spring 1959, alongside other prominent French critics at the time (Jean Starobinski, Jean-Pierre Faye, and Lucien Goldmann), Maurice Blanchot replied to a questionnaire from the neo-Marxist quarterly *Arguments*.[2] Blanchot's response, put forward on the basis of having to deal on a daily basis with some of the most challenging texts of the post-war years, was characteristically incisive.

Literary criticism, the writer argued, mindful of his own increasingly anomalous position on the margins of the one and outside the sphere of the other, is an activity that takes place at the uncertain and sometimes problematic intersection between two separate but equally powerful institutions: the world of journalism – what today would be called the media – with its dynamic, but largely ephemeral interest in day-to-day events, and academia or the university, with its sedate, but more durable commitment to verifiable knowledge.[3] To be active as a critic, Blanchot continued, was to derive legitimacy and authority from one or other, sometimes both, of these complementary yet competing bodies. In this sense, he concluded, criticism had less to do with literature itself – assuming such a thing to exist at all – than with the political aspirations of the media or the academy and the ambitions of such institutions to exploit artistic production for their own purposes, which they did (and do) by translating art or literature into a discourse whose main function, explicitly or implicitly, was to legitimate a set of cultural, political, or ideological positions. Which is why literary criticism, as its history attests, ultimately reveals more about its own assumptions and values and the state of society embodied in them than about the literature it professes to take as its object. Claiming to speak to literature, it more often ends up merely talking about itself.

There remains, however, an underlying paradox. Despite their status as centres of discursive power, Blanchot observes, the institutions of literary criticism derive their prestige finally not from the persuasiveness of their own acts, but from something much less assured, at the limit of their authority, upon which they are nevertheless dependent for their survival: "literature" itself. In a word, criticism needs "literature" far more than "literature" needs criticism. This secondariness or belatedness of criticism is one of its key distinguishing traits, its dependency or contingency one of its most essential features. Criticism is always circumstantial. Even when it adopts an air of knowing superiority over the object it claims to evaluate, criticism can never take precedence over the singularity of the case it endeavours to address. By a strange reversal, the would-be universality of aesthetic judgements finds itself reliant here on the texts to which its verdicts are meant confidently to be applied. The result, as both the media and the university are aware, is that literary criticism comes to exist in an odd twilight world, halfway between seriousness and frivolity, professionalism and amateurism, hovering uncertainly between description and prescription, and where what comes first are not criticism's own arguments or truth claims, but the ignorance or unruliness of that upon which it claims to legislate. As Blanchot explains:

> The language of criticism has this strange characteristic that the more it realises, develops, and asserts itself, the more it must efface itself; eventually, it breaks down. Not only does it not impose itself, attentive as it is to the requirement that it should not take the place of its object; it accomplishes and achieves its end only when it disappears. And this movement of disappearance is not the simple discretion of the servant who, having finished his tasks for the day and tidied the house, then withdraws: it is the very sense of its accomplishment which means that, in realising itself, it disappears.[4]

Thus Blanchot in 1959. True enough, over the last forty-five years, much has happened to transform the daily routines of the literary critic. In particular, in response to developments in disciplines such as anthropology, linguistics, philosophy, psychoanalysis, and sociology, enormous strides have been made in providing criticism with better

and more rigorous theoretical foundations and guaranteeing the professionalism of its procedures and the coherence of its methodology. The
effects of these changes are plain to see in any modern university syllabus.
The impressionism and obscurantism that characterised literary criticism
in a previous epoch are increasingly subject to challenge. But perhaps
most startling of all about this invasion of literary criticism by so many
eclectic and hybrid discourses, each having its origin and specificity
elsewhere – and I refer here to everything that makes up the strange
multi-headed monster ubiquitously described as Literary Theory – is
the short-lived fragility of each and every theoretical discourse that in
recent years has been set to work defining "literature." No sooner does
one way of addressing the so-called literary text gain currency, it seems,
than it is immediately superseded by another. Competitiveness is the
order of the day. Confusion may sometimes result; but more often the
outcome is radical imponderability. But this is arguably not the fault of
theoretical discourse; it rather derives from the problematic character of
the so-called object of criticism itself.

Literature, it appears, is possessed of a kind of spectral indeterminacy,
which allows it to be traversed by this or that critical methodology, even as it
mutely slips away. Critical fashions pass; so-called literary texts obstinately
remain; but, more importantly, so does the question of literature: what it
is (if anything), where it starts or ends. It could even be argued that what
has most notably been achieved by the current proliferation of theoretical,
or pre-, post-, post-post-, or anti-theoretical accounts of literature,
rather than a conceptually more rigorous understanding of the thing we
call literature, is an awareness of the mysterious unfindability – not to
be confused with ethereal transcendence – of criticism's obscure object
of desire: literature, which cannot be presented or made present "as
such," and which exists (if it exists at all) only as a non-finite collection
of examples primarily exemplifying themselves. This is perhaps not
surprising. Already Kant, in considering the possibility of aesthetic
judgements of the sort that might be addressed to literature, was obliged
to do so in enigmatically self-cancelling and aporetic terms: as pleasure
without interest, a perception of purposiveness without purpose in
the artwork, appealing to a moment of necessary universalisation that
remained however without guarantee or confirmation. Far from being
self-identical, then, the object of aesthetic judgement, on this evidence,
displays an extraordinary degree of instability – and inevitably so, since
without such mutability on the part of its putative object, the theoretical
revolution in criticism that is such a feature of recent decades would

barely have been possible at all. Today, however, no less than in 1959, notwithstanding the many radical changes in critical thinking that have occurred over the last forty-five years, one troubling and impertinent fact still remains, as many a critic can attest, irrespective of whether he or she writes as an academic or a journalist. It is that criticism's very existence is inseparable from a sense that it is always already on the brink of erasure. It is by nature redundant and expendable. It lives and dies with the works that prompt it, and rarely outlasts the historical conjuncture to which it belongs. Far from embodying indispensable truth, it is never very far from worrying irrelevance.

This instant disposability of so much literary criticism, Blanchot goes on to argue, is not mere circumstance. It says something about the strange structure of the literary work itself. For it is apparent that any literary work, in order properly to exist at all, requires a (future) reader, without whom it would remain empty and inert. And if reading is a necessary feature of any work, perhaps even to the point of founding the work *as* a work, as Benjamin claims, the same arguably also goes for literary criticism. It too is inseparable from the work as a work. After all, a critic, in the first instance, is little more than a reader, albeit a reader of a peculiar kind, as Blanchot puts it, whose relationship to the work is doubly mediated: both through the reading of a writing and the writing of that reading. Criticism begins, in other words, with reading: by responding to the implicit appeal made by the work (or, better perhaps, the promise of the work-to-be) to the contingent, always future reader dormant in each and every one of us.

This act of reading, Blanchot explains, is both more dutiful and less inhibited than might first appear. For if the intervention of a reader is required for the work fully to be what it is, the work may be said not only to imply the reader, but to obligate him or her, who cannot *not* respond to what he or she is reading, since reading is already by way of being that response. To read, in this sense, is always to be indebted to the work. But the nature of this debt is enigmatic. The work does not instruct the reader how to read. On the contrary, while the reader's involvement is a necessary moment in the unfolding of the work, it is also, as far as the work is concerned, quite superfluous. The work itself cares little about how it is read, or even if it is read at all. This insouciance can often be bewildering. No sooner is the reader called upon to respond than he or she is told that response is unnecessary, redundant, or indifferent. No sooner is the reader put in the work's debt, then, than he or she is released from that debt; the obligation to the work is cancelled, and submissive constraint gives way to untrammelled freedom. "Read the text!", students are urged. "But how?" "Any way you like! Just keep reading!"

Admittedly, a reader can respond to this double bind of necessity and irrelevance, obligation and redundancy, by retreating into admiring or disapproving silence. That is the prerogative of any reader. The critic, however, who has decided to write about his or her reading, enjoys no such luxury; by definition, he or she is enjoined to address the work. But in what way? Minimally, taking on the role of mediator, a critic might endeavour merely to repeat the work. But it is soon apparent, as Borges shows in his famous story, "Pierre Menard, Author of the *Quixote*," that any such fidelity to the text is impossible, since any repetition, however rigorous, always adds to what it is repeating a hair's-breadth displacement, which is the effect of repetition itself. Exact repetition is impossible; to repeat is always already to transform.[5] Once the critic begins addressing the work, then, it is always to say something in response to the work which is not said by the work. This is the task of the critic; indeed there can be no other. It implies no originality on the part of the critic, is rather a function of the critic's supernumerary existence as a reader both internal and external to the work.

Here, too, there is ambivalence. The work, we know, is complete in itself; and nothing can be added or subtracted from the work without altering it fundamentally. But the work is also incomplete; for without the evidence of such incompletion, it would not be available to any critic to speak about the work in a way not always already anticipated by the work. Which is also to say the work is necessarily inhabited by an enigmatic silence, a withholding of language that says both everything and nothing, and which the critic, warming to the task, is enjoined to translate into words of his or her own (and it is at this stage, no doubt, that academic or journalistic discourse intervenes, if it has not done so already, to channel, inflect, or appropriate the critic's speaking or provide the critic's reading with institutional, ideological, or methodological legitimacy). Whatever a critic's response – enthusiastic, hostile, or indifferent – and whatever the discursive context of the critical act – praise or polemic, demonstration or analysis – it will never be possible for criticism to overcome the incompletion that is an irreducible feature of the work. Criticism can never speak in place of the work, nor can it put an end to the work's own garrulous silence. Which is why criticism, in order to exist at all, is condemned to remain forever provisional: undecided – enjoined to decide, that is, but granted no power of decision over the work.

The critical relation, then, is the site of a strange inconsistency. The intervention of the critic is necessary, yet superfluous; the critic must respond to the work, but that response is in vain; the critic's task is to translate the work, but all criticism uncovers in the work is evidence of the work's untranslatability. These paradoxes are revealing. For what criticism makes apparent in the work, embodied in the work's endless potential for commentary and interpretation, is not the self-identity of its object – as an example or instance of literature or literariness – but what Blanchot in 1959 described as the work's essential non-coincidence with itself, "sa non-coïncidence essentielle avec elle-même," the effect of which, he adds, is to make the work itself perpetually "possible-impossible." The work is finite, yet also infinite. It is readable, yet essentially unreadable.[6] True enough, criticism has always known this, since it holds the secret to criticism's own longevity. For if it were possible once and for all to exhaust the text to which criticism endeavours to respond, this would spell the end not only for the work but criticism too. It may be that the task of critics is to decide upon the meanings and value of literary works, but what criticism encounters in the work, by necessity, is its own failure to decide once and for all. Criticism, then, may be a discourse that seeks to impose the self-evidence of its judgements; but it is also, at the same time, a discourse that harbours within itself the necessity of its own impotence.

The fact is, Blanchot argues, the literary work always eludes the finality of judgement. An abiding duplicity separates the artwork from itself. Writing for Blanchot obeys at least two masters, which is to say it properly serves the interests of neither. The writer explains the workings – or, better, the unworkings – of this strange logic in a famous six-page chapter from *L'Espace littéraire*, first published in June 1953, entitled "The Gaze of Orpheus [*Le Regard d'Orphée*]" (see *EL* 179–84/ *SL* 171–6). It is towards this section in the book that Blanchot directs the reader's attention as the ever mobile, secret centre of his inquiry. The Orpheus story is of course familiar to readers of literature – of Virgil, Ovid, Rilke, Cocteau, many others – as one of writing's most enduring self-images or tales of origin. Orpheus, the poet, is given permission by the gods to descend to the underworld in order to retrieve his loved one, Eurydice, who is more properly dead, and lead her back into the light of day, in return for which he must promise not to look back – "or else," says Ovid, "the gift would fail."[7] Like countless earlier commentators, Blanchot uses the story as a fable dealing with the achievement – and cost – of poetic inspiration. But Blanchot's retelling of the story is not simple. It lays bare a dual, dissymmetrical logic. On the one hand, he says, art speaks of loss, and therefore of the possibility of redemption. It records grievous absence but, as it does so, it transfigures the object of mourning by substituting for it an image that retains the essential features of the absentee. Art, then, saves from death and represents light's victory over dark. True enough, success is indirect, since what is salvaged is not the object of desire itself but an intangible representation of it. But such obliqueness is inescapable; it is the price paid for the hubris of the work, which otherwise would not survive, and which, since it does survive, is able to preserve both loved one and poet, who are remembered, in their absence, in the work.

But this familiar story conceals a more compelling, properly sub-terranean plot. Orpheus' purpose in descending to the underworld, Blanchot points out, was not in fact to produce a work at all. More simply, more radically, it was in order to see Eurydice again – not an image of Eurydice, but Eurydice herself, as she is (or *is* not) in death: irretrievable, invisible, impossible, and irreducibly other. This, Blanchot insists, is the more powerful injunction: not to produce the work, but to travel to the limit of the visible in order to see what precisely cannot be seen. The act of mourning or poetic retrieval is traversed by a ghostly presence it can neither grasp nor renounce. And this is why, according to Blanchot, despite agreeing to avert his eyes, Orpheus nevertheless looks again, at which point Eurydice is lost twice over. Death is therefore double. From the perspective of the work, Orpheus' impatient transgression is an act of madness, carelessness, and irresponsibility. But that betrayal is merely a response to a more exacting requirement. As Blanchot explains:

> assuredly, by turning round to gaze at Eurydice, Orpheus ruins the work, the work immediately unravels, and Eurydice returns once more to the shadows; and as Orpheus looks on, the essence of night is no longer what is essential. He thus betrays the work, and Eurydice, and the night. But *not* to turn around to gaze at Eurydice would be no less a betrayal, no less an infidelity to the immeasurable, careless force of his movement, which does not want Eurydice in her daytime truth and everyday attraction, but wants her in her nocturnal obscurity, in her remoteness, with her body closed and face locked away, wants to see her not when she is visible, but when she is invisible, not as the intimacy of a familiar life, but as the strangeness of that which excludes all intimacy, and wants, not to give back her life, but to have the plenitude of her death living on in her. (*EL* 180/*SL* 172)[8]

Orphic impatience, here, is not the opposite of patience; it is its hyperbolic intensification. "True patience," comments Blanchot, "does not exclude impatience, it is its intimate core: impatience suffered and endured without end. Orpheus' impatience is therefore also a fitting gesture [*un mouvement juste*: a just movement or impulse]: it marks the beginning of what will become his own passion, his greatest patience, his infinite lingering in death" (*EL* 181/*SL* 173).

If Orpheus breaks his promise not to look upon Eurydice, it is in order to fulfil another promise, that of his undying passion for Eurydice. But Eurydice is doubly dead, and, though each promise is affirmed without reserve, neither of them can in fact be kept. The work is sacrificed on the altar of its own dissolution. This entails, however, no covert resurrection. The promise of the work cannot be realised; indeed this is what gives it its status as a promise. Promises cannot be made present; they belong only to the future. Despite appearances to the contrary, then, there is no dialectic at work here, or rather the dialectic of the art work that Blanchot presents is itself more properly – improperly – unhinged by something that exceeds it. (It is, so to speak, paralysed, suspended, neither realised nor destroyed, and the fate of the poet, in Blanchot's retelling, is strongly reminiscent of the impasse confronted by the Kafka of *L'Espace littéraire*, who finds himself, says Blanchot, in the position of Abraham – who, in sacrificing Isaac to God, is at the selfsame time seemingly compelled to sacrifice God's own possible, earthly future...)[9]

The work may be all, then, but for the poet it is still not enough. "The work is everything for Orpheus," says Blanchot, "– except for the desired look into whose depths it plummets, such that only in that look is the work able to go beyond itself, reach back to its origin, and be consecrated in impossibility" (*EL* 182–3/*SL* 174). So though the work is an act of deliberation, which must begin and end, it can do so only by abdicating its extremity, which remains unfathomable; yet that extremity, which is nowhere explicit, is what gives the work its singular appeal, and Orpheus' song relies for its existence on something it cannot therefore embody. The work resists elucidation. It alludes to a secret which cannot be divulged by the work, but which nevertheless lies within the work at an intangible distance from the work, as a kind of secret without secret, simultaneously veiled yet unveiled, and in itself irreducible to any disclosure or disclosing of truth, visible or invisible.

It might be said that to uncover this absent secret of the work's singularity is criticism's task. But though it constitutes (and dissolves) the work as such, the secret remains forever inaccessible. Like "literature" itself, it is not an object, indeed it hardly exists at all, which is why criticism's lot is constantly to pursue it while never grasping it.

At this point in Blanchot's text it is no doubt telling that, in drawing on myth, fable, or allegory, the critic is driven to blur the boundary between fiction and criticism in his own writing. As Blanchot makes plain in the prefatory note from *L'Espace littéraire* identifying the importance of Orpheus' gaze in his exposition, the pages recounting Orpheus' story themselves necessarily gesture towards something of which they cannot speak directly.

This is proof of the fact that the Orpheus legend for Blanchot is not simply a convenient crux on which to hang a theory of literary creativity, but that the writer's retelling of the story actively partakes in the problematic it describes. In other words, Blanchot's own Orpheus story is an abyssal reflection of that which it is describing, and it is as though as a result the critical essay that is *L'Espace littéraire* is also possessed of a secret it cannot reveal or make present, not because Blanchot's text has somehow acquired prophetic status, but because simply, and without any kind of privilege, the text the reader is reading, irrespective of whether the text offers itself as criticism or as fiction, is that secret itself in its absolute withdrawal from presence and as an ever futural event. Which is to say that criticism here finds itself in exactly the same predicament as the literature about which it once claimed to say so much. In its indispensable inadequacy, criticism shares ultimately in literature's enigma and incompletion. Criticism is no pedestrian insult to literature – no, more radically than that, it is an extension of literature (if it exists) by other means, a vacuous yet unavoidable replication of what it once sought to transform into its own proper object, and which in its turn wreaks on its offspring its own final, paradoxical vengeance, which is to transform literary criticism into a minor branch of imaginative or imaginary literature. For in the end, the fate of criticism, Blanchot says, is merely to display the radical yet demanding void that, if such exists, lies at the very heart of literature.

Is this to say that criticism – not as external legislation, but immanent possibility – is a necessary culmination of the work? This, it may be remembered, was how Benjamin in 1920 sought to explicate the critical thinking of the Jena Romantics. For Friedrich Schlegel and Novalis, Benjamin wrote, "criticism, in its central intent, is not a judgement [*Beurteilung*] of the work, but both the fulfilment [*Vollendung*], completion [*Ergänzung*], and systematisation of the work, and its dissolution in the absolute." "The problem of immanent criticism," Benjamin added, "loses its paradoxical character in the Romantic definition of the concept, according to which criticism does not mean judging the work, since if it did so it would be nonsensical to announce a criterion immanent in the work. Criticism is rather a reflection [*Reflexion*] of the work, one that of course can only bring to fruition the germ immanent within it."[10] Elsewhere, Benjamin argued, it was the pure criticisability or *Kritisierbarkeit* of the work that, for the Romantics, constituted the work as such: "So long as a work is criticisable [*kritisierbar*] it is an artwork [*Kunstwerk*], otherwise not."[11] What was implied here, of course, was the status of the artwork as a provisional stage in a spiralling process of infinite reflection culminating in the absolute Idea. In this respect, as Daniel Payot suggests, the criterion of criticisability, for Benjamin, was proof of the necessity of a progressive movement of aesthetic transcendence. "In other words," Payot explains, "the particular work, constitutively and in essence, is a form that is 'sublatable' ['*relevable*']: it is what it is – unity, completeness, solidity – and maintains itself as a work only in so far as within it empirical (contingent) form may be dissolved ('consumed') into the sphere of absolute form. A sublation of this type [*une telle relève*] is not something that affects finished form [*la forme achevée*] after the event: the possibility of sublation is much rather the condition, the transcendental ground of the work's own completeness [*complétude*]. The work is a work only to the extent that, by its very constitution, it has always already received the status of a consumable form: its very completeness is nothing other than what might be termed its 'sublatability' ['*relevabilité*']."[12]

In Blanchot, however, there is little trace of any such ambitions of transcendence. On the contrary, the upward movement of infinite reflection as articulated by the Romantics remains decisively blocked by the persistent and infinitely retrocessive movement not of the Idea, but of what, with Levinas, Blanchot addresses as the *il y a*: that always prior affirmation that escapes negation, is irreducible to being or non-being, cannot be absorbed into truth or (for Blanchot at any rate) become the basis for any transcendence whatsoever. "Above all," writes Blanchot in *L'Écriture du désastre*, "the *there is* [*l'il y a*], as neuter [*en tant que neutre*], defies the question relating to it: if challenged, it ironically absorbs the challenge, which has no power over it. Even if it allows itself to be overcome, it does so because defeat is what is improperly proper to it [*est sa convenance inconvenante*], just as bad infinity [*le mauvais infini*] in its perpetual repetition determines it as true to the extent that it (falsely) imitates transcendence and thus exposes [*dénonce*] its essential ambiguity and the impossibility of subordinating that ambiguity to what is either true or just" (*ED* 108/*WD* 65).[13]

The neuter, then, in Blanchot, this movement of simultaneous inscription and effacement, withdrawal and supplementarity, and which the writer describes elsewhere as what makes literature possible and yet impossible at the same time, interrupts decisively, by dint of its irreducible indecision, all forms of aesthetic transcendence. Literary criticism and literature alike are returned to the endless finitude that is their common lot. For if literary criticism is an institution without justification or purpose, other than that of asserting its own fragile authority, then, it is because this is already true of literature. Literature, too, is bound to disappearance. Its only essence, Blanchot says somewhere, lies in its essential non-essentiality, its lack of self-presence, identity, or worth. Literature is flummery. For the institutions of literary criticism, this is a troubling diagnosis. It suggests that, far from validating those values for which critics and readers display such voracious appetite, "literature" just as often treats them with disrespect, scepticism, or indifference.

This at any rate, Blanchot argues, is what the history of modern literature shows. Time and again, literature has fallen short of the many worthwhile causes it was once thought to be promoting. Even in those cases where, seemingly for the very best of reasons, literature undertook to intervene politically – the canonic example, in France, during the 1940s and 1950s, was the committed literature of Sartre, de Beauvoir, and others – there too, writing has the disquieting effect of undermining the very positions it was meant to protect. The decisiveness of action, as each of Sartre's novelistic or theatrical protagonists belatedly discovers, is always dissipated by the indecisiveness of words, those very words that Sartre, late in his literary career, in a reversal whose irony was far from being lost on the author, was minded to renounce by writing a book entitled precisely: *Les Mots* (*Words*). Sartre's ambition may have been to overcome the unruly awkwardness of writing, its failure to endorse the writer's ethico-political project, by appealing to the dialectic of "qui perd gagne," "loser wins," but there was little guarantee, as Sartre was secretly aware, that even his own words would prove so compliant as to allow themselves to be contained by philosophy.

"The situation is clearer now," Blanchot observed in 1945, referring to Sartre's (then, and since, unfinished) tetralogy of committed novels, *Les Chemins de la liberté* (*The Paths of Freedom*), "the novel has nothing to fear from a didactic proposition [*une thèse*], provided the proposition is willing to be nothing without the novel. For the novel has its own rule of behaviour [*sa morale propre*], which is ambiguity and equivocation. It has its own reality, which is the power to discover the world in the unreal and imaginary. And, finally, it has its own truth, which obliges it to assert nothing without seeking to take it back, and to allow nothing to succeed without first preparing its failure, so that every didactic proposition that triumphs in a novel immediately ceases to be true" (*PF* 203/*WF* 207). Bataille says something similar in an essay on Emily Brontë. Literature, he writes, is not civic duty; it is precarious, abyssal exposure to what lies at the edge of human experience: "Being inorganic," he says, "it is irresponsible. Nothing rests upon it. It can say anything [*Elle peut tout dire*]."[14] Which does not exclude, it must be said, the enigmatic possibility or even necessity, notwithstanding (or, more accurately, precisely because of) the absence of any legislative authority competent to decide where responsibility here either begins or ends, that to write might also imply having to take responsibility for literature's own irresponsibility, or, as Blanchot puts it in *Le Pas au-delà*, without specifying whether this is an impossible injunction or an unanswerable question: "[to] assume responsibility [*répondre*: i.e. to both be responsible and take responsibility, responsibility therefore as both state and act, and in that sense a disposition, so to speak, that precedes both state and act] for that which escapes responsibility" (*PD* 168/*SNB* 123). But for what else, one might respond, is it possible to assume responsibility, if not for that for which we are *not* responsible? Responsibility in this sense is no longer a form of moral ownership of one's actions or those of another: it is impossibility itself.

But faced with the radical disobedience of the putative object of his or her concerns, how is a critic to respond? As for all things, there would appear to be always at least two choices. The first is straightforward enough. Whether by preference, moral or political conviction, or sheer laziness, it is no doubt possible to read so as to allow the object of reading to confirm, either positively or negatively, the reader's prejudices – those prejudices which, as Blanchot concedes, are an indispensable part of any act of understanding. As all readers know, it can be sometimes intensely pleasurable, after a moment's trembling hesitation, to rediscover familiar convictions in this way; whole literary genres, such as melodrama, thrive on these effects. But at some point any reader must stop, either because, for whatever reason, he or she simply abandons the act of reading, or because, excessively challenged or affronted by the work, the reader refuses to continue reading, and passes to something less taxing or less offensive. On occasion, to cease reading in this way can no doubt seem – and quite plausibly often is – a responsible course of action: in the face of repugnant propaganda, pornography, or mass-produced kitsch. But in the end, all reading encounters a limit; it is bound to define itself therefore not simply in terms of what it can or will read, but also in terms of what it cannot or will not read. If so, a second option stands facing the reader, who, instead of giving up, once he or she reaches the limit of the readable, may attempt instead to carry on, and expose his or her experience of reading to the promise or threat of the unreadable, thereby endeavouring to measure up to the demands of the text, which may mean relinquishing, at least provisionally, the assumptions that are among readers' most cherished and necessary possessions – if only then, at times, to retrieve them and revert to them as before.

At this stage it is apparent that the choice facing the reader – to read or not to read? – is less of an alternative than it may seem. To cease reading, for whatever reason, is already an act of reading and decided while reading, just as any act of reading is itself always a confrontation with what cannot be read. In either case, reading is haunted by the spectre of the unreadable. That spectre is a necessary one. Without the prospect of the unreadable, no reading would be able to delimit its own task or purpose, and it would have no object to which to apply itself. It is well known that readers often skip passages they believe they have already read. To read at all, it may be argued, is to encounter the unfamiliarity, the strangeness, the otherness of the unreadable. In other words, to read is by necessity to strain towards the point at which its own possibility is put into crisis. When this happens, as it eventually must, it becomes apparent that to read is not simply to scrutinise an object, it is also to be scrutinised by that object in turn; it is no longer to circumscribe the object of reading within an interpretative horizon grounded in familiarity, but to suspend that interpretative horizon by treating it in its turn as an object of reading. At this extreme point, in the name of justice itself, all critical decision-making has necessarily to be deferred, and the values underpinning decisions put into abeyance, without there being any guarantee that any decision will finally be made, or the values in question rehabilitated or reasserted.

All of this, Blanchot repeats, does not arise as a consequence of the superior value of literature or the aesthetic with respect to other modes of discourse. It is rather because "literature" is not the self-identical, aesthetic object criticism assumes it to be, but a kind of corrosive vacancy that resists all positing and positioning. And this is also why "literature," however much the institutions of literary criticism claim otherwise, is not in itself a source of value or values, and why to read is to be exposed to an essential inessentiality that can only ever be affirmed in its very weakness. As Blanchot writes:

it is precisely the essence of literature to escape any determination of
its essence, any assertion which might stabilise it or even turn it into a
reality: literature is never given, but remains always to be rediscovered
or reinvented. It is not even certain that the word literature, or art,
corresponds to anything real, or possible, or important.

And he goes on:

> Whoever affirms literature in itself affirms nothing. Whoever seeks it
> seeks only that which slips away; whoever finds it finds only what falls
> short of literature or, even worse, what lies beyond it. This is why, in
> the end, it is non-literature that each book pursues as the essence of
> what it loves and yearns passionately to discover. (*LV* 244 / *BC* 201)

Writing, then, for Blanchot, is far from the autonomous activity as which
it is sometimes portrayed. For at least three reasons: first, because it is
subject to no legislation, external or internal, that it does not contest:
"writing," Blanchot notes in *L'Entretien infini*, recalling Moses' broken
tablets, "in this respect, is the greatest violence, since it transgresses the
Law, all law, and its own law" (*EI* viii / *IC* xii); second, because, being
essentially inessential, it has no self-identity which might be the basis for
autonomy; and third, because it is not yet at all clear in what sense, if any,
writing for Blanchot is an activity, a making or doing, whose objects (if
they exist) belong to the practical world of means and ends.

Blanchot's purpose in all of this is not to bind the fate of literature
and criticism to nihilism, as impatient commentators have sometimes
assumed. On the contrary, literature for Blanchot is inseparable, in
its simultaneous possibility and impossibility, from the question that
literature itself becomes for Hölderlin, Mallarmé, Kafka, Beckett, and
many others. It is not premissed therefore on the realisation or belief,
in Nietzsche's famous charge, frequently cited by Heidegger as a key
diagnosis (and symptom) of technological modernity itself, "that the highest values are being devalued [*Daß die obersten Werte sich entwerten*]."[15]
Indeed, writes Blanchot in 1973, referring perhaps indifferently to writing, literature, or the *neutre*, "he [*il*: he or it] is too lacking in scepticism
to entertain hope [*trop peu sceptique pour espérer*]. He does not hope
enough to be content with nihilism [*Il n'espère pas assez pour s'arrêter au
nihilisme*]. The unknown without hope" (*PD* 91 / *SNB* 64). But nor is it
grounded in the contention that art's uncertainty, its forfeiting of self-
evident legitimacy, ought rather to be understood as an indictment of
modern capitalist society, mirrored in a culture industry that grants art
autonomy the better to enslave it, severing its time-honoured bond with

the social world, with the result that art's role can henceforth only be one of melancholy, unreconciled negativity. This, it will be remembered, was the point of departure of Adorno's *Aesthetic Theory*, which precisely begins with the philosopher's dismay at the essential self-questioning – judged here to have itself become an article of unquestioned faith – which art in the modern era has become: "It is everywhere assumed to be the case today that nothing concerning art can be assumed any longer to be the case," writes Adorno, "neither in itself, nor its relation to the whole, nor even its right to exist." So far so good, at least up to a point, Blanchot might rejoin; but Adorno continues in rather different vein: "The loss of what could be done without reflexion or unproblematically has not been compensated for by the open infinitude of new possibility that reflection confronts. In many regards, expansion appears as contraction."[16]

For Blanchot, however, and crucially so, literature is not bounded by philosophical horizons of this kind, whether ontological or sociological, deriving from the history of Being or the dialectics of history. Indeed, the philosophical (and by that token more than philosophical) importance of literature – of Hölderlin and Mallarmé, among others – according to Blanchot, lies precisely in the extent to which, while set within the philosophical horizon, it necessarily also, by the appeal it makes to words, punctuates or disperses that horizon itself. This is why from 1960 onwards Blanchot was increasingly drawn to address literature under the rubric of what he terms "a change of epoch [*un changement d'époque*]," implying not simply that literature here enters into a fresh periodisation or new epoch (from the Greek *epokhè*, meaning: a stoppage, or station, the position of a planet, or a fixed point of time), a claim which, relying simultaneously, as it does, on saturnine certainty and terrestrial uncertainty, is at best aporetic (but has nevertheless in recent years given rise to an inordinate amount of inconsequential, self-promoting debate among literary critics concerning the differences between so-called modernity and postmodernity, not to mention so-called post-postmodernity, when it is plain to see that the one is merely the repetition of the other: albeit not as tragedy but as farce), but also, more importantly, that literature is henceforth thinkable only according to its own suspension (from the same Greek word, *epokhè*, meaning: suspension of judgement). And as Blanchot later reminds the reader in *L'Écriture du désastre*, *epokhè* also refers to messianic time: this time of perpetual indecision whose fate will never be resolved, this ever future epoch that will never be present, even though the time to which it belongs is necessarily always: now, today, this forever impending instant of my dying.[17]

The story that literature tells, then, in so far as it is a story at all, is not one of dispiriting decline, but of interruption, withdrawal, difference: not the past, but the future, not the historical forgetting of Being nor the negativity of the dialectic, but radical openness. So if it is true, for instance, as Blanchot suggests in 1963 apropos of Louis-René Des Forêts's story, *Le Bavard*, that such a work, like some of its contemporaries, is traversed by what he calls "an almost infinite nihilism," it is essential to read in these words a trembling doubt, an erasure even, as signalled by the peculiarity of an adverbial modifier (for what is an infinity that somehow falls short of itself?), and to set this re-marking of infinity alongside the desolate, ravishing joy that such emptiness, according to Blanchot, implies (see *A* 139, 149/*F* 119, 128).[18] To say that literature asserts nothing, then, is not to fall prey to the lure of a substantified absence or *deus absconditus*. Far more radically, it is to bind literature to a more essential kind of affirmation, no longer dependent on the authoritative imposition of value or values, and belonging therefore not to the certainties of the past, but to the unpredictable demands of the future.

But what kind of future is at stake here? Futurity is not futuristic imagining, and responsiveness to the future is not prediction or predication; to affirm the future is to affirm exposure to that which is without name, without example, and cannot be evaluated in advance – but without which justice itself cannot be affirmed in its turn. It is a decision that decides on behalf of undecidability. And this is what is essentially at issue in Blanchot's own critical account of literature, writing, poetry. Writing, he says, glossing the poems of René Char in 1953, and in so doing invoking Heraclitus' description of the impersonal, anonymous speaking of the oracle at Delphi, consists neither in saying nor concealing, but in pointing, giving a sign:

> The language in which the origin speaks is essentially prophetic. This does not mean that it dictates future events, it means that it does not base itself on something which already is, either on a currently held truth, or solely on language which has already been spoken or verified. It announces, because it begins. It *points* towards the future, because it does not yet speak, and is language of the future to the extent that it is like a future language which is always ahead of itself, having its meaning and legitimacy only before it, which is to say that it is fundamentally without justification.[19]

There is nothing sure or self-evident about Char's poetry. The affirmation it demands or requires of either reader or writer cannot be reduced to any given discursive position. In this respect there is nothing assertive about affirmation as Blanchot formulates it. It is, so to speak, neither positive nor negative. Like the *il y a* or the neuter in Blanchot, it both precedes and exceeds the dialectic of yes or no, even as it may manifest itself as a yes: a yes to the unpredictable, futural otherness of the event, as betokened by the singular injunction "viens," "come," addressed to a thought that may be a person, or to a person that may be a thought, which falls at the end of *L'Arrêt de mort*. Affirmation in this context takes on a strange intensity, singular and irreducible. It leaves intact neither the who, the what, or the how of reading: neither the putative reading subject, nor the supposed aesthetic object, nor the recourse to any pre-established critical method. It implies an interpretative decision, but one that is necessarily exposed at every stage to radical indecision. Reading here becomes an enigmatic event, which can no longer be simply configured as the encounter between a conscious, responsible subject and a stable object according to a regulated process of understanding.

This is not to say that affirmation in Blanchot's sense is not selective. But the differences within texts or between texts at stake here escape any proper aesthetic or moral codification; they imply no evaluation or legislation. Writing, however, is not arbitrary. Whether as literature or criticism, it falls subject to an imperative that does not however rely on any essential determination. As Blanchot formulates it, writing obeys a strangely indeterminate and fragile injunction, which is not moral, nor aesthetic, but perhaps rather ethical (though this word too is barely adequate) in a sense that owes nothing to the aesthetic or the moral in any determinable sense, if only because any such injunction cannot be unified or reduced to any logic of unity such as ethics or morality strive to reach. Indeed it is an imperative without imperative which is radically suspicious of all forms of (aesthetic, moral, political) transcendence. Affirmation in Blanchot's sense (which is also that of Bataille) affirms nothing other than affirmation: it challenges myth, aestheticism, moral authority, any kind of established political order, all homogeneity or unity.

Affirmation then speaks for Blanchot not as renewed assertiveness, nor as a desire to impose a new set of values, be they viewed by some as dangerously transgressive, but by way of the *neutre*, that withdrawal from all positionality that is in excess of all affirmation and negation (which it merely juxtaposes without being exhausted by them), but which, nevertheless, has a secret complicity or affinity with affirmation: affirmation understood as that which affirms that which is undecidable, and always in excess of the unity of the one, forever dedicated to the otherness of the other, that which is perpetually other than any other (see

PD 104/*SNB* 74). If indecision hesitates, it is not because it is unable to select the one rather than the other; it hesitates rather because it refuses the necessity of that choice. "'Which of the two?'", asks a voice in *Le Pas au-delà*. "'– Neither the one nor the other, the other, the other'," comes the answer (*PD* 108/*SNB* 77). Indecision, then, does not constitute itself as a gesture founded in negativity, but as a fragile response to plurality, as a more radical form of affirmation than that which is bound to asserting the same or its double. "What might be thought to respond or correspond to the neuter," says Blanchot, "is the fragility of what is already in the process of breaking [*la fragilité de ce qui déjà se brise*]: a passion more passive than anything else that may be said to be passive [*plus passive que tout ce qu'il y aurait de passif*: it is worth emphasising here this recourse, albeit in the conditional, to the *il y a* in Blanchot's text], a yes that has said yes [*oui qui a dit oui*] prior to all affirmation, as though the passage of dying had always already passed, preceding all consent" (*PD* 162/*SNB* 118). Radical indecision in Blanchot, then, is not embarrassed uncertainty; it is in fact radically decisive: it intervenes, incisively, to withdraw from all positing or positioning.

Such, then, is Blanchot's conclusion in 1959. As readers will know, invoking critical indecision did not imply on his part any undecisiveness, any retreat from the decisions history or politics demanded. On the contrary, speaking of the future challenges of literature and criticism in *Arguments*, Blanchot was careful also to evoke the political struggles (against de Gaulle's undemocratic return to power in France in 1958 and France's on-going colonial war in Algeria, a war that, it is well known, was never *named* as such) occurring at the time at – and accordingly within – literary criticism's own gates:

> criticism – literature itself – to me [wrote Blanchot] seems to be closely related to one of the most difficult, but important tasks of our time, which is being acted out in a process that is itself necessarily undecided: the task of both preserving thought and releasing it from the notion of value, and consequently opening history up to that which, within history, is already moving beyond all forms of value and is preparing for a wholly different – and still unprecedented – kind of affirmation.[20]

And in 1959, in a passage excised from subsequent versions, whose political implications at the time were hard to miss, Blanchot continued:

> Of what, then, does the literary work speak when it rejects all evaluation? Why do we feel ourselves bound by it to the concern for anonymous

existence, to being as a neutral and impersonal power, excluding all distinct interest, all determined speech, and calling on the violent equality of becoming? And, if indeed this is the direction it opens up for us, is it not strange that we should then be led to rediscover, in the most superficial kind of criticism, that which in journalistic form is part of the murmur of everyday experience [*la rumeur quotidienne*] and of life outside [*la vie du dehors*], the just continuation [*le prolongement juste*] of the movement of profound indeterminacy that seeks to communicate in the creation of the work in order to affirm in the work the future of communication and communication as future?[21]

Criticism today, Blanchot suggested, by dint of its necessity and impossibility, is faced with an exacting challenge: either of reasserting, after all, those moral, political, and aesthetic values that are under threat from the joyful scepticism of a literature which fails to validate them; or else of embarking on the more difficult course of affirming the otherness (beyond presence, identity, or sense) of an act of language no longer authorised by morality or truth, and thus no longer subject to a logic of identity or a dialectic of completion. Numerous are the critics, journalists and academics alike, who have preferred the former of these paths; but many too, often in silence, are the writers and readers who have sought to meet the challenge synonymous with the second. The alternative, one might say, still remains; and there hangs, for Blanchot – and (dare I say it?) the author of these lines – the future prospects of any critical writing on literature at all.

ENDNOTES

Although I have provided references to the English editions of Maurice Blanchot's works, for reasons of accuracy or stylistic consistency I have modified the translations in most cases.

[1] Blanchot, "Je juge votre questionnaire remarquable...," from a response to a questionnaire on the critical method of Henri Guillemin, *Les Lettres nouvelles* (24 June 1959), 9–10 (10).

[2] Blanchot, "Qu'en est-il de la critique?," *Arguments*, 12–13 (1959), 34–7. Blanchot's response is reprinted, with slight modifications, as a preface to the revised edition of *Lautréamont et Sade* (*LS* 9–14), and in English as "The Task of Criticism Today," trans. Leslie Hill, *Oxford Literary Review*, 22 (2000), 19–24; the remarks that follow, unless otherwise indicated, are based on this later version of the essay. For the allusion to Mallarmé, see Stéphane Mallarmé, *Œuvres complètes*, ed. Henri Mondor and G. Jean-Aubry (Paris: Gallimard, 1945), 645. Blanchot comments:

"When Mallarmé asks, 'Does something like Literature exist?,' this question is literature itself – literature when it has become the concern [*le souci*] for its own essence. The question is one that cannot be avoided. What happens [*Qu'arrive-t-il*] by virtue of the fact that we have literature? How do matters stand with regard to being [*qu'en est-il de l'être*], if one says that 'something like Literature exists'?" (*EL* 35/*SL* 42–3). Heidegger's preliminary question or Vor-frage: "How does it stand with Being? [*Wie steht es um das Sein?*]," is articulated in the opening chapter of the 1935 lecture course (first published 1953), *Einführung in die Metaphysik* (Tübingen: Niemeyer, 1987), 25; *An Introduction to Metaphysics*, trans. Ralph Manheim (New Haven: Yale University Press, 1959), 32.

3 By the late 1950s Blanchot's institutional position as a critic had become increasingly uncertain. He had never been a member of the academic élite, unlike his co-respondents of 1959 and most of the influential thinkers of subsequent decades (Foucault, Barthes, Deleuze, Derrida, Lyotard, or Kristeva), though it is worth noting that some of these occupied surprisingly modest positions in the French university system. After leaving university in the early 1930s, Blanchot was mainly active as a political journalist, and after the war derived his livelihood from his activities as a literary reviewer and his association with the Gallimard publishing house. Admittedly, this was not an unfamiliar pattern in France during the first half of the century (Sartre is another prominent example of a writer and philosopher without university affiliation), as Régis Debray shows in *Le Pouvoir intellectuel en France* (Paris: Ramsay, 1979). But by the late 1950s it had begun to be a thing of the past. By that time, too, though it continued to appear regularly in *La Nouvelle Revue française* in (oblique) response to this or that recent publication, Blanchot's critical writing had largely left behind the usual constraints and methods of literary journalism. The writer's lack of enthusiasm for book-reviewing as such was the main reason for his withdrawal from *Critique*, the monthly journal he had been instrumental in helping Georges Bataille to launch in 1946, but to which he ceased contributing after 1953.

4 Blanchot, "Qu'en est-il de la critique?," 35/"The Task of Criticism Today," 20.

5 See Jorge Luis Borges, *Labyrinths*, ed. Donald A. Yates and James E. Irby (Harmondsworth: Penguin, 1970), 62–71.

6 Blanchot, "Qu'en est-il de la critique?," 36/"The Task of Criticism Today," 22.

7 Ovid, *Metamorphoses*, trans. A. D. Melville (Oxford: Oxford University Press, 1985), 226.

8 For a more detailed account of Blanchot's Orpheus story, see Chantal Michel, *Maurice Blanchot et le déplacement d'Orphée* (Saint-Genoulph: Nizet, 1997). Other critics have been less sympathetic. In a feminist reappraisal of Blanchot's retelling ("Blanchot's Mother," *Yale French Studies*, 93 [1998], 175–95), Lynne Huffer takes issue with what she considers to be the sexual politics of Blanchot's analysis. "Blanchot's description of a fragmented and dispersed Orphic voice," she writes, "in fact hides its own foundation in the binary and gendered structure of the origin and its loss." "That structure," she continues, "is the structure of nostalgia. The

lost origin – Eurydice, the mother – is recuperated, as loss, into a form that is not only thoroughly human but, like humanism itself, decidedly masculine as well" (194). This is, however, to miss the point. It privileges the first part of Blanchot's presentation, where what indeed counts (as Blanchot agrees) is the abolition of the real object (in this case, the other person or other sex) as a precondition of the emergence of the work. But what above all else motivates Blanchot's Orpheus is not the work, but rather the otherness or inaccessibility of Eurydice in herself, as she appears (without appearing) outside, beyond, or before the work. Here, the sexual and political implications of Blanchot's writing are indeed crucial. But far from conspiring in what Huffer calls "the homogenization of the feminine" (195), Blanchot does something infinitely more challenging, which is to confront and articulate in his writing the very question of the alterity of the other body. In fact Blanchot does not present the relation with the other primarily in terms of the bipolarity of gender; indeed, as he makes clear in a number of places, gender, if it is to affirm the possibility of (sexual) difference, can only be articulated on the basis of a thought of alterity, which is why what he says about Eurydice in *L'Espace littéraire* reworks what Blanchot had already said about the raising of Lazarus in *La Part du feu* (*PF* 316/ *WF* 327). Blanchot's treatment of Orpheus and Eurydice ought not to be seen in isolation; it resonates with a number of other fictional or non-fictional texts where sexuality is at issue, as I argue in *Bataille, Klossowski, Blanchot: Writing at the Limit* (Oxford: Oxford University Press, 2001), 200–5.

[9] On the question of myth and sacrifice in Blanchot, see Gisèle Berkman, "Le Sacrifice suspendu: à partir de *L'Écriture du désastre*", in *Maurice Blanchot: récits critiques*, ed. Christophe Bident and Pierre Vilar (Tours: Farrago, 2003), 357–75.

[10] Walter Benjamin, "Der Begriff der Kunstkritik in der deutschen Romantik", *Gesammelte Schriften*, ed. Rolf Tiedemann and Hermann Schweppenhäuser (Frankfurt: Suhrkamp, 1974–89), 1.1: 78, translation mine.

[11] Benjamin, "Der Begriff der Kunstkritik", 79, translation mine.

[12] Daniel Payot, *Anachronies: de l'œuvre d'art* (Paris: Galilée, 1990), 120, translation mine.

[13] On the relationship between the *il y a*, literature, and the promise, see Blanchot, "Notre compagne clandestine," in *Textes pour Emmanuel Lévinas*, ed. François Laruelle (Paris: Jean-Michel Place, 1980), 79–87 (86); *Face to Face with Levinas*, ed. Ralph A. Cohen (Albany: SUNY, 1986), 41–50 (49). Already in 1948, in the famous essay on "La Littérature et le droit à la mort [Literature and the Right to Death]", in *La Part du feu (The Work of Fire)*, one of the prime effects of the *il y a* was to impede the forward march of the Hegelian dialectic. In later writings, the *il y a* comes to be treated rather differently by Blanchot and Levinas. In the case of the latter, it is reformulated as an account of the ethical transcendence of the Other. In Blanchot, however, it remains a decisive moment in the refusal of all transcendence. I examine the covert *différend* between the two friends in my *Blanchot: Extreme Contemporary* (London: Routledge, 1997), 167–84. I explore some of the further implications of this divergence with regard to transcendence in "'Distrust of Poetry': Levinas, Blanchot, Celan", *MLN* (2005), forthcoming.

14 Georges Bataille, *Œuvres complètes* (Paris: Gallimard, 1970–88), 9: 182.

15 See for instance Martin Heidegger, *Holzwege* (Frankfurt: Klostermann, 1950), 218. I discuss Blanchot's complex debate with Heidegger on the question of nihilism in *Bataille, Klossowski, Blanchot*, 237–43.

16 T. W. Adorno, *Ästhetische Theorie*, ed. Gretel Adorno and Rolf Tiedemann (Frankfurt: Suhrkamp, 1970), 9; *Aesthetic Theory*, trans. Robert Hullot-Kentor (London: Athlone, 1997), 1, translation modified. These are the opening words in Adorno's unfinished book.

17 On this motif of "a change of epoch," see *EI* 394–418/*IC* 264–81; as well as *ED* 158–60, 215/*WD* 101–3, 142. Blanchot glosses the relationship between messianic time and the indecision of dying in a fragment from *Le Pas au-delà*: "What is the meaning behind [Moses'] broken tablets?," asks Blanchot.

> Perhaps the breaking apart of dying [*la brisure du mourir*], the interruption of the present that dying has always already [*toujours par avance*] introduced into time. "Thou shalt not kill" evidently means: "do not kill whoever in any case will die" and means: "because of this, do not abuse dying [*ne porte pas atteinte au mourir*], do not decide in the place of indecision [*ne décide pas de l'indécis*], do not say: now it is done, thereby assuming a right over what is "not yet" [*t'arrogeant un droit sur "pas encore"*]: do not presume the last word has been said, time brought to an end, the Messiah come at last." (*PD* 149/*SNB* 108)

18 For a polemical *mis*reading of Blanchot's essay on Des Forêts, which bizarrely presents it as a naive exercise in nihilistic textualism, see Yves Bonnefoy, *La Vérité de parole et autres essais* (Paris: Gallimard/Folio, 1988 and 1992), 123–279. I have discussed Blanchot's essay on Des Forêts in a similar context elsewhere: see Leslie Hill, "D'un nihilisme presque infini", in *Maurice Blanchot*, ed. Bident and Vilar, 77–93.

19 Blanchot, *Une voix venue d'ailleurs* (Paris: Gallimard/Folio, 2002), 57/"The Beast of Lascaux", trans. Leslie Hill, *Oxford Literary Review*, 22 (2000), 12.

20 Blanchot, "Qu'en est-il de la critique?", 36–7/"The Task of Criticism Today", 24.

21 Blanchot, "Qu'en est-il de la critique?", 37. Why does Blanchot delete this concluding passage in 1963? Did it seem rhetorically redundant, given the allusion to "unprecedented affirmation" in the preceding passage? Was Blanchot, four years later, unwilling, in the name of affirmation itself, to subscribe to such problematic values as the impersonality of *being* and the future as *communication*, both formulations that Blanchot in subsequent texts would abandon?

AN IDYLL?

Michael Holland

*Éternellement, mot qui requiert une pensée
très nouvelle ou plus qu'ancienne.*
Jacques Derrida[1]

IN THE CONCLUSION TO *DECEIT, DESIRE AND THE NOVEL* (1961), RENÉ GIRARD observes that, at the time of writing *Notes from the Underground*, Dostoevsky "was traversing Maurice Blanchot's 'literary space'." This he defines as the space of a literature "doomed to inconclusiveness," one whose exemplary representative is Kafka, and in which the impossibility of concluding is directly related to what Blanchot calls "an inability to die in the work and to free oneself in death."[2] Without referring directly to them, Girard is clearly quoting Blanchot's reflections in *The Space of Literature* (1955), a work in which Blanchot's own writing traverses a "space" occupied not only by Kafka, but also Mallarmé and above all Rilke, and where Dostoevsky's Kirilov is encountered as an illustration of how "freeing oneself in death" (suicide), though apparently a means of rendering death possible, is also perhaps "the experience ... of a radical reversal, where [Kirilov] dies but cannot die, where death delivers him to the impossibility of dying" (*SL* 100). Whence what Blanchot calls "the hauntingly repetitive [*ressassante*] character of suicidal gestures" (*SL* 102).

It is this inability to conclude which Girard places at the heart of the "Romantic lie" to which the original title of his book refers. It reflects "a particular historical and metaphysical situation" which he calls "our time of anguish" (309), and whose literature is summed up by him in (unattributed) Barthesian terms as "'l'écriture blanche' and its 'degré zéro'" (264). And it is this cultural and aesthetic condition which the novel overcomes: "In all genuine novelistic conclusions," Girard claims, "death as spirit is victoriously opposed to the death of the spirit" (305) . Despite superficial affinities therefore, "there is an irreducible opposition between Dostoevsky and contemporary fiction" (259). If *Notes from the Underground* contains "characters doomed to inconclusiveness," and if, as Girard will later claim, in this work Dostoevsky is still caught up in a Romantic urge to "rehash his old certainties and to justify himself in his own eyes by continuing to take [*ressassant*] the same point of view about others and about himself,"[3] like all great novelists, he "cross[es] the literary space defined by Blanchot but [does] not stay there", pushing "beyond that space toward the infinity of a liberating death" (309).

The status which Girard accords Blanchot in his argument is deeply ambiguous. Although he enlists Blanchot's help in the task of rehabilitating the novel, he can only do so by blanking out an entire dimension of the argument of *The Space of Literature*, as his blindness to what Blanchot says about Kirilov attests. More fundamentally, by acknowledging the pertinence of Blanchot's category of "literary space," only to posit another space, that of the novel, which in effect lies outside and beyond it, he neglects to acknowledge that Blanchot's "literary space" is first and foremost, and in advance of all categorisation on his part, the "space" of his own fiction (which has already been included by Barthes under his category of "l'écriture blanche").[4] And crucially, when Blanchot traverses that space, it is in the opposite direction to the one proposed by Girard: away from the novel towards the first-person *récit* and the inconclusiveness which Girard abhors. And at a key turning-point in his fictional writing, at precisely the juncture where he leaves behind the novel considered as a way beyond what is interminable, it is in fact Blanchot who "traverses the literary space" of Dostoevsky in order to reach the point in that space where Girard eventually encounters him as it were head-on.

"L'Idylle" (The Idyll), a short story first published in 1947,[5] unmistakably brings to mind Dostoevsky's novel *The House of the Dead*, which was published three years before *Notes from the Underground*, in 1861. As Gary Mole has set out in some detail,[6] there are remarkable similarities between Dostoevsky's story and Blanchot's: the hospice in "The Idyll" closely resembles the prison camp in *The House of the Dead*; the name of the stranger who is incarcerated there, Alexandre Akim, combines that of Dostoevsky's narrator, Alexander Petrovitch Goriantchikov, and that of a fellow prisoner, Akim Akimytch; a number of other proper names used by Blanchot are borrowed from Dostoevsky's novel; and each story contains a very similar song.

It would seem safe to assume, however, that Blanchot has found, in the literary space he is exploring in 1947, a very different Dostoevsky from the one Girard places there. The space of literature which is his would seem much rather to accommodate the Dostoevsky whom Mikhail Bakhtin will first present in 1963 in *Problems of Dostoevsky's Poetics*, and subsequently in a late set of "Observations" (1973) attached to his 1937–1938 essay "Forms of Time and of the Chronotope in the Novel."[7] This is a Dostoevsky whose literary space is governed by what Bakhtin calls a "chronotope of the threshold and of other related figures: the staircase, the corridor, the front hall" (*DI* 248). It is a chronotope of crisis, of a break in life (*DI* 248), of "radical change" (*PDP* 169). It is a time of the instantaneous, "it has no duration and falls out of the normal course of biographical time" (*DI* 248). The latter is the time of novelists such as Tolstoy, whose space is that of the domestic interior. In a novel like *Crime and Punishment*, however, "absolutely nothing ... ever loses touch with the threshold" (*PDP* 170). And in the triptych of *récits* which Blanchot publishes between 1948 and 1953, as Jacques Derrida points out, the same figural chronotope is to be found: "The *room* is the privileged place of *la Chose* in all these stories, domestic but utterly foreign (*unheimlich*) ...; outside, corridors and stairways."[8] Bakhtin even extends his description of the space to be found in Dostoevsky to the very story from which the setting of "The Idyll" is borrowed, relating it to another story by Dostoevsky, *The Gambler*:

> Both the life of convicts and the life of gamblers – for all their differences in content – are equally "*life taken out of life*" ... And the time of penal servitude and the *time* of gambling are ... an identical *type of time*, similar to "the final moments of consciousness" before execution or suicide, similar in general to the time of crisis. All this is time on the *threshold*, and not biographical time, experienced in the interior spaces of life far from the threshold. (*PDP* 173)

If all of this raises important questions about Girard's conception of literary space, it raises much more significant questions about the status and indeed the nature of Blanchot's story. For "The Idyll" would hardly seem to conform to Girard's (or Bakhtin's) conception of a narrative of the interminable and the inconclusive, towards which I have claimed that all of Blanchot's fictional writing tends. Whereas both of the novels which appear before 1945 render their own limits or borders uncertain,[9] "The Idyll," set as it is in a penal colony lying within a town, and whose narrative concerns the arrival of an outsider, his incarceration, failed assimilation and eventual suppression, offers by contrast a relation between story and form of the most conventionally self-contained sort. The only sign that "The Idyll" does not sit undemandingly within the timeless dimension of the tale or fable, is the date which the story bears on its closing page: "juillet 1936." As fiction, it is given a grounding in history. In 1947, however, this temporal indication appeared merely to identify "The Idyll" with another era, making it seem at the time of publication like little more than a *fond de tiroir*, dating from a period when Blanchot was still in search of a narrative style. And "The Idyll" does indeed appear still to be caught within the version of literary space to which Girard seeks to confine Dostoevsky, one in which narrative points away from inconclusiveness towards what he calls "novelistic revelation."[10] Yet for Girard, *The House of the Dead* belongs to the phase in Dostoevsky's writing when his turn towards the novel had not yet occurred, when he is still in thrall to the ressassement of narrative inconclusiveness. Furthermore, it has been pointed out that Dostoevsky is "no idyllist,"[11] and indeed for Bakhtin, the chronotope of the threshold clearly differentiates between Dostoevsky and writers like Tolstoy, for whom it was "the family-idyllic chronotope and even the chronotope of the labour-idyll" which had most significance (*DI* 249–50). In short, "The Idyll," despite its clear relation to *The House of the Dead*, would seem to conform to neither of the versions of Dostoevsky which emerge in the post-war period, nor either to the pattern of its own author's fictional development. It thus appears suspended rather uncertainly within the "literary space" of Blanchot's writing in 1947: anchored forlornly in another historical era, while harbouring beneath its smooth and unassuming surface a fundamental uncertainty as to where its generic border lies.

But things were not to remain there. However much of an anachronism "The Idyll" may seem, it remains, along with "Le Dernier Mot" (The Last Word) which was published in the same year,[12] the single most reworked piece of writing in Blanchot's *oeuvre*. However inert and self-contained its outer appearance, it has resurfaced on repeated occasions along the extraordinary trajectory of Blanchot's fictional practice, coming to the fore again with the publication of *The Instant of my Death* in 1994, thanks to the association between the episode recounted in that brief fiction and that which led Dostoevsky to write *The House of the Dead*: the experience of almost being executed by firing squad.

The process of reworking began in 1951, when Blanchot brought together "The Idyll" and "The Last Word," with modest revisions, in a single volume entitled *Le Ressassement eternel* (*RE*).[13] The title was not taken from the stories themselves, but echoed a passage omitted from an article published in the same year, "Les deux versions de l'imaginaire," when it was annexed to *The Space of Literature* in 1955:[14]

> Mais avant le commencement, il y a le recommencement qui fait de la lumière une fascination, de l'objet son image et de nous le cœur vide du ressassement éternel.

[But before beginning there is beginning again, which turns light into fascination, the object into its image and us into the empty heart of eternal repetition.][15]

This would seem to provide clear confirmation that the direction in which Blanchot's fiction was moving through "literary space" in these years was the very opposite to that which will be promoted by Girard shortly afterwards. By reactualizing two narratives taken from his novel-writing past,[16] Blanchot appeared at the time to be situating them in a continuing process, during the course of which they had been left behind as his writing turned away from a search for novelistic conclusiveness, and entered the restless, turbulent space of the *récit*.[17]

And there things were set to remain for quite some time. Then in 1970, *Le Ressassement éternel* was re-edited in facsimile by Gordon & Breach, with a brief paragraph of presentation on the back cover:

> Le récit répond, toujours indirectement, à l'attrait du signe unique. Signe que la pensée désigne comme sa parfaite cohérence, mais qui, lui-même, se refuse à toute spécification et ne spécifie rien. Dans "l'inéquivalence" des deux récits: "L'Idylle" et "Le Dernier Mot," écrit [*sic*] à partir de 1935, vient s'inscrire, en tiers, l'écho répercuté d'un titre: "Le Ressassement éternel," qui, dans son ambiguïté, désigne moins l'espace commun d'une recherche, que le déploiement de celle-ci, son espacement sans perspective – sa propre force de dépassement.

> [The *récit* responds, always indirectly, to the draw of the single, unique sign. A sign which thought points to as its perfect coherence, but which itself eludes all specification and specifies nothing. Within the "non-equivalence" of these two *récits*, "The Idyll" and "The Last Word," written from 1935 onwards, is inscribed a third element, the repeated echo of a title: "Le Ressassement éternel," which, in its ambiguity, points less towards the common space of a search, than to the deployment of the latter, its spacing without perspective – its inherent power of overcoming.]

Finally, thirteen years later, in 1983, the volume entitled *Le Ressassement éternel*, which incorporated the two stories "The Idyll" and "The Last Word," was itself incorporated in a new work, *Après coup* précédé par *Le Ressassement éternel*, published once more by the Editions de Minuit.[18]

On one level, this was the same book which had appeared in 1951 and then in 1970 (there were again no textual variants), accompanied this time by a postface which in effect replaced the paragraph on the 1970 back cover, and whose title, "Après coup" (After the Fact), reflected both the temporal and compositional relations between itself and the original book. By also making this the title of the 1983 re-edition of *Le Ressassement éternel*, however, Blanchot was doing something less straight-forward. For although the composition of the new book reflects the chronological relation between *Le Ressassement éternel* (1951) and "After the Fact" (1983), its title disrupts this relation, turning *Le Ressassement éternel* into no more than a preamble to the later postface. *Après coup* thus transfers the already turbulent space of *Le Ressassement éternel* into one in which time and space are in tension with each other. In the 1983 volume, what comes *after* is not only given textual priority ("After the Fact" is "preceded by," rather than coming after, the 1951 work);[19] by substituting itself for and encompassing the original title: *Le Ressassement éternel*, it specifies and refines upon the temporality of Blanchot's narrative as it is reflected in the title from 1951. The adverbial rather than substantival status of the words "après coup" (their separation by a space rather than a hyphen) serves, I would argue, to indicate that the eternal *ressassement* of literary space does not merely provide an escape from historical time: it incessantly generates an original, non-chronological relation to history from somewhere beyond its end.

Once this becomes clear, it throws into relief something that has almost never been remarked upon:[20] from the moment *Le Ressassement éternel* appeared, the relationship between fiction and time changed √ fundamentally in Blanchot's writing. For whereas in 1947 "The Idyll" bore the date "juillet 1936," in *Le Ressassement éternel* it is without any date marker whatsoever, while at the end of "The Last Word," Blanchot adds: "1935, 1936." Were the order of stories in the book "The Last Word," "The Idyll," this change would be unremarkable. But the opposite is the case: between "1935, 1936" and "The Idyll," "The Last Word" there is an inverse relation. What is more, this inversion is not a neat or self-contained one. In both the note on the back cover of the 1970 re-edition and in "After the Fact" itself, an element of uncertainty accompanies the reference to dates: the back cover of the Gordon & Breach edition reads: "ces deux récits: 'L'Idylle' et 'Le Dernier Mot', *écrit* à partir de 1935" (my emphasis). This singular (where one might have expected a plural) may simply be a typographical error. As it stands, however, while it signifies that the second story, "The Last Word," was written from 1935 onwards, it gives no date for "The Idyll." The different historical reference in *Le Ressassement éternel* thus places between "The Idyll" and its original date, 1936, not just a separation but an absolute break.

In *Après coup* thirteen years later, the provenance of the two stories is confirmed when Blanchot speaks of "these two old stories, so old (nearly fifty years old)" (*VC* 63), and then refers to "'The Last Word' (1935)" (*VC* 64). When he comes to "The Idyll," however, things are less straightforward, since he refers to it as "the story that seems to have been named – by antiphrasis? – 'The Idyll,' or the torment of the happy idea (1936)" (*VC* 65). Strangely, whereas "The Idyll" is the story whose chronological status originally appeared more established, at the point where "The Last Word" finally acquires the unambiguous historical marker "1935," it is cut loose from its chronological grounding, since its date, 1936, from which it was separated through inversion in 1951, has by 1983 been transferred on to an experience described as "the torment of the happy idea" with which it is said to be synonymous, while at the same time its title itself has become the site of an inversion and an interrogation ("by antiphrasis?") which render its status uncertain.

What emerges therefore, when *Le Ressassement éternel* is incorporated into *Après coup* in 1983, is that the 1951 volume did not simply sever the link which originally anchored "The Idyll" in history: in inverting the chronological order of the stories and removing "juillet 1936" from "The Idyll," it also wrenched "The Idyll" out of history, placing between it and "The Last Word" not merely the reversibility of equivalence, but the "non-equivalence" of a radical break. If this was initially indicated by no more than the comma separating 1935 and 1936 in 1951, what Après coup throws into light is that through this slim interval, the 1951 book created an opening onto the dimension it refers to in its title as "le ressassement éternel," and which appears in retrospect as the formal equivalent or enactment of "the torment of the happy idea," projected beyond the historical moment (1936) when it was experienced, into an absolute, eternal moment of time. If 1935 turns out to be the secure anchor point for both *Le Ressassement éternel* and *Après coup* in 1983, between 1936 and "The Idyll" a complex relation therefore emerges. Something about "The Idyll" and history seems to be at stake in 1951. More precisely, between 1947 and 1951, the idea that an event or moment in history gives rise to and is reflected in a work of fiction,[21] yields to a relation between narrative and history marked by reversal and interruption.

Après coup thus reveals that the simple relation between narrative and history, reflected in the dating of "The Idyll" in 1947, is superseded with the publication of *Le Ressassement éternel*. By incorporating the story within the 1951 volume, Blanchot in effect *renarrates* it. In so doing, he transfers it to the particular time which narrative occupies, and which by

1951 appears to him as a form of restless eternity. This alters its relation to history fundamentally. For what *Le Ressassement éternel* looks back to is not a moment in time – juillet 1936 – which has led progressively to the point from where it can be recollected in tranquillity, but a moment when history, understood chronologically, seems somehow to have stopped. If that moment led to the moment in 1951 when *Le Ressassement éternel* appeared, it did so not along a linear development marked by successive publications, but immediately, consigning all of Blanchot's writing to a single spatialized moment which has since endured "eternally." In short, the moment in history which put a stop to history became the endless, eternal present moment at which history will remain trapped, for Blanchot, henceforth.

What *Le Ressassement éternel* allows, therefore, is not simply an act of retrospection ("1935, 1936" seen from 1951). In so far as all renarration is retrospection, it occurs not "in" 1951, but rather from within what the Gordon & Breach back cover will call in 1970 a "spacing without perspective" which has taken the place of time. Seen from the perspective of *Après coup* in 1983, 1951 is thus no more than the point in a now superseded historical time-scale when/where the moment which has stopped history and divided time can come fully face to face – or rather: into phase – with itself by means of narrative, and thus designate itself as a break in time, "1935, 1936," through which linear continuity (history) was both reversed and displaced into endless repetition. Beneath the surface of Blanchot's "literary space" as it evolves between 1945 and 1951 there thus lies not a gradual, orderly transition from third-person novel writing to first-person *récit*, but a fundamental reorientation in which language, in the form of narrative, is brought into phase with the experience out of which it arises, an experience which is nothing other than a collapse of the present dating back to 1936.

The question remains, however: what is it that brought about this change of perspective in 1951? Nothing *happens* in either of the stories themselves to precipitate the change (the variants are minimal). The answer to this question requires a brief excursion into the post-war phase in Blanchot's writing, during which he thoroughly revised his narrative practice. In 1948, he simultaneously published his last novel, *Le Très-Haut* (*The Most High*), and his first récit, *L'Arrêt de mort* (*Death Sentence*). Then in 1949, he published a story entitled "Un récit(?)" in which, as Jacques Derrida demonstrates in "The Law of Genre,"[22] the principle of narrative inconclusiveness which Girard attributes to Blanchot's "literary space" is enacted as a "textual event."[23] As Derrida clearly demonstrates, in "Un récit(?)," genre itself yields to the question it raises, a question which goes to the heart of the idea of law in general. As a result, "Un récit(?)," a story which emerges from the heart of the changes which were going on in Blanchot's fiction, is nothing but the enactment of its own "non-equivalence":

> *Récit* of a *récit* without *récit*, a *récit* without edge or boundary, *récit* all of whose visible space is but some border of itself torn from itself, without "self," consisting of a framing edge without content, without modal or generic boundaries – such is the law of this textual event. (242; translation modified)

By the time Blanchot includes "The Idyll" and "The Last Word" in *Le Ressassement éternel* in 1951, therefore, it may be said that the space of his fiction has already become the reality to which the title of that work refers. But this still does not entirely answer the question: How? Derrida's analyses of "Un récit(?)" are indispensable for any reading of Blanchot's fiction. However, the fictional process he describes at one point as "an analysis ... [which is] insatiably recurring [*ressassante*]" (237), though powerfully disruptive of time, has no direct bearing on time as history.[24] What is it that allows Blanchot to take two stories from the historical past, sever their anchorage and set them adrift in the space of eternal *ressassement*?

The answer, I believe, is to be found in the *récit* which Blanchot published the year before "Un récit(?)," *Death Sentence*, and which begins: "These things happened to me in 1938" (*DS* 1). It is the story of a young woman referred to as J., whose dying forms the first part of the *récit*, and of whom the narrator says: "Her doctor had told me that from 1936 he had considered her dead" (*DS* 5). With the same simplicity as "The Idyll," *Death Sentence* anchors the story it tells in history, which is to say in the immediate pre-war past (there is precise reference to the Munich crisis [*DS* 4]). In the same year, 1947, two works of narrative fiction are thus given a clear historical grounding by Blanchot in 1936. In *Death Sentence*, this relation to history is part of the story, and the narrator goes on:

> I should recall that I once managed to put these events into writing. It was in 1940, during the last weeks of July or the first weeks of August. Inactive as a result of stupor, I wrote this story. But once it was written I reread it and immediately destroyed the manuscript. (*DS* 1, trans. modified)

In *Death Sentence*, narrative looks back from 1947 at events in 1938 involving France and a woman who should have been dead in 1936, but before doing so, it evokes a previous attempt to look back at these events by means of narrative in July–August 1940 (which is when the Vichy government was installed). It thus both inverts the chronological order of these two moments, and separates them absolutely, since what lies between 1938 and 1940, as both historical event (the *débâcle*) and personal ordeal (the narrator's bereavement), is presented as total disaster, as the absolute end. There would seem here to be a close parallel with the temporal structure of *Le Ressassement éternel*, which can be expressed most simply as follows:

$$[1947 (1938, 1940)] = [1951 (1935, 1936)].$$

In other terms, it is clear that *Death Sentence* both anticipates the focus on the interruption of history which *Le Ressassement éternel* will enact and, like that work, relates it to a previous attempt to "put events into writing" ("The Idyll" (1936), "this story" (1940)). 1947 thus sees a fundamental break in the relation between narrative and time in Blanchot's writing. Simultaneously in that year, he will publish a story that looks back continuously to 1936, and a *récit* that narrates the failure of narrative which seeks to do so. A relation to history as something on which it is possible simply to look back, coexists with one in which looking back historically has ceased to be possible.

There is still some way to go, however, before it can become clear how *Death Sentence* both affirms and severs the link between narrative and history. So far, the story has concentrated on the failure of narrative to give a retrospective account of events across the divide opened up between September 1938 (Munich) and July 1940 (Vichy). Eventually, however, having traced out the parallel decline of J. and France until each ceases to exist, the narrative of *Death Sentence* fails in its turn: "I have said nothing extraordinary or even surprising. What is extraordinary begins at the moment I stop. But I am no longer able to speak of it" (*DS* 30). The *récit* would seem, therefore, to get no further than *The Most High* which appeared alongside it, and which ends with its narrator, as he is shot, crying: "It's now, now that I speak" (*TH* 243). In both works, the moment at which narrative "speaks" is a moment when it can only be silent.

But of course, the end is not the end: *Death Sentence* has a second, longer part. A voice begins: "I will go on with this story, but now I will take some precautions" (*DS* 31). In the first part, the closer the narration of events came to the moment when everything would founder in disaster, the closer it came, seemingly inevitably, to its own suspension. In the second, a way will be found of narrating that suspension of narrative, by tapping in to what will a few years later be termed *le ressassement éternel*. On the surface, it is not clear how this will occur. The second part resumes the historical narrative:

> I must, however, not forget events. They were becoming more and more serious: thinking and living no longer went hand in hand. (*DS* 61, trans. modified)

There are also references to the bombardment of Paris and to the need to take shelter in the Métro (*DS* 61, 64). It would appear as if the second part is simply renarrating the fatal slide into disaster which eventually reduced the first part to silence. The difference is that this time, the narrator can speak of the disaster itself:

> I am talking about things which seem negligible, and am ignoring public events. These events were very important and they occupied my attention every day. But today, they are rotting away, their story [*histoire*] is dead, and the hours and the life which were then mine are dead too. What speaks is the present moment and the moment that will come after it. The shadow of yesterday's world is still pleasant for people who take refuge in it, but it will fade. And the world of the future is already falling in an avalanche on the memory of the past. (*DS* 46)

This passage, with its Proustian resonances, marks an absolute advance on the end of the first part. What the narrator then was "no longer able to speak of" is here spoken. He is not the speaker though: as the text makes clear, it is "spoken" both *by* and *as* the break in time itself which lies between the present moment and the one that comes after it. Furthermore, the temporality of this moment is totally original, consisting as it does of a moment experienced as to come in so far as it has already happened. In the second part, therefore, disaster, given futurity by the impossible attempt to look back at it from a present which it has already annihilated, opens, by way of this reversal, on to the disjunction of a non-chronological present from within which it is time itself ("the present moment and the moment that will come after it") that speaks.

Having identified the voice that speaks in the second part in the way he does, the task the narrator sets himself is to make the language of his narrative progressively divest itself of everything except what constitutes that voice: namely, a reversal which breaks the succession of time and opens on to an endlessly fractured present. Whereas the fate of J. in the first part followed events into catastrophe, leaving the narrator speechless, the narrator's relationship with Nathalie in the second part survives catastrophe, but only after a crucial parting of the ways. For Nathalie, by now reduced to the initial N., ceases to figure in the story as it reaches its conclusion. As if wanting to "tear apart with a vigilant hand the pretences we were living under" by talking to him about what she calls his "plan [projet]" (*DS* 79), N. has vanished, and in place of a living being there remains only a thought. Nathalie is now a memory, and what the entire narrative of his memory of her projected into the future, as a separation between thinking and living (*DS* 61), has now come to embrace the whole of time.

Unlike in the first part, however, the invasion of the present by a future which is borne along on the wave of narrative as it recounts the past, does not silence narrative. An ability to say remains, which is that of "voice" reduced entirely to a non-chronological succession of moments, and which is jubilantly reflected in the closing words of the book: "to it [that thought], I say eternally, 'Come,' and eternally, it is there" (*DS* 80, trans. modified). These are without doubt the "ten words" that the narrator has been grappling with since 1938 (*DS* 2) – "eternally" counting once only, as nothing other, in the French original, than the stuttering repetition to which it gives rise: "éternellement . . . et, éternellement . . . ." Now he is no longer even their narrator, merely one of a pair of pronouns (I – her) to which time itself gives voice in the process of endlessly thinking and saying itself, through narrative, as reversal and interruption.

There seems little doubt that what occurs at the end of *Death Sentence* in 1947 prefigures and renders possible what becomes *Le Ressassement eternel* in 1951. The final sentence of the *récit is* that *ressassement*, not in the abstract form of a category but as a real, spatialized moment in language, where speech is henceforth merely the performative of a silent inscription.[25] If Blanchot can place "The Idyll" and "The Last Word" inside that moment, therefore, it is quite simply because by 1951, the language of his narrative now inhabits it totally. The relation to time consisting of a reversal and an interruption which is perceptible in the separate stages of the publication of *Le Ressassement éternel* (1951, 1983) is actualised and made permanent by *Death Sentence* in 1947.

Two questions still remain, however, and they are related: what is the significance of the shift from 1938, 1940 in *Death Sentence* to 1935, 1936 in *Le Ressassement éternel?* And why "The Idyll"?

A clear answer to the first question suggests itself, though it can only be speculative at this stage. In *Death Sentence*, the disaster in which everything founders after 1938 is that of the French nation. In the light of Blanchot's own nationalist sympathies in the 1930s, this can be read as a reflection of the personal ordeal occasioned by the collapse of France. From that perspective, the reference to 1936 as the date when J. should have died evokes the Front Populaire, Blanchot's bitter hostility to it and to Léon Blum, and for many readers since the 1980s, the suspicion that Blanchot shared and was guilty of the anti-Semitism which informed nationalist discourse at the time. The conclusion of *Death Sentence* can be convincingly read as a redemptive eschewal of that entire history on Blanchot's part; a rejection of mourning in favour of a mode of subjectivity grounded in affirmation and open to the other.

As it stands, however, that development remains open to question and criticism, and does not fully offer satisfaction to those for whom Blanchot's turn away from his pre-war position is merely opportunistic: a way of concealing a structure of thought rather than expiating it (to use a term attributed to Blanchot by Bataille). For however rigorous the process which takes place in *Death Sentence*, it seems merely to put an end to reflection as far as the pre-war past is concerned; to do no more than make it possible for subjectivity, an "I," just to keep afloat on the tide of destruction which has put an end to history and ushered in an endless post-apocalyptic present. In short, the jubilant conclusion to the *récit* appears inherently nihilistic. The *ressassement éternel* which it inaugurates is just as much the experience of "horror, confusion and uncertainty" which characterizes it in *The Space of Literature* (238) as it is "the hymen or the alliance in the language of the other" of which Derrida speaks in "Living On" (77).[26]

The replacement of "1938, 1940" by "1935, 1936" in 1951 discreetly but decisively transforms this state of affairs. In *Death Sentence*, the collapse of history enters language in such a way that the present of writing and the present of history become (a fractured) one. Narrative in its reflexivity becomes historical at the moment where history ends. Disaster may thus become reflexive, but its reflexivity cannot be reflected on its turn: it can simply inscribe, in an eternal *ressassement*, the fractured voice which says "come ... it is there."[27] With the shift to "1935, 1936" in 1951, a further dimension is introduced. 1936 remains the "fatal" date, but rather than leading, in a series of delayed actions, to disaster in 1940, it now points back, to 1935. The question then arises: what happened in 1935 to make a gap open up between that year and 1936, just as one did between 1938 and 1940? If the history of France at the time is examined, no event of "historic" significance occurs in that year. On what then is Blanchot focusing when he writes "1935, 1936"?

In both *Death Sentence* and *Le Ressassement éternel* Blanchot simultaneously anchors his writing in 1936 and releases it into the eternal. In *Death Sentence*, however, this historical anchorage is at the same time presented as uncertain: "I must say that for me it did happen that way, setting aside the question of dates, since everything could have happened at a much earlier time" (79). Crucially, it emerges, reversal and discontinuity are not characteristics of a given historical event, allowing say 1936 to emerge as the date when history came to an end. Rather, they are what historical subjects bring to bear on events. And what *Le Ressassement éternel* reveals, three years later, is that *Death Sentence* does not simply allow Blanchot to write history off in favour of the endlessness of the present: rather, it makes possible a return to history from the vantage point of the eternal *ressassement* which his narrative brings to it. More precisely, *Le Ressassement éternel* displaces the break, which for *Death Sentence* lies between 1936/1938 and 1940, in such a way that this break, which initially signifies merely the failure of narrative in 1940 to account for the disaster which begins to happen in 1936/1938, can be moved around as it were heuristically through history. Narrative will henceforth not merely generate endless *ressassement* in a present cut off from history; in return, it will allow a reflection on the *idea* of history considered as the site of an interruption which has brought it to an end.

By replacing "1936/1938, 1940" with "1935, 1936" Blanchot is, therefore, not simply going back in time in search of a more original moment in the history of disaster. He is locating the break which is now the site of his writing in such a way in relation to history, that it is no longer simply the reality of the nation which is mourned, it is the very *idea* of a nation which is reflected upon. For the date 1935, I would argue, does not refer to the history of France at all, but to the history of Germany. In September 1935, Nazi Germany passed the so-called Nuremberg decrees which deprived Germany's Jews of their citizenship. Nationhood was affirmed in Germany by depriving certain Germans of their nationality. The following year Spain and France, purporting to rise above nationalism in the name of an ideology of internationalism, elected a Popular Front government. From the perspective of the first part of *Death Sentence*, the sole interpretation of these events was that 1936 sealed the fate which eventually overtook France in 1940. From the perspective which *Death Sentence* eventually opens up, and which *When the Time Comes* and *Le Ressassement éternel* both adopt, what comes to the fore is the blindness which conditions both the nationalist and the internationalist positions in France from 1936 onwards, since neither was able to see what nationalism had perpetrated in Germany in 1935. In a reversal of perspective in relation to the break marked by 1936, *Le Ressassement éternel* reveals that the very idea of the nation, whether affirmed or contested, is constructed out of blindness to the apocalyptic thought-processes from which it stems, and which condition the nation to see what lies outside of it, its "other," as the site of unspeakable disaster. As result of that blindness, between 1935 and 1936 history considered as the history of nations did indeed come apart, swallowing up its other (the Jew) in the abyss which it had become.

If it is possible to put forward what remains a hypothesis concerning the shift from "1938, 1940" to "1935, 1936," it is firstly because there are discrete signs, in Blanchot's post-war writing, which point to an increasing consciousness of the reality of the Holocaust.[28] *The Most High*, with its reference to the State as "our promised land" (*TH* 172) and its theme of sabotage, would seem to reflect the events in Palestine leading to the foundation of the State of Israel in 1948. And in 1951, Blanchot wrote the following in *When the Time Comes*:

> I would sometimes stare through the window for a long time at the disfigured facade of the synagogue (one shouldn't forget the bomb) – that black wall, those beams supporting the entrance or closing it off, a merciless image. Certainly the truth does not die easily. (*WTC 32*)[29]

Ever since the publication of *Après coup*, the issue of whether "The Idyll" anticipates or at least bears a relation to the reality of the camps has been approached and shied away from. The above hypothesis allows an answer to that question which disengages it from the impasse into which it has tended to lead: despite appearances, it is not "The Idyll" but *Le Ressassement éternel* itself which offers a reflection on the camps, by redirecting the narrative reflexivity, which is now Blanchot's response to the end of history, back into history considered as the site of a break which the present has proved so far incapable of confronting, with disastrous results.

The answer to the second question: "why 'The Idyll'?" appears to confirm this hypothesis. The question of the idyll is in fact much more a German one than a French one. More precisely, from the late eighteenth century onwards, it accompanies the powerful struggles which led to the emergence of Modern Germany as a nation, providing a focus for the complex and contradictory attitudes to France (the France of 1789) which marked this historical turning-point, and which found their cultural and political adversary in Rousseau. There are two moments in the emergence of the idyll as a problematical focus at this time. In 1784, Johannes Heinrich Voss published the first "modern" version of the pastoral idyll in German, *Luise*, which offers a picture of middle-class life sealed off from contemporary political turmoil (it is noteworthy that the female protagonist of "The Idyll," like others in Blanchot's fiction, is called Louise). For Hegel,[30] this "modernised" idyll was merely a distraction, and Schiller is not far from sharing his view.[31] However, Voss's example gave rise to a second, more positive response, which led writers such as Jean Paul[32] and even Goethe to produce self-conscious, ironic or "critical" idylls[33] in response to contemporary social and political realities.

Though this is often overlooked,[34] it was Schiller who encapsulated this dual response. In *Über naive und sentimentale Dichtung* he denounced the "modernised" idyll on the one hand, whose model he saw in Rousseau's *Julie*, for appealing to a desire for physical tranquillity rather than moral harmony (477). But he then went on to project, as a possibility whose *theory* remains to be worked out (501), an idyll which would reconcile the innocence of the outmoded form with what he calls the subject of contemporary culture (500), which is to say, the modern self:

> Der Begriff dieser Idylle ist der Begriff eines völlig aufgelösten Kampfes .... *Ruhe* wäre also der herrschende Eindruck dieser Dichtungsart, aber Ruhe der Vollendung, nicht der Trägheit; eine Ruhe, die aus dem Gleichgewicht, nicht aus dem Stillstand der Kräfte, die aus der Fülle, nicht aus der Leerheit fliesst und von dem Gefühl eines unendlichen Vermögens begleitet wird. (500).

> [The concept of this idyll is the concept of a struggle that has been entirely resolved. ... The dominant impression afforded by this type of poetry would thus be one of calm, but the calm of perfection not of inertia, the calm which results from a balance of forces, not from their cessation, from fullness not emptiness, the calm which is accompanied by a feeling of endless power.]

In French translations of Schiller's work, *die Ruhe* is usually translated as *le calme*.[35] In 1955, Blanchot published a short extract of what would become the beginning of Part II of *Le Dernier Homme*, which he entitled "Le Calme."[36] I would argue that it is by going back to the era when Schiller's project for an idyll was still in search of its theory, that Blanchot found a generic counterpart for the "textual event" which gradually emerges in his fiction in the years following 1945. This both provides a model for the simultaneous closure and interruption which Jacques Derrida identifies in his *récits* from 1949; and establishes the inseparability of this endlessly reflexive process of narrative from a reflection on the politics of modernity.

ENDNOTES

[1] Jacques Derrida, "Pas" [1975], in *Parages*. Nouvelle édition revue et augmentée (Paris: Galilée, 1986–2003), 93.

[2] René Girard, *Deceit, Desire, and the Novel: Self and Other in Literary Structure*, trans. Yvonne Freccero (Baltimore: Johns Hopkins University Press, 1965), 309.

[3] René Girard, in *Resurrection from the Underground: Feodor Dostoevsky*, ed. and trans. James G. Williams (New York: Crossroad, 1997), 32.

[4] See Roland Barthes, *Writing Degree Zero*, trans. Annette Lavers and Colin Smith (London: Jonathan Cape, 1967), 11.

[5] "L'Idylle", *La Licorne*, 1 (Spring 1947), 33–58.

[6] Gary D. Mole, *Lévinas, Blanchot, Jabès: Figures of Estrangement* (Gainesville: University Press of Florida, 1997). See in particular the section entitled "Blanchot, *L'Idylle* and the play of ambiguity", 30–54.

[7] Mikhail Bakhtin, *Problems of Dostoevsky's Poetics*, trans. C. Emerson (Manchester: Manchester University Press, 1984) (hereafter *PDP*); "Forms of Time and of the Chronotope in the Novel", *The Dialogic Imagination: Four Essays by M.M. Bakhtin*, ed. Michael Holquist (Austin: University of Texas Press, 1981), 84–258 (hereafter *DI*).

[8] Derrida, "Living On. Border Lines", trans. James Hulbert, in *Deconstruction and Criticism*, ed. Geoffrey Hartman (New York: Seabury Press, 1979), 75–176 (here 121–2). Derrida also points out that in Blanchot's *récits*, "rien ne reste finalement au seuil, le pas sans pas ne s'arrête pas à une simple pensée du limen [in the end, nothing remains on the threshold, the step without step does not stop at a simple thought of the *limen*]" ("Pas", 5). Correspondingly, if the staircase is a key figure, "cet escalier, cette structure d'escalier ... reste infiniment éloigné de tout escalier perceptible, présentable, familier [that staircase, that staircase structure remains infinitely remote from any perceptible, presentable, familiar staircase]" (69–70). In these narratives, he says in "Living On," "the event ... takes place place*less*ly" (146), according to the "phoronomie atopique [atopic phoronomia]" which makes every "pas" a "va-et-vient [coming and going]" ("Pas", 25).

[9] Echoing the end of Kafka's *Trial*, Blanchot's first novel, *Thomas l'obscur* (1941), ends with the words "comme si la honte eût commencé pour lui [as if shame had just begun for him]" (*TOI* 232). His second novel, *Aminadab* (1942), ends by leaving hanging a question which has recurred throughout the narrative: "Qui êtes-vous? [Who are you?]" (*Ab* 226).

[10] Girard, *Deceit*, 268.

[11] Julius Bramont, introduction to Fyodor Dostoevsky, *The House of the Dead* (London: J. M. Dent & Sons, 1933), viii.

[12] "Le Dernier Mot", *Fontaine*, 60 (May 1947), 33–75.

[13] "The Last Word" had already appeared as a volume in the collection "L'Âge d'Or," published by Editions Fontaine, in 1947, though this was never put on sale.

[14] See "The Two Versions of the Imaginary" in *SL* 254–63, and *Cahiers de la Pléïade*, 12 (1951), 115–25. The following year, it is again evoked when Blanchot speaks of "the horror, the confusion and the uncertainty of eternal repetition [*du ressassement éternel*]" in which the writer is adrift ("Literature and the Original Experience" *SL* 238).

[15] I keep Ann Smock's translation here for reasons of consistency, though it leaves out much of what *le ressassement* signifies.

[16] "The Last Word" contains an episode in which the narrator writes on a school blackboard an extract from a narrative concerning a character called Thomas.

[17] This dual perspective is clearly indicated in the *dédicace* which Blanchot inscribes in Denise Rollin's copy of *Le Ressassement éternel*: "Ces pages d'un autre temps [these pages from another time]", followed by the closing words of "Les deux versions de l'imaginaire," again not included in *The Space of Literature*, where Blanchot evokes the giant turtles described by Melville in terms of "le piétinement de la monotonie, [le] harcèlement gigantesque au sein du recommencement [the endless tread of monotony, the gigantic harrassment at the heart of recurrence]." See Jean Rollin, *Le Dialogue sans fin*, précédé de *Quelques souvenirs sur Georges Bataille, Maurice Blanchot et Michel Fardoulis-Lagrange* (Treillières: Le Pigeon Blanc, 1997), 29.

[18] Translated by Paul Auster as *Vicious Circles. Two Fictions and "After the Fact"* (*VC*).

[19] It must be noted that the title of the English translation eliminates this structural dimension.

[20] Mole is the exception. See *Lévinas, Blanchot, Jabès*, 50.

[21] Evelyne Londyn simply asserts that "L'Idylle", which she dates from 1935, is inspired by the Spanish Civil War (July 1936). See *Maurice Blanchot romancier* (Paris: Nizet, 1976), 189.

[22] Jacques Derrida, "The Law of Genre", translated by Avital Ronell, in *Acts of Literature*, ed. Derek Attridge (New York: Routledge, 1992), 223–52. This is an abridged version of the original essay, which appeared in French and in English in *Glyph*, 7 (1980).

[23] "Un récit(?)", *Empédocle*, 2 (May, 1949), 13–22 (the question mark is only present in one of the three mentions of the title in the journal). Published as *La Folie du jour* (1973; 2002). Translated by Lydia Davis as *The Madness of the Day*.

[24] Indeed, Derrida positively warns against treating the "moment" to which "Un récit(?)" confines itself as a simple moment *in* history. To do so would be to reveal that "on ne s'est pas délivré de l'héritage romantique [we are not yet free of the Romantic legacy]," which he defines as "la mise en ordre téléologique de l'histoire

[the teleological ordering of history]," *Parages*, 240–1 (this passage is omitted from "The Law of Genre" in *Acts of Literature*).

25 The closing words of *When the Time Comes* (1951) reflect this change, by comparison with those which close *The Most High*: "even if I had to write this eternally, I would write it in order to obliterate eternity: Now, the end" (*WTC* 74).

26 Derrida is also aware of the ambivalence of what concludes *Death Sentence*. The *hymen* is at the same time a crime: "The violence of a truth stronger than truth. The crime of the *hymen* takes place without taking place and repeats itself endlessly" ("Living On," 155).

27 The eternal present of this two-fold enunciation (whose complexity is formulated in *When the Time Comes* by the words "What! You were here! Now!" (9)) describes an unrepresentable distortion of space and time (of "chronotope"), since what is to come is already there. "Perspective" is simultaneously retrospective and prospective. It is prefigured by a passage from *Death Sentence* already cited: 'the world of the future is already falling in an avalanche on the memory of the past' (*DS* 46).

28 From the perspective of this essay, it is difficult not to remark that in 1945, the following anonymously authored book appeared: *Souvenirs de la maison des morts. Le massacre des juifs. Documents inédits sur les camps d'extermination* (Paris: L. Simon). The most recent translation of Dostoevsky's novel dated back to 1936: *Souvenirs de la maison des morts*, trans. Henri Mongault and Louise Desormonts (Paris: Gallimard, 1936).

29 Christophe Bident relates this passage to the bombing of the synagogue in the rue de la Victoire on the night of 2–3 October 1941. See *Maurice Blanchot, partenaire invisible* (Seyssel: Champ Vallon, 1998), 75.

30 "Der Mensch darf nicht in solcher idyllischen Geistesarmut hinleben, er muss arbeiten [man should not waste his life in such idyllic spiritual impoverishment, he must work]." G. W. F. Hegel, *Ästhetik*, ed. Georg Lukács (Frankfurt-am-Main: Europäische Verlagsanstalt, 1966), 1: 255.

31 Friedrich Schiller, "Über naive und sentimentale Dichtung" (1795), in *Über Kunst und Wirklichkeit. Schriften und Briefe zur Ästhetik* (Leipzig, Reclam, 1975), 435–534 (499).

32 Jean Paul's early work *Wutz*, contained in *Die Unsichtbare Loge* (The Invisible Lodge) (1793), is subtitled "eine Art Idylle" (a sort of idyll).

33 See Peter Morgan, *The Critical Idyll: Traditional Values and the French Revolution in Goethe's "Hermann und Dorothea"* (Columbia, SC: Camden House, 1990).

34 In "The Image of Rousseau in the Poetry of Hölderlin", Paul de Man's discussion of the idyll is constrained by his presentation of only the negative side of Schiller's response to it. See *The Rhetoric of Romanticism* (New York: Columbia University Press, 1984), 19–46 (especially 43).

35 See for example Schiller, *Poésie naïve et sentimentale*, trans. Robert Leroux (Paris: Aubier-Montaigne, collection bilingue des classiques étrangères, 1947), 211: "L'impression dominante que procurerait ce genre poétique [Schiller's second

version of the idyll] serait donc le calme, mais le calme qui résulte de la perfection non de l'inertie."

36 "Le Calme", *Botteghe Oscure*, XVI (September 1955), 28–36. In *DH* 106–21.

BLANCHOT'S "THE INDESTRUCTIBLE"

Christopher Fynsk

IN THE CONVERSATION BLANCHOT PURSUES WITH LEVINAS, THERE IS NO apparent response to what might be termed the first word of *Totality and Infinity*. Where Levinas speaks of peace,[1] we find reference only to a staying of violence and something Blanchot terms "the exigency of another relation." But the form of this latter relation is elusive, and far more prominent is Blanchot's disconcerting formulation of the impossibility of destroying its exigency as it comes to us obliquely in the presence of *autrui*: "man is the indestructible, and this means that there is no limit to the destruction of man."[2]

Especially striking is the fact that this latter formulation (which punctuates several dialogues in *The Infinite Conversation* in different phrasings) is pursued most directly and at greatest length in a brief essay, "Humankind" ("L'Espèce humaine"), coupled to another bearing the heading "Being Jewish" ("Être Juif") – the latter constituting what is probably Blanchot's most significant statement on Judaism. The essays are joined with the chapter-title "The Indestructible." Since "Being Jewish" may be construed as the description of a *form of existence* that bears witness to the exigency to which I have referred, the meaning of Blanchot's gesture of coupling the essays should give us pause. We may presume that something quite significant in Blanchot's relation to Levinas is played out in these pages. Unfortunately, we do not find in these essays significant clues as to whether "the other relation" to which Blanchot refers bears any resemblance to Levinas's notion of a "sabbatical existence" (which is one point from which the question of peace may be addressed). I will have to pursue this topic elsewhere. But I will use this question regarding the theme of peace as a means of introducing the two essays by Blanchot because the socio-historical circumstances that have undoubtedly driven me to it are addressed powerfully by Blanchot's essays. In a time when acts of torture and other forms of barbarism are normalized in our societies, the meaning of Blanchot's discreet response to Levinas via the motif of "the indestructible" seems critically important.

I will not review the beautiful pages from the beginning of *Totality and Infinity* that set Levinas's notion of peace against the privilege accorded to war in philosophical thought. I will retain only his critical assertion that peace comes about when human beings are able to answer for themselves, rather than lend their voices to the anonymous words of history and their totalizing demands. Peace, he tells us, is nothing other than "an aptitude for speech."[3] By the latter, Levinas refers to the promptness of responsive saying in what he will later term the diachrony of transcendence. As a giving over of language itself, and with it the time, the world, even the finitude of the responding subject, it is a kind of unconditional surrender. But it is a surrender to no power, and thus it is more like an unconditional offer. And even though Levinas claims that the visage communicates a commandment ("thou shalt not kill"), the offering to the other cannot be predicated on some obedience (the prohibition can only be articulated in the relation), or take form against the horizon of possible hostilities. The offering, in this ethical relation, is absolute.

But here, already, we meet a question. In what sense, precisely, is this offering one of peace? What is *given* in peace, or is it merely an absence of conflict or of some form of violent appropriation? Does peace inhere in a *time* given, or something like the gift of finitude? When Levinas constructs this offering as an alternative to violence in *Totality and Infinity* ("we speak or we kill," he says on numerous occasions), he seems to limit his meditation on peace. What might we learn from Blanchot's meditation on the encounter with *autrui* and the possibility of learning an "aptitude for speech"?

We find the latter scene of encounter, staged as a matter of speaking or killing, at numerous points in *The Infinite Conversation*. The dialogue "Keeping To Words," for example, introduces it as "something terrible" by reason of its radical character inasmuch as *nothing* stands between the individual and *autrui*. We speak to the other or we kill because nothing upholds the relation prior to our act. In worldly affairs, what Heidegger named *Mitdasein*, relations are always mediated, be they of rivalry or cooperation. But in the moment of encounter, the mediating barriers fall:

> The walls have fallen: those that separate us, those too that permit us to communicate, and those, finally, that protect us by keeping us at a distance. In a sense, man is now the inaccessible, but the inaccessible is in a sense the immediate; what exceeds me absolutely is absolutely at my mercy. Here is man come forth in his presence, that is to say, reduced to the poverty of presence. . . . My intervention – that of the

self – will not be limited to the partial violence of work, nor to the limited and veiled negation of refusal; there, if I assert myself still as a power, my power will extend to death, and this is not a partial but a radical death. (*IC* 60)

I speak or I kill. But the act of speaking cannot be construed as an act of communication since it is the reception of a presence that precedes all signification and hovers at the limit of insignificance. And it is not an act of mediation since it preserves the naked presence before it from any appropriation, any accommodating power. It is an act that effectively renders possible something like the alternative, speech or violence. Deferring a lengthier consideration of this act of speech, Blanchot gives the following to one of the voices in his dialogue:

> This isn't the moment for us to give an account of it. But I will say two things: first, if speech is weighty, it is because, being bare presence, it is what lays presence bare, what thus exposes it to radical violence in reducing it to the fragility of what is without power. To speak at the level of weakness and of destitution – at the level of affliction – is perhaps to challenge force, but also to attract force by refusing it. And second: in this situation, either to speak or to kill, speech does not consist in speaking, but first of all in maintaining the movement of this *either . . . or*; it is what founds the alternative. To speak is always to speak from out of this interval *between* speech and radical violence, separating them, but maintaining each of them in a relation of vicissitude. (*IC* 62)

So, the speech to which Blanchot refers is a kind of speech before speech, opening the space for speech, or violence. "What is that speech?" Blanchot's interlocutors ask at various moments. How do we understand the saying that occurs in the encounter with *autrui*, and how might we understand a speech that responds to the exigency it carries and unfolds within it?

An answer to these questions would carry us through the whole of Blanchot's work and into a region left largely unthought by Levinas, who leaves the structure of saying in its relation to the said relatively undeveloped. In Blanchot's text, it becomes, for example, the question of writing. Needless to say, the topic is far too vast to cover here. But elements of it must be addressed because they hold a key to Blanchot's divergence from Levinas on the question of peace and are vital for a reading of "The Indestructible." The essential point might be summarized in Blanchot's Hegelian-inflected vocabulary by noting that the structure of saying, which is the path of an opening to the other, could never be thought apart from the mortal power of the negative. At the scene of encounter, where before *autrui* we speak or we kill, death has already entered. It speaks in the very exposure of *autrui* to the other human being, saying its own suspension before what escapes its power. There is an interruption here, but the deferral is like a fold in what seems an inevitable violence. A passage from *The Infinite Conversation*, to which I am compelled to return once again, captures the way in which saying, at its origin, stays its own violence and says this arrest. The context is a meditation on Camus's *The Rebel*, specifically on the character Kaliayev's expression of his initial inability to commit murder:

> We sense that the recoil of violence – its arrest in front of the children's weakness, Kaliayev's "*I cannot*" – coincides with the moment at which violence lays bare the visage and makes man this extreme destitution before which death draws back because it cannot reach it, because this weakness is this arrest, this drawing back itself. The children and the wife, their innocence, are nothing other than the visage of the grand duke, the naked visage that Dora had made Kaliayev see in advance: nothing other than the nakedness that is man in proximity with death's revelation, nothing other than the "*moment at which you will look at him.*" What we are left with is this moment. This is *the time* of the word, the moment at which speech begins, lays bare the human visage, says the encounter that is this nakedness and says man as the encounter with the extreme and irreducible limit. ... "*I cannot*" is the secret of language where, outside all power to represent and to signify, speech would come about as what always differs from itself, and, as difference, holds back. It does not merge with the moral interdiction against killing, nor with the fact that one cannot really kill. "*I cannot*" is death speaking in person, an allusion that death formulates when, in the act of killing, it comes up against the evidence of the visage as though it were its own impossibility; a moment that is death's own drawing back before itself, the *delay* that is the site of speech, and where speech can take place. (*IC* 186–7)

This is indeed terrifying, as the next paragraph underscores in the strongest manner.[4] One could only conclude that talk of peace in such a context would be simply fatuous. But the passage also affirms that the instant of encounter, the time of speech at its origin somehow remains. It forms what Blanchot names earlier in the volume a "reserve" in thought that is not a point of dissipation or seizure, but rather the point of a possible turn: "The impossible is not there to make thought capitulate, but to let it announce itself according to a measure other than that of power" (*IC* 43). Thus, in the moment shadowed by "radical violence"

– the power of the negative proper to language itself – there would subsist or survive the ground of a different, perhaps affirmative opening to alterity, and thus perhaps the possibility of a hosting (the grace of hospitality), or perhaps an approach that offers peace.[5] But how do we think the maintenance and affirmative assumption of that instant relation to the "impossible," a form of being not founded in the exercise of the power of the negative, or being, thought as possibility? How do we think an affirmative reception of *autrui?*

Blanchot's essay "Being Jewish" provides an approach to this question that is astonishing in its force. Moreover, Blanchot's gesture of linking it to his meditation on Robert Antelme's *L'Espèce humaine* under the title "The Indestructible" suggests strongly that the mode of existence he calls "being Jewish" would exceed any relation of power and be *other* than a relation of power (and any "being possible," in Heidegger's sense). But can "being Jewish" fully testify to the experience Blanchot finds evoked in Antelme's volume, or does this latter experience somehow oblige us to rethink the forceful claims made in Blanchot's essay on Judaism? What happens when Blanchot links these two stunning essays? I will approach these questions by reading each of the essays in turn, and by then considering, albeit briefly, how Blanchot's last words from the second essay fold back on the first.

[1] BEING JEWISH

"Being Jewish" offers itself quite demonstratively as a philosophical statement; indeed, it is far more avowedly philosophical than most of the sections of *The Infinite Conversation.* Answering the "denegations" of anti-semitism (the effort to reduce Judaism to some negative essence, and to move from this negation to active annihilation and effacement), and countering a Sartrean effort that Blanchot describes respectfully as "rigorous" to make any Jewish "difference" a mere reflection of the anti-semitic gaze, Blanchot affirms in Judaism a ground of "'historical' reality and authenticity" that derives from the manner in which Judaism engages "the relation of every man to himself" (*IC* 124). Being Jewish is an historical event with an import of universal character; it designates a "grave truth" that must be brought forth in an always personal engagement.

> This can only be the fruit of long work and a meditation that is more personal than erudite. There is a Jewish thought and a Jewish truth; that is, for each of us, there is an obligation to try to find whether

in and through this thought and this truth there is at stake a certain relation of man with man that we can sidestep only by refusing a necessary inquiry. (*IC* 125)

A Jewish thought and truth, and an obligation to undertake them in order to determine whether the relation to the other, the human relation as such, is at stake there for us. This strong, almost redundant statement ("an obligation ... a necessary interrogation" – one is historically based, the other ethico-philosophical) appears to condense three assumptions that Blanchot will develop in the course of his essay and which can only be summarized here as we move toward their meaning. It affirms, first, a "truth" in the revelation that is assumed as Judaism, and the founded character of the tradition of reflection devoted to it. It does this, however, in such a way as to evoke the philosophical essence of Judaism (as opposed to any religious commitment or some cultural significance). Second, it interprets the thought and truth of Judaism along the lines of something Blanchot will name a "Jewish humanism," suggesting that "being Jewish" may offer the means to address a responsibility that is general in nature. This second step does not suggest that all humanism – if so we may name a thought of a just relation to the human other – must be Jewish or that the "authentic" human relation must be a "being Jewish," but it does suggest that Judaism reveals the truth of what we might term "humanism." Third, it links the thought and truth of Judaism to a history of oppression that gives the affliction suffered by the Jewish people, throughout history and in every society, a *general* significance; it thus implicates every individual in a relation of responsibility to what Blanchot terms "being Jewish." Thus, to an exigency that speaks already in the Jewish "truth" (and thus calls upon each of us in the manner described by Levinas), there is a moral and societal imperative that is historically founded to face that to which being Jewish testifies.

These claims are challenging enough, and we will need to return to them. But another step, also triply articulated, follows immediately as Blanchot asserts that everything he would want to convey is held in that dense expression "being Jewish" and the factical meaning to which it testifies. Answering Pasternak's question: "What does being Jewish mean? Why does it exist?," Blanchot writes:

I believe that among all the responses there is one in three parts that we cannot avoid choosing, and it is this: [being Jewish] exists so that the idea of exodus and the idea of exile should exist as a just movement; it exists, through exile and through the initiative that is exodus, so that the experience of strangeness should affirm itself close

> at hand as an irreducible relation; it exists so that, by the authority of
> this experience, we should learn to speak. (*IC* 125)

"Being Jewish" testifies, it would seem, *from the beginning*. It stands witness to the just character of the act of exodus (as a movement of response) in and by this movement's manner of offering itself or going out to an event whose occurrence both founds this justice, and takes on, through this founding, the authority of a teaching. In its testimony, we might say, being Jewish *institutes* – from the beginning. It stands witness to its own possibility. In this, it is a "quasi-transcendental" of sorts (and thus, "Être Juif" is also aptly translated as "Jewish Being"), a way of being that is a structure of relation. It does not institute a relation between two terms or some teaching (in the sense of a doctrine), rather, it institutes the way of a relation that may become a teaching.

Blanchot remarks in one of the earlier dialogues from *The Infinite Conversation* that prepare the argument of "The Indestructible" that only the recognition of the privilege and distance of *autrui* can teach me both what humankind is, and the infinite that comes to me from the other human being. I must accept the other as other (exalted or abject) if I am to begin to learn what the human is and the nature of the alterity its presence brings. This statement implies that the question of the human opens only in an *event* (this is a crucial point to which we must return), and it suggests that this event must be prepared. How am I to recognize the other before knowing who or what the other is? Levinas urges that teaching occurs in the sheer presence of *autrui* (the Torah is given in the light of a face to which acquiescence must inevitably be accorded, if only to be refused). He also tells us that the path of this teaching is a form of prophetic witness: "we will do and we will hear." Fully historical in its instantiation, but of the same temporal order, "being Jewish" would name the ground of that latter act. Bearing witness to that possibility from the start (thus anticipating itself as a discipline of witness), it would found an ethical praxis.

These formulations may not fully capture Blanchot's manner of displacing Western ontology with this account of a self-founding praxis of truth. But however imprecise they might be, they point to a question that is difficult to avoid: can the practice of Judaism be so subsumed philosophically and not surrender its specificity? The question is not a simple one, as we will continue to see, but it is vital to underscore here Blanchot's understanding of the historical ground of this form of relation. For, while Blanchot describes it as a *form* of being (of life?), he emphasizes that it is revealed only in the course of a history and through the exigency of response. Justifying the first of the three points addressed to Pasternak's question, Blanchot points to the painful evidence offered by history: "If Judaism is destined to take on meaning for us, it is indeed by showing that, at whatever time, one must be ready to set out, because to leave (to go to the outside) is the exigency from which one cannot escape if one wants to maintain the possibility of a just relation" (*IC* 125). Here, the *nomadic* essence of Jewish being is asserted against those forms of paganism (both Levinas and Blanchot situate Heideggerian ontology here) that link truth to a rooted dwelling and permanence. And in this nomadism, in the dispersion it implies, there emerges a form of truth: "Just as it calls for a sojourn without place, just as it ruins every fixed relation of force with *one* individual, *one* group, or *one* state, it brings forth, before the exigency of totality, a different exigency and finally prohibits the temptation of Unity-Identity" (*IC* 126). Needless to say, this is an exigency difficult to reconcile with the directions taken in the contemporary state of Israel.[6]

Two points in Jewish history define this form of being: Abraham's act of separating from his Sumerian world and his passage to a "not yet world," his act of beginning (an act that "founds the human right to beginning, the sole veritable creation" [*IC* 126]), and then Jacob's "enigmatic contact" whereby he takes the sign of election. Here, the response to the Foreign becomes a form of solitary responsibility. Israel's solitude, Blanchot writes, derives not only from its relation to surrounding peoples, but from "this particular relation with itself that placed this extreme, infinite distance, the presence that is other, in its proximity" (*IC* 126). That self-relation, once again, is the assumed responsibility of exodus, of going out. This is a positive relation to truth, Blanchot emphasizes, that diverges radically from that of philosophy in its Greek provenance:

> The words exodus and exile indicate a positive relation with exteriority, whose exigency invites us not to be content with what is proper to us (that is, with our power to assimilate everything, to identify everything, to bring everything back to our I). Exodus and exile express simply the same reference to the Outside that the word existence bears. ... Facing the visible-invisible horizon Greek truth proposes to us (truth as light, light as measure), there is another dimension revealed to man where, beyond every horizon, he must relate to what is beyond reach. (*IC* 127)

Again, we see described a form of relation that becomes, in its historical unfolding, a form of life.

Yet it is with regard to the revelation of Judaism that Blanchot's philosophical gesture is most dramatic (his own word here is "brutal"). What we owe to Jewish monotheism, he asserts, "is not the revelation of the one god, [but] the revelation of speech as the site where men hold themselves in relation with what excludes all relation: the infinitely Distant, the absolutely Foreign" (*IC* 127). Jewish thought, he tells us, countering Hegel's infamous words about the "insurmountable abyss" in the Jewish spirit, honours the separation that language preserves as it gives relation to the infinite without reducing it to the same. It teaches us, he says, that speech inaugurates an "original relation." It teaches us what it means to speak:

> To speak to someone is to accept not introducing him into the system of things or of beings to be known; it is to recognize him as unknown and to receive him as foreign without obliging him to break with his difference. (*IC* 128)

Earlier in *The Infinite Conversation*, in the dialogues that prepare the thought of "The Indestructible," Blanchot asserts that such an understanding of language constitutes the "unique dignity" (*IC* 51) of the relation philosophy invites us to entertain with the unknown. The "philosophy" Blanchot is reading in Judaism is "existential," in a certain sense, but it is essentially a philosophy of language which holds that language takes its meaning (meaning itself) from the "absolute" relation it measures, without any form of reduction or mediation of that radical alterity. As such a philosophy, it is essentially ethical in the sense of the term proposed by Levinas. Only shortly after the statement about the "unique dignity" of the philosophical relation, Blanchot introduces Levinas's name and asserts that it constitutes a new beginning for philosophy: "We are called upon to become responsible for what philosophy essentially is, by receiving, in all its brilliance and in the infinite exigency that are proper to it, precisely the idea of the other, that is to say, the relation with *autrui*" (*IC* 51–2).

We would appear to be moving in a circle. Blanchot reads the history of Judaism from philosophy, but he does so with an understanding of philosophy he has drawn from Levinas. Still, Blanchot breaks the circle when he refuses the religious commitment of Levinas's thinking and brackets the name of God. We have read this gesture in "Being Jewish," and we may find it expressed more "brutally" elsewhere in *The Infinite Conversation* when Blanchot asserts that only the other human being brings me before an in-finite, only the presence of *autrui* communicates an absolute difference. If the revelation of language at stake in Jewish monotheism is a revelation about the manner in which language *maintains* difference, it is also a revelation about the relation to the other human being, since difference comes to us only by the other, by *autrui*.

Accordingly, there follows in Blanchot's essay a brief meditation on what he calls "Jewish humanism," which is astonishing, in relation to Greek humanism, by reason of a concern for human relations that is so constant and so preponderant that, even where God is nominally present, it is still a matter of man, of what lies between human beings when nothing stands between them. The marvel, as Blanchot comments in relation to Jacob's remark to Esau, "I have seen your face as one sees the face of Elohim," is human presence, that Other presence that is *autrui* – a presence that is terrible, he reminds us, for the fact that the issue of such an encounter can only be either speech or violence. Does a philosophical humanism, finally shorn of the name of God, gain the final word here? We recall that Blanchot began by affirming a thought and a truth in Judaism that obliges each of us to confront a certain relation of man with man at stake there. The thought and the truth, as we have seen, are borne in, and *occur* in a "being Jewish" that is inseparable from a recognition of the privilege of *autrui* and an opening, an exposure, to the question of the human via a teaching that is a "learning to speak." But Blanchot does not claim in conclusion that humanism is the truth of Judaism. Sensing that he has ventured a bit far, perhaps, in letting the name of God dissipate, and perhaps stopping short of Judaism for this very reason (this point appears to be marked by his citation of Rosenzweig [*IC* 128]), he concludes with the statement that the "truth" of what he has sought to convey in speaking of the affirmation of separation at the heart of "being Jewish" is that whoever seeks to read the history of the Jews *through Judaism* must reflect on the way the Jews bear witness to the difference brought to us by the presence of the other human being. They recall to us, he says, "the exigency of strangeness ... designating as pure separation and pure relation what from man to man exceeds human power, which is capable of everything" (*IC* 129). This manner of bearing witness to the indestructible is itself indestructible: "no form of force can have done with [it] because no force is able to meet up with it" (*IC* 129). Hence the furore of anti-Semitism, he suggests, which is fuelled by an anxious need to submit to the all-power of death what cannot be measured in terms of power and to efface the responsibility to which it testifies.

[2] HUMANKIND

["*I cannot*"] coincides with the moment at which violence lays bare
the visage and makes man this extreme destitution before which death
draws back because it cannot reach it, because this weakness is this
arrest, this drawing back itself. ... What we are left with is this moment.
This is the *time* of the word, the moment at which speech begins, lays
bare the human visage, says the encounter that is this nakedness and
says man as the encounter with the extreme and irreducible limit. ... "*I
cannot*" is the secret of language, where outside all power to represent
and to signify, speech would come about as what always differs from
itself, and, as difference, holds back. ... "*I cannot*" is death speaking in
person, an allusion that death formulates when, in the act of killing,
it comes up against the evidence of the visage as though it were its
own impossibility; a moment that is death's own drawing back before
itself, the *delay* that is the site of speech, and where speech can take
place.   (*IC* 187)

I propose that we read "the indestructible" in relation to what Blanchot
says here of these words, "*I cannot*." It names what exceeds power, as we
have seen, but also an exposure that *remains*, and the burden of this remainder, which is an ineffaceable ethical responsibility. When enunciated
in the presence of the human, "the indestructible" does not name an
essential trait of some kind, any more than do "simplicity," "poverty," or
"innocence." When Blanchot states in "Humankind" that "man affirms
himself at that limit where possibility ceases: in the poverty, the simplicity
of a presence that is the infinite of human presence" (*IC* 132) he is describing the irreducible trace of an exposure. This relational structure,
occurring in language, as language, does not give us a substance to which
could be attributed the term "indestructible"; rather, "the indestructible"
would first name something of the manner of this giving. It is salutary to
recall here Blanchot's words regarding the designation "*autrui*":

"When we ask ourselves 'who is *autrui*?', we question in such a
way that the question necessarily distorts what it means to call into
question. *Autrui* cannot designate a nature, it cannot characterize a
being or an essential trait ... it is not a certain type of man whose task
it is to occupy this role – in the manner of the saints and prophets,
delegates of the Most High – opposite the clan of the "I's." This must
be recalled ... because our language substantifies everything. (*IC* 70)

What cannot fail to strike the reader of "Humankind," the second section of "The Indestructible," is Blanchot's articulation of the way the human relation will remain a burden for those who seek to rise above it and an effaceable responsibility for those who are called to bear witness to it. Blanchot's assertion, early in The Infinite Conversation, that only the presence of the human other brings us before an infinite and confronts us with a radical difference, is here joined by a complementary ethical assertion as Blanchot insists that one cannot be rid of this presence. The torturer, for example, cannot become a god and assume the objective powers of a fate or nature – they remain human, subject to the indestructible which emerges at the limits of their power. And the tortured, who become bearers of this unattained infinite, will hold to the indestructible in the knowledge that only human power can torture in this way, that violence is an irreducibly human choice in the scene of the encounter where one speaks or kills. "Indestructible" says that for the human being, there is no escaping the human. Where Levinas would ultimately assert, after the Psalmist, that there is no escaping the presence of God, Blanchot insists that there is no escaping the human that is there in the scene of encounter wherein one speaks or kills. Both, in turn, seek to convert this powerlessness into an affirmation. The indestructible to which "I cannot" bears witness is the ground of an irreducible ethical affirmation that must be brought to language. This is what it would mean to learn to speak.

It is crucial to underscore that it is in and from such responsibility that Blanchot attempts to approach the question "who is *autrui?*" in *The Infinite Conversation* (a question, he says at the start of "Humankind," that leads him back to Antelme's volume every time it is articulated [*IC* 130]). This is why his thinking diverges so dramatically from an argument like that proposed by Giorgio Agamben in *Remnants of Auschwitz*.[7] And this is why he considers Robert Antelme's testimony in *L'Espèce humaine* so essential, for the question *happens* there as a question. The book thus "teaches" as it introduces us to the understanding "that man is the indestructible, and that nevertheless he can be destroyed." It leads us to the indestructible via its account of affliction.

It is vital for a reading of this essay to see what Blanchot means by "destruction," for it is through this destruction that humankind emerges as the indestructible. Destruction is not immediately annihilation; it is the reduction of the human being to an affliction wherein the human subject is stripped of its power to posit itself as subject and say "I." The human being who afflicts in this manner is capable of everything in the sense that he or she can strip another of their relation to the world (the whole of relations of power and meaning by any number of means, including torture), unmooring the hold of the self.

> In affliction – and in our society affliction is always first the loss of social status – the one who suffers at the hands of men is radically altered. Having fallen not only below the individual, but also below every class and every real collective relation, the person no longer exists in his or her personal identity. In this sense, the one afflicted is already outside the world, a being without horizon. (*IC* 131)

In a sense, there is no limit to destruction, since affliction is a kind of abyss, and there is no end to the fall (*IC* 133). But a limit to power appears in that the act of destruction cannot alter the inexorable affirmation that emerges as humankind slips from the world:

> That man can be destroyed is certainly not reassuring; but that despite this and because of this, in this very movement, man should remain the indestructible – this fact is what is truly overwhelming, *for we no longer have any chance of ever seeing ourselves relieved of ourselves or of our responsibility.* (*IC* 131, my emphasis)

There is the meaning of the "indestructible" to which I pointed above; it emerges in and as the presence of the human, which the oppressor cannot reach. Antelme: "*But there is no ambiguity; we remain men and will end only as men. ... It is because we are men as they are that the SS will finally be powerless before us. ...* [The executioner] *can kill a man, but he cannot change him into something else*" (*IC* 131).

In this self-identification, as Antelme understands it (for Blanchot, as we will see, it cannot be the act of a self, and certainly not a self-identification), the afflicted retains the capacity to know that his or her affliction is of human doing. This is the last recourse for the afflicted: "to know that he has been struck not by the elements but by men, and to give the name man to everything that assails him" (*IC* 131). Affliction is abyssal, and inasmuch as the afflicted loses all sense of self, this last recourse is like a handhold that must give way. Here, we glimpse that Blanchot actually diverges from Antelme, who holds firmly to the prisoner's consciousness of the oppressor. But Blanchot retains the latter relation in his own way, and does not allow the dissolution of self in affliction (which he describes quite radically) to eliminate a relation to one's own presence, which is not a presence to self, but relation to the other in oneself: the presence of *autrui*. Here, a speech occurs that *reserves* itself from the language of power, not just by the fact that it escapes that language essentially, but by a kind of refusal. Thus, the tortured, Blanchot asserts, will refuse to cede to the language of the torturer (except in an extreme passivity that cannot give satisfaction to the latter and only reiterates the refusal) in order to preserve the "true speech" that they know is confounded in this instant with their silent presence, which is that of *autrui* in them:

> A presence no power, even the most formidable, will be able to reach, except by doing away with it. It is this presence that bears in itself and as the last affirmation what Robert Antelme calls *"the ultimate feeling of belonging to the species [espèce]."* (*IC* 132)

These are astonishing words for Blanchot to take over. But let us translate *espèce*, here, as "kind" and ask: what is this feeling of belonging? Is this an affect? And does it entail a sense of community? Blanchot's answer, which he claims to find in Antelme as "the book's most forceful truth" (*IC* 133), is that affliction reveals a radical *need*. When man is reduced to the extremity of need, "we see [*l'on aperçoit*] that he is reduced to himself, and reveals himself [*se découvre*] as one who has need of nothing other than need in order to maintain the human relation in its primacy, negating what negates him" (*IC* 133). Blanchot, as we see, side-steps the question of the subject of this "self-discovery" in this phrase (even while he maintains the relation to the oppressor with a problematic evocation of a dialectical "negation of negation"). But he insists that a relationality endures. The afflicted being who knows radical need maintains "the human relation in its primacy" (the phrase is repeated at *IC* 135) – a kind of pure exposure "where all relation is lacking" (*IC* 135). This is not a relation to the other human being, then, but the "impossible experience" of becoming *"autrui* for oneself" (*IC* 135), not a self-possession (or a sense of belonging), but a dis-possession. Or, as Blanchot puts it in an even more stunning formulation: "It is as though I received the Other [*l'Autre*], host not to myself but to the unknown and the foreign" (*IC* 133).

This is a terrifying account of the (non)ground of human community, and Blanchot does not attenuate it in the least. He argues that need, the "most terrible kind of egoism," must be distinguished from *jouissance* as Levinas describes it, inasmuch as the latter relation always maintains and affirms a relation to *self*. For Blanchot, on the contrary, need in its radical form is nothing more than a "naked relation to naked life" that is not some bare life in a corporeal sense, but "human existence pure and simple," and as such, a relation to the other. I cite once again to underscore the "primacy" of the relation:

> One can therefore say that when, through oppression and affliction, my relation with myself is altered and lost – making of me this foreigner,

this unknown from whom I am separated by an infinite distance, and making of me this infinite separation itself – at this moment need becomes radical: a need without satisfaction, without value, that is, a naked relation to naked existence; but this need also becomes the impersonal exigency that alone bears the future and the meaning of every value or, more precisely, of every human relation. (*IC* 133)

I touch, in affliction, the (non)ground of all community and all hospitality, which Blanchot will name, later in *The Infinite Conversation*, desire. I live (I eat), not *for myself* but *for the other*, and what affirms itself in my place is the strangeness of *autrui*, the affirmation of an infinite exigency (*IC* 132). This, once again, is Blanchot's interpretation of that "last affirmation" that is "*the ultimate feeling of belonging to the species.*" "I" incarnate a kind of pure ethical exigency in relation to which no sufficient answer or act of solidarity will ever be possible.

I noted above that Blanchot takes something of a distance from Antelme when he defines the structure of self-relation in affliction. We see this distance open in the light of a reading such as that of Sarah Kofman when she interprets the notion of belonging to humankind in relation to a notion of community that is based not on a common ground of any kind, but rather upon "a shared power to choose, to make incompatible though correlative choices, the power to kill and the power to respect and safeguard the incommensurable distance, the relation without relation."[8] She draws here on Blanchot's notion of community, but she also emphasizes a power of choice that is foreign to Blanchot's account and she justifies this, appropriately in the terms of her argument, with a remarkable assertion by Antelme. Following a remark on the offence constituted by forms of intimacy (such as music or sport) with the oppressors and a citation of Blanchot's devastating sentence ("There is a limit at which the practice of any art becomes an affront to affliction"), she continues:

> The camps also taught a lesson about the abyss that can separate one detainee's judgment from another's, one choice from another choice, for the necessity of choice was greater there than it has been anywhere else: "Here is where we'll have known both the greatest esteem and the most definitive contempt, both love of mankind and loathing for it, with a more total certainty than anywhere else, ever. ... The more transformed we become, the farther we retreat from back home, the more the SS believe us reduced to the indistinctness and irresponsibility of which we certainly present the appearance – the more distinctions our community does in fact contain, and the

stricter those distinctions are. The inhabitant of the camps is not the abolition of those differences; on the contrary, he is their effective realization."[9]

Blanchot's account does not allow this claim of differentiation. He acknowledges that a sporadic society could appear among the deported that would afford them a sense of self-relation in relation to others and against the powerful. But the *truth* of the situation, he says, speaking in strongly dialectical terms of a structure that is not dialectical, and thus wilfully seeking a relation to the language of political action, is that the death camps housed a sea of others who had become *autrui* for a murderous Subject:

> Between these men who are Other and the Self of Force, no language was possible; but neither is there any possibility of expression. What is then said is essential, but *in truth* heard by no one; there is no one to receive as speech (save through the momentary exchanges in which, through camaraderie, a self is revived) the infinite and infinitely silent presence of *autrui*. Now each has no relation with words other than the reserve of speech that he must live in solitude. (*IC* 135)

Blanchot argues here that an external subjectivity must emerge to receive the silent word of *autrui* and to bring its truth to speech.[10] He then adds, in a step that recalls Levinas's struggle with the notion of justice, but seems almost to despair of it, that a collective subject must emerge that recognizes in the affliction of the other an injustice committed against all and thereby finds the point of departure for a *"common demand [revendication commune]"* (*IC* 134). For a just political response, he suggests, must be totalizing (*IC* 448, n. 7).

The step Blanchot makes here is a disconcerting one in that it seems to short-circuit possible developments of the argument of "Being Jewish," or even suggest that the form of existence described in that essay is incommensurable with political imperatives (a possible conclusion to which Blanchot's long footnote hesitantly pointed, but also skirted). Moreover, it is hard to see the justification for passing so imperatively from the need for the singular act of testimony (Antelme's for example), or a conceivably communitary form that might be latent in the thought of "being Jewish" and the task it enjoins of "learning to speak," to the totalizing terms of traditional political action that Blanchot evokes with his reference to "class consciousness" (*IC* 134).[11] However, the dialectical turn in his argument appears to serve more than a political statement; it seems also designed to expose in absolute terms what Blanchot names for a second time, "the human relation in its primacy." This does not make it less problematic, to be sure, but the effect would be to draw forth the ethical exigency that speaks in the event of the Shoah by drawing forth the silence of the word, the saying of the presence of *autrui* – to draw it forth to such a point that an abyss opens between this silence and the just speech that would bring it to expression. This is a wound, Blanchot infers, that language itself would have to bear, without ever saying it (or closing it). It is a pain that would afflict every event of speech.

Blanchot makes this last statement by commenting on Antelme's expression of his inability to bridge the distance between the silence of the camps and a just speech that would represent its truth. "Hardly had we begun to recount and we were choking." Blanchot's interlocutors take this up as follows:

> – Why this wrenching? Why this pain always present, and not only here in this extreme movement, but already, as I believe it is, in the simplest words?

> – Perhaps because, as soon as two individuals approach one another, there is between them some painful formulation, of the sort we expressed in beginning. They speak, perhaps, in order to forget it, to deny it, or to represent it.

> – That man is the indestructible who can be destroyed? (*IC* 135)

Our leitmotif, we see now, is something like the saying of a pain that can never be fully articulated, of that "terrible responsibility" that is the presence of the other – a responsibility to which I cannot be sufficient and cannot escape. It is a "saying," as I have suggested, of a very particular order since it would be haunting every instance of speech addressed to the other; the "simplest words" would bear it as the latent expression of an origin of meaning they cannot fully speak. In this sense, though it is given by Blanchot's interlocutors as an attempted "formulation," a necessarily inadequate rendering whose opacity is the only "adequate" sign of its weakness, its status would be comparable to that of the "I cannot" Blanchot isolates in the passage I have re-cited as an epigraph to this section – words (also figural or "formulaic," in their way) that bear "the secret of language." It would be comparable to the phrase, "no, it would not suffice," from the magnificent opening dialogue of *The Infinite Conversation*,[12] and even to "a child is being killed" from *The Writing of the Disaster* (*WD* 71–2). All of these are phrases that speak in some sense "before" signifying language, sayings of the rending from which language opens.

To read Blanchot, I believe, we must learn to read in the instant of the appearance of such phrases, or simply *from* such linguistic events. I will want to say a brief word on what this might mean for the texts at hand before concluding. But we should first pause to consider what is communicated in the formula offered in "Humankind." For what haunts in it is not merely the difficulty of the too-patent antinomy it offers (the juxtaposition of an "impossible" that is infinite – the indestructible – with the finite order of the "possible": "man is the indestructible who *can* be destroyed") and what it tells us of humankind. What is devastating in the phrase is what it communicates of an exposure to violence, or a vulnerability: the fact that the presence of the indestructible *delivers man to infinite destruction*. The final phrasing of what it teaches us, strongly underscored by one of the interlocutors ("Yes, I believe we must say this, hold onto it for an instant" [*IC* 135]), brings home this dimension of the phrase. A reader could have expected the interlocutor to turn from the terrible testimony it gives as the dialogue reaches its conclusion; that is to say, they might well have anticipated after the "man is the indestructible," something on the order of: "and therefore cannot be touched even as he is subject to endless destruction."[13] Instead, we have an assertion that reinforces the vulnerability that is given each time in encounter: man is the indestructible and *this means* ("*cela signifie*" – and how *literally* may we read the reference to signification here?) there is no limit to the destruction of man. To be sure, this is a kind of descriptive statement that honors Antelme's staggering account of his experience. But the furore of the Nazis testified to something more.[14] Humankind is open to limitless destruction, it seems, inasmuch as every act of violence – every effort to impose a term to human finitude – makes the horizon-less character of its presence both surge and recede; the latter presence provokes to further violence, *delivers humankind up* to further violence, without term. The indestructible seems even to offer itself to destruction inasmuch as a limitless destruction is directed at it.[15] Thus, the human is, from the first opening of its presence, delivered to violence, and the phrase seems to say: because man is the indestructible, *there will be* a violence without term. Again, "this means…" seems to hint at the *provocation* of presence and the violence that inevitably follows.

But a further step must be taken, for we must also recall Blanchot's words regarding the phrase "*I cannot*" – words that would seem to pertain to every formulation of its kind. We must recall, in other words, that in the exposure of *autrui* violence *already awaits* inasmuch as the exposure of presence is nothing but a violence deferring itself – that the infinite is only exposed in and to violence (might this be why the presence of the indestructible is said to *signify?*). As Blanchot's explication of "*I cannot*" suggests, the imminence of violence is inherent to the instant of exposure as it is given in speech. Violence necessarily haunts the indestructible, almost as its aura; it is already gathering. We may *learn to speak* in such a way as to defer the destruction, but in every encounter with the other, "as soon as two individuals approach one another," there is the rending that is the exposure of the infinite offering of human presence to violence. "Tragic" cannot capture what speaks in these words since we are beyond the order of tragedy, but it is not easy to find another word that expresses their weight.

Can "being Jewish" bear such a truth? Or does Blanchot's meditation in "Humankind" require us to rethink in some manner the ethical praxis Blanchot describes in the essay that precedes it? At first appearance, "Being Jewish" and "Humankind" stand almost as complementary statements, counterparts (this impression is underscored by the concluding paragraph of the former essay in that it seems to establish a firm bridge between them). The former describes a mode of self-relation that is a relation to the other. The latter describes the exigency of the other to which the former responds. But can "being Jewish," as it is described, become the path of a relation that escapes the violence that haunts this encounter as it is evoked in "Humankind"?[16] Returning to the discussion of the Jewish revelation in "Being Jewish," we note that language is thought as the site of a non-violent encounter with alterity, an encounter where an absolute distance is preserved in its purity and the other is received as other. From here, Blanchot can evoke a form of promise: "In this sense, speech is the promised land in which exile is accomplished as dwelling, since it is no longer a matter of being at home, but always Outside, in a movement in which the Foreign offers itself without renouncing itself" (*IC* 128). Is this promise possible from the ground of what is said in "Humankind"? And if so, how do we think this form of dwelling? Does the latter essay perhaps even force us to recast the "positive truth" Blanchot ascribes to Judaism and rethink somewhat more severely what it reveals of language? To be sure, formulas such as "*I cannot*," or "man is the indestructible…" are translations of an interruption (which Blanchot describes at one point as "hyperbolic") that preserves difference. The statements from "Being Jewish" concerning the revelation of language do not betray numerous other accounts in *The Infinite Conversation* of the manner in which language "measures" an immeasurable distance.[17] But the movement of "formulation" or "translation" to which I have referred (a movement that is a staying of violence, but in which violence gathers) is inevitable; it is always already occurring even as the "reserve" of the other takes form. All "learning to speak" must pass through this arrested movement and maintain it somehow.

I do not know whether it would be appropriate to say that the meditation in "Humankind" is meant to subject his statements in "Being Jewish" to some kind of trial. But I believe we have to ask whether the experience of the *Shoah*, as Blanchot encounters it through the testimony of Antelme, among others, forces us to go much farther in thinking a "practice of peace" than does the "Jewish humanism" Blanchot takes over from Levinas in the first essay. For while it does not invalidate the previous description of the revelation of language, it does oblige us to entertain the exigency of a terrible responsibility and a necessary assumption of powerlessness; it obliges us to conceive of a mode of proceeding *from* the arrest of an "I cannot," and in the space of this irreducible linguistic remainder. The notion of a "sabbatical existence" can be developed in this way, I believe, and it can be conceived affirmatively, but the step that must be taken here leads us into a quite radical reconception of ethics.

ENDNOTES

[1] I refer here to the opening statements of the Preface to Emmanuel Levinas's *Totality and Infinity*, trans. Alfonso Lingis (Pittsburgh: Duquesne University Press, 1969), 21–30.

[2] I cite here the final explication of a phrase that appears more frequently and concisely as: "Man is the indestructible who can be destroyed." These citations are from the essay, "Humankind" (*IC* 130–5). Blanchot's allusion to "the exigency of another relation" appears on *IC* 192. I have on occasion throughout this chapter modified the translations in *IC*.

[3] Levinas, *Totality and Infinity*, 23.

[4] "This is a speech, assuredly, of which we are not directly aware and, it must be said again, a speech that is infinitely hazardous, for it is encompassed by terror. Radical violence is its fringe and its halo; it is one with the obscurity of the night, with the emptiness of the abyss, and so doubtful, so dangerous, that this question incessantly returns: why the exigency of such a language? What have we to do with it?" (*IC* 187).

[5] In *Infant Figures* (Stanford: Stanford University Press, 2000), where I have previously turned to the last two citations from Blanchot, I try to develop the possibility that the self-annunciation of thought according to "another measure" might take the form of (or proceed from) an acquiescence, a kind of affirmation or assent. The central dialogue of the volume is directed toward this notion.

[6] One must consider here a tortuous footnote that concludes Blanchot's essay and in which he asserts that "the question expressed by the words 'being Jewish' and the question of the State of Israel cannot be identified, even if they modify one another" (*IC* 447). While recognizing the necessity of political response to the afflictions suffered by the Jewish people, particularly after the Shoah, Blanchot does not consider the state form a sufficient response to the question of being Jewish, which he terms "universal." The concluding sentence is particularly interesting in that it urges reserve before philosophy's temptation to try to hold its own with political powers in deciding on the meaning and future of the "truth" offered by Judaism: "I would be tempted to conclude by saying that in the society that is being tried in Palestine – a society caught up in struggle, under threat, and threatened by nothing less grave than the necessity of this struggle for 'safeguarding' (as is also the case in societies that have issued from Marxism or have been liberated from colonial bondage) – it is philosophy itself that is being dangerously measured against power inasmuch as this society, like the others, will have to determine the meaning and the future of 'nomadic truth' in the face of the state" (*IC* 448). The point would seem to be here, once again, that "being Jewish" cannot be commensurate with the order of "powers" or any political program.

[7] Giorgio Agamben, *Remnants of Auschwitz: The Witness and the Archive*, trans. Daniel Heller-Roazen (New York: Zone Books, 2002). While this book clearly owes a great deal to Blanchot's meditations on the Shoah, its one reference to them consists in a charge that Blanchot "misunderstands" his own words in "The Indestructible" (135). There is little point in dwelling on the merits of this curious and rather murky claim. It seems, simply, that Blanchot's meditation on the inhabitant of the camps is insufficiently radical for Agamben in that it does not meet his understanding of the experience (beyond experience) for which he finds an exemplary figure in the "Muselmann." Blanchot's meditation on the exposure of *autrui* (which Agamben never really confronts) fails to capture the Muselmann's "inhuman" state and does not measure up to Agamben's effort to push the categories of ethics into the "grey zone" described by Primo Levi (an effort that should recall to us the work of Lawrence Langer, who is not cited by Agamben). Beyond the fact that Agamben is hardly consistent in evoking this abyss (how could he write, for example, that the Muselmann, who touches inhumanity in suffering the impossible, "has much to say but cannot speak" [120]?), a confrontation between these texts would have to take up their discursive structures. One can certainly find points in Blanchot's work where a pleasure in speculative paroxysm seems to overcome him, but one also finds a crucial sobriety. These words, for example, after a return to the motif of need in *The Writing of the Disaster*: "But the danger (here) of words in their theoretical insignificance is perhaps that they claim to evoke the annihilation where

all sinks always, without hearing the 'be silent!' addressed to those who have known only partially, or from a distance the interruption of history. And yet to watch and to wake, to keep the ceaseless vigil over the immeasurable absence is necessary, for what took up again from this end (Israel, all of us) is marked by this end, from which we cannot come to the end of waking again" (*WD* 84). Or these words, after commentary on the fact that musical concerts were organized in the camps that momentarily effaced the distance between executioners and victims (like the soccer games that so offend Agamben): "There is a limit where the practice of any art becomes an affront. Let us not forget this" (*WD* 83). While there are many arresting and haunting formulations in Agamben's book that honor Blanchot's imperative in important ways ("Nevertheless, one must..."), it remains hard for me to grasp how Agamben can give himself over so freely to theoretical and speculative analogies in such a context, or write a sentence like this one: "Let us then formulate the thesis that summarizes the lesson of Auschwitz" (133). Further, it would seem to me that rhetoric is one of those "arts" where cognizance of the limit to which Blanchot points is critical.

[8] Sarah Kofman, *Smothered Words*, trans. Madeleine Dobie (Evanston: Northwestern University Press, 1998), 70.

[9] Kofman, *Smothered Words*, 71–2.

[10] "There must be restored – beyond this self that I have ceased to be, and within the anonymous community – the instance of a Self-Subject: no longer as a dominating and oppressing power drawn up against the 'other' that is *autrui*, but as what can receive the unknown and the foreign, receive them in the justice of a true *speech*" (*IC* 133–4). The point is reiterated in the concluding page of the essay.

[11] This point turns on a reading of Levinas's notion of justice. I have tried to show elsewhere (in an essay that is as yet unpublished) that Levinas's struggle with this term can be resolved without an appeal to a totalizing notion of commensurability. I would add that I raise the question of the communitary dimension of "being Jewish" with considerable caution (deferring a proper treatment of it), but with the sense that it is unavoidable. At this point in Blanchot's essay, there appears to be an unthought implication in Blanchot's gesture of linking the two parts of "The Indestructible."

[12] The passage that follows the appearance of these words reads as follows: "From the instant that this word – a word, a phrase – slipped between them, something changed, a history ended; an interval should be placed between their existence and this word, but the word always comprises this very interval, whatever it may be, and also the distance that separates them and separates them from it" (*IC* xiv–xv).

[13] As we see earlier in *The Infinite Conversation*, for example p. 61.

[14] Blanchot refers here to "A denial so absolute, it is true, that it does not cease to *reaffirm* the relation with the infinite that being-Jewish implies" (*IC* 129).

[15] How are we to understand what happens at the most extreme points, when humankind has fallen even below need and has reached the zone of a living death? Surely, there is a limit to devastation. And yet, Blanchot clearly wants to suggest

that something remains, even beyond this point. Here we would have to approach his meditations on the corpse and consider how he would treat the Nazi effort to eradicate even the trace left by the "*Figuren.*"

[16] The question is not meant to be "rhetorical," but if the answer proves negative it must be followed by this other one: must the Jews somehow be consigned to bearing witness to this impossibility?

[17] I would refer the reader, in particular, to "Keeping to Words" (*IC* 59–65).

A MATTER OF LIFE AND DEATH:
Reading Materiality in Blanchot and de Man

Hector Kollias

> *Yes, literature is unquestionably illegitimate, there is an
> underlying deceitfulness in it. But certain people have discovered
> something beyond this: literature is not only illegitimate, it is also
> null, and as long as this nullity is isolated in a state of purity,
> it may constitute an extraordinary force, a marvellous force.*
>
> Blanchot[1]

> *The critical deconstruction that leads to the discovery of the
> literary, rhetorical nature of the philosophical claim to truth is
> genuine enough and cannot be refuted: literature turns out to be
> the main topic of philosophy and the model for the kind of truth
> to which it aspires. But when literature seduces us with the freedom
> of its figural combinations, so much airier and lighter than the
> laboured constructs of concepts, it is not the less deceitful because
> it asserts its own deceitful properties.*
>
> Paul de Man[2]

ON THE FACE OF IT, THESE TWO STATEMENTS ABOUT LITERATURE APPEAR
to be complementary. "Deceitfulness," writes Blanchot; "deceitful properties," echoes de Man a propos of Nietzsche. A closer reading may yet
complicate the issue, insisting, perhaps, on the rigorous provenance of
de Man's argument about literature from an argument which is strictly
about philosophy and its "claim to truth," whereas Blanchot is concerned
with literature itself, and not in conjunction with any philosophical
parentage. And yet, a further turn of reading may show that the context
of Blanchot's statement is indeed a confrontation with the philosophical
questioning of literature, philosophy's question: "what is literature?"
It then becomes apparent that behind the surface agreement as to the
deceitful or illegitimate nature of literature lie rather different concerns.
De Man is chiefly demonstrating that philosophy's "claim to truth" is
implicated in the essential deceitfulness of literature, whereas Blanchot
is arguing for a radical turning away from the essential philosophical

question about literature, a turning away effected by literature itself.[3] But is it not the case that de Man's last cited sentence, itself starting with a "but," also points to a turning away, a turning away from the last vestige of possible truth for philosophy, the truth of and about literature, since literature itself cannot, in its deceitfulness, accommodate that truth? Both writers are faced with the irremediable condition that, for reasons of "nullity" or "deceitfulness" (it remains to be seen how far these two conceptions can be taken to be synonymous or coextensive), literature is that which cannot harbour the seeking after essences that is philosophy's idiom. Literature cannot bear the question "what is literature?"

There are, of course, several other possibilities of opening and conducting a "dialogue" between Blanchot and de Man.[4] Nevertheless I think it is eminently arguable that all such possibilities would need to converge in a reflection on both writers' treatment of a singularity (literature, or the textual event) falling outside the purview of philosophy, and in the subsequent ramifications of such an exclusion for both philosophy and literature. My approach here will be to focus on an arguably very specific, although not marginal, aspect of Blanchot's and de Man's theoretical writings on literature – this is the notion of materiality, the materiality of literary language, of language in general, of the word, and of the letter. Studies on de Man's idea of such a materiality are already abundant, but the same cannot be said about Blanchot.[5] My aim here is not to "rectify" this situation and thereby claim materiality to be as central an issue in Blanchot as it is in de Man. Rather, I propose a reading of Blanchot's appeal to materiality (notably in *The Work of Fire* in general and "Literature and the Right to Death" in particular), a reading which could perhaps, in tandem with de Man's much more rigorously articulated conception, shed light on what remains a controversial notion, and stake a claim for its centrality with regard to the questions posed by both writers about literature and to literature. What if the singularity of literature, as advocated in several and differing ways by both Blanchot and de Man, were to be connected to, if not hinged upon, such a notion of "literary materiality"?

[1]

Blanchot mentions the words "materiality," "material," or "matter" in his critical writings only a few times. Most of these mentions, in fact, come from the early volume *The Work of Fire*, and it could be argued that, if one accepts the *tour de force* of "Literature and the Right to Death" as a cornerstone in Blanchot's critical itinerary, what that essay mainly sought to bring forth – what Leslie Hill calls "the philosophical account of literature as pre-conceptual singularity" – becomes the bedrock of all Blanchot's critical endeavours, at least until the arrival of the fragmentary (and no longer simply "critical") writings of the late 1960s and onwards.[6] What I wish to argue for is that in the midst of this seminal exploration of the singularity of literature, the few (seven, all in all) references to "materiality" or "matter" in "Literature and the Right to Death" are indeed central, and, what is more, the focus on materiality may allow us not simply to perceive modes of connection between Blanchot and de Man's theoretical enterprises, but also to recognize where the points of convergence in their thought turn into divergent trajectories, and finally, perhaps, to understand what the relation between this convergence and this divergence may be. This would be the "programme" then – to begin it, it is imperative first to examine the use Blanchot makes of the notion of materiality.

It would seem, at least on the surface, that all seven references in the essay are concerned with the materiality of language, in one way or the other. Blanchot writes of either "the materiality of language," or of the "material weight" of words, their "material value," or of meaning having become "material." We know already that the whole argument of the essay, although seemingly progressing "dialectically" along the lines of Hegel's exposition of consciousness in the chapter from *The Phenomenology of Spirit* entitled "The Spiritual Animal Kingdom" and running, so to speak, alongside the dialectic, never simply coincides or runs parallel, as it has been shown many times before, with any dialectical moves.[7] In a similar way, Blanchot's references to materiality are particularly nuanced by their exact position in the overall argument, and cannot simply be taken to be references to the same "thing" or notion. And just as the whole argument of the essay is intentionally ambiguous, duplicitous, complicated in its successive adumbrations, so Blanchot's references to materiality, if read all together, also end up being a tantalizingly ambiguous affair. It also needs to be noted that, alongside "Literature and the Right to Death," the essay providing us with the most numerous and most significant references to the notion of language's materiality is the essay Blanchot devoted to Mallarmé in the same volume, entitled "The Myth of Mallarmé." That Mallarmé's own conception of literary language, its aims, functions, and particularity, as well as his own distinction between "brute" and "essential" language form (along with Hegel, of course) a basis for Blanchot's moves in

"Literature and the Right to Death" is already known and need not be discussed further.[8] But it is not without significance that materiality comes to the fore when Blanchot is, implicitly or explicitly, staging a dialogue with Mallarmé – it is Mallarmé who can be found, in different guises perhaps, on *both* "slopes" Blanchot articulates in his essay, and it is Mallarmé's foregrounding of the material properties of the word that give Blanchot the impetus for his consideration of the distinction, and consequent entanglement, of the two "slopes" of literature.

In the first instance, Blanchot claims that language, all language and therefore literary language too, is an attempt to annihilate the existence of things through their transformation into the ideality of the concept, or of meaning. To speak the language of structural linguistics that Blanchot hardly ever used, the operation of literature in this, its first slope, is to negate, nullify the objective and material existence of a thing or person, of an "*existant*," as Blanchot writes after Levinas, transforming it into the material absence and ideal presence that characterize the signified. In this sense, materiality is what referents leave behind, what is annulled in a thing for the thing to become idea, and to obtain meaning. This is an essential operation of signification in general, but literature in particular, if it is to grasp this movement of negation in its fullness, has to interrogate the absence of a thing in its meaning. Mallarmé attempts to think that in the renowned formulation from "Crise de vers": "I say: a flower! And, beyond the oblivion to which my voice relegates any contour, as far as it is something other than known chalices, musically there arises, the idea itself and suave, the one absent from all bouquets."[9] What appears in language is not the thing, the flower, but the absence of the thing, its negation, "absent from all bouquets." In this way, Blanchot argues, something, an existant, a thing of material and objective presence, has been lost, annihilated into its absence as idea and meaning. But the word that bears the meaning of the thing's absence, the word that carries absence *as* its meaning, is not itself absent. Literary language, Blanchot quickly understands, "observes that the word 'cat' is not only the nonexistence of the cat, but nonexistence become *word*, that is, a perfectly determined and objective reality" (*WF* 325). Thus this first "slope" of literature comes up against what turns out to be an ineluctable and constitutive paradox, an aporia: its power of negating existence is itself reliant upon the existence of words that carry the absence of existence in them. A certain form of existence, which it would not be precipitate to call a *material* existence, is necessary for the negation of existence that is essential to literary language on this slope.

But this is not all. On the second slope, Blanchot argues, literary language finds solace in that which, just previously, marked its failure to negate totally the objective reality of things – in words. Literary language, Blanchot postulates, "is a search for this moment which precedes literature" (*WF* 327), it is the search, in language, of what language leaves behind in order to appear as such – existence, objectivity, materiality, which now makes its first appearance in the essay. Blanchot cites Mallarmé:

> *I say a flower!* But, in the absence where I mention it, through the oblivion to which I relegate the image it gives me, in the depths of this heavy word, itself looming up as an unknown thing, I passionately summon the darkness of this flower, I summon this perfume that traverses me and which I do not breathe, this dust that permeates me but which I do not see, this colour which is a trace and not light. Then what hope do I have of attaining the thing I push away? My hope lies in the materiality of language, in the fact that words are also things, a nature, that which is given to me and gives me more than I understand of it. (*WF* 327)

In the materiality of words lies the hope that what gets lost in language's operation of conveying meaning may yet not be lost. Literary language thus becomes the possibility of contact with what Blanchot calls "the existence before the day" (*WF* 335), the existence of things before they became things, of a world before it was constituted into a world, dust which permeates without being visible and colour that is not illumination. This possibility is afforded by the materiality, the "thing-ness" of words, and although Blanchot explicitly names this materiality as what makes words the bearers of an objective existence, "a nature" that is equivalent to that of things, it is already apparent that the function, or the *work* of this materiality is to bear the trace of an "existence" before existence, of an "existence" that survives the annihilation of existence. If words, on the first slope, are the bearers of an absence, the workers of a negation which would be the ideality of meaning, on this second slope, the materiality of language bears the mark, not of the existence of things as such, but of an "existence before the day," of an existence which both predates and survives things.

It is in his further discussion of this second slope of literature that Blanchot once again refers to materiality. Just as the first slope was shown to result in an inexorable aporia or double bind, so will the second slope, when literary language may at last hope to capture the meaningless existence of things by forging an alliance "with the reality of language"

(*WF* 330), but in doing so turns language into "matter without contour, content without form" (*WF* 330). "Brute," formless existence thus appears on the scene, but with its appearance something disappears and is lost, namely the power of words to signify in their ideality the absence of a thing – meaning, signification itself is lost. Words on this slope no longer have meaning, they *no longer signify*: "opacity is their answer, the flutter of closing wings is their speech; in them, material weight is present as the stifling density of a heap of syllables that has lost all meaning" (*WF* 331). The material property of the word weighs heavily, and it weighs against the lightness of meaning, it stifles meaning that depends on absence with " a heap of syllables." But the paradox is that this loss of meaning is itself meaningful. Blanchot writes:

> Literature has indeed triumphed over the meaning of words, but what it has found in the words taken apart from their meaning, is meaning become thing: and thus it is meaning detached from its conditions, separated from its moments, wandering like an empty power, a power no one can do anything with, a power without power, simple inability to cease to be, but which, because of that, appears to be the proper determination of indeterminate and meaningless existence. (*WF* 331)

This is the moment, as Blanchot will write a little later, where "meaning becomes more material than words" (*WF* 335), the moment when materiality is no longer a hope but a catastrophe, a destruction of the meaning of individual words, in a manner which can perhaps be appropriated to the Hegelian "negation of negation," if one considers that what the word negates and carries as absence ("I say: a flower!"), that is to say meaning, is now itself destroyed. But once again, this apparent proximity with the operation of the dialectic is misleading. Nothing is here "carried over," "sublated" (*aufgehoben*) into a further, and higher stage of development. Meaning itself becomes material, and this, for Blanchot, means both *present*, with a presence that weighs down and is palpable, and, at the same time, *opaque*, inaccessible to cognition, a presence that cannot be phenomenally apprehended.

Since both slopes in Blanchot's account end up being aporetic, the reference to materiality can be itself taken to be an integral part of the aporia. Materiality is thus both situated in the word, as what gives the hope of capturing the existence of things that begins the movement of the second slope, and in meaning, at the end (if end there is) of the movement, when it is what betrays communicability, cognition, and reference, and makes the absence of meaning the only sense of meaning. And if the materiality of the word as it appears in the beginning of the movement may seem to have a "classic" determination ("words are also things"), this is by no means to be taken as the final word on the issue. For the moment, the materiality of meaning proves to be enough of a turn, enough of a complication. If meaning itself is to be viewed as material, then its materiality is quite different, even contradictory to the "thing-ness" of the word. For meaning to be a thing, opaque and intractable, it has to renounce meaning itself, it has to signify the negation, the absence, the annihilation of signification. "Material" meaning is thus only the bearer of the absence of meaning, and as such, its materiality is not existence, despite the heaviness, the palpability, the opaqueness – it is, to cite Blanchot "existence before the day," existence predating the necessary conditions of possibility for existence, existence in the absence of its own horizon. And yet, at the same time, a further ambiguity arises. Writing about Ponge and his avowed intention to take "the side of things" in his poetry which thus makes him another exemplary "inhabitant" of literature's second slope, Blanchot writes that Ponge thereby expresses "not the existence before the day, but the existence after the day: the world of the end of the world" (*WF* 335). This materiality of meaning is aligned to a future survival after the annihilation of all existence, just as the materiality of the word comes from the existence that predates all existence. Materiality is therefore nothing other than what Jacques Derrida would call a *trace*. Despite the "classic" referral, often explicit in Blanchot's text, to a metaphysical concept of materiality, that is to say despite the connotations of presence, existence, palpability, physicality, *this* materiality is the "simple inability to cease to be," the principle of the eternal conservation of matter underlying all matter. Blanchot has another phrase for this principle, and it is the phrase made famous by Hegel: "the life which supports death and maintains itself in it" (*WF* 336). Language is that life, and if it is, it is so because of language's materiality. Due attention has already been paid to Blanchot's appropriation and transformation of this Hegelian dictum for the sake of language and of literature. This shows that Blanchot's concept of materiality, the materiality of word and of meaning, is concomitant with that of "life," since materiality is the bearer, in language, of life that maintains itself in death, meaning's life in the word's death, and the word's life in meaning's death.

[2]

Perhaps the claims advanced in the previous paragraph are schematic, and in need of further elaboration. In order to achieve this, and in order to situate, as I wish to do, the notion of materiality at the core of Blanchot's enterprise in "Literature and the Right to Death," I propose to take a detour through a discussion of a thought where materiality plays a much more pronounced role. This thought is Paul de Man's, and although, as it will become apparent, the differences in the conception of materiality between Blanchot and de Man may at first seem insurmountable, my aim is to trace possible lines of connection organized around the ways in which materiality, for both writers, finally becomes a marker for much more than it would initially refer to. This is already quite easy to perceive when dealing with de Man, even though the appearance of the notion of materiality in his writings is late, and achieves pre-eminence only in the posthumously published collection of essays under the title *Aesthetic Ideology*.[10] Here, de Man offers at least three discrete formulations of materiality: the "materiality of the letter," the "materiality of actual history," and finally the materiality associated with what de Man calls "the material sublime" in Kant's *Critique of Judgment*. Initially it must be noted that all of those references to materiality occur in discussions of philosophical and not literary texts, but this does not mean that materiality for de Man, especially the "materiality of the letter," is only to be located in philosophy. In fact, if I may be allowed to refer back to the epigraph of this article, my contention is that de Man's notion of materiality plays a central role in his understanding of the singularity of literary language as excluded from the "totalizing" gestures of philosophy, just as, perhaps, Blanchot's notion of materiality is a conduit for the forceful resistance that he unmistakably ascribes to literature, a resistance to the philosophical seeking after essences. Materiality then, can be seen, pre-emptively, as a notion with which both writers seek to demarcate what is irreducibly singular about literature – even if this can be the "literature" found in philosophical texts, in de Man's case.

What de Man means when he employs the notion of materiality is not simple. In short, materiality first refers to "the prosaic materiality of the letter" (*AI 90*), in a sense which initially simply repeats the gesture made by Blanchot when discussing the "thing-ness" of the word, but which will, like Blanchot's counterpart, in due course need to be seen as rather more complicated than its initial appearance. Second, as is the case in his reading of Kant, and also, arguably, in his discussion of the materiality of history, materiality refers to an occurrence, within the confines of a text, and which interrupts it, leaving, as de Man says "a trace on the world" (*AI* 132). As Jacques Derrida shows, these two (or three) differing conceptions of materiality seem to point to a paradoxical synthesis of two elements that ordinarily are not thought of in conjunction: on the one hand, the materiality of the letter pertains to what de Man, from much earlier in his career, sought to establish as the machinic codes operating in a text, materiality as machine, and on the other hand, the materiality as occurrence and as disruption of a textual system points to a notion of event.[11] If "materiality" is able "to join the thinking of the event to the thinking of the machine" it is easy to see how large the stakes are in attempting to formulate such a notion. My task is here more modest, and it is, in the first instance, to find a common ground between these differing conceptions of materiality in de Man's work. Such a common ground can be found if materiality is "defined" in opposition to phenomenality, as de Man himself does in his reading of Kant. In two related essays, "Phenomenality and Materiality in Kant," and "Kant's Materialism," (the latter being actually the transcript of a lecture) de Man focuses on Kant's use of the word *Augenschein* to describe how objects of nature, the ocean and the sky, are to be judged sublime. Kant insists on the sublime being possible only if one sees such objects "as poets do, merely in terms of what manifests itself to the eye."[12] De Man reads this as an instance of "formal materialism" (already a paradoxical notion), by which he means that the *Augenschein* marks a moment where all possible phenomenalization of the sublime is rendered impossible: "Kant's looking at the world just as one sees it is an absolute radical formalism that entertains no notion of reference or semiosis" (*AI* 128). This is what de Man calls "a material vision" (*AI* 82), a vision which paradoxically does not engage with what vision is meant to bring forth, that is the world of phenomena. Instead, in de Man's reading, in order for the judgment of the sublime to occur for Kant, what is necessary is an impossible abstraction from the phenomenal, a "material vision" which would render the sublime accessible to what is programmatically its proper domain, the moral law. What is significant in all this is that "material," and "materiality" designate an *interruption* of phenomenal proceedings, an arrival from an unreachable exteriority which nevertheless is what makes the world of phenomena appear as well as being able to link it, as was Kant's programme, to the noumenal world of reason.

How is this connected to the notion of "the prosaic materiality of the letter"? In his examination of textual "systems" and rhetorical codes, as exemplified in his cardinal *Allegories of Reading*, de Man's main concern is with finding another instance of interruption, what he calls a "textual event," which is the moment when the "tropological" systematicity of the text, the arrangement of tropes and figures which the text deploys in its development, cannot account for the text's own generation, and where the text has to make a leap from a constative to a performative gesture. De Man always associates tropological systems, the rhetoric, in other words, of texts, with cognition, with the constative mode. As he explains in his lecture on "Kant and Schiller," and as he also discusses in the closing pages of *Allegories of Reading* which deal with Rousseau's *Confessions*, the move from constative to performative is what texts are required to do in order to attempt to account for their own generation, and what always interests him in this is the very fact of the *passage* from one mode to another. This passage, found, de Man insists, in all texts, is what he calls a textual event, the interruption of the flow of rhetoric by that which comes from outside it, which we can now assimilate to the interruption of phenomenal proceedings by a "material vision" in the course of the judgment of the sublime. Materiality then, appears to denote an interruption of an otherwise closed system or progressive movement, by a radical exteriority which thereby transforms, fortuitously or not, the workings of the system and its progression, it marks, as de Man writes apropos of Kant's sublime, "the moment when the infinite is frozen into the materiality of stone" (*AI* 127). Perhaps a certain affiliation between this materiality that interrupts the flow of phenomenal presentation, and Blanchot's obscure materiality of meaning which is also radically exterior in relation to phenomenal or cognitive processes, can already be seen. For this material inscription, or this material vision, to occur as textual event, be that in Kant or in Rousseau, what is necessary is a materiality of the first, simpler or more "classic" order – the materiality, in other words, of the letter or the word. The textual event occurs *as* and *in* language, and as such it has recourse to linguistic "matter" for its support. Although de Man never proposes such a reading of his own thought, I would like to suggest here another connection between him and Blanchot on the notion of materiality. Blanchot's aporia of materiality, as we have seen, is that the materiality of meaning, in a sense, disrupts and destroys the operations of the materiality of the word, in that the "meaning-thing" is what finally forbids words from having meaning; at the same time, and in a circular movement which has nothing to do with the sublations of the dialectic, this "meaning-thing" only ever obtains through and because of the support of the word-thing.

In de Man, the exteriority that in a sense characterizes the thought of the event fundamentally dislocates and disarticulates the workings of textual systems – but, and the circularity is here the same, the event only ever becomes manifest in language, it needs the material support of words. To frame this in another way: in Blanchot "the existence before the day," or "the life which supports death and maintains itself in it," as language is formed, takes place with the material support of words, when words become opaque and "heavy," or finds resistance in the same words, when that material support is denied and language pertains only to the ideality of transparent meaning. In de Man, the interruption of the textual event finds both its support and its resistance in the sheer "matter" of words. The materiality of the word, therefore, far from being a simple reference to a physicality or an objectivity, becomes, in the hands of both writers, the bearer of a trace of radical exteriority (the exteriority of the event, or of "the existence before the day"), and it bears it both as support and as resistance.

Leaving de Man behind, for a moment, and returning to Blanchot, there is no avoiding the particularly *negative* slant assumed by this consistently aporetic and duplicitous nature of language. "An art which purports to follow one slope is already on the other," Blanchot writes (*WF* 332). Caught between the incessant, deathless veering of the two slopes towards one another, despite their evident irreconcilability, literary language always seeks after what precedes it. "Literature . . . dedicates itself, not to the resurrection embodied in conceptual thought, but to the unthinkable singularity that precedes the concept as its simultaneous condition of both possibility and impossibility."[13] This singularity is what finds support and resistance in materiality. But the result of the encounter between this unthinkable singularity, which could be called a singularity from *outside*, pure exteriority that necessarily needs to become manifest in language, and language itself in its materiality – is not a work. If it is a work, it is one which constantly self-deconstructs, or, as de Man would perhaps say, a work where the encounter with such a singularity "is extended over all the points of the figural line," where the interruption of the encounter becomes "permanent parabasis" and thus "unworks" the text from within at every single one of its points of development.[14] Blanchot, as is well known, names this essential self-deconstructing nature of every work "worklessness," *désoeuvrement*. And yet, this worklessness is itself the necessary condition of both possibility and impossibility for there to be work, *oeuvre*. As "Literature and the Right to Death" makes painstakingly clear, the possibility of literature, of a work, only arrives alongside its impossibility as worklessness. Similarly, de Man's insistence on the destructive power of the "prosaic materiality of the letter" must be seen as indissoluble from the production of text in general – there is no text without materiality, and there is no text, or work, without this destructive power which is thus also, and this is a further double bind, *enabling*. Derrida, although writing on de Man, puts it in unmistakably Blanchotian terms: "The materiality in question . . . is nothing, and yet it works, *cela oeuvre*, this nothing operates, it forces, but as a force of resistance."[15] And this resistance is itself double: it is the resistance that materiality, in a first moment, shows to the radical exteriority of the event, the resistance, in Blanchot's terms, of meaning's ideality to "the existence before the day" without which there would be no meaning; and it is also the resistance to, as Derrida puts it, "both beautiful form and matter as substantial and organic totality," the resistance to closure and substantiality, or the inexorable failure of a text to account for its own constitution.[16] The materiality of language is both a boon and a curse, it is the one *because* it is the other, as work exists because of worklessness, and vice versa.

Have we then arrived at a point where the conception of materiality as it is implicit in Blanchot's work can be wholly aligned to that explicitly foregrounded by de Man? I would like to suggest that the relation between the two writers' notions of materiality is yet another double bind, or, to borrow Blanchot's metaphor, that their formulations of materiality can be viewed as two slopes, two slopes that remain, in a fundamental sense, irreconcilable and never reach a plateau, despite the fact that they constantly veer towards each other. For Blanchot, as his most persistent references to materiality in his essay on "The Myth of Mallarmé" show, materiality is itself a double figure of resistance and support: resistance in the sense he attributes to Mallarmé's doomed attempts to make silence manifest in writing, leaving behind "the material emblem of a silence that, in order to allow itself to be represented, must become thing and that thus remains the scandal, its insurmountable paradox" (*WF* 37); and support in the sense that, as he perceives again of Mallarmé's idea of absence and ideality in meaning, "as if words, far from turning us away from things, had to be the things' material tracing" (*WF* 38). What is being resisted or supported, in both cases, by the materiality of language, is precisely worklessness, the arrival of "the existence before the day," the advent of irreducible singularity. In de Man, materiality is both resistance and support also: resistance to the totalizing gesture of the closed tropological system which thus becomes an impossibility, "the systematic undoing, in other words, of understanding";[17] and support for the singular "textual event" which, although it is absolutely exterior to the tropological or cognitive system, requires the materiality of words for its happening. But this is no longer a parallel trajectory. For Blanchot the irreducible singularity of worklessness operates on, works the material properties of language towards the production of a work always already contaminated by a worklessness that is its birth and its death at once – "the life which supports death and maintains itself in it." This is perhaps why in most cases Blanchot uses "material" and its cognates as *attributes*; even when the substantive "materiality" is used, it is always predicated *of* language, of meaning or of the word. De Man's materiality, although it can be said to gesture towards the same worklessness that Blanchot writes about, is nearly always substantive, and when it is an attribute, as in the phrase "material vision," it becomes an attribute that invades what it is meant to describe, so that, as de Man himself suggests, "material" vision is no vision at all. Thus, de Man's materiality, even if it is, as Derrida proposes "without matter" or without a metaphysical concept of matter, is not the bearer of worklessness, it *is itself the* undoing of work and of a worklessness that would be productive. It is not a "life" of any sort but "the moment when the infinite is frozen," interminable death maintained on every living point of a text.

ENDNOTES

[1] Blanchot, "Literature and the Right to Death", *WF* 301. I have occasionally modified the translations in *WF*, particularly at the points where Blanchot's use of "material" and its cognates is obscured by its translation into "physical," "physicality," and so on.

[2] Paul de Man, *Allegories of Reading: Figural Language in Rousseau, Nietzsche, Rilke, and Proust* (New Haven: Yale University Press, 1979), 115.

[3] For a consideration of the same argument in Blanchot, and which also serves as the opening for an article on "Literature and the Right to Death", see Rodolphe Gasché, "The Felicities of Paradox: Blanchot on the Null-Space of Literature," in *Maurice Blanchot: The Demand of Writing*, ed. Carolyn Bailey Gill (London: Routledge, 1996), 34–69.

[4] A particularly challenging possibility is that referred to precisely as a challenge and a possibility by Paul Davies in a note in his entry on Blanchot in *A Companion to Continental Philosophy*, ed. Simon Critchley and W.R. Schroeder (Oxford: Blackwell, 1998), 304–16; namely that of comparing the two writers' conceptions of allegory and symbol.

[5] For de Man's notion of materiality see especially the essays collected in the volume *Material Events: Paul de Man and the Afterlife of Theory*, ed. Tom Cohen, J. Hillis Miller, and Andrzej Warminski (Minneapolis: University of Minnesota Press, 2001) and also Rodolphe Gasché's discussions in his *The Wild Card of Reading: On Paul de Man* (Cambridge, Mass.: Harvard University Press, 1998).

[6] Leslie Hill, *Blanchot: Extreme Contemporary* (London: Routledge, 1997), 118.

[7] For Blanchot's use of, and deviation from, the structural progressions of Hegelian dialectics see Gasché, "The Felicities of Paradox", and also Andrzej Warminski's "Dreadful Reading: Blanchot on Hegel", *Yale French Studies*, 69 (1988), 267–75.

[8] See Leslie Hill, "Blanchot and Mallarmé", *MLN*, 195 (1990), 889–913 for the most thorough investigation of Mallarmé's influence on Blanchot.

[9] "Je dis: une fleur! Et, hors de l'oubli où ma voix relègue aucun contour, en tant que quelque chose d'autre que les calices sus, musicalement se lève, idée même et suave, l'absente de tous bouquets." Stéphane Mallarmé, *Œuvres complètes*, ed. H. Mondor and G. Jean-Aubry (Paris: Gallimard, 1945), 368. The translation is my own.

[10] Paul de Man, *Aesthetic Ideology*, ed. Andrzej Warminski (Minneapolis: University of Minnesota Press, 1996). All references to this volume will be made in the main body of the text, indicated by the abbreviation *AI* followed by the page number.

[11] See Jacques Derrida, "Typewriter Ribbon: Limited Ink (2) ('within such limits')", in *Material Events*, ed. Cohen et.al., 277–360.

[12] Immanuel Kant, *The Critique of Judgment*, trans. Werner Pluhar (Indianapolis, Hackett, 1987), 130.

[13] Hill, *Extreme Contemporary*, 112.

[14] Paul de Man, *Allegories of Reading*, 300–1. The figure of "permanent parabasis" is one de Man takes from Friedrich Schlegel's most tantalizing definition of irony. How and if Schlegelian irony comes into play in these considerations of materiality is a fascinating issue for which there is no scope in the current study.

[15] Derrida, "Typewriter Ribbon", 350.

[16] Derrida, "Typewriter Ribbon", 350.

[17] Paul de Man, *Allegories of Reading*, 301.

BLANCHOT, READER OF BAUDELAIRE:
"Baudelaire's Failure"

Alain Toumayan

GIVEN THE IMPORTANCE OF BAUDELAIRE AS ONE OF THE FIGURES COMMONLY mobilized to define the notion of literary modernity, and given the often striking congruence in themes and images between Blanchot and Baudelaire, it is somewhat perplexing that he does not figure more prominently in the Pantheon of major literary and philosophical influences on Blanchot, along with Sade, Lautréamont, Mallarmé, Rilke, Hölderlin, Kafka, Hegel, Heidegger, Beckett, Artaud, and so on. While Blanchot has, to be sure, written several articles on Baudelaire, his engagement with Baudelaire generally appears neither deep nor sustained. For example, he identifies many Baudelairian references as sources of Lautréamont in his *Lautréamont et Sade*, muses on the Baudelairian practice of intertextuality in a review of Jacques Crépet's edition of *Les Fleurs du Mal* (*Fp* 180–6/*FP* 156–62), and, in "Vaste comme la nuit," a review of Gaston Bachelard's signature study *La Poétique de l'espace*, Blanchot takes issue with Bachelard's analysis of the synthetic power of the word "vaste" in the poem "Correspondances" (*EI* 465–77/*IC* 318–25). Of these texts, only "Vaste comme la nuit" presents a recognizably Blanchotian analytic procedure. In that essay, Blanchot's questioning of Bachelard, and, more generally, his revision or correction of the phenomenological method that informs his enquiry, involves an investigation of the problem of the image, of the relation of the image to the *neutre*, and the explicit positing of the figure of enigma (*EI* 471, 476–7/*IC* 321, 324–5) to approximate the image's mode of signifying in lieu of the synthesizing, totalizing, and unifying dialectic assumed by Bachelard. The correction that Blanchot brings here to Bachelard evinces a characteristic gesture in Blanchot's readings which involves substituting a figure of non-dialectical opposition to the dialectic, thus disabling or displacing it.

In what follows, I propose to consider Blanchot's most sustained examination of Baudelaire, a review of Sartre's monograph *Baudelaire* (1947), entitled "Baudelaire's Failure" [*L'Échec de Baudelaire*], which appeared in the February and March 1947 issues of *L'Arche* (*PF* 133–51/*WF* 132–52). I will argue that this essay reproduces much of the development of Blanchot's most significant study of that period, "La Littérature et le droit à la mort." In particular, I will suggest that Blanchot's reading of Baudelaire *contra* Sartre parallels the development of Blanchot's analysis in "La Littérature et le droit à la mort" and that the strategic importance of Levinas in Blanchot's revision of both Hegel and Sartre correlates with Blanchot's examination of Baudelaire. In other words, if it is principally Levinas who supplies to Blanchot the conceptual means to revise Hegel and Sartre in "La Littérature et le droit à la mort," as Hill and Libertson in particular have brilliantly demonstrated,[1] it is in Baudelaire that Blanchot will locate the means to effect a similar displacement in "L'Échec de Baudelaire." It is not accidental that Baudelaire and Levinas are thus associated as Blanchot's examination of Baudelaire is, in part, mediated by Levinas.

The dates of publication of "L'Échec de Baudelaire" correspond to a particularly fertile period in Blanchot's critical writings and to a rich moment of intellectual exchange with Levinas which informs both a pivotal rethinking of Hegelian negativity and a subtle displacement of Blanchot's reading of Heidegger. In addition to corresponding to the dates of "La Littérature et le droit à la mort," the dates of publication of "L'Échec de Baudelaire" coincide with or follow closely those of Levinas's *De l'existence à l'existant* (of which the exposition of the *il y a* figures so prominently in "La Littérature et le droit à la mort") as well as of Levinas's *Le Temps et l'autre* in which Levinas pointedly reworks Heidegger's Being-towards-death as "impossibilité de la possibilité."[2] They coincide also with Sartre's *Qu'est-ce que la littérature?* to which Blanchot also responds in "La Littérature et le droit à la mort," as Hill has shown.[3]

Among those themes sketched by Blanchot in "L'Échec de Baude-laire," which are given fuller development in "La Littérature et le droit à la mort" and in *L'Espace littéraire* in particular, are: the definition of the imaginary *contra* Sartre as the apprehension of the real in its totality (*PF* 140/*WF* 139); the play of incompatible logics of totalization and incompletion (or "inachèvement") which Blanchot will, in subsequent essays, formulate in various guises, among others as the "oeuvre" and the "livre" (*PF* 140–1/*WF* 140); and the figure of an essential ambiguity identified with poetry itself: "it is in ambiguity that poetry becomes creation [*c'est dans l'ambiguïté que la poésie devient création*]" (*WF* 141/*PF* 141).

The most striking feature of the analysis of Baudelaire, however, is the manner in which, in Baudelaire's poetry, Blanchot, in essence, locates figures of Levinas's *il y a*. According to Blanchot, Baudelaire too has explicitly challenged the principle of negativity: "Baudelaire never trusted nothingness [*Baudelaire n'a jamais eu confiance dans le néant*]" and he has, in particular, questioned the equation of death and negativity: "He has the very profound feeling that the horror of living cannot be consoled by death, that it does not encounter an emptiness that exhausts it, that this horror of existing that is existence has as its main signification this feeling that one does not stop existing, one never leaves existence, one exists and one always will exist which is revealed by this very horror."[4] This particular formula recalls the one given in "La Littérature et le droit à la mort" where, identifying two distinct and opposed characteristics of literature, Blanchot formulates the normally hidden dimension it manifests in which negativity does not obtain: "it is the presence of things before the *world* exists, their perseverance after the world has disappeared, the stubbornness of what remains when everything vanishes and the dumbfoundedness of what appears when nothing exists."[5] Later, in a formulation which will be linked to Levinas's *il y a*, Blanchot notes: "it manifests existence without being, existence which remains below existence, like an inexorable affirmation, without beginning or end—death as the impossibility of dying."[6] Blanchot's comment in "L'Échec de Baudelaire" is supported by a reading of "Le Squelette laboureur," a poem in which, musing on the disconcerting and uncanny impression elicited by anatomical plates which represent flayed human bodies and skeletons in various poses as if engaged in different sorts of labour, Baudelaire pointedly enquires if the concept of nothingness is not, in fact, a fraudulent promise, if death as the "sommeil promis" is not a lie and if its association with nothingness in this guise does not in fact serve to dissimulate the even greater horror of a kind of perpetual, laborious "existence" beneath existence.

> Do you want (terrible, clear
> Emblem of a fate too hard)
> To show that even in the grave
> The promised sleep is far from certain?
>
> That to us Nothingness is traitor;
> That everything, even Death, lies to us. . . . (*WF* 148)
>
> [Voulez-vous (d'un destin trop dur
> Epouvantable et clair emblème!)
> Montrer que dans la fosse même
> Le sommeil promis n'est pas sûr;

> Qu'envers nous le Néant est traître;
> Que tout, même la Mort, nous ment. ...][7]

Both "Le Squelette laboureur" and "Obsession," in which Baudelaire observes that the darkness of night is never empty or dark enough but composes the background against which is detected a perpetual murmur, and against which occurs the appearance of the disappeared, thereby, once again, suggesting a weakness of negativity, will be marshaled by Blanchot, in "L'Échec de Baudelaire," to serve as explicit counter-examples to Heidegger's "Being-towards-death" as "authentic possibility." While Baudelaire's examination in "Obsession" of the nocturnal excess over nothingness – "But darkness itself is a canvas/ Where live, spurting from my eye by the thousands,/ Vanished beings with familiar looks!" (*WF* 148) ["Mais les ténèbres sont elles-mêmes des toiles/ Où vivent, jaillissant de mon oeil par milliers,/ Des êtres disparus aux regards familiers" (*CB* 76)] – suggests Blanchot's extensive and very rich examinations of the themes of night, the other night, the apparition, and the darkness, the attempt to disable, revise, or undermine Heidegger's "Being-towards-death" as possibility indicates an equally extensive horizon of Blanchot's thinking and certainly composes one of the questions, along with the *il y a*, about which there is a lengthy and productive exchange of views between Blanchot and Levinas.

In *De l'existence à l'existant*, Baudelaire supplies to Levinas also some salient figures of his argumentation. The poem "Le Voyage" provides Levinas with an image of evasion and "errance" ("But the true voyagers are those who move/simply to move...." [*FE* 179]) ["Mais les vrais voyageurs sont ceux-là seuls qui partent/ Pour partir (*CB* 130)] and "Le Squelette laboureur," with its unusual and uncanny imagery of effort in perpetuity, is used by Levinas to investigate the phenomenology of effort, fatigue, asseveration,[8] and the condemnation to being which is developed so emphatically in the essay "Il y a" in which the image of horror is, in Levinas's words, conceived as an explicit answer to Heidegger's *es gibt*. Thus, as in the case of "La Littérature et le droit à la mort," Levinas and, in particular, Levinas's thinking of the *il y a* supply to Blanchot a conceptual tool to revise Sartre, Hegel, and Heidegger and, as both Blanchot's and Levinas's texts suggest, this path has been charted by Baudelaire's particular examination of death and negativity.

Co-extensive with, if somewhat subsequent to, his elaboration of the *il y a* is Levinas's identification of a temporality which, as he puts it, falls in the interval, an interval between present and past, present and future, even, on closer scrutiny, an interval within the present itself. The temporality of *l'entretemps*, which suggests an insufficiency of negativity formulated in the context of the problem of time, is examined in a short essay on aesthetics and criticism entitled "La Réalité et son ombre."[9] Levinas here starkly describes a temporality of death that would be an entrapment in the empty interval of the *entretemps*, a perpetual approach, never-ending anguish, something akin, Levinas notes, to the temporality of nightmare, to the phobia of being buried alive: "something inhuman and monstrous [*quelque chose d'inhumain et de monstrueux*]" (786). The work of art, particularly the work of plastic art, expresses this particular experience of time, according to Levinas: Niobe frozen in her grief and the figure of Laocoon's horror immortalized in the grip of tormenting snakes.

I would like to relate this thematization of temporality to Blanchot and to his reading of Baudelaire by first examining the temporality of awaiting and the problem of death in both Blanchot and Baudelaire; and second, by considering the problem of the temporality expressed by the work of plastic art in Blanchot's "L'Échec de Baudelaire."

The temporality of approach and awaiting, especially in relation to the approach of death and, once again, as an alternative to or correction of Heidegger's "Being-towards-death" as authentic possibility, "élan," "anticipation," or *vorlaufen*, is one of the figures one finds most consistently throughout Blanchot's fiction and essays – from *Thomas l'obscur*, *L'Arrêt de mort*, *L'Attente l'oubli*, and *L'Écriture du désastre*, to the "mort toujours en instance" of his short *L'Instant de ma mort*. I will examine one short example, though many others of similar form could be adduced. In an excerpt from *L'Attente l'oubli*, Blanchot undermines death as negativity by associating awaiting and death through the pun on the words "attendre" and "atteindre": "Death, considered as an event that one awaits, is incapable of putting an end to waiting. Waiting transforms the fact of dying into something that one does not merely have to attain in order to cease awaiting."[10] The attempt to seize the event of death through the awaiting of death, as "élan" and anticipation, becomes the experience of death as awaiting. Though Blanchot does not consider the text in "L'Échec de Baudelaire," Baudelaire's poem "Le Rêve d'un curieux" presents this very scenario and is worth considering for the remarkable congruence in theme and image with Blanchot's examination of death. Indeed, recording an attitude of burning intellectual curiosity before death's event through a striking series of oxymorons: "douleur savoureuse," "Angoisse et vif espoir," "désir mêlé d'horreur," "torture âpre et délicieuse" (*CB* 128–9), Baudelaire's poem thematizes an attitude of anxious anticipation, "élan" or *vorlaufen* in relation to death. Unbearable suspense, excitement, and fear combine in the desire to apprehend the mystery of death, to face death in its absolute otherness, to annex death within the horizon of consciousness. The titillation and excitement of this intellectual curiosity is formulated in the expectation of the "froide vérité" of death's revelation: "I seemed a child, so keen to see the Show/ He feels a deadly hatred of the Curtain" (*FE* 178) ["comme l'enfant avide du spectacle/Haïssant le rideau comme on hait un obstacle..." (*CB* 129)]. The poem's structure itself enacts the suspense and the delay with the "event" of death played out progressively in the text. Expressed in the imperfect tense, it is announced in the first stanza: "I was due to die [*J'allais mourir*]" and emphasized in its progression in the second: "and as the sands of life ran low [*Plus allait se vidant le fatal sablier*]"; the event itself is recorded in the first verse of the last tercet: "J'étais mort" with the "revelation" of death's "truth" deferred to the last verse: "I felt that dreadful dawn around me glow/With no surprise or vestige of a thrill./ The curtain rose—and I stayed waiting still" (*FE* 178) ["J'étais mort sans surprise, et la terrible aurore/M'enveloppait.–Eh quoi! n'est-ce donc que cela?/La toile était levée et j'attendais encore" (*CB* 129)]. Thus Baudelaire enacts what both Levinas in *Le Temps et l'autre* and Blanchot in *L'Espace littéraire* refer to as "le paradoxe de l'heure dernière": "if you are, it is not; if it is, you are not [*si tu es, elle n'est pas; si elle est, tu n'es pas*]."[11] Yet what is more interesting here is the way in which Baudelaire has represented this event and dramatized the failure of a consciousness presented as only too eager to grasp it. To seize the event of death within the horizon and parameters of consciousness would be to apprehend it within the present, to be present to it (as the formula noted above suggests: "si tu *es*"). The manner in which Baudelaire undermines this particular operation is through the present's deferral or collapse into a perpetual "à-venir" with the perpetuity of the awaiting expressed both by the adverb and the imperfective aspect of the past tense: "j'attendais encore." What undermines the apprehension of death is a temporal structure in which a weakened negativity immobilizes consciousness in an empty interval comparable to Levinas's *entretemps*.

As noted above, it is in sculpture that Levinas finds the most salient illustrations of the *entretemps* and it is by way of Rodin's sculpture that Levinas represents the obtrusiveness of the *il y a* in *De l'existence à l'existant* (88). Against a conventional concept of the sculpted figure as representing a form captured within the present (as in a freeze-frame), Levinas argues in "La Réalité et son ombre" that the sculpted form expresses instead "un avenir éternellement suspendu ... un avenir à jamais avenir" (782). The instant or present moment, here, collapses into the inhuman and monstrous experience of a time without negativity. Blanchot shares this fascination with statuary. His stories frequently describe characters acquiring a statuesque demeanor, a mask-like aspect, a hardness in appearance, or an immobile or frozen mein, often to figure an alteration of the parameters of time which is generally, though not exclusively, related to the proximity of death. In both *L'Arrêt de mort* and *Thomas l'obscur*, for example, the narrator describes J. and Anne as resembling statues as death progressively claims each one. While Baudelaire has written extensively on painting and drawing, he has not written as extensively on statuary. It is significant, therefore, that among the poems that Blanchot examines in "L'Échec de Baudelaire" is Baudelaire's "Le Masque." Dedicated to sculptor Ernest Christophe and presenting as outstanding an example of literary ekphrasis as one will find in the nineteenth century, the poem describes the statue of a female figure executed by Christophe which presents a smiling demeanor. A slight change in the viewer's perspective of the statue shows that the smiling face is a mask, revealing beneath it a tortured expression of sadness and anguish, a figure frozen in her grief. Whence the "blasphème de l'art" and the "fatale surprise" exclaimed by the poet. In the poem's concluding verses, cited by Blanchot, Baudelaire asks and then emphatically answers the question: "But why is she weeping?" ["Mais pourquoi pleure-t-elle?"]:

> –She weeps, madman, because she has lived!
> And because she lives! But what she is lamenting
> Above all, what makes her tremble to her knees,
> Is that tomorrow, alas! She will have to live again!
> Tomorrow, the day after tomorrow and forever!—like us!
> (*WF* 149)

> Elle pleure, insensé, parce qu'elle a vécu!
> Et parce qu'elle vit! Mais ce qu'elle déplore
> Surtout, ce qui la fait frémir jusqu'aux genoux
> C'est que demain, hélas! Il faudra vivre encore!
> Demain, après-demain et toujours! – comme nous!
> (*CB* 24)

Like the figures of Niobe and Laocoon for Levinas, Ernest Christophe's statue described by Baudelaire figures for Blanchot "the despair of existing endlessly, in the dissolution of all form and all existence, a dissolution that, by still being form and existence, continues, beyond all life,"[12] or, again, Blanchot notes that "the horror of existing discovers in existence what is already below death, beyond its own end, and in the 'numbness of nothingness' a pseudo idea and false hope,"[13] in other words, the very horror figured so dramatically in "Le Squelette laboureur" and "Le Rêve d'un curieux" and examined in Levinas's *il y a* and *entretemps*. Indeed, in Levinas's terms, one could say that the statue in Blanchot's reading articulates both the *entretemps* and the *il y a*, and that it even raises Levinas's analysis to a higher degree of abstraction, since what the statue figures and immortalizes (in her frozen posture expressing the *entretemps*) is the very horror of her apprehension of the perpetuity of existence, the intrusiveness of the *il y a*. Thus does the statue serve as a prototype of art and of its function according to Blanchot: "art and the work of art (that the statue of Christophe represents in these verses)."[14] The serene face we might normally associate with statuary turns out to be an illusion, revealing the anguish and horror of the apprehension of the "pseudo idea and false hope" of the nexus of death and negativity or, as Baudelaire puts it in "Le Squelette laboureur," of the treachery of the idea of nothingness and the falsity of death. Blanchot's reading of "Le Masque" identifies two opposite functions of art, both related to negativity, and outlines the relation between them. On the one hand, the serene, calming, humanizing appearance of vitalizing negativity, on the other hand, the intrusion of a darker, more threatening meaning associated with a weakness of negativity (an *il y a* or an *entretemps*), and finally, the tendency to confuse the two, to take the latter for the former, or to articulate their relation in terms of negativity. Thus does this reading run rigorously parallel to the development of "La Littérature et le droit à la mort" in which the definition of literature is given, after many detours and after a circuitous exposition through Sartre, Hegel (and some of his commentators), and Levinas, as the locus in which death is enunciated as impossibility, and, beyond that, as the locus of an ambiguous play of death as possibility and as impossibility that is not resolvable by dialectical means.[15] It likewise runs parallel to the analysis of the duplicity of image in *L'Espace littéraire*, which derives from the "initial double meaning which the power of the negative brings with it and from the fact that death is sometimes truth's elaboration in the world and sometimes the perpetuity of that which admits neither beginning nor end."[16]

Central to Sartre's reading of Baudelaire and, as it happens, to his definition of poetry, is the notion of failure. Such a view is in part predicated upon the notion that literature is a form of action and that, for Sartre, Baudelaire appears to be the polar opposite of the "man of action": "Personne n'est plus éloigné de l'action que Baudelaire."[17] In a long footnote in the first section of *Qu'est-ce que la littérature?* Sartre emphatically and repeatedly characterizes poetry in contrast to prose as failure, since it is solipsistic and self-referential; its hermeticism prevents the active engagement with the world in real time, so to speak, that, in Sartre's view, should characterize literature.[18] Sartre's monograph on Baudelaire is, essentially, a case history and a demonstration of this proposition, whence the title of Blanchot's essay – "L'Échec de Baudelaire" – which is a good example of those statements by Blanchot that are to be read simultaneously as declarative and interrogative phrases. It is Blanchot's merit to discredit Sartre's reading of Baudelaire essentially by pointing out the obvious: if Baudelaire's career can be considered an earned and self-inflicted failure with its odd inconsistencies and laughable idiosyncracies, if he is a pathetic "self-tormentor" and a feckless poser, his verse poetry – to say nothing of his prose works, essays, and criticism – *Les Fleurs du Mal*, one of the most astounding works of the century, must somehow be related to this failure.

The examination of the problem of artistic inspiration in the opposition of a world of will, action, and accomplishment to a world of inaction or failure, passivity, powerlessness, *désœuvrement*, and impossibility is one of the richest problems examined by Blanchot throughout his career and developed with the most elegance and concision in *L'Espace littéraire* and most notably, in that work, in his reflection on Orpheus. Here, Blanchot makes the following observation about Baudelaire in response to Sartre: "the writer who attributes a great deal of poetic value to work is also the one who, not managing to work, discovers a form of activity more profound than work, from which his body of work came in part, and to which it bears witness,"[19] comments which outline the opposing logics of totalization or negativity and incompletion examined throughout Blanchot's work and in whose play the event of inspiration, like Levinas's trace, are to be found. This particular opposition may indeed be illustrated by various elements of Baudelaire's biography or comments in his correspondence, diaries, and journals. But it composes also one of the central themes of both prose and verse works and frames his examination of the phenomenon of artistic inspiration. In "Le Confiteor de l'artiste," for example, the event of artistic inspiration is figured thus: "The study of the beautiful is a duel in which the artist shrieks with fright before succumbing [*L'étude du beau est un duel où l'artiste crie de frayeur avant d'être vaincu*]" (*CB* 279).

In as much as the work of art itself can be associated with this shriek or "cri" (a word used also in the poem "Les Phares" to characterize the work of art), it is apparent that this model begins by situating the work within an economy of power, control, and technique (a duel) but locates the authentic artistic "event" of inspiration at the moment when the limits of this economy are reached. Clearly, such a "cri" is uttered by none other than the artist; he or she is its author and origin and it may even represent an authentic expression of its author's subjectivity. Just as clearly, however, it exceeds its author's initiative, conception, and power. No such "cri" can be intended, planned, or executed according to plan. This very scenario is enacted in Blanchot's treatment of Orpheus as well as in the following formula (and series of characteristic puns) in *L'Espace littéraire*: "what he is to write delivers the one who has to write to an affirmation over which he has no *authority*" [*ce qui s'écrit livre celui qui doit écrire à une affirmation sur laquelle il est sans autorité*]" (*SL 26/ EL* 16, my emphasis).

The Baudelaire that emerges from Blanchot's analysis in "L'Échec de Baudelaire" is of course partial, even idiosyncratic; "Le Squelette laboureur," "Le Masque," "Obsession" are not the most frequently cited examples of Baudelairian poetics. On the other hand, the extent to which Baudelaire's figurative terminology accurately anticipates problems examined extensively by Blanchot (and Levinas) is revealing. Most dramatic perhaps is a critical examination of duality, often at a high level of abstraction and involving both the explicit questioning of negativity and a challenging of the dialectic as an articulation of duality (it would be interesting to speculate about what Baudelaire could have meant by his one terse and pejorative reference to Hegel in *Mon Cœur mis à nu* [*CB* 688]). Thus, while Baudelaire anticipates some of Blanchot's most original and creative formulas, the latter's texts cast also a unique light on some of the most provocative, unusual, and problematic themes in Baudelaire's poetry.

ENDNOTES

I wish to thank the Institute for Scholarship in the Liberal Arts at the University of Notre Dame for generously supporting my participation at the "Blanchot, the Obscure" conference with an international travel grant.

[1] Joseph Libertson, *Proximity: Levinas, Blanchot, Bataille and Communication* (The Hague: Martinus Nijhoff, 1982), 132, 166–7, 206–7, 243. Leslie Hill, *Blanchot: Extreme Contemporary* (London: Routledge, 1997), 109–114.

[2] Emmanuel Levinas, *Le Temps et l'autre* (Paris: Presses Universitaires de France, 1994), 59 and 92 n5.

[3] Hill, *Extreme Contemporary*, 106–8.

[4] *WF* 147/*PF* 147:
[I]l a le sentiment très profond que l'horreur de vivre ne peut pas être consolée par la mort, qu'elle ne rencontre pas de vide qui l'épuise, que cette horreur d'exister qu'est l'existence a pour principale signification le sentiment d'un: on ne cesse pas d'exister, on ne sort pas de l'existence, on existe et on existera toujours, qui est révélé par cette horreur même.

[5] *WF* 328/*PF* 317:
[L]a présence des choses avant que le *monde* ne soit, leur persévérance après que le monde a disparu, l'entêtement de ce qui subsiste quand tout s'efface et l'hébétude de ce qui apparaît quand il n'y a rien.

[6] *WF* 328/*PF* 317:
[E]n elle se montre l'existence sans l'être, l'existence qui demeure sous l'existence, comme une affirmation inexorable, sans commencement et sans terme, la mort comme l'impossibilité de mourir.

[7] Charles Baudelaire, *Œuvres complètes* (Paris: Gallimard, Pléiade, 1974), 1: 94. Hereafter this edition and volume cited parenthetically as *CB*. *The Flowers of Evil*, ed. Marthiel and Jackson Matthews (New York: New Directions, 1989), 119. Hereafter this edition cited parenthetically as *FE*.

[8] Levinas, *De l'existence à l'existant* (Paris: Vrin, 1981), 32 and 49.

[9] Levinas, "La Réalité et son ombre", *Les Temps modernes*, 38 (Novembre 1948), 771–89.

[10] *AwO* 27/*AO* 55:
La mort, considérée comme un événement attendu, n'est pas capable de mettre fin à l'attente. L'attente transforme le fait de mourir en quelque chose qu'il ne suffit pas d'atteindre pour cesser d'attendre.

[11] Levinas, *Le Temps et l'autre*, 59. And *EL* 122.

[12] *WF* 149/*PF* 149:
[L]e désespoir d'exister sans cesse, dans la dissolution de toute forme et de toute existence, laquelle étant encore et toujours forme et existence, continue au-delà de toute vie.

[13] *WF* 150/*PF* 149:
l'horreur d'exister lui découvre dans l'existence ce qui est déjà en-dessous de la mort, au-delà de sa propre fin, et dans 'l'insensibilité du néant' une pseudo-idée et un faux espoir.

[14] *WF* 149/*PF* 149: "l'art et l'œuvre d'art (que représente dans ces vers la statue de Christophe)."

[15] Rodolphe Gasché, "The Felicities of Paradox: Blanchot and the Null-space of Literature", in *Maurice Blanchot: The Demand of Writing*, ed. Carolyn Bailey Gill (London: Routledge, 1996), 63–5.

[16] *SL* 261/*EL* 355:
Double sens initial qu'apporte avec soi la puissance du négatif et ce fait que la mort est tantôt le travail de la vérité dans le monde, tantôt la perpétuité de ce qui ne supporte ni commencement ni fin.

[17] Jean-Paul Sartre, *Baudelaire* (Paris: Gallimard, 1963), 52.

[18] Sartre, *Qu'est-ce que la littérature?*, in *Situations II* (Paris: Gallimard, 1948), 85–7.

[19] *WF* 144/*PF* 145:
L'écrivain qui met une grande part de la valeur poétique dans le travail, est aussi celui qui, n'arrivant pas à travailler, découvre une forme d'activité plus profonde que le travail, d'où son œuvre est sortie partiellement et dont elle témoigne.

BETWEEN HÖLDERLIN AND HEIDEGGER:
The "Sacred" Speech of Maurice Blanchot

Robert Savage

ON 22 JANUARY 1988, AN OPEN LETTER FROM MAURICE BLANCHOT TO Catherine David was published in the Parisian newsmagazine *Le Nouvel Observateur*. It represented his contribution to the "French Heidegger Wars," the controversy regarding Heidegger's fascism, and its implications for his philosophy, that raged through the late 1980s before petering out in the nineties. Coming from a man who once professed to have dedicated his life entirely to literature, such a statement carries a weight not usually accorded the musings of the professional feuilletonist. In a postscript to his letter, Blanchot recalled the excitement he had experienced some sixty years earlier, when he and Levinas had read *Being and Time* together. According to Blanchot, the most terrifying quality of the recently republished speeches from the rectorate period, which reveal Heidegger's overzealous commitment to the national awakening proclaimed by the Nazis, is the reappearance of the "*very* language and the very writing by which, in a great moment of the history of thought, we had been invited to participate in the questioning designated as the most high – that which would come to us from Being and Time."[1] Heidegger's crime is thus not only political but also linguistic. That he may temporarily have subscribed to an abhorrent politics is regrettable; but the nazification, perhaps simply the *politicization*, of "the most high" language of fundamental ontology irreversibly transforms that language into so much cheap rhetoric, degrading the philosophy it heralded.

So Blanchot. Yet Blanchot had been aware for decades of Heidegger's political activities in the Third Reich, and had read Heidegger's infamous speech "The Self-Affirmation of the German University" by 1960 at the latest, when it was republished by Guido Schneeberger. We know this because Blanchot tells us as much in a long footnote to *The Infinite Conversation*, a footnote that repeats, word for word, the charge against Heidegger I have just quoted (*IC* 451). The *very* language and the *very* writing he used in 1969 would thus find their way, practically unaltered, into the letter from 1988 – with one important difference. For whereas the footnote concludes with the remark about the damning proximity of Heidegger's political and philosophical language, the later text adds a sentence: "Yes, the same sacred language, perhaps a bit more crude, more emphatic, but the language that will henceforth be heard even in the commentaries on Hölderlin and alter them, but for still other reasons."[2] Blanchot's letter breaks off at this point.

What are these "still other reasons" to which Blanchot alludes, which presumably are only indirectly related to Heidegger's dalliance with Hitler? Is Blanchot renouncing his own earlier texts on Hölderlin, which praised Heidegger's commentaries and helped mediate them to a French public?[3] Or can a more critical and nuanced relationship to Heidegger already be found within those texts, such that the final sentence in Blanchot's letter, like its precursors, reads like a transcription from his earlier work? In that sentence, Blanchot attributes a "sacred" quality to Heidegger's language in connection with the Hölderlin commentaries. This is hardly surprising, considering the immense significance Heidegger accords "the Sacred" (*das Heilige*) in his *Elucidations to Hölderlin's Poetry*. But Blanchot's coupling of "le même langage sacré" with Hölderlin also recalls the title of an essay from 1946, "La Parole 'sacrée' de Hölderlin," in which he discusses at length Heidegger's interpretation of the poem "Wie wenn am Feiertage." If, earlier in the letter, Blanchot had tacitly quoted a passage from *The Infinite Conversation*, he reaches back still further in the last sentence, and this second intertext may point toward an answer to the questions I have raised.

The quotation marks within which Blanchot confines the Sacred in the title appear again at the end of the essay: "Such is the 'sacred' speech of Hölderlin" (*WF* 131). The gesture of distancing performed at both ends of the text is ambiguous. On the one hand, we can read *la parole "sacrée"* as meaning "this particular word 'sacred'" – certainly, says Blanchot, a "fundamental word" in Hölderlin's poetry, but still one word among many employed by the poet, capable of being analyzed across specific contexts and semantic fields. *La parole "sacrée"* would therefore limit the Sacred to a trope, an element of Hölderlin's discourse, rather than signifying a sacral language (such as Heidegger's) which imbues all its utterances with holy pathos. Blanchot seems to sanction this approach when he gives Hölderlin's optative "*das Heilige sei mein Wort* [the Sacred be my word]" the narrowest possible meaning, taking *Wort* at its word. Immediately after quoting the line, Blanchot writes: "If this term 'the Sacred,' designating gods, nature, the day, is constant in the poems, it remains very rare as a fundamental word" (*WF* 119). *Wort* means this particular word, "the Sacred," not language in general, oath, or creed.

Even if we stick to this strictly literal translation, however, a counter-interpretation suggests itself. For the quotation marks around *sacrée*, while interrupting the movement of transcendence by nailing the Sacred to its linguistic appearance, also express a need to keep the Sacred free from the vicissitudes of chatter; they indicate typographically the unique status of this auratic word in Hölderlin's vocabulary. When it is worn out through repetition and misuse, the Sacred – *das Heilige* – regresses into the sanctimonious – das *Scheinheilige*; this may well be the accusation behind the final line of Blanchot's letter. Quoting "*das Heilige sei mein Wort*" once again, this time in "The Great Refusal," Blanchot continues: "Das Heilige, the Sacred, an august word charged with lightning and as though prohibited, serving perhaps only to conceal with the force of a too-ancient reverence the fact that it can say nothing" (*IC* 36). The Sacred, like Hölderlin's Fatherland, is forbidden fruit; yet the profane act which reveals the word's emptiness might also restore and exalt, beyond religious convention, its inexhaustible richness. The Sacred's contentual poverty may be precisely what distinguishes it from common language and makes it "an august word charged with lightning," in the same way that Being, saying nothing, allows in its essence all saying (and all not-saying as well). Although and because it eschews its phenomenalization, the Sacred engulfs language as its ordinarily forgotten condition of possibility.

On the other hand, "*sacrée*" can be understood as a quotation from Heidegger, such that the title means: "Hölderlin's speech that Heidegger calls 'sacred.'" Blanchot cites this Heideggerean concept – *das Heilige* – in order to differentiate his own understanding of the Sacred from the philosopher's. The latter's holy language is, borrowing the terms of the 1988 letter, a bit more crude, more emphatic: "Let us add that the unparalleled soaring of [Hölderlin's] language, this rhythm that is its superior truth, this surge upward are in their turn ignored by the commentary" (*WF* 114). Unlike Paul de Man, Blanchot never charges Heidegger with ventriloquizing through Hölderlin, for anything lent by the philosopher to the poet's text "had been borrowed from it" (*WF* 119). He also agrees with Heidegger's circumscription of the Sacred in Hölderlin as a creative totality anterior to both gods and mortals.[4] They part company, however, in determining the relationship between the Sacred, the law, and speech. Heidegger argues that the Sacred is the immediate and incommunicable, hence, from the law's point of view, chaotic. "Chaos is the Sacred itself," which forbids every handhold and withdraws from every dialectical movement.[5] Yet for Heidegger, we should not rush to equate chaos with lawlessness, for the immediate is at the same time the mediacy of the mediate, that which makes possible in its essence the mediated and the communicable, the *Mittelbar* and the *Mitteilbar.*[6] As such, chaos is the law – not just any law, but "the most high." Heidegger writes in his commentary to "Andenken": "The Most High is *the Sacred*, the law, which posits in another manner to human law."[7] Chaos (the Sacred) is not outside, above or beyond the law, but the law itself as the sending power, prior to all statutes, regulations and prohibitions.

This analysis of the Sacred, notes Blanchot, takes its "inspiration from a prose fragment of Hölderlin," namely "Das Höchste," the Most High, one of the Pindar fragments (*WF* 120). Namely "Das Höchste" – yet Blanchot fails to mention "Das Höchste" by name, as if the name were unimportant or irrelevant to the business at hand. Heidegger cites most of the fragment and devotes to it a laborious exegesis; Blanchot refers, almost dismissively, to "a prose fragment of Hölderlin," as if it little mattered which. Let us recall, however, another "sacred" word of Hölderlin, one that simultaneously names the Sacred and revokes its naming: "I will not speak of the Most High [*Vom Höchsten will ich schweigen*]."[8] More than Heidegger's volubility, Blanchot's reticence concerning "The Most High" may indicate his fidelity to the poetological principles he has gleaned from the fragment. Blanchot's (non-)naming of "Das Höchste" comes just two sentences before the essay's most critical moment, in which he describes Heidegger's reading of "Das Höchste" – a reading which charts precisely the becoming-language of the immediate, the possibility of naming the Most High – as "more sensitive to tradition than to Hölderlin's experience" (*WF* 120). Blanchot's silence regarding the "inspiration" for the Heideggerean notion of the "Sacred" anticipates the argument formulated at the end of the essay: that the Sacred's reconciliation with speech is impossible (*WF* 131).

If that is correct, then "Das Höchste" must be understood, contrary to appearances, as the most high and most important, because silenced, reference in Blanchot's essay, and the caesura in his conversation with Heidegger. In order to test this hypothesis, I will have to follow Heidegger's example, rather than Blanchot's, by citing Hölderlin's text at some length. Like the eight other Pindar texts, it begins with a heading invented by Hölderlin and continues with a translation of a sententious fragment by the Greek poet Pindar, before offering Hölderlin's own commentary on the fragment. The relation between title, translation and explication is by no means straightforward, for the title given to each fragment often finds little support in the translation that follows, which in turn is already an interpretation of the Greek original. In place of philological clarification, the commentary goes on to present a semi-autonomous chain of philosophical and poetological reflections. The fifth such fragment reads as follows:

THE MOST HIGH

> The law,
> The king of all, mortals and
> Immortals; which for that very reason
> Guides with violence
> The most just right with the very highest hand.
> The immediate, taken strictly, is impossible for both mortals
> and immortals; the god must differentiate between
> different worlds, according to his nature, because heavenly
> possessions, on their own account, must be sacred, unmixed.
> The human, in that he knows, must also differentiate
> between different worlds, because knowledge is only possible
> through opposition. The immediate is therefore, taken
> strictly, impossible for mortals and immortals alike.
> But strict mediacy is the law.
> But for that reason it violently guides the most just right with the very
> highest hand. . . .
> "King" means here the superlative which is only the sign for the
> highest epistemic ground [*den höchsten Erkenntnisgrund*], not
> for the highest power.[9]

Among the most puzzling aspects of this difficult text is that its title does not unequivocally correspond to anything that follows. Hölderlin does not provide us with a statement of the sort: "The Most High is . . ." As we have seen, Heidegger elucidates the fragment in just this manner: "The Most High is *the Sacred*, the law." To what extent is he justified? The law is the king of all, writes Pindar, and Hölderlin elaborates: the highest ground of knowledge, *but not the highest power*. Hölderlin grounds human knowledge in the positing of something I am not as something I am not, that is, in the act of recognition. Only insofar as I venture outside myself, self-alienated, can I know myself, "because knowledge is only possible through opposition." Hölderlin was among the first to reject Fichte's absolute ego by referring it to a primordial Being, which cannot be brought to consciousness because it cannot be known, only intuited.[10] The law is thus the highest "epistemic ground" in two radically different (though not opposed) senses.[11] There might be something higher than the law, "the highest power" which precedes all opposition and discloses itself solely to intellectual intuition, but the law, as strict *mediacy*, is the highest ground *for* knowledge qua op-position. In the eighth Pindar fragment, Hölderlin draws an implicit etymological connection between Themis, the goddess of law, and the Greek verb tithenai, to posit.[12] At the same time, the law is *strict* mediacy, or the mediacy of the mediate, as Heidegger says, hence the immediate and unpositable, the highest un/ground of knowledge, which looks chaotic simply because we tend to ascribe any indigestible difference to chaos. The highest epistemic ground, the law, is either knowledge's knowable ground or its unknowable abyss; the gatekeeper before the Most High or the Most High itself; a hierarchy of contractually defined relationships and obligations – or the Sacred.

Curiously enough, Blanchot challenges Heidegger's equation of the Sacred with chaos, and hence of chaos with the Most High, on experiential grounds:

> On this point, it seems that the commentator was more sensitive to tradition than to Hölderlin's *experience* [*expérience*]. Chaos, assuredly, opens up in a profound way in the poems and hymns: it is given a very strange name: *das freudigschauernde Chaos*, chaos in which trembling is made into joy. But to seek in this an *experience* of chaos as such an *experience* of night might completely distort the poet's *experience*. Neither chaos nor night lets itself be *felt* in it in such an absolute way. On the contrary, night and chaos always end up testifying to the law and form of light. (*WF* 120, italics added)

Blanchot appears at this point to out-Heidegger Heidegger. The philosopher's commentaries have been accused time and again (with some justice) of philological inaccuracy, unscrupulousness, and interpretative violence, but at least Heidegger professes his utter servitude before the text.[13] Blanchot seems to be demanding of us that we read Hölderlin through the prism of his experience, which of course is strictly unknowable, except insofar as it becomes word, in which case Blanchot should chastise Heidegger for failing Hölderlin's poetry, and not his feelings. The importance thus accorded experience as the source and measure of criticism transforms literary production, however indirectly, into a means of self-expression. Unavoidable and undeniable as this moment may be, its persistence at the center of Blanchot's argument with Heidegger runs counter to the essay's general (and Heideggerian) argument on poetry's unique ontological status: "wherever poetry asserts itself, existence, considered as All, also begins to assert itself" (*WF* 115).

Before subscribing to such objections, we need to examine the connection between the appeal to Hölderlin's experience, which occurs within Blanchot's discussion of "Das Höchste," and the propositional content of that text. This connection will help us to clarify what Blanchot means by "experience." Blanchot maintains that the poet's experience of night and chaos cannot be posited as absolute, for the law and the light always shine through the darkness. We can certainly conceive of day and night as "different worlds," as when we talk of Hölderlin's "dark night of the soul"; we can theorize this dichotomy in different ways and build philosophical systems around it – but Hölderlin *felt* the night in a different, more differentiated fashion. This nameless experience resists its diremption into opposites, and hence its sublation into knowledge, which is only possible through opposition. Blanchot invokes here a non-oppositional (or non-mediate: neither mediate nor immediate) form of knowledge which, because incapable of its polarization, its *taking strictly*, can only be brought to consciousness as knowledge after the event. Hölderlin's "experience" of night, the way he "felt" it (an experience closer to *Erlebnis* than *Erfahrung*, and closer still to non-experience), cannot be taken "in such an absolute way," that is, strictly. Hölderlin's is not the night in which all cows are black, nor is it the night as the day's oppositional or dialectical counterpart; his impossible knowledge (and Blanchot's impossible knowledge of this knowledge) goes past the point at which knowledge generated through opposition meets its limit – the law as the highest ground of knowledge – but without lapsing into absolute indifference.[14] It neither bursts into the plenitude of Being, nor plunges into the void, but finds itself in the existential twilight zone which Blanchot associates with daybreak: "The Sacred is the day: not the day as it contrasts with the night, ... but anterior to the day, and always anterior to itself; it is a before-day, a clarity before clarity to which we are closest when we grasp the dawning, the distance infinitely remote from daybreak, which is also what is most intimate to us, more interior than all interiority" (*WF* 121).

Knowledge struggles in vain to catch the Sacred as it crests on the brink of its actualization. A little later, Blanchot describes the Sacred in distinctly Heideggerian terms as the "shining power whose outpouring is the law, principle of appearance of what appears, origin of all ability to communicate" (*WF* 122). The Sacred, the law as origin of the law, requires a mediator, the poet, that it not lose itself in boundless totality. Once again quoting "Das Höchste" while still declining to name it, Blanchot writes: "The possibility of communicating, such as it emanates from the law, is too large to be truly communication; it is 'absolute mediatedness,' says Hölderlin" (*WF* 124).

Blanchot has not simply reached the same conclusion as Heidegger – the Sacred is the law which spawns the law – via a different route, following the day's gleaming awakening instead of the night's turbid confusion. The originary law of which they both speak harbours a radical difference. Heidegger's law, impersonal and authoritative, thunders down the ages and commissions the poet to be its voice; it authorizes this man Hölderlin, whose life-and-times we need investigate no further, to accept the lightnings sent by the Most High and so become the immediate's mediator and poet of the poet, who looms before the Germans as their national task and destiny.[15] Blanchot resists this pathetic upswing from mortal to agent of Being by locating the liminal condition in which the poet becomes aware of the Sacred in experience, before it has been swept into a speculative economy. "More sensitive to tradition than to Hölderlin's experience," Heidegger failed to see that the law beyond law which shines through this condition would also be irreducibly personal, "more interior than all interiority," for even interiority presupposes its opposite. Yet Blanchot's critical move comes at a high price: it turns upon the critic by hypostatizing the very experience that should be utterly singular. Blanchot can only claim a special insight into Hölderlin's incommunicable experience through his own feelings, yet this means he can never know if his experience of non-experience – what he will later call the neuter – is the same as the poet's.

We can draw from this two consequences for Blanchot's relationship to Heidegger. Firstly, "sacred" speech, the mediation and mediatization of the unmediated, is impossible. Heidegger writes: "The Sacred gifts the word and comes itself into this word."[16] Blanchot would only consent to the first part of the proposition. Hauled into language, subjected to the law it precedes, the Sacred shrivels into a figure of speech. To the three interpretations of the quotation marks around "*sacrée*" I suggested earlier may thus be added a fourth: they are bars prohibiting the word's access to what they defend and imprison. The poet's task would be incessantly to assail the Sacred with language, that the Sacred at last be said and, being said, cast aside language like a veil;[17] the poet's lot, however, is an incessant not-saying, while poetry's is the tenacity of discourse.

Secondly, against Heidegger, the arche-law, which discloses itself as undisclosable to an experience so intimate that it falls under the jurisdiction of its duplicitous other as soon as it is posited, cannot unequivocally be designated the Most High. One could just as legitimately identify (and deify) as the Most High the poet through whom alone this law arises. The poet calls the Sacred into being that the Sacred may have called into being the poet who calls it: "the poet must exist as a presentiment of himself, as the future of his existence" (*WF* 117). But this is madness *par excellence*. "The poet," writes Blanchot in the essay of that name, "is the locus of a dialectic of derangement, which reproduces and makes possible the very movement of the true."[18] As such, he stands higher than the limitless height which, first constrained by his word, allots measure to mortals and immortals alike; without his intervention, we could not speak of the Most High at all. Moreover, the originary law as much created as reproduced by the poet is literally worthless, incapable of founding a history or legislating for a people because inseparable from the poet's knowledgeless experience. For Blanchot, the Sacred can *only* be approached as touch, smell, feeling, as the sublime or the abject, and cannot be abstracted from these obscure borderline states, at the risk of dissipating into theological speculation and problems of logic – and hence into mediation.

Beyond the law, then, Blanchot discovers a law that is for me alone, tactile and fleshy: "not the law everyone knows, which is severe and hardly agreeable"; not Being either; but the woman known as *la loi*, who abases herself before the narrator of *The Madness of the Day* (*MD* 14–5). A similar figure, Jeanne Galgat, appears in another work of fiction from the same period, *Le Très-Haut*, translated into English as *The Most High*. Ever since Klossowski pointed out that the name of its narrator, Sorge, means "concern" in German, commentators have recognized the presence of a Heideggerian subtext in the novel, *Sorge* being the term Heidegger uses to describe the basic relation of Dasein to the world in which it finds itself thrown.[19] Aside from Leslie Hill's suggestion that the novel's title be read as a translation of "Das Höchste," however, the existence of an overlapping Hölderlinian subtext remains ignored.[20] Yet the novel, written around the same time as "The 'Sacred' Speech of Hölderlin" and published in 1948, not only demands to be understood as a gigantic commentary on Hölderlin's fragment; it makes quite precise references to other Pindar fragments as well.

Take, for instance, this strange woman Jeanne Galgat, Sorge's nurse, worshipper and assassin. Galgat steps into the foreground of the narrative in Chapter Eight. After appearing to rape her – "strictly speaking, she didn't resist" (*MH* 202) – Sorge signs a document at her behest, giving her sole rights to care for him. Galgat, who had remained silent up to this point, now decides to speak. Toward the end of the chapter she tells him: "Yes, I see you, I hear you, and I know that the Most High exists"

(*MH* 231). The similar behaviour of *la loi* in *The Madness of the Day* has invited several commentators to identify Galgat with the law.[21]

This identification finds more solid textual support in Chapter Eight's Hölderlinian intertext, the eighth Pindar fragment. Hölderlin entitles this fragment "Die Asyle," the sanctuaries; its French cognate, "*asiles,*" which Blanchot had not used on a single occasion hitherto, crops up three times in the chapter (*MH* 204, 214, 216). Pindar's text tells how Themis, the Greek goddess of law – Hölderlin calls her "the lover of order" in his commentary – bore "the silent places of rest," the sanctuaries named in the title; in Blanchot's chapter, Sorge withdraws entirely into his room and watches Jeanne go about her chores in methodical silence (*MH* 203). That Jeanne takes the part of Themis is also suggested by the legal document she urges Sorge to sign (*MH* 208–9). Hölderlin says of "die Asyle" that "nothing foreign can touch them"; Jeanne commands Sorge not to leave his room while she is away (*MH* 230). Most importantly, Hölderlin argues that man's spirit finds "no peace until ... god and man know each other again"; Sorge's asylum is precisely the site of their recognition.[22]

Similarly, the ninth and final chapter of Blanchot's novel corresponds exactly to the ninth and final Pindar fragment. The chapter opens with the extended description of a rag that absorbs all the water dripping onto it, evoking in the narrator the "vague depths of a hollow filled with water" (*MH* 240). The text then teems with images of outbreak and fluvial movement, of a liquid mass "surging" out of a "cavernous void," the "always saturated and inundated places" "overflowing," "smothering and inundating me." When Galgat and Sorge set out across the city by night to find new, even more isolated lodgings for the patient, the road itself takes the form of a river: "Then the passion of forward movement overcame it again, and it changed course, stretched out, narrowed" (*MH* 240). Even in his new room, Sorge remains haunted by "an enormous sticky stain ... which was heading in all directions, spreading itself out, to its own horror, more and more in broad daylight." At the height of the ordeal, Sorge sees, "completely and not its image," a muddy, flowing mass (*MH* 248). It is as if all the stain and sweat imagery in the novel, the oozing and odiferous tropes lurking on the margins of the text and the narrator's consciousness, had finally burst their banks.

This amorphous mass may well be the *Stromgeist,* the river-spirit that is the subject of the last Pindar text. Hölderlin's commentary begins with the description of a landscape "rich in rocks and grottoes" in which the river had to "stray around [*umirren*]" before it could break a path through the mountains. Such regions were therefore full of "damp meadows and hollows" in which "the waters longingly sought their direction." The moment of release came when the roots of trees and shrubs growing alongside it allowed the erring liquid to assume a particular form, gather momentum, and charge through the weakest link in the mountains. At this point, "the formed wave swept aside the peace of the pond" and forged a path through the forests, shaking up "the idle life of the plain" and creating the conditions for agriculture and human settlement. The industrious and well-ordered life of the city thus has as its origin the restless wanderings of the *Stromgeist* before it acquires direction – in the terms of Blanchot's account, before it becomes image. After his encounter with the *Stromgeist*, Sorge writes: "Then I saw that I was alone; no one was holding me back, not an order, not a thought, not an obstacle, and I knew something was going to happen, something vile, and I saw and understood everything…" (*MH* 248–9). Complete freedom of movement collides here with the premonitory awareness of an ultimate determining event, just as the river, pure spirit until it "took on a determination," then "makes paths and boundaries, with violence, on the originally trackless upwardsgrowing earth."[23]

A detailed investigation of other such correspondences is beyond the scope of this essay. I mention them only to demonstrate the pervasive presence of Hölderlin's Pindar fragments in *Le Très-Haut*. I can now attempt to sketch in more detail the ways in which the themes Blanchot drew from "Das Höchste," and first explored in "The 'Sacred' Speech of Hölderlin," are taken up again in the novel. That Blanchot should introduce his Hölderlin interpretation into his fiction is hardly surprising, given that he had already introduced fiction into his Hölderlin interpretation. Hill observes that, while the first line of verse quoted by Blanchot at the end of the 1946 essay comes from Hölderlin, the second is pure invention.[24] In a similar sleight-of-hand, Blanchot translates the same verses from "Germanien" three times in *The Work of Fire* (the collection of essays in which "The 'Sacred' Speech of Hölderlin" was taken up), each time slightly varying his translation (*PF* 7, 69, 129–30). Considering the minute revisions to which he subjected the essays before republication, it seems unlikely that Blanchot unintentionally gave three different renderings and then forgot to homogenize them. The triple transcription reflects instead the content of the translated verses: "One time a truth should appear to you, / In a triple metamorphosis transcribe it; / Though always unexpressed, as it is, / O innocent, so it must remain" (*WF* xi).

Blanchot again tests the boundaries between criticism and literature in
Le Très-Haut, this time from the other side, by extending and deepening
the conversation with Heidegger and Hölderlin begun in "The 'Sacred'
Speech of Hölderlin." Blanchot's novel depicts a totalitarian society
in which the law permeates the most trivial aspects of life, turning a
stroll into "the application of a public decree" (*MH* 80), an insignificant
bureaucratic post into the embodiment of the entire administration
(*MH* 125). It is a state in which, paraphrasing Pindar, the law is king
of all, mortals and immortals, in which it guides justice with the very
highest hand. Yet as the novel progresses, the law comes increasingly
to resemble its opposite, lawlessness. Revolutionary political activities
are tolerated, even condoned, by the state, because infringements of the
law merely confirm its power. When there is nothing outside the law,
there are also no outlaws; when the law is king of all, no-one can stand
up to challenge its sovereignty. As Peter Köppel writes: "At the end, no
more antitheses appear in this order. It is therefore no longer positional-
thetic, but thoroughly permissive."[25] The law merges with chaos, and
chaos becomes the law.

Translated into Heideggerean terminology, the post-historical
Dasein portrayed in *Le Très-Haut* "stands as everyday being-with-one-
another under the dominion of others," that is, under the dictatorship
of *das Man*.[26] The fungibility of each citizen before the law indicates
Dasein's fallenness. "That everyone was equally faithful to the law,"
writes Sorge, "– ah, that idea intoxicated me" (*MH* 18). So interpreted,
the devastating progress of the epidemic brings the citizens back to
their "ownmost," their mortality. Sorge's last words, "'Now, now I'm
speaking'" (*MH* 254), would signal the recovery of authenticity in
being-unto-death, in which "Dasein relates to *itself* as to a distinct ability
to be."[27] This ecstatic, auto-affective moment arrests the expropriative,
self-dissimulating movement of chatter (*Gerede*). Grounding authentic
speech, it reveals that Sorge has not truly spoken to this point, and so
makes possible the entire narrative: *Le Très-Haut* retrospectively emerges
as a circular novel. Sorge's first words, "I wasn't alone, I was anybody.
How can you forget that phrase?" follow upon his last as their condition
of utterance. *Gerede* (this phrase "I was anybody") is always a deficient
modus of *Rede* ("Now, now I'm speaking").[28]

Neat as this reading may be, it raises more questions than it answers.
Sorge's fallenness, if such it be, is not his strickenness in the existent
but his obsession with totality; he is not "intoxicated" with the law as it
reveals itself in regulations and by-laws (as it manifests itself ontically,

one might say), but with its incessant circulation: Sorge is "solicitude for and of the law," writes Foucault.[29] Further, the novel's circularity, which mimics that of the law, means that Sorge never actually dies: the endless swansong released by the instant of his death ensures that death never arrives. The "now" of "Now, now I'm speaking" flattens out into an impossibly vast, distended present, while the spoken "I" leaves its suffering speaker behind to expand into anonymity. Despite appearances, then, we are worlds away from being-unto-death. Sorge's dying words are precisely his *dying* words: they express an impersonal, infinitely protracted dying rather than a death that is ever my own;[30] they emerge from a suspension, rather than a plenitude of Being; they tarry in a bloated now-time, rather than testifying to the anticipatory temporality characteristic of Dasein that has accepted its finitude.

"Now, now I'm speaking": this is "sacred" speech, in the rigorously contradictory Blanchotian sense outlined above. In "The 'Sacred' Speech of Hölderlin," in lines which anticipate Sorge's dying, Blanchot writes: "Impossible, the reconciliation of the Sacred with speech demanded that the poet's existence came nearest to non-existence. That is when, for one moment, it itself seemed possible, when, before foundering, it agreed to assert itself in song, come from an already silent body, uttered by a dead voice, so that the only hymn worthy of the essence of day rose from the depths of the vanished day ... not because the most high is darkness ... but because the All made itself language to say it" (*WF* 131, trans. amended). In a somewhat later essay, "Hölderlin's Itinerary," he imagines the Sacred, again in silent reference to "Das Höchste," as an "empty and pure place which distinguishes between the spheres" (*SL* 274). Taken together, these comments describe the deathless dying of the Most High. Poised between life and death, godhead and mortality, Being and beings, Sorge gives birth to the narrative *Le Très-Haut* and everything contained within it. His enactment of pure immediacy in speech, at once rapturous and horrified, brings forth the infinitely complex web of legal relationships from which no-one in the novel may escape. At the same time, it withdraws from that web, for Sorge, dying, is this no-one, and only no-one, non-Being, is privy to the immediacy that, taken strictly, is impossible for mortals and immortals alike.

I mentioned earlier that, while the becoming word of the Sacred is impossible, it is so for me alone, through an experience I could only describe as unknowable, incommunicable, worthless, sublime. This experience can now be examined more concretely. Blanchot presents Sorge's (non-)encounter with the Sacred, at the end of *Le Très-Haut*, as the culmination of the epidemic sickness which progressively ravages the city, from which Sorge himself suffers, and which contaminates every sentence of the novel.[31] The isolated space to which Jeanne drags Sorge at the beginning of the final chapter, and in which he meets his interminable end, is by no means disinfected and quarantined from the rest of the book; the fluvial imagery that dominates the chapter suggests precisely the opposite. Suffering, denied the dignity of a cause or meaning, calls into question the absolute sovereignty of the law by sinking into the embodied experience of abject contingency.[32] While the law effortlessly assimilates Bouxx's revolutionary movement, sickness alone escapes its grip, and it is in and through sickness that Sorge comes at last to "speak."

This statement must immediately be qualified by remembering that it is not the disease that kills Sorge – before he accepts Jeanne's dubious protection he seems on the verge of convalescence. Dorte notices his "air of health," his "radiant appearance," and, a few pages later, Sorge "again felt almost good" (*MH* 173, 179). It is instead the law, as Jeanne/Themis, that violently intervenes, with the very highest hand. The law cannot tolerate that the Most High lie outside its jurisdiction, so it eliminates the threat by taking care of it, in both senses of the term (as nurse and murderess; this may even be an obscure pun: *Jeanne sorgt sich um Sorge*).

Her twin functions are not so contradictory as they appear. In her capacity as nurse, Jeanne/Themis takes it upon herself to be Sorge's sole intermediary. She does everything in her power to guide the Most High back into the law, so that, reintegrated into a system of knowledge, he abdicates before it. She confines him to his room and demands he sign what she calls "a pact, an alliance" requesting her to stay. Having signed it, Sorge sees her assume "an incredible expression of shrewdness, pride, and satisfaction, her head held high ... As if to humiliate, she gazed triumphantly at everything here, one after another, everything" (*MH* 209–10). The law's gloating cannot arise from the content of the document, which expresses merely the wish that Galgat continue in her service, "if she is available" (*MH* 209). Imperiously surveying everything, the law believes it has wrested back the title of the Most High through the binding force of the signature itself.

When this belief proves premature, the law adopts the most cunning strategy of all: she addresses Sorge openly as the Most High, as if admitting defeat by stripping him of his incognito. Were the law to interpellate Sorge in this manner, and were Sorge to translate its flattering claim into self-knowledge, then the experience of non-experience through which alone he merits this distinction would again submit to mediation. Sorge would henceforth bring a firm identity to every experience, the now illusory "I, the Most High," and this identity would call forth an equally rigid opposite. The law sets the trap nicely: "'What I'm going to say is true. Take me at my word, tell me you'll believe me, swear to it.' – 'Yes, I'll believe you.'" Sorge nonetheless manages to thwart the danger, and sidestep his promise, by refusing to ac-knowledge his interlocutor in the first place: "'*I know that you are the Unique, the Supreme One. Who could stay standing before you?*' I turned away so as not to meet her eyes" (*MH* 233).

At last, the law is driven to contract murder. The execution of this decree, however, is what first makes the Most High the Most High – or rather, it catapults *le Plus-Haut* into *le Très-Haut*. The phrase *le Plus-Haut* takes on two meanings in the novel, corresponding to the two interpretations of "Das Höchste" offered above. On the one hand, *le Plus-Haut* designates the State, the law as an uncircumventable network of relations and obligations; this is the sense in which Sorge uses it (*MH* 120). On the other, *le Plus-Haut* names Sorge, the Hölderlinian hero who calls the Sacred into being by encompassing both the law and the meaningless suffering that eludes it; this is the sense in which Jeanne/Themis uses it (*MH* 231). The word *le Très-Haut*, a Jewish honorific which according to Köppel designates an intensification of *le Plus-Haut* – the Most Most High, as it were – appears only in the title.[33] *Le Très-Haut* thus signifies the narrative in which *les Plus-Hauts* uneasily cohabit; as such, it stands higher still than both. But this narrative exists only because the law destroys *le Plus-Haut* that it may speak (the law). The undecidable duplicity which characterises the law dwells within the Sacred itself and tears it apart. The Sacred rises above the law and falls prey to it ad infinitum, for the Sacred is *also* the law. Again, a Pindar text provides the model for this spiralling ambiguity:

THE INFINITE

Whether I scale
The law's wall, the high,
Or crooked deception's,
And thus transcribing myself,
Live onward, on that point
I am of two minds,
To say it precisely.[34]

Blanchot's critical reflection on the Sacred, as I have traced it through "The 'Sacred' Speech of Hölderlin" and *Le Très-Haut*, does not share

Heidegger's faith that the Sacred is the Most High. Sorge will never be finished scaling the wall of the law, nor will he ever be able to separate into different worlds the law which brings forth the law (the Sacred), and that begotten law. The Sacred, maintains Heidegger in his letter against humanism, "comes to appearance only when Being itself, beforehand and after long preparation, has become clear in itself [*sich gelichtet hat*] and has been experienced in its truth."[35] Nothing could be both closer to, and further from, Blanchot's conception of the Sacred than this epochal experience of light and truth. The mutual parasitism (or symbiosis) of the Sacred and the law undercuts Heidegger's insistence on the Sacred's primordiality: we can never quite be sure that the Sacred, the origin of the law, is not deceiving us by denying *its* origins. Who (or what) is *le Plus-Haut*? We cannot tell. If ambiguity, according to Blanchot, is "the essential movement of poetry," then this movement pushes all the way through to the loftiest realms of poetic expression (*WF* 156); if "sacred" speech is the blinding moment in which the poet founds what endures, then it is also crooked delusion, black as the light absolutely anterior to day.[36] For Blanchot, the poet inhabits this fundamental ambiguity, demonstrating over and again the necessity and impossibility of "sacred" speech, that in the experience of non-experience – in the suspension of Being – he may (re)discover and (re)affirm the futility of his striving.

In the late 1940s, then, the intensive study and creative adaptation of Hölderlin's writings helped Blanchot articulate his distance from Heidegger. The importance of the Pindar texts in this process, particularly "Das Höchste," can hardly be overestimated. They constitute the pivot upon which Blanchot's assent to key theses of Heideggerian poetics – the founding power of poetic language; the poet's exceptional, quasi-heroic existential status; the Sacred's all-embracing antecedence – swings into disagreement. As such, they already form the site of a critical engagement with Heidegger that anticipates the later, much more forcefully enunciated statements of 1969 and 1988.

One nagging doubt remains. Walter Benjamin once attended a meeting of the College of Sociology at which Georges Bataille was speaking on the Sacred. Benjamin leaned over to Pierre Klossowski during the speech to whisper the chilling and sober words: "In the end, you are working for the fascists."[37] Does his judgment hold true for Bataille's close friend Blanchot? Must *le Très-Haut* be fertilized with the blood of *le Plus-Haut*? Does a thinking, which, despite all manner of reservations and complexities, celebrates suffering as the unavoidable pathway to authentic expression, and invokes a sacred discourse, a rhetoric of sacrifice and martyrdom, to describe this suffering, betray a deeper complicity with fascism? I will not endeavour to answer this question here, which has bedevilled European thought since long before the Heidegger controversy. I am wary, too, of the atmosphere of condemnation and vilification that often chokes such debates. I will instead, and for the last time, give Blanchot the floor: "What, then, is above Transcendence, what below Transcendence? Well (let us hasten to respond, as haste alone will caution the response) it is that before which all evaluation reveals itself to be inadequate, be it the most high or the most low; that which, therefore, strikes all possibility of evaluating with indifference and, in so doing, challenges all the guardians of value, whether they be celestial, terrestrial, or demonic and whatever their authority derive from reason, unreason, or surreason" (*IC* 395, trans. amended).

Such is the "sacred" speech of Maurice Blanchot.

ENDNOTES

1 Maurice Blanchot, "Letter to Catherine David", trans. Paula Wissing, *Critical Inquiry* 15.2 (1989), 479, trans. amended.

2 Blanchot, "Letter to Catherine David", 480, trans. amended.

3 See Herman Rapaport, *Heidegger and Derrida: Reflections on Time and Language* (Lincoln: University Nebraska Press, 1989), 112.

4 Heidegger, *Erläuterungen zu Hölderlins Dichtung* (Frankfurt/M: Klostermann, 1984), 59.

5 Heidegger, *Erläuterungen*, 63; *WF* 120.

6 Heidegger, *Erläuterungen*, 62.

7 Heidegger, *Erläuterungen*, 104.

8 The line comes from the late fragment "Einst hab' ich die Muse gefragt." Friedrich Hölderlin, *Gedichte*, ed. Jochen Schmidt (Frankfurt/M: Insel, 1984), 215.

9 Friedrich Hölderlin, *Theoretische Schriften*, ed. Johann Kreuzer (Hamburg: Felix Meiner, 1998), 113–4.

10 "Where subject and object are absolutely and not just partially unified, so that no separation at all can be undertaken without violating the essence of that which is to be separated – there, and nowhere else, can one speak of an absolute Being, as is the case with intellectual intuition." Hölderlin, *Theoretische Schriften*, 7–8. See also Dieter Henrich, "Hölderlin on Judgment and Being", in *The Course of Remembrance and other essays on Hölderlin*, ed. Eckart Förster (Stanford: Stanford University Press, 1997).

[11] Schestag argues that the phrase traces "the oxymoronic outline of the law": "*Der höchste Erkenntnisgrund* can mean both the highest, most certain knowledge about the ground of all knowledge and the highest, most unknowable ground that is subject to all knowledge – in which knowledge, since the phrase *highest ground* is impossible for it, is suspended." Thomas Schestag, "The Highest", in *The Solid Letter. Readings of Friedrich Hölderlin*, ed. Aris Fioretos (Stanford: Stanford University Press, 1999), 380.

[12] "Wie der Mensch sich setzt, ein Sohn der Thetis..." Hölderlin, *Theoretische Schriften, 116, 129–30.*

[13] "The last, but also most difficult step of every interpretation consists in disappearing ... before the pure standing-there [*Dastehen*] of the poem." Heidegger, *Erläuterungen*, 8.

[14] See Hölderlin's critique of Schelling, which predates Hegel's by several years: "But the wise men who only differentiate generally, with the Spirit, hasten back into pure Being, into an indifference which is all the greater because they believe themselves to have sufficiently differentiated, and who take the non-opposition to which they return as eternal." *Theoretische Schriften*, 16.

[15] See Heidegger, *Erläuterungen*, 71. Leslie Hill frames the differences between Heidegger's and Blanchot's conception of the law in terms of unicity/duplicity: "It is this univocity of the law which doubtless allowed Heidegger to think of the poetic act as a founding political initiative, capable of revealing to the Volk the truth of its destiny. ... For Blanchot, on the other hand, the question of the law is never simple, always double." Hill, "'Ein Gespräch': Blanchot depuis Heidegger jusqu'à Hölderlin", *Revue des sciences humaines*, 253 (1999), 205–6.

[16] Heidegger, *Erläuterungen*, 76.

[17] See Gerald L. Bruns, *Maurice Blanchot: The Refusal of Philosophy* (Baltimore: Johns Hopkins University Press, 1997), 49.

[18] Blanchot, "Madness *par excellence*", in *BR* 123.

[19] Klossowski's essay on Blanchot was first published in 1949 as a review of *Le Très-Haut*. Pierre Klossowski, *Un si funeste désir* (Paris: Gallimard, 1963), 171; see also Michel Foucault and Maurice Blanchot, *Maurice Blanchot: The Thought from Outside / Michel Foucault as I Imagine Him*, trans. Brian Massumi and Jeffrey Mehlman (New York: Zone Books, 1987), 37. For Heidegger's analysis of *Sorge*, see *Sein und Zeit* (Frankfurt/M: Klostermann, 1976), §39 to §44.

[20] Hill, "'Ein Gespräch'", 202.

[21] See François Brémondy, "*Le Très-Haut* ou l'incognito de Dieu," *Revue des sciences humaines*, 253 (1999), 55.

[22] Hölderlin, *Theoretische Schriften*, 115–6.

[23] Hölderlin, *Theoretische Schriften*, 116–7.

[24] Blanchot writes: "Enigma is the pure gushing of what gushes out / Profundity that shakes everything, the coming of the day" (*WF* 131). The first line might pass for a translation of *Ein Räthsel ist Reinentsprungenes*; the second finds no textual

support whatsoever. Hill charitably concludes that Blanchot wants to tell us we should rewrite Hölderlin, not continually reread him. Hill, "'Ein Gespräch'", 131.

25 Peter Köppel, *Die Agonie des Subjekts: Das Ende der Aufklärung bei Kafka und Blanchot* (Wien: Passagen, 1991), 87. Blanchot spells this logic out elsewhere, in relation to Kafka: "Everyone, says Olga, belongs to the Castle; from which it must be concluded that there is no Castle." Blanchot, *The Infinite Conversation*, 396.

26 Heidegger, *Sein und Zeit*, 168 (§27).

27 Heidegger, *Sein und Zeit*, 335 (§51); Blanchot, *MH*, 254.

28 See Heidegger, *Sein und Zeit*, §34–§35.

29 Foucault, "The Thought from Outside", 37.

30 See Jacques Derrida, "Demeure" (*ID 51*).

31 For a comparison of the thematics of plague in *Le Très-Haut* and Camus's roughly contemporaneous *The Plague*, see Evelyne Londyn, *Maurice Blanchot romancier* (Paris: A.-G. Nizet, 1976), 187–190.

32 See Köppel, *Die Agonie des Subjekts*, 84.

33 Köppel, *Die Agonie des Subjekts*, 117–8.

34 Hölderlin, *Theoretische Schriften*, 115.

35 Martin Heidegger, *Wegmarken* (Frankfurt/M: Klostermann, 1976), 338–9.

36 See Emmanuel Levinas, *Proper Names*, trans. Michael B. Smith (Stanford: Stanford University Press, 1996), 137. Levinas accounts for the difference between Heidegger and Blanchot in the following terms: "To Blanchot, death is not the pathos of the ultimate human possibility, the possibility of impossibility, but the ceaseless repetition of what cannot be grasped, before which the I loses its ipseity. The impossibility of possibility." Although Levinas takes pains to salvage Blanchot from the murky depths of fundamental ontology – Blanchot's critical reflection is "an invitation to leave the Heideggerian world" – he mentions his Hölderlin writings solely in connection with that world: "The affinity with the German philosopher can be felt in all kinds of ways; including Blanchot's choice of the texts of Rilke and Hölderlin to write on." Levinas, 132, 135, 129.

37 Quoted by Philippe Lacoue-Labarthe, "Poetry's Courage", in *The Solid Letter*, ed. Fioretos, 79.

"WHAT TERRIFYING COMPLICITY"
Jean Paul as Collocutor in *Death Sentence*

Dimitris Vardoulakis

> *... friends to the point of this state of profound friendship in*
> *which a forsaken man, forsaken by all his friends, meets in life*
> *the person who will accompany him beyond life, himself*
> *lifeless, capable of free friendship, detached from all bonds.*
>
> Georges Bataille

IT IS NOT PROPER TO BEGIN WRITING ON *DEATH SENTENCE* WITH A PLEA about the difficulty of the text, for this *récit* attains such a simplicity of plot and description that it is anything but difficult. Nor is it proper to begin with the anxiety of addressing a text which has been dealt with by so many critics, despite the fact that *Death Sentence* is perhaps singular in the fascination that it has exercised over the readers of Maurice Blanchot. The reason that any *captatio benevolentiae* is inappropriate has more to do with what J. Hillis Miller has referred to as the "double bind."[1] For, if the "double bind" is an injunction whose very articulation is simultaneously its transgression, it would be inappropriate to augment with it an article whose title – the terrifying complicity ("*quelle complicité pleine d'horreur*") – refers to what seeks to outdo the "double bind." Not by denying the double bind. A denial will always be inadequate, because, as Blanchot told his readers in 1948, it will only provoke the return to what has been denied. Rather, the complicity has to do with a "third" element, always unnamed and unnamable, never to be beheld, like the secret hidden away in the narrator's closet (*armoire*) (*DS* 132/*AM* 10). An element of "nocturnal obscurity [*obscurité nocturne*]" (*SL* 172/*EL* 180), since it responds to an absence which, although in itself can never become present, is nevertheless linked to a kind of presence, the writing hand – of which Blanchot did not see fit to remind his reader in 1971.[2]

The question is: how can one address this absence? If something is completely absent, there can be no reference to it. The quandary is even more pronounced for the critic: for how is writing about something that is not "on the page" possible? The force of the secret in the closet is shown at the beginning of the *récit*, when an unnamed woman "made a move to open it [the closet], but at that moment she was overcome by a strange attack."[3] She fell helpless on the bed, breathing hoarsely, like a death rattle (*à râler*). The secret is dangerous. In a reaction that recalls the unnamed woman's reaction, Nathalie "began to tremble, her teeth chattered, and for a moment she shivered so violently that she lost control of her body." At this point Blanchot distinguishes between law and justice: "I could do nothing to help her; by approaching her, by talking to her, I was disobeying the law; by touching her I could have killed her. To struggle alone, to learn, as she struggled, how through the workings of a profound justice the greatest adverse forces console us and upraise us, at the very moment that they are tearing us apart: that is what she had to do."[4] What is remarkable about the "profound justice" is that it also makes the secret imperative, but without it being related to any content whatsoever. Instead, the only thing that matters is the locus where the adverse forces manifest themselves, in a way such that the subject is torn apart. The critic, then, need *not* posit a *complete* absence. All that is needed is a regulative absence, certainly contentless, moreover threatening and terrifying, but which has nevertheless the capacity to console and upraise. The torn subject along with the regulative absence constitute together a "double unbind," a locus where the law cannot hold but without excluding the law. This place can be called justice – a justice which is registered doubly. First, in the text itself, in the manner in which the characters both follow and are followed by the law. "I had no idea whether I was following her or if she was following me" (*MH* 222), says Henri about Jeanne, a figure that in large measure stands for the law in *The Most High*. Second, the interpretability and criticizability of the work depends on the "double unbind" of justice. The critical task is broader than an extrapolation of that which is expressed by the legal entity who signs and owns the copyright of the work. The writing hand, as it will be shown, belongs also to a friend, an accomplice, or a collocutor. Yet this accosting presence re-configures the legally constituted agent, the autonomous individual. Where justice emerges, then, the subject – as a character in the work *and* as the author of the work – will have already been in a process of dissolution. Justice appears at the point – never distinct, constantly negotiated, always here and to come – of subjective disappearance.

Yet the subject remains. There is no absolute disappearance of the subject, nor of the law. Otherwise there will be no consolation, no upraising. The argument here will be that the subject in "an instant of distraction [*un instant de distraction*]" (*DS* 182 / *AM* 137) is indeed able to experience this "double unbind." But the experience is one where self-identity is no longer operative; identity figures in a relation of difference. The subject now *is* difference. To approach this difference, attention needs to be paid to the relation between the narratorial I (what Blanchot calls the "*voix narratrice*") and Nathalie, the two subjects between which there exists the "terrifying complicity." Since not much is actually known of either, it is expedient to start with the one who at least has a name. Nathalie is a name that has a double register, its etymology and its literary precedents. It comes from the Latin verb *nascor*, to originate, to be born, but also to grow, to rise up. Nathalie is a certain origin and an upraising. At the same time, there are two famous Natalies in romantic literature, the one in Goethe's *Wilhelm Meister's Apprenticeship* and the other in Jean Paul's *Siebenkäs*.[5] Goethe and Jean Paul, along with Valéry, are designated by Blanchot as the only non-classical authors with whom he was familiar as he was taking his first steps in writing (*VC* 490–1/*AC* 92). However, as will be shown shortly, Goethe's Natalie does not sit happily next to the Nathalie in *Death Sentence*. Conversely, the Natalie in Jean Paul's novel tallies with a number of motifs and themes that have a compelling resonance in Blanchot's *récit*.

A tentative approach to the name Nat(h)alie has to start with an exposition of some of these motifs. First, there are remarkable parallels in the first meeting between the narrator and Nathalie in *Death Sentence* and Siebenkäs and Natalie in Jean Paul (*DS* 157–9/*AM* 74–9; *S* 364–6). In both texts, the female character appears at night, at a place that is hardly described, and without any explicit reason. The meeting is contingent, accidental, unintended. Both women are clad in black, and both are likened to a statue. They are both shrouded in mystery, not only because they turn their back to the male character, but also because in *Siebenkäs* Natalie wears a veil that hides her face, while in *Death Sentence* there is the conspicuous absence of a hat on her head "(which was more uncommon [*plus rare*] than it is now)," as it is proffered in a parenthesis. Further, while in both cases the female is unacquainted with the male, there is nevertheless a moment of *déjà vu*, a kind of recognition beyond the normative rules of recognition accompanied by the appearance of a very strong feeling within all parties that vacillates between a threatening strangeness and an irresistible appeal. In both scenes there is a glass surface, the window in the hotel room, and the glass door through which Siebenkäs walks and the mirror though which he contemplates the unknown woman. Sight features heavily, as well, since Blanchot's Nathalie cannot see well at night, while the other Natalie cannot discern Siebenkäs's characteristics so that she has to approach him closely and lift her veil. In addition, a number of other motifs are introduced which, while they do not have a direct correspondence in both meeting scenes, are nevertheless related to other themes in the two works. Natalie's veil has already been mentioned, and there are a number of references to veils in *Death Sentence*. And roses and casts of the dead, which feature throughout *Death Sentence*, are also present in the meeting between Natalie and Siebenkäs. But the most important feature is perhaps Natalie's fiery eyes, a characteristic of Nathalie's as well, underlined after the encounter at the métro, when the narrator enters his hotel room to feel the presence of someone there (*DS* 177 / *AM* 124).

If this register of motifs from the first meetings is incomplete, the whole register of themes common to Natalie and Siebenkäs, on the one hand, and Nathalie and the narrator, on the other, is verily incompletable. It is certainly important to note the autobiographical references in the male characters, since the narrator, like Blanchot, is a journalist, and Siebenkäs is the author of the *Selection from the Devil's Papers*, an early work by Jean Paul.[6] There are several additional similar "details," such as the presence of a doctor character who is somewhat derided (*S* ch. 20), and a key of decisive importance (*S* 531). Along with certain stylistic similarities, such as a proclivity for repetitions and the repeated framings of the narrative, for instance with the use of apostrophe. Not to mention a preoccupation with the narrative's end in *Siebenkäs*, to the extent that the story spills over into subsequent novels and that Jean Paul significantly revised the text for the 1818 edition – a preoccupation fully shared by Blanchot. Further, the Siebenkäs character is arguably linked to contemporary political concerns of Jean Paul's,[7] just as the dates in *Death Sentence* give it a strong – even if ambiguous – sense of temporality and topicality.[8] And, considering also other works that were composed in the same period as *Death Sentence*, it can, for instance, be noted that the first name of the protagonist of *The Most High* is Henri, while Siebenkäs's original name, which he re-assumed after his staged death, is Heinrich.[9] There is also the rhyming of Lenette, Siebenkäs's first wife, and Collete, the narrator's neighbour in the hotel in *Death Sentence*, and the echoing of Jean Paul's own first name by Jeanne's name in *The Most High*.

The slide here into what may be just arbitrary coincidences is not unintentional. The list of common "motifs" can be expanded further-more. What is presented here will only be a foretaste to someone who delights in such comparisons and compilations. Ultimately, all these themes and motifs can advance criticism only slightly, they are but a first empirical step. Jean Paul's Natalie might form part of the inspiration for *Death Sentence*, but the theme-based procedure will always be lacking in approaching a *récit* in which regulative absence holds sway. For a "theme" of necessity is dependent on content, there is always a *certain* reference made by way of the theme. And to stay on the thematic level would be precisely to insist on the content. Whereas it has already been noted that the regulative function of the secret in *Death Sentence* does not allow for such an adherence. It is not as if *Death Sentence* is a kind of *roman à clef*, in which the dates, the self-references to Blanchot's journalistic activities, and the references to Blanchot's reading of Jean Paul provide a "key" to unlock the "meaning" of the text. For the dates, as Leslie Hill has shown,[10] are anything but straightforward; and, given that the *récit* already moves towards an effacement of subjectivity, the autobiographical reference cannot be strictly speaking historical, or even symbolic of a specific historical occurrence. This is not to say that there are no autobiographical elements to the story.[11] Rather, it shows that what has to be resisted is to assume that the empirical aspect is all that there is. There is no reduction to the empirical.[12] And it is here that a crucial difference from Goethe's Natalie is encountered. For the crux of the plot of Goethe's novel is that, unbeknown to Wilhelm Meister, he is cultivated by a secret society, to the extent that every chance occurrence can be attributed to that society's intervention. Natalie is part of this dialectic of concealment and unconcealment, of Wilhelm's journey in an inexplicable world that becomes finally extricated when he is initiated into the sect. The secret, then, pertains to the context of Wilhelm's journey and to his actions. What is excluded is any idea of a regulative and contentless secret. As Walter Benjamin argued in the appendix to his dissertation on German Romanticism, a similar structure is applicable to Goethe's notion of criticism, whereby a work is underwritten by a primordial substance which is forever inaccessible since its content is uncognizable.[13] Goethe's adherence to content in terms of plot and in terms of a presupposition of criticism is never entertained by Blanchot.

Moreover, the inadequacy of staying with the thematic analysis would have had to contend with the plain fact that, despite certain similarities, Blanchot and Jean Paul are separated by significant differences as well. For instance, the latter's novels unfold in an exuberant and serendipitous meandering that does not accord with the simplicity of a condensed narrative like *Death Sentence*. Jean Paul's injunction to "Write everything down"[14] seems foreign to Blanchot's universe, where silence reigns supreme. Further, Blanchot has taken Jean Paul to task about the relation of death to subjectivity. Thus, in "The *Igitur* Experience" Blanchot observes that the dignity of pure dying does not accord "to the ideal of Jean-Paul Richter, whose heroes, 'lofty men,' die in a pure desire to die, 'their eyes gazing steadfastly beyond the clouds' in response to a call of a dream which disembodies and dissolves them."[15] What Blanchot objects to seems clear enough: the purity of dying is not guaranteed by a beyond which sets the rule. There is no glimpse of any kind of heaven. However, a look at Jean Paul's text will show that this objection is not unambiguous. Blanchot is referring to the chapter "The Dream in a Dream," perhaps the most discussed chapter of *Siebenkäs* along with the preceding chapter, "The Speech of the Dead Christ."[16] The ambiguity of Blanchot's citation is twofold. First, it is doubtful whether the text here represents *prima facie* Jean Paul's ideas. Not only did Jean Paul relocate these two little chapters in the second edition of the novel – whereas in the 1796 edition they are the opening chapters in *Siebenkäs*, in the 1818 edition they appear in the middle of the novel, at the end of book two.[17] As if this repositioning is not enough to undermine any straightforward identification of these ideas with Jean Paul's own views, the very ideas expressed here are explicitly ridiculed later on in the novel (*S* 513–4). Second, it should be noted that the ambiguity in Blanchot's use of quotation marks is even more pervasive. For, in fact, despite Blanchot's use of quotation marks, the text is not a direct citation. Thus, the "'lofty men'" who are "heroes," according to Blanchot, are actually, according to Jean Paul, "two sublime friends" who have sacrificed everything, including their lives, but not their country.[18] Maybe this sacrifice makes them heroes – although this is a moot point, not least because of the historical circumstance bracketed by the dates of the two editions of the novel, the years from 1796 to 1818 – but nevertheless the word "heroes" is not used by Jean Paul. The case of the second phrase placed in quotation marks by Blanchot, "'their eyes gazing steadfastly beyond the clouds,'" is even more unclear. According to *Siebenkäs*, the two friends are sent clouds by the earth to obscure their views (*S* 279). Blanchot seems to be summarizing the next paragraph, where a series of questions allude to a vision beyond the clouds. But the rhetorical questions in *Siebenkäs* are addressed to Mary, who has been dreaming these "two friends" and the clouds that occlude them. As one of the questions puts it, are you happy, Mary, "because the storm clouds are turning into rainbows?" The answer is, adhering to the logic of the rhetorical question, "No" (*S* 280). This may be partly the reason, Jean Paul writes, but the real cause of happiness is that Mary thinks of her child, Christ. And this thought is what precipitates the end of the dream. The vision has dissipated, and Mary embraces her real child. The "resolution" is not provided by something beyond, but by the return to the corporeal. Remarkably, then, Blanchot extracts from the passage he misquotes a meaning that is almost antithetical to what Jean Paul seems to suggest.

What is important here has nothing to do with the fact that Blanchot may have made a simple mistake – this would have been the only assertion that a reduction to the empirical could have legitimately made. Instead, what is important is that Blanchot seems here to be citing from memory – he is mis-"quoting." Jean Paul has become part of Blanchot's vocabulary. To the extent that Blanchot is referring to Jean Paul as the real person who authored a specific corpus, then here Blanchot is speaking in Jean Paul's language. And to the extent that this dialogue unfolds in such a particularized language, which apparently Blanchot does not master, the use of that language is irresponsible. However, this irresponsibility should not be seen as a simple mistake, a lack of mastery. Irresponsibility has much more to offer, especially in the way that the subject of the utterance relates to the other subject whose language he has worked with in a way that does not exclude the other. There is a collusion or complicity between Blanchot and Jean Paul; they become not merely interlocutors but collocutors, each of whose personal identity is inextricably linked, at the moment of the utterance, to the identity of the other. Otherness is no longer a differentiation of attributes, but the very identity as such. There is a forgetting operating here, which results, among other things, in the impossibility of attributing statements directly to one or the other party of this partnership of complicity.

Such a state of affairs alludes to *Death Sentence* and the episode in the métro, where the narrator's use of Nathalie's language, a language he is not fluent in, is characterized precisely as irresponsible. What is asserted here is not merely a motif, a thematic congruity. Rather, the point is broader and touches upon Blanchot's conception of criticism and literature. What is enacted here is a re-articulation of the literary canon. A canonical author for Blanchot is not whoever has been designated by the academy, the Alexandrian scholar, or even the general history of reception. The canonical author is rather one like Jean Paul, whose name is never mentioned in *Death Sentence* but which nevertheless can be brought into play therein, as the collocational Other who collocutes (in) the text.[19] In addition, precisely because this is not a procedure to fix the identity of the author "Blanchot," this does not allude to any subjectivist extrapolation of the canon. Jean Paul's elided name is not just a manifestation of the fancy of Blanchot, the reader of Jean Paul in the 1930s. If there is a conversation going on here between Blanchot and Jean Paul, it is a conversation without any goal, a silent conversation of gestures, whose effect is to strip the work of both authors from any obvious referential meaning other than the gesture itself. As Eleanor Kaufman writes, "personhood and subjectivity are absent, yet a material energy of thought is excessively present." "Such a coexistence of the absence of the person and the presence of thought as materiality" is what regulates, she adds, the *encomia* written by French post-war thinkers about their peers.[20] However, the canonicity that this form of interplay establishes need not be confined to a specific genre of writing. Rather, it can be broadened so that the interplay becomes that which defines both canon and genre through a notion of absent subjectivity. This broadening is suggested by Blanchot himself in *The Unavowable Community*. Blanchot cites an anecdote from Bataille, in which Bataille's "interlocutor is not named, but he is shown in such a way that his friends recognize him, without naming him." Blanchot first observes that, through the unnamed interlocutor, Bataille thus "represents friendship as much as a friend." And then Blanchot goes on to suggest that this is a form of "not-doing" that is "one of the aspects of unworking, and friendship, with the reading in darkness" (*UC* 23). Collocution is taken here to mean precisely this non-naming of the interlocutor that leads to an interplay of singularity and universality – an interplay that asserts both the negation of the name as subject and at the same time emphatically affirms the presence of the non-named.

Precisely such an interplay emerges in Blanchot's relation to Jean Paul. As it figures in *Death Sentence*, *Siebenkäs* is specifically not the key that will unlock the secrets of the *récit*, nor reveal the contents of the closet, nor what dispels the stormy clouds that would have allowed the two friends, Blanchot and Jean Paul, to regard some metaphysical heaven – such a secret would still have asserted presence and the old conception of canonicity. *Siebenkäs* is a key only insofar as it does not unlock anything, a regulative secret that leads reference and representation to failure. It is an absent presence, not present in the form of a "determinate negation" but present only as a collocution. Therefore, the silent presence of Jean Paul in *Death Sentence* is an example of Blanchot at his most rigorous, adhering closely to the law of his own narrative – the "double unbind" that articulates a secret that is no secret at all, since it is absent, without even its very absence being named. Jean Paul, then, is like "the background figure" that Foucault places next to Blanchot, "a companion who always remains hidden but always makes it patently obvious that he is there; a double that keeps his distance, an accosting resemblance."²¹ It is especially pertinent to talk about such a double of Blanchot when the reference is to *Siebenkäs*, the novel in which the word "Doppelgänger" is used for the first time, in which appellation ceases to designate one character, and where identity is given instead by "this wandering name [*wandernden Namens*]" (*S* 385) and by the anonymity that pertains to the differential relation of otherness.²²

The impact of the reformulation of the canonical in literature finds an additional register, one that is already announced in the Greek word *kanon*, meaning measure, the rule whereby something is measured, the law that generically legitimates literature. However, according to Blanchot, this law is radically different between a novel and a narrative or *récit* such as *Death Sentence*. Genesis and temporality feature in Blanchot's distinction. While the novel is born out of a chronologically arranged sequence of episodes so that what precedes is the cause of what follows, the *récit* eschews such teleology. Thus, the récit is "not the relating of an event but this event itself, the approach of this event, the place where it is called on to unfold, an event still to come."²³ What holds the *récit* together is not the documentary accuracy of a witness–like account. Instead, the "secret law of narrative" is precisely this "delicate relationship" introduced by the subversion of linear chronology whereby the product, the producing, and the producer of the narrative are co-implicated and are impossible to steadfastly distinguish. This interruption of time and in time introduces a temporality that escapes the hold of presence as a thing to be beheld in the now, and instead installs a presence always "to come," never stabilized, incessantly differential. Hence, it is imprecise to call Blanchot's *récits* a genre, since the legislating authority is solely ascribed to a futural relation that is never completely fulfilled.²⁴ Such a relationship is what operates in *Siebenkäs* as well, designated as the "harmonious key [or, the fork, *Stimmpfeife*]" of the narrative (*S* 450). Reminding the reader that his novel is part imaginary and part real, Jean Paul explicates the interplay between the two as the authorial inventions vis-à-vis the temporality of the events due to the lack of documents and witnesses. This interplay as it unfolds in *Siebenkäs* will never find a resolution, as is the case with the different accounts by the four Gospels. Nevertheless, Jean Paul's metaphor continues, this discord is given by the regulative presence of a "harmonious key" that would have resolved the discord of the Gospels. Yet this "key" is only a futural presence, a law of Jean Paul's novel that will never be encountered in the novel itself, only assigned to a harmonized relation that eschews teleological narration. That his key, in turn, will never be able to designate a genre can be shown by a work such as *Clavis Fichtiana* ("the key to Fichte"), which addresses the subjectivity of the Doppelgänger character in *Siebenkäs* while treading the line between literature and philosophy.[25] What takes place, then, between Blanchot and Jean Paul under the rubric of the *canon* is at least twofold: on the one hand, they both insist on a law about narrative relation that bypasses presence in the present by assigning presence to the future – an absent presence; at the same time, this absent presence is precisely what the companionship of Jean Paul in *Death Sentence* also enacts – Jean Paul as Blanchot's double.

This twofold aspect of the canon could be expressed by saying that the experience of writing is linked to the experience of reading. The duplicity that underlies Blanchot's reformulation of canonical literature is what pertains between the reader/author and the other author/companion. Linked to this is the dual relation to law, a duality that seeks to capture the just relation of a futural presence in a present absence. This law, the law of narrative given by the "other night," is also an intricate balancing act towards the image. This is a relation where, while the image is necessary, it is still found wanting compared to the aural experience of reading. It is the relation extrapolated by the Orphic logic of failure. This is not to say that Blanchot in "Orpheus's Gaze" constructs a dialectic. The opposite is the case, since the emphasis on failure, which affirms that "as if to renounce failure were much graver than to renounce success,"[26] is a non-dialectic, a movement of suspension. The suspension takes place between the demand of writing, on the one hand, which leads Orpheus to the underworld to rescue Eurydice with his art on condition that he does not turn back to look at her. Yet this injunction the work is always already going to disobey, the work's exigency is the failure to obey the law. Simultaneously, it is in this night of the deep that the origin of the work is located, an origin as uncertain as it is certain that the work will fail. On the other hand, this first "sacred night" that "follows" Orpheus and "binds" his work is not the only night. The other night is given by Orpheus's unbinding gaze, the unintentional turn of the head back towards Eurydice. "It is in this decision that the origin is approached by the force of the gaze that unbinds night's essence, lifts concern, interrupts the incessant by discovering."[27] Thus, Eurydice is the origin of this journey, she is another Nathalie. However, this is not a foundational origin but one that liberates only by a "glad accident," or what Blanchot also calls a "leap" – just as the meeting between the narrator and Nathalie in *Death Sentence* is completely unintentional, their relation not grounded in any teleology. But the leap is not a law, the movement is non-dialectical, and thus it is able to hold onto the work and onto work's lawlessness at the same time, as in a "magic dependence [*dépendance magique*]" (*SL* 173/*EL* 181). This is a logic of disjunction, where the activity of work and writing is always asymmetrical to the gestural language of the deep night, where unworking unfolds at the moment that reference and meaning break down. The same logic is also described in Jean Paul's *Preschool to Aesthetics*. Thus, in §13 a pure self is said to be creative, productive.[28] But also such a self is always bound to encounter "something dark" that is not created but an origin. This point or "instinct" is "the sense of the future." Jean Paul points out that the deficiency in the negation of the presence of the work is not a dialectical one, because "only a true deficiency makes possible the impulse towards it [that dark point]." This is an earthly or worldly something. Yet at the same time it is something infinite which cannot be named. "The common people say simply, 'The *shape*, the *thing* makes itself heard' [*'Die* Gestalt, *das* Ding *lässet sich hören'*]. Indeed, to express the infinite, they often simply say: 'It [*es*].'" This neuter cannot be found simply in the day on earth, nor in a "deep heaven [or sky, *in tiefen Himmeln*]" – it is not something visible, nor invisible as such, it is something aural and nocturnal. This poetical instinct takes place in the suspension between the embodied spiritual world, and the deified physical world. If the former alludes to the dialect of the "double bind" and the latter to mythopoetic origin, the point of their mutual suspension – not sublation – is precisely the liberation offered by the instinct. What Jean Paul calls instinct here is precisely the disjunction and asymmetry between the dialectic of clarity and the obscurity of origin.

What holds the disjunct elements together is desire. A desire for writing as a desire for the prohibited image, the image that can never be seen in the deepest night, and yet is always seen despite the night, despite the brevity of the gaze. This is the logic of Jean Paul's *Siebenkäs*, a novel about writing, where a series of injunctions are placed so that writing can take place. These are laws against sight, against seeing the most treasured other. Siebenkäs, the aspiring author, is not allowed to see the object of his desire, Natalie. Nor is he allowed to see his *sosie*, and best friend, his Doppelgänger Leibgeber – the word Doppelgänger is used for the first time when this injunction is initially made (*S* 66–7). This visual prohibition is often described as a journey or a path, one that leads to the pursuit of the other.[29] The second and final time that Siebenkäs and Leibgeber part company, Siebenkäs is compelled to follow his friend surreptitiously (*S* 541). While Siebenkäs and Natalie follow each other without even knowing it, "not like a shadow, because a shadow disappears sometimes,"[30] but ineluctably, until they meet by chance, at the very end of the novel, in front of Siebenkäs's own empty tomb, his cenotaph whose door opens only by the small key he carries.[31] If the Orphic logic is enacted in *Siebenkäs*, the mannerist sprawl of Jean Paul's novel is nevertheless different from the cold precision with which the Orphic logic is carried out in *Death Sentence*.[32] But what *Siebenkäs* and *Death Sentence* share as an essential aspect of this logic is that desire which prompts a certain type of experience that cannot be extricated from the desire of writing – the author's desire to write as well as the desire embodied in that writing itself.

This experience faces the difficulty of beginning. Action is from the start caught in a circular movement that seeks to establish a law that frames the narrative while at the same time the narrative itself is framed to transgress this law. The condition of the possibility of action is linked in *Death Sentence* with the possibility of singular experience. The narrator has to go to the theatre "for a reason connected to work [*pour une raison de travail*]", and there he unexpectedly catches sight of Nathalie in the company of a young man. This perception is "as if it were behind a window [*comme derrière une vitre*]" (*DS* 172/*AM* 112), framed by a context that circumscribes the parameters of action. Yet the other is not present completely, but present infinitely close and yet infinitely far at the same time. "She remained in my presence with the freedom of a thought . . . and what tacit understanding was therefore established between her and my thought, what terrifying complicity."[33] Action then includes sight, but the sight is as if it comes from "behind the eyes [*une reconnaissance de derrière les yeux*]"; not the recognition of a real person but "a recognition of thought [*une reconnaissance de la pensée*]" (*DS* 172/*AM* 113). The framing of the window experience has put the female object of desire in an extremely precarious position. For the law that allows for the recognition is given by thought, a movement of thought, not an action in the world, and thus in danger of losing her (the female, the thought) in this world. Although there is a complicity of desire, this complicity is terrifying as it installs the danger of the annihilation of the desired other. It is at this point that action is imperative. The next episode unfolds in a very specific time and locale: the métro "at the moment Paris was bombed" (*DS* 173/*AM* 113). However, it remains unclear how much time had elapsed between this moment and the previous moment of the window experience in the theatre. Was it the next day? Had the narrator met Nathalie before the descent into the shelter of the métro? Or, was this their first meeting since the narrator's encounter with her as his thought at the theatre? These questions are in a sense redundant. What matters is that the entry point into the logic given by the window experience is pursued here with the utmost rigour: the threat of the non-action of thought gives way here to an imperative to act. And to act in a singular manner. The narrator proposes marriage to Nathalie, using her own language that he hardly knows. And this is an act of complete irresponsibility, not only because he is not fond of wedlock, but also because the meaning of the language he has used is elusive. It is an almost meaningless language, but for the same reason all the more meaningful, it has a meaning that can never be translated into any other context. This is the moment of pure action, if such a kind of action exists at all, where words and acts are almost fused. The narrator acknowledges this fusion when he concedes that "inwardly I committed myself to honouring these strange words; the more extreme they were, I mean alien to what might have been expected of me, the more true they seemed to me because they were novel, because they have no precedent."[34] The paradox of this extremity of meaning, of the utterance without "precedent" and without "responsibility" is that, despite the singularity that ensues, the singularity is not one of a subject alone in the world. Rather, the singularity is established between the actor and the other, whose alien language has been used. The only thing that matters in this singular experience is the relation of otherness that persists, even as the narrator reverts back to his familiar French.[35] But even now the French words are strange, exercising a power of madness because the actor "was driven by something wild [*de furieux*], a truth so violent [*une vérité si violente*]" that is unequal to any language (*DS* 175/*AM* 180). There is surely a failure here, at least of signification. But this failure erases the identity of each party, since the lack of communication turns them into anonymous entities, subjects that cannot utter meaningful names. Nevertheless, this failure is what made it possible to begin, since it was premised on their "complicity" that compelled action.

The singularity of the pure experience of otherness fails, and it is a necessary failure that can achieve much more than any success. Simultaneously, this failure has to be complete, to the extent that success cannot figure in it in any way that re-posits the subject. Otherness has to be maintained; success can only figure as the anonymity of the initial complicity in the relation to the other – although this is not a success by intention, since nothing has been accomplished that was not established at that originary moment. However, despite the meaninglessness of the language in the singular experience of otherness, does not the danger still persist that action carries with it a detritus of intentionality? Is not every utterance, even in its nonsensicality, still a "hermeneutical" event that takes place between agents? Blanchot is happy to concede this point. Once action has started, its cessation is problematic.

The narrator is in the full grip of action after the marriage proposal at the métro. He looks for Nathalie without success with a madness that arose "from an impatience [*impatience*] which grew with each passing minute" (*DS* 175–6/*AM* 120). Accosting this impatience is a series of prohibitions about where Nathalie is allowed to be (she has to be in her loft when her daughter is in town, she is not to go to one of the narrator's hotel rooms). Yet at the same time the prohibitions are transgressed. Everyone acts – and acts madly. Not only has Nathalie gone to the prohibited hotel room; she has entered the room only because she has stolen the key from the narrator's wallet. Yet this "imprudence of desire which forgets the law [*l'imprudence du désir qui oublie la loi*]" (*SL* 173/*EL* 182) leads to the closest possible encounter between the narrator and Nathalie. And the narrator is fully complicit: although he knows that "by touching her, I could have killed her" (*DS* 167/*AM* 99), and in spite of the fear that she would "break [*briserait*] in my hands" *(DS* 178/*AM* 126), he still touches her, and she touches him back. Their encounter may be a sexual scene remarkable in its non-sensual description. What compensates and makes this one of the most powerful sexual scenes in literature is that every act, every movement, from the silent look to the non-trembling hand, is an act of transgression. As the encounter is prolonged beyond any expectation, it even becomes possible to address the other – and to address her with a command: "Come." A command that is obeyed, even for a moment, since "as I came near her she moved very quickly and drew away (or pushed me back)."[36] Of course, this has already accomplished much more – but also infinitely less – than the non-perception of the gaze of Orpheus. Yet the transgressive desire has still not been satisfied. It persists unabated when Nathalie wakes up cheerful the next morning, and for a whole "week after that day" (*DS* 181/*AM* 135). As the narrator puts it, he endeavours to "remain a little longer in the realm of things,"[37] even by getting involved in the negotiations of a duel. (Is not this reference to a duel proportionally even more anachronistic than Nathalie's not wearing a hat at their first meeting? Or, is it merely an allusion to the duel as a trade-mark scene of the Doppelgänger and by implication a thematic reference to

Jean Paul?) Yet as the Orphic logic dictates, "impatience links desire to insouciance."[38] Action is liberated – it is no longer transgressive – so long as it is linked to an instant where care and intention are absent. The narrator is aware of this, as well as of the consequent loss of the "realm of things." "And the most terrible thing is that in those minutes I was aware of the insane price I was going to pay for an instant of distraction."[39] It was an instant of absent-mindedness that brought about the breaking of the law, the madness of action, and the enactment of desire. Lamenting for this instant of distraction – the complicity of the window experience? or, the moment that Nathalie stole his key? – is really a last attempt to intend a prolonged stay in the "realm of things." However, any intention has already been forestalled, the "plan [*projet*]" will have already been carried out: Nathalie has already had a cast made of her hands and face. She is already dead. And yet, upon realizing this, the narrator admits that "I was no longer in the least interested; all that belonged to another world."[40] What has been accomplished by the "plan" is no longer in the realm of things; it concerns a space of complete indifference.

The carelessness and carefree loss of interest, the distracted subject in the midst of dramatic revelation, the experiencing of a joyful abandon in the face of death, this forgetting of the "realm of things," even the forgetting of the instant of distraction itself that brought about thingliness, the forgetting of forgetfulness – this state in which the narrator finds himself is no longer transgressive. It is the very suspension of transgression in the name of justice. The work has taken place, writing has happened. But the only thing that is thereby affirmed is the augmenting impetus that brought about the work. Unhappiness is no less than happiness at this detour, as the narrator affirms in the final statement of the second part of the *récit* – the final part of the 1971 edition. Like words and like actions, the passions suffered through things have already been done and undone. There is no sad fate operating here, because the "thought" established at the moment of the "terrifying complicity" between the narrator and Nathalie "if it [she] has conquered me, has only conquered through me, and in the end has always been equal to me."[41] It is the origin, then, it is Nathalie, that has given and has been given. This gift and sacrifice is the liberation of the law.

The sacrificial gift should not be seen as something dutiful. There is no categorical imperative established here ("act as if you are distracted all the time"). Not only would this be impossible, since action has long been abandoned; more importantly, absence has to be maintained. If there is a non-commanding and non-imperative justice that authorizes no laws, it is justice as this absence. This justice can become "visible" as the thought, as the Nathalie. But it also has to remain invisible – this is the justice of the secret, justice as the secret. If that was not the case, the whole narrative would have been in the grips of the double bind – in the grips of a command impossible to break and yet impossible to obey. The "unbinding" by the secret is not an ethical or moral command. It is here that the function of writing becomes important: as a prelude to the maddening transgression that takes place between the narrator and Nathalie, an apostrophe installs a prohibition to the narration itself: "I will say very little about what happened then."[42] This prohibition *qua* law can never be followed and will always be broken. But this prohibition *qua* absence can be both followed and broken at the same time – for nothing is there. This absence, this nothingness, is like Nathalie whom the narrator's hands cannot touch and yet touch. Blanchot returns to the hands in the third section of the novel that he saw fit to delete in the 1971 edition of *Death Sentence*. In the form of a command, or even a curse, whoever reads "these pages" is warned not to look for unhappiness in it: "And what is more, let him try to imagine the hand that is writing them: if he saw it, then perhaps reading would have become a serious task for him."[43] Whose are these hands? Are they really Blanchot's? How could Blanchot be so careless as to reinstate the actative of "writing" when all action had given way to absence? Perhaps this third section is not a "mistake" at all, perhaps it is not a *coda* revealing the secret of *Death Sentence*. In which case the hands are not Blanchot's, but belong perhaps to Blanchot's companion, Jean Paul. But if that is really the case, then why did Blanchot delete this third section from the subsequent edition? Maybe he forgot that the hands belonged to Jean Paul. In which case, while Blanchot was re-reading *Death Sentence* for the revised edition, he would have thought that the narrative would have been indeed self-cancelling. And in a moment of terror and madness Blanchot decided to act: to delete. Or, maybe Blanchot did not forget the absent hands, maybe he chose to forget the very forgetfulness of Jean Paul's name in *Death Sentence*. In which case the deletion of the third part is not an action in any proper sense. Rather, it is the very enactment of the forgetting of forgetfulness, and hence the affirmation of the absent presence, the obscurity, the absence stronger than presence of Jean Paul – the affirmation of a liberating complicity.[44]

ENDNOTES

I am indebted to Leslie Hill, who gave me the idea for this article. I am also grateful for suggestions by Andrew Benjamin, and for comments on an earlier draft by Chris Danta, Andrew Johnson and Walter Veit. A note on Jean Paul's name: his real name was Johann Christian Richter. Later he assumed the pseudonym Jean Paul. However, his real surname is often added to his pseudonym: Jean Paul Richter. In France, a hyphen is often added to his pseudonym: Jean-Paul. Throughout this chapter I have opted for "Jean Paul," as is customary in German scholarship, unless I cite an author who uses one of the variant spellings.

[1] J. Hillis Miller, "Death Mask: Blanchot's *L'Arrêt de mort*" in *Versions of Pygmalion* (Cambridge, Mass.: Harvard University Press, 1990), 179–210. On the "double bind" in *L'Arrêt de mort* see also Jacques Derrida's compelling article "Living On: Border Lines", trans. James Hulbert, in *Deconstruction and Criticism* (New York: Seabury Press, 1979), 75–176.

[2] Since the 1971 edition of *L'Arrêt de mort* the final two paragraphs were deleted. These two paragraphs constituted in the 1948 edition a separate section that has customarily been viewed as a metatext or as *coda* to the text. References here are to the original 1948 printing of the story.

[3] *DS* 132/*AM* 11, "cette armoire, elle l'a vue, elle a fait un geste pour l'ouvrir. Mais à cet instant, elle fut prise d'une crise étrange."

[4] *DS* 167/*AM* 99, "Elle se mit à trembler, à claquer des dents et, pendant un moment, frissonna à perdre le commandement de son corps. . . . Je ne pouvais l'aider en rien; en m'approchant, en lui parlant, j'agissais contre la loi; en la touchant, je pouvais la tuer. Lutter seule, apprendre, dans cette lutte, à connaître par quelle profonde justice les plus grandes forces adverses, au moment où elles nous déchirent, nous consolent et nous relèvent, c'est là ce qu'il lui fallait faire."

[5] Johann Goethe, *Wilhelm Meister's Apprenticeship*, trans. Eric A. Blackall and Victor Lange, in *Goethe's Collected Works*, vol. 9 (New York: Suhrkamp, 1983). Jean Paul, *Blumen-, Frucht- und Dornenstücke, oder Ehestand, Tod und Hochzeit des Armenadvokaten F. St. Siebenkäs* [1796], in *Sämtliche Werke*, div. 1, vol. 2, ed. Norbert Miller (Darmstadt: Wissenschaftliche Buchgesellschaft, 2000), hereafter abbreviated as *S* and cited parenthetically in the text; all references to Jean Paul are to the Miller edition and all the translations are mine unless otherwise stated. Of interest here is Michael Holland, "Nathalie ou 'le supplément du roman'", in *L'Œuvre du féminin dans l'écriture de Maurice Blanchot*, ed. Eric Hoppenot (Grignan: éditions Complicités, 2004), 133–56. Holland briefly discusses the figure of Nathalie as it appears in Jean Paul, concentrating on Goethe's novel and specifically in comparison to the way it was appropriated by the Romantic project of Schlegel in his review of the novel in *Athenaeum*.

[6] Jean Paul, *Auswahl aus des Teufels Papieren* [1789], in *Sämtliche Werke*, div. 2, vol. 2.

7 For a discussion of the political aspect of Jean Paul's novel *Titan*, see Heinz Schlaffer, "Epic and Novel: Action and Consciousness. Jean Paul's *Titan*", in *The Bourgeois as Hero*, trans. James Lynn (Cambridge: Polity, 1989), 8–38. In *Titan* Jean Paul continues the story of the central male characters in *Siebenkäs*.

8 See Leslie Hill, *Blanchot: Extreme Contemporary* (London: Routledge, 1997), 142–57.

9 Heinrich was also the name of Jean Paul's brother, whose suicide had a profound influence on Jean Paul.

10 Hill, *Blanchot*, 145–50.

11 See Christophe Bident, *Maurice Blanchot: partenaire invisible* (Seyssel: Champ Vallon, 1998), 103–9 and 291–5.

12 This reduction to the empirical, whereby "themes" are related to historical events as if the meaning of both is given solely through their reciprocity, is what makes suspect the efforts to read in *L'Arrêt de mort* either a supposedly rejected fascist ideology (Jeffrey Mehlman, *Genealogies of the Text: Literature, Psychoanalysis, and Politics in Modern France* [Cambridge: Cambridge University Press, 1995], ch. 6), or even "the narrator's passivity as a historical agent" (Steven Ungar, *Scandal and Aftereffect: Blanchot and France since 1930* [Minneapolis: University of Minnesota Press, 1995], 72).

13 Walter Benjamin, "The Concept of Criticism in German Romanticism", in *Selected Writings*, ed. Marcus Bullock and Michael W. Jennings (Cambridge, Mass.: Belknap, 1997), 1: 178–85.

14 This is Fragment 1 in the collection of Jean Paul's previously unpublished material *Ideen-Gewimmel: Texte und Aufzeichnungen aus dem unveröffentlichten Nachlaß*, ed. Thomas Wirtz and Kurt Wölfel (Frankfurt am Main: Eichborn, 1996), 25.

15 *SL* 111/ *EL* 111, "non pas toutefois selon l'idéal de Jean-Paul Richter dont les héros, 'les hommes hauts,' meurent dans un pur désir de mourir, 'les yeux fixés au delà des nuages,' par l'appel d'un rêve qui les désincarne et les désorganise."

There are various other references to Jean Paul in Blanchot's work. However, the most important is maybe the short text "De Jean-Paul à Giraudoux", *Journal des débats* (3 February 1944), 2–3, reprinted in *Maurice Blanchot: récits critiques*, ed. Christophe Bident and Pierre Vilar (Tours: Farrago, 2003), 29–32. Blanchot starts by pointing out that Jean Paul has a "sosie exalté" in Giraudoux. For Blanchot, Jean Paul represents a "principle" within Romanticism whose "main characteristic is the recognition of an experience proper to literature." Blanchot mentions Jean Paul's family of humble origins, as well as the vision of his own death, and advances a dual typology of Jean Paul's works. There follows a discussion of metaphor in Jean Paul, which assigns a "véritable frénésie" to his prose. Also, Blanchot mentions in the article contemporary translations of Jean Paul's works into French and pays tribute to Stefan George's assessment of Jean Paul. For a reading of this article by Blanchot, which concentrates, however, on the figure of Giraudoux, see Christophe Bident, ". . . au point de vacillement (d'un écart de Blanchot à Giraudoux)", in *Maurice Blanchot: récits critiques*, 505–22.

[16] Cf. Blanchot, "De Jean-Paul à Giraudoux", 29.

[17] See the editor's note in *S* 1153. "The Speech of the Dead Christ" has an extremely complex development in Jean Paul works, as is often the case with ideas or themes that preoccupied Jean Paul. The first draft of this piece bears the title "The dead Shakespeare's Lament to dead listeners about the non-existence of God," in Jean Paul, *Sämtliche Werke*, 2.2: 589–92; according to the editor's note, it was first written in 1791 (*Sämtliche Werke*, 2.4: 419–20). It will not be expedient to digress here into an examination of the development of this speech, not least because its rendering in *Siebenkäs* is the most famous one and the one referred to by Blanchot. J. W. Smeed traces the different versions in *Jean Paul's Dreams* (London: Oxford University Press, 1966), *passim*, but see in particular 18–31.

[18] *S* 279. Blanchot uses the phrase "'les hommes hauts'" (in quotation marks) also in "De Jean-Paul à Giraudoux" (30), where the phrase "lofty men" indicates those characters of Jean Paul who are prodigious but who nevertheless have to suffer life's difficulties. This seems to be a fair description of Siebenkäs and Leibgeber in *Siebenkäs*, although it represents for Blanchot one of the two mains types of characters to be found in Jean Paul's work. The two uses of "'les hommes hauts'" are not incompatible, but it is also not inconceivable that Blanchot has mixed up his references when he quotes from memory in the later article.

[19] This is not to say that the only name of an author, the name "Kafka," that appears in *L'Arrêt de mort* does not make an impact that is beyond a mere reference to the author of the *Castle* and which touches on Blanchot's very understanding of literature, as Leslie Hill has shown in *Bataille, Klossowski, Blanchot: Writing at the Limit* (Oxford: Oxford University Press, 2001), 206–26.

[20] Eleanor Kaufman, *The Delirium of Praise: Bataille, Blanchot, Deleuze, Foucault, Klossowski* (Baltimore: Johns Hopkins University Press, 2001), 54.

[21] Michel Foucault "Maurice Blanchot: The Thought from Outside", trans. Brian Massumi, in *Foucault/Blanchot* (New York: Zone Books, 1987), 47.

[22] The first time that Jean Paul writes the word in *Siebenkäs* (*S* 66–7), it is spelled with a 't' between the two compounds: *Doppeltgänger*. Later on p. 532, the 't' is elided and the word is spelled in its customary way: Doppelgänger. However, the passage on p. 532 is an addition of the second edition of *Siebenkäs* in 1818, by which time, of course, the word "Doppelgänger," spelt without the *t* between the two compounds, had been in wide use.

[23] *BC* 6/*LV* 13, "Le récit n'est pas la relation de l'événement, mais cet événement même, l'approche de cet événement, le lieu où celui-ci est appelé à se produire, événement encore à venir."

[24] Cf. Derrida's discussion of *La Folie du jour* in "The Law of Genre", trans. Avital Ronell, in *Acts of Literature*, ed. Derek Attridge (New York: Routledge, 1992), 223–52.

[25] For a discussion of the *Clavis Fichtiana* as it relates to the genesis of the word Doppelgänger, as well as to the relation between subjectivity, literature and

philosophy, see my "The Critique of Loneliness: Towards the Political Motives of the Doppelgänger", *Angelaki*, 9.2 (2004), 81–101.

²⁶ *SL* 173–4/*EL* 182, "comme si renoncer à échouer était beaucoup plus grave que renoncer à réussir." If there is here an affirmation of failure, there is also in Blanchot a suspicion about success. For instance, see in *Le Très-Haut* the story of the general who is worried only when his orders seem to be carried out: "So our success just demonstrates the fact that we're still in our hole, still totally impotent" (*MH* 218).

²⁷ *SL* 175/*EL* 184, "C'est dans cette décision que l'origine est approchée par la force du regard qui délie l'essence de la nuit, lève le souci, interrompt l'incessant en le découvrant."

²⁸ Jean Paul, *Horn of Oberon: Jean Paul's School of Aesthetics*, trans. Margaret R. Hale (Detroit: Wayne State University Press, 1973), 38–40; *Vorschule der Ästhetik*, in *Sämtliche Werke*, div. 1, vol 5, 60–2. All subsequent reference to the *Vorschule* are to §13.

²⁹ The word "Doppelgänger" literally means a double walker, like a man and his shadow.

³⁰ *DS* 181/*AM* 134, "Je ne la suivais pas comme une ombre, car l'ombre parfois disparaît."

³¹ Leibgeber gave Siebenkäs this key in *S* 531. For the meeting between Siebenkäs and Natalie, see *S* 572 ff.

³² This is not meant as a criticism of Jean Paul. Instead, as will be obvious to any reader of Jean Paul and Blanchot, their respective projects are evidently not the same.

³³ *DS* 172/*AM* 112, "Elle se tenait en ma présence avec la liberté d'une pensée . . . et quelle connivence s'établissait donc entre elles, quelle complicité pleine d'horreur."

³⁴ *DS* 174/*AM* 117, "je m'obligeais intérieurement à faire honneur à ces mots étranges; plus ils étaient excessifs, je veux dire étrangers à ce que l'on pouvait attendre de moi, plus ils me paraissaient vrais à cause de cette nouveauté sans exemple."

³⁵ On singularity in Blanchot, see Andrew Benjamin, "Figuring Self-Identity: Blanchot's Bataille", in *Other than Identity: The Subject, Politics and Art*, ed. Juliet Steyn (Manchester: Manchester University Press, 1997), 9–31. Although Benjamin looks at the way Bataille figures in *L'Entretien infini*, his analysis is still pertinent since is deals with the more general problematic of subjectivity and difference.

³⁶ *DS* 179/*AM* 129, "à mon approche, elle eut le mouvement le plus rapide et s'écarta (ou me repoussa)."

³⁷ *DS* 182/*AM* 136, "toutes ces circonstances et les interprétations que j'en donne ne sont pour moi qu'un moyen de rester un peu plus longtemps dans le domaine des choses qu'on peut raconter et vivre."

³⁸ *SL* 175/*EL* 184, "Le désir est lié à *l'insouciance* par *l'impatience*".

[39] *DS* 182/*AM* 137, "Et le plus terrible, c'est qu'en ces minutes j'avais conscience du prix insensé que j'allais payer pour un instant de distraction."

[40] *DS* 184/*AM* 141, "je ne m'y intéressais plus du tout, cela concernait un autre monde."

[41] *DS* 186/*AM* 146, "car cette *pensée*, si elle m'a vaincu, n'a vaincu que par moi, et finalement elle a toujours été à ma mesure…"

[42] *DS* 177/*AM* 123, "Je dirai peu de chose de ce qui arriva ensuite."

[43] *DS* 187/*AM* 149, "Et plus encore, qu'il essaie d'imaginer la main qui les écrit: s'il la voyait, peut-être lire lui deviendrait-il une tâche sérieuse."

[44] In other words, Jean Paul's hands come to interrupt the "persecution" of the writing hand and by the non-writing hand that Blanchot describes in the first chapter of *The Space of Literature*. If the mastery of the non-writing hand consists in interrupting the writing hand and restoring primacy to the present, then the absent hand complicates this interruption, infusing the present with the past and the future (see *SL* 25/ *EL* 19).

FIGURES OF THE WORK
Blanchot and the Space of Literature

Caroline Sheaffer-Jones

> *Literature would begin where one no longer knows who writes
> and who signs the story of the appeal, and of the "Here am I!,"
> between the absolute Father and Son.*
> Derrida, *The Gift of Death*

> *as if, by this inspired movement, he had indeed captured
> from Hell the obscure shade and had, unknowingly,
> led it back into the broad daylight of the work.*
> Blanchot, *The Space of Literature*

THE SUBJECT OF NARRATION

WRITING AND THAT WHICH IT ENTAILS ARE THE SUBJECT OF COUNTLESS
texts by Maurice Blanchot. In particular, Blanchot has focused on the
notion of the work, or more precisely on a groundlessness or an absence
of the work,[1] which he has designated from different perspectives over
the course of more than half a century. In various ways, Blanchot has
conceived of the work as an affirmation of its undoing. The question
of narration, often about a confrontation with death, is fundamentally
important, as is evident for example in Blanchot's *Death Sentence* (1948),
The Madness of the Day (1973) or *The Instant of My Death* (1994). In
a sense, it is bound up with the possibility of the work. In "Narrative
Voice (the 'it' ['il'], the neutral)," in *The Infinite Conversation* (1969),[2]
Blanchot describes a groundlessness or decentring of the work which is
not conceived of as a unified whole. However in writing on authors such as
Henry James and Hermann Broch in *The Book to Come* (1959), Blanchot
focuses on a very different conception of the absence of the work which
certainly relates to the writer's difficult struggle to narrate all, to tell the
truth. Indeed it concerns that limit of existence near death at which the
work might be the revelation of everything. My reading of Blanchot's
"The Gaze of Orpheus" in *The Space of Literature* (1955) will draw on
these texts. With reference to certain writings by Derrida and Bataille, as

well as Blanchot's "Narrative Voice," I will put forward an approach to the work in "The Gaze of Orpheus" to show that alongside the project of realising it as a totality, Blanchot exposes a more radical conception of non-totalization of the work whose borders are uncertain. It is in this way, through a deconstructive reading, that Blanchot can be shown to step beyond an impossible conception of the absence of the work.

What is repeatedly in play in Blanchot's discussions of the work from various perspectives is the question of its limits. However in Blanchot's early text "Literature and the Right to Death," in *The Work of Fire* (1949), it is Hegel's *Phenomenology of Spirit*, more especially Alexandre Kojève's reading of it,[3] which takes on a key role. Literature is conceptualized in terms of the phenomenology of spirit with all of its figures of meaning. It would be absolute knowledge in the form of a Book. The work is not in the world, but is the realisation of everything, that is the absence of everything, of nothing; it is "the meaning of meaning of words," *"that life which supports [porte] death and maintains itself in it."*[4] In later texts, Blanchot's writing testifies to a marked shift away from Hegel and Kojève, firstly towards Heidegger and the question of Being, evident in some texts of *The Space of Literature* and *The Book to Come*, then to Levinas and also Nietzsche, as is already apparent in *The Infinite Conversation*. This ongoing displacement is important, since no text states the last word.

It is a certain displacement which I will underline in my reading of Blanchot's "The Gaze of Orpheus" by examining different conceptions of the groundlessness of the work which can be considered to coexist in the text. This double reading is clearly of importance in a deconstructive approach in which there is no simple step beyond metaphysics. In "Structure, Sign and Play in the Discourse of the Human Sciences," in *Writing and Difference*, Derrida defines two aspects of play. In his discussion of structuralism, Derrida opposes its negative, nostalgic, Rousseauistic side of thinking of play to the Nietzschean "affirmation of the play of the world and of the innocence of becoming, the affirmation of a world of signs without fault, without truth, and without origin which is offered to an active interpretation." Derrida adds: *"This affirmation then determines the noncenter otherwise than as the loss of the center."*[5] While one side is directed towards a truth or dreams of this origin which escapes play, the other does not search for the beginning or end of play but affirms the game. Presence or absence is not thought prior to the game but as a function of it. Derrida insists that the two irreconcilable interpretations of interpretation share the field of the social sciences and that it is not simply a matter of choosing between them.[6] I will indicate the way in which Blanchot's text on Orpheus points not just to a nostalgic conception of play but also beyond it.

In "Narrative Voice (the 'it' ['il'], the neutral)," in *The Infinite Conversation*, Blanchot emphasises the way in which narration as conscious vision has been brought into question. If Flaubert still believed in narration, in telling as showing, without really dwelling on its limitations, Thomas Mann already began to challenge it (*IC* 382–3/ *EI* 560–1). Insisting that telling is certainly not self-evident, Blanchot contests the use of a centralized perspective in a story in the form of a privileged "I," or perhaps also in the guise of a third person. For the problem is that these stories equate the narrative act and the transparency of a consciousness, as if telling were only being conscious or revealing. What takes place with Kafka, for Blanchot, is a distancing of the main character from himself, the other characters and events. This decentres the work and brings into the narration a different speech or speech of the other (*IC* 383–4/*EI* 561–2). It is then the narration itself which comes into play.

Blanchot associates the neuter with Kafka's narration: in it speaks an "il," a third person which is neither a third person nor simply impersonality. The subjects are in "a relation of non-identification with themselves": "something happens to them which they can only seize again by letting go of their power to say 'I,' and what happens to them has always already happened to them" (*IC* 384–5/*EI* 564). Narrative voice (*narrative*), to be distinguished from narrating voice (*narratrice*), is thus not that of a particular subject. The "il" is dispersed and mobile. "'Its' place" is both where it is always missing, therefore empty, and a "surplus of place" or "hypertopia" (*IC* 385, 462 n.2/*EI* 563–4 n.1, 565). Blanchot states that this voice signals an emptiness in the work like Marguerite Duras's "absence-word": "'a hole-word, hollowed out in its center by a hole, the hole in which all the other words should have been buried'." It is "a neutral voice that speaks the work from out of this place without a place, where the work is silent" (*IC* 385/*EI* 565).[7] "Spectral, ghostlike," although clearly in a different sense from Blanchot's description of narration and James, narrative voice is "the indifferent-difference that alters the personal voice," decentring it (*IC* 386/*EI* 566). The work thus lacks a centre and does not form a whole.

In contrast to this notion in which an affirmation of play is apparent, Blanchot's conception of the work of various authors in *The Space of Literature* and *The Book to Come* involves a nostalgic search to narrate everything or to reach end-game. The writer is engaged in an interminable task, one which is about his ruin. In Blanchot's text on Henry James entitled "The Turn of the Screw," in *The Book to Come*, everything is at stake in the work, or is it nothing? Blanchot quotes James as saying: "'The subject is everything – the subject is everything'" and asks what could be understood by these words (*BC* 126/*LV* 187; see also *BC* 153/*LV* 227–8). Blanchot gives his impressions of James's notes, *The Turn of the Screw*, and also of the essence of this writer's art. The notes are considered to be James's initial work in which his pen exerts a kind of magic pressure. In secret confidence with himself, James is supposedly in touch with the "pure possibility" of the work of art which powerfully draws him in; that is the "fullness of the story [*récit*] which has not yet begun" (*BC* 132/*LV* 195). This region of possibility is "this ghostly and unreal life of what we have not been, figures with whom we always [*toujours*, also 'still'] have an appointment" (*BC* 132/*LV* 195). It would seem that it is not only the children in *The Turn of the Screw* who are haunted by ghosts, by scary images or figures, but that everyone, including the governess, James and the author in general, is swept into an eerie, unreal space.[8] In Blanchot's reading of James, there is indeed an unattainable authenticity or truth of the work which is linked to this ungraspable region.

Narration is this imaginary and indistinct realm and, for Blanchot, perhaps "the evil heart [*le cœur malin*] of every story" (*BC* 130/*LV* 192). Blanchot notes that James applies "pressure" to the work of art to make it speak and that this writer refers to it in a general sense as the "turn of the screw" (*BC* 133/*LV* 196–7). This general meaning is no doubt operative in Blanchot's use of James's title *The Turn of the Screw* as the title of his own text on James. For Blanchot, the pressure which the governess exerts on the children in James's story to snatch away their secret is essentially the pressure of narration that is

> the marvellous and terrible movement which the act of writing exercises on truth, torment, torture, violence which finally lead to death where everything appears to be revealed, where everything however falls back into doubt and the void of the shadows. (*BC* 133/*LV* 197)

The pressure of narration is, according to Blanchot, the "'subject'" of James's story (*BC* 133/*LV* 197). Of course the subject is everything and narration, it would seem, must be at the border of silence, death, which engulfs all. It involves a search for a force beyond the work of a writer.

It is about arriving at a point of revelation, as in the passage cited above, however elusive it may be.

Narration is associated with death, thus it is no coincidence that Blanchot ends his text on James by quoting the dying writer of *The Middle Years* (*BC* 133, 259 n.3/*LV* 197), a character from whose text James takes the title of his story. Many of the authors to whom Blanchot turns his attention in *The Book to Come* are depicted in particular at the close of their lives. It is by focusing on a glimpse of death, which writers would somehow have at the end of the road, that Blanchot broaches the essential question of telling everything and nothing. It is when the authors lose themselves, or perhaps rather gather their lives together, that telling would come into its own and the voice from the abyss might be heard. As time passes, James, according to Blanchot, "moves in a more deliberate way towards himself" (*BC* 131/*LV* 195). The evanescent truth of his life story might be realised in his disappearance. Virginia Woolf's suicide is also a source of intrigue for Blanchot and she may even paradoxically have avoided a certain failure and infidelity to herself in her demise (*BC* 104/*LV* 154). It is this point of death, or indeed birth, which is central in Blanchot's text. It is as if there were an instant at which the work might be converted into the infinite and vie with creation. In this nostalgic endeavour of the writer lies the realisation of the work.

In *The Book to Come*, Blanchot considers Broch's description of Virgil's last days. Broch supposedly senses the salvation which would bring his monologue to its centre and point of simultaneity where the beginning and end would join up: "the return to the sources, the happiness of rediscovered unity" (*BC* 120/*LV* 176–7). For Blanchot, there is indeed a centre which might bring unity. Orpheus, the poet *par excellence* in *The Space of Literature*, is not the only one who descends into the depths in the accomplishment of his deadly mission. The "dying poet" whom Blanchot describes when discussing Broch's *The Death of Virgil* is in fact the quintessential writer of *The Book to Come*, for he approaches that point at which his work will become a possibility. Blanchot writes:

> There will be no true communication, nor song, if song cannot descend below all form, toward the formless and toward that depth where the voice outside all language speaks. It is therefore this descent – descent toward the undetermined – which the dying poet seeks to accomplish by his death. The space of song and the space of death are described to us as linked and grasped through each other. (*BC* 123/*LV* 182)[9]

Writing in general is bound up with death, or birth, and a descent into the depths at the limit of the world. There the song is no longer, or not yet, language. Blanchot's conception of writing, or narration, hinges on death when all might be revealed as infinitely possible. The work would be the representation of such a point at which everything, or perhaps its absence, might be disclosed. In this nostalgic vision, it is indeed "pure absence" which is at stake. Referring to Blanchot, Derrida writes: "Only *pure absence* – not the absence of this or that, but the absence of everything in which all presence is announced – can *inspire*, in other words, can *work*, and then make one work" (*WrD* 7/*EcD* 17). The writer's task would be to pursue some ultimate moment of truth which is clearly difficult to grasp.

LIMIT ENCOUNTERS

The opening text of *The Book to Come*, *"Encountering the Imaginary*,"[10] one of two texts in the first section entitled "The Song of the Sirens," is also about the precarious approach of the writer or narrator towards an intangible point of revelation. The writer's task is no more straightforward than that of the traveller who is attracted to a source and through which he will navigate more or less successfully. In this story, there is indeed a "point of encounter" (*BC* 5/*LV* 12), which Blanchot defines as belonging intrinsically to the *récit* (story) in contrast to the novel,[11] but it is almost impossible to reach. Although the goal is mapped and supposedly exists, some try to get to it too early, others too late; some impatiently say: "it is here; here, I will cast anchor" (*BC* 4/*LV* 10) whereas for others, Blanchot insists, it was always beyond the right point. Blanchot opposes Homer's Ulysses in his encounter with the Sirens to Melville's character Ahab in his pursuit of the great white whale in *Moby Dick*. Everything is at stake. Of particular interest is the way in which it all appears to hinge on the relationship between the writer and the character. In Blanchot's analysis, it is as if the writer could see himself in his character and to a certain extent realise his work. It is as if he could associate with the character to such a point that the space of narration would virtually disappear and the imaginary would be indistinguishable from the real.

It is evident that both Ulysses and Ahab are engaged in an extremely hazardous mission. However Ulysses is cunning and calculating: "He will be everything, if he maintains a limit and this interval between the real and the imaginary which, precisely, the Song of the Sirens, invites him to go through" (*BC* 8/*LV* 16). By establishing a boundary, and then somehow passing through it, Ulysses will come home victorious and attain "everything." By being tied to the mast, that is through technique, Ulysses is not engulfed by the Sirens' song and realises "*a sort of* victory" (*BC* 8/ *LV* 16, my emphasis). In contrast, Ahab pursues his goal to the end, goes under, achieving a "somber disaster" (*BC* 8/ *LV* 16). Blanchot writes that Ulysses, unlike Ahab, does not undergo a metamorphosis, in which he loses himself, but seems to travel full circle to find himself as he was. Ahab, Blanchot states, "does not find himself again and, for Melville himself, the world incessantly threatens to sink into that worldless space toward which the fascination of a sole image draws him" (*BC* 8/ *LV* 17). However, it is apparent that neither Ulysses nor Ahab could really tell the "point of the encounter" (*BC* 5/ *LV* 12). If Ulysses artfully survived by failing to make contact with the treacherous region and Ahab died while carrying out his mission, it is evident that there simply is no revelation and the very existence of a so-called meeting point is brought into question. Blanchot's story is about two "heroes," neither of whom can fulfil the nostalgic dream of truth and search for presence, characteristic of the negative side of thinking play to which Derrida has drawn attention.

It is significant that Blanchot focuses not just on Ahab but also on Melville who, like his protagonist, seems to be drawn into an unreal, solitary space at the end of the world. It is as if the writer, in his tale of the voyage recounting nothing but the imaginary space, were dragged into the depths by Ahab's encounter. What is indeed at stake is the limit, not simply between Ahab and the whale or Ulysses and the Sirens' song, but between Ahab and Melville, Ulysses and Homer. The problematic difference between narrator and character is like the ungraspable limit, described in the two adventures, between a navigator and some mysterious frontier. One of the section headings of "Encountering the Imaginary" is "When Ulysses becomes Homer" and Blanchot asks what would happen if Ulysses and Homer were "one and the same presence" (BC 7/LV 15). Blanchot writes:

> To hear the Song of the Sirens is to become Homer, from Ulysses, who one was, but it is nevertheless only in the story of Homer that is accomplished the real encounter, in which Ulysses becomes the one who enters into a relationship with the force of the elements and the voice from the abyss.
>
> That seems obscure, it evokes the predicament of the first man if, in order to be created, he needed to pronounce himself, in an entirely human way, the divine *Fiat lux* capable of opening his eyes. (*BC* 7/ *LV* 15)

It would seem that there is a source of creation, at which the difference between narrator and character is not operative. Homer and Ulysses would both be born at once; Ulysses is a creation of Homer; through the writing Homer himself would come to life. It is in the very narration of the story that the author, and not just the character, is fashioned. In this sense, Blanchot writes of the first man who would divinely pronounce the *Fiat lux* himself, enabling him to see.[12] Yet in Blanchot's text the character is necessarily also separate from the author and is more or less a means by which the author may arrive at lucidity. In the navigation through the unknown, it is as if the author could really only have the chance to accomplish his life and work through another, through the character, thereby taking on the role of the other; and yet this substitution of places is also that which threatens to jeopardise the achievement of his own goal.

The limit between the author and character is not clear-cut. In writing about Broch, Blanchot states that this writer wants to make "literary expression" into an "experience" and is of the belief that in writing he will reach "the unique point of presence where, in absolute simultaneity, the infinity of the past and the infinity of the future will open up to him" (*BC* 124/*LV* 182). At this "point" the boundary between Broch and his character would certainly disintegrate. Indeed in relation to Broch's *The Death of Virgil*, Blanchot states: "Virgil, that's Broch" (*BC* 125/*LV* 184). How might one speak of the interchangeability of Broch the writer and Virgil who dies? The possibility of simply collapsing the writer and character into each other is not so evident in some texts of *The Book to Come*. Blanchot writes that Musil was contemplating using a first person where the "I" represented neither the character nor the novelist but rather their relationship, that is, a selfless voice of impersonality (*BC* 147–8/*LV* 218–9). This would be a more neutral voice. Would the narrative voice of "Encountering the Imaginary" be Ulysses, Ahab, Homer, Melville and others in the meetings of extremes, or perhaps not one voice nor another? When Blanchot writes "When Ulysses becomes Homer" (*BC* 7/*LV 15*), can the text be read differently, so that it is not simply dependent upon an imaginary and nostalgic point of encounter, "the point where singing will cease to be a deception [*leurre*: also meaning lure]" (*BC* 9/*LV* 17)?

FACING DEATH

It is evident that many of Blanchot's writers are involved in an ultimate confrontation or are depicted on the verge of death when they supposedly express the soul of their life's work. It is as if then they had virtually travelled full circle and might somehow be closest and most true to themselves. In writing about Artaud, Blanchot discusses the possibility that this writer is the "absolute witness of himself" (*BC* 38/*LV* 59). "The Gaze of Orpheus,"[13] in *The Space of Literature*, can be read not simply as the writer's pursuit of unity, but also as a different exposition of groundlessness in the work. In this double reading, it is not simply the nostalgic search for revelation which is described, but a movement which exceeds this understanding. Conscious vision is brought into question as in the neutral narrative voice where subjects, instead of striving to find themselves, face up to being radically decentred.

Blanchot writes about Orpheus's descent,[14] into the depths of hell, towards Eurydice who is for him

> the extreme that art can reach. Under a name that hides her and a veil that covers her, she is the profoundly obscure point toward which art and desire, death and night, seem to tend. She is the instant when the essence of night approaches as the *other* night. (*SL* 171 /*EL* 227)

Orpheus's work is not simply to approach this "point": "His *work* is to bring it back to the light of day and to give it form, shape [*figure*] and reality in the day" (*SL* 171/*EL* 227). Orpheus's work is to expose this spectre alive in the work. No single name nor figure could ultimately define her. In a sense forgetting the work, which nevertheless remains consistent with the extravagant demands of his art, Orpheus would supposedly face the ultimate "point." Blanchot calls this gaze of Orpheus "inspiration" (*SL* 173/*EL* 231), as if there were some pure spirit which could be grasped.

Orpheus's approach towards the ultimate point would be the instant at which the work or indeed the life of the poet Orpheus is in the balance. Blanchot writes:

> The work is everything to Orpheus except that desired look where it is lost so that it is also only in that look that the work can surpass itself, be united with its origin and consecrated in impossibility. (*SL* 174/*EL* 232)

This gaze of Orpheus designates the search for the origin and sanctification of the work. Blanchot's text can be read in the nostalgic sense in which the work is considered "lost" and that loss, the gaze of Orpheus, indeed Eurydice, is the noncentre defined in terms of a "loss" of centre as discussed by Derrida in "Structure, Sign and Play." Eurydice is "lost," "twice lost" (*SL* 173/*EL* 230–1) or retrievable, a dream which Blanchot entertains in this act of looking, as "regarder" also means "to keep again." However, there is also a sense in which Blanchot's text supports the reading of a noncentre which is an affirmation of play. The writer's work would not be focused on rectifying a loss or on the realisation of absolutely everything. It would not be centred on point zero, pure absence as presence. Thus, if Orpheus's work is the progression to the limit, this limit is a moving one which cannot simply be thought teleologically. Eurydice is not an "instant" in which revelation might take place. It is not Orpheus's nostalgic desire for her presence which needs to be stressed, but the admission that, however elusive Eurydice may be, outside the song there simply is no relation: "He is Orpheus only in the song; he can only have a relation with Eurydice within the hymn" (*SL* 172/*EL* 229). The gaze of Orpheus cannot just be conceived of as an event in which Orpheus, momentarily, turns towards Eurydice to reveal a presence, or indeed absence, of the work. Rather Eurydice is the dispersion which Orpheus faces throughout the work: "in reality, Orpheus has not ceased to be turned toward Eurydice" (*SL* 172/*EL* 229). The gaze of Orpheus traverses the work. It is not merely a point at which the work is lost or consecrated, but the detour of writing in which Eurydice is neither simply present nor absent.

Blanchot's writing on the gaze of Orpheus takes on an importance which extends well beyond these central pages of *The Space of Literature*. In the preamble to the text, Blanchot states that in a book there is a "centre" which is both moving and fixed and which is displaced by the "pressure" of the book and its circumstances. The author is ignorant of this centre and reaching it may be an illusion. This lack of clear-cut knowledge of a centre is compounded by the fact that in Blanchot's text, as stated in the preliminary remarks to *The Space of Literature*, the focal "point" to which the book appears to direct itself is "here, towards the pages entitled 'The Gaze of Orpheus.'" "Here" implies in the instance of this book where the "point" is the gaze of Orpheus and that which it entails, but at the same time "here" can be read in terms of the already decentred gaze of the preliminary remarks of the book describing the uncertainty of the centre, one which is more like a noncentre. Indeed, Blanchot, as writer, inscribes the unseeing gaze of Orpheus as that centre of the space of literature which cuts across *every* "point" of the text, including "here" in this preamble and beyond. It is evident that this narration is not simply about conscious vision, but about the fathomless, unknowing gaze of the work of Orpheus. The borders of "The Gaze of Orpheus" extend right across *The Space of Literature*. It is therefore as if the gaze of Orpheus, of the character in "The Gaze of Orpheus," were already in a sense that of the narrator Blanchot, and yet the limits between the two are uncertain. Blanchot would be this Orpheus who would occupy a double position.

In this gaze of Orpheus, writer and character, Orpheus would incessantly cross the limit to see the end of the world, as it were, in a movement in which he would be neither alive nor dead. It is as if Orpheus were telling Orpheus's death; Broch telling *The Death of Virgil*, when Virgil is Broch. The writer's work would always involve stepping across the borders of life and death, the real and the imaginary. It is as if there were absolute simultaneity in which, perhaps like Homer and Ulysses, the narrator and character would be "one and the same presence" (*BC* 7 / *LV* 15). They would be born in a situation similar to the one described by Blanchot in which the first man might pronounce the divine *Fiat lux* to bring himself alive. Yet the difference between the narrator and character must also be affirmed. It is evident that the existence of the work is at stake at that impossible limit between narrator and character, the limit of undecidability.[15] The work would be the image of that ungraspable circle in which now, and yet never, or perhaps "straight away although little by little" (*BC* 16–7 / *LV* 27–30), Orpheus becomes Blanchot, indeed Blanchot becomes Orpheus, the author of his own work of death and creation.

The story of Orpheus is one of writing and dying, or writing and creation. In a sense, it involves a face to face which necessarily speaks its own impossibility. However, most importantly, death is not a simple event which arrives at an extreme "point" in the writer's journey, but rather that which is always an integral part of it. The gaze must be read not merely as a final gesture in which Orpheus dies, striving like other writers to communicate the definitive work, but as that which is always in play in the work. In the unrecognisable gaze of Orpheus, the fixed stare of death is always inscribed in the vision. Indeed the work is that gaze of Orpheus, showing not just Orpheus alive contemplating his death, but also that already unseeing, impersonal gaze of Orpheus dispersed.

The space of literature centred upon the gaze of Orpheus is impossible to circumscribe. The work incorporates within it an abyss in which it is engulfed, as the gaze of Orpheus designates not only vision but limitless blindness. As in Blanchot's conception of narrative voice, there is an emptiness which pervades the text and exceeds it. "The Gaze of Orpheus" can be read not simply in terms of the nostalgic project to approach an extreme point and to narrate everything, but as that which has no ultimate point and is unable to be grasped once and for all. In opposition to Blanchot's depiction of writers in pursuit of unity, pure inspiration and meaning at the instant of death, another side of the writer's endeavour is apparent. What is in play is not pure absence and the presence of everything. A different notion of groundlessness already traverses the work. Rather than a vision which would encompass the whole world, it involves a blindness always inherent in the gaze.

It is apparent that the unseeing gaze which testifies to a lack of recognition and consciousness cannot be considered to be a point, but rather something much more fundamental in Orpheus's vision. Indeed revelation could be considered a comedy.[16] There is, as Bataille affirms in *Inner Experience*, a blindness which cannot be contained in knowledge, but rather knowledge is absorbed in this blind spot.[17] It is in this sense that Orpheus, at once knowing yet necessarily ignorant, is not unified but absolutely torn[18] throughout his work in a way which exceeds any "restricted economy." In his reading of Bataille in "From Restricted to General Economy: A Hegelianism without Reserve," in *Writing and Difference*, Derrida underlines the vast difference between, on the one hand, certain texts of Bataille, which to some extent simulate Hegel, and on the other hand, Hegel, who was blind to absolute loss which exceeds the closure of absolute knowledge. For Derrida, Bataille does not "overturn" the phenomenology of spirit, with its sphere of absolute knowledge, but rather this restricted economy is "comprehended" or inscribed with its figures within a general economy. In this economy, the "horizons of knowledge" and "figures of meaning" are related not to the grounds but to the "nonbasis of expenditure, not to the *telos* of meaning, but to the *indefinite* destruction of value" (*WrD* 343–4/ *EcD* 398–9). The "we" of the *Phenomenology of Spirit* "develops the sense, or the desire for sense, of natural consciousness, the consciousness that encloses itself in the circle in order to *know* sense; which is always where it comes from, and where it is going to. It does not *see* the nonbasis of play [*le sans-fond de jeu*] upon which (the) history (of meaning) is launched" (*WrD* 349/ *EcD* 406).[19] It is evident that if what is at stake in Blanchot's *The Book to Come* and *The Space of Literature* differs from the conception of the absence of the book in "Literature and the Right to Death" in *The Work of Fire*, it relates nevertheless to the realisation of the absolute, however fleeting or ungraspable it may be. Yet an affirmative side of play also emerges in Blanchot's space of literature in the gaze of Orpheus. Orpheus's dispersion is at the heart of the work: this senseless unworking, this "ordeal of eternal unworking" (*SL* 173/ *EL* 230) has always already begun.

The work of Orpheus is not simply about the approach to the extreme limit at which all might be narrated and truth disclosed, the dream of escaping play. The "point," to which Blanchot repeatedly refers in *The Book to Come* and *The Space of Literature*, can be read not as a simple moment of conversion for the writer, but rather as one which is incessantly transgressed. In "seeing" Eurydice, Orpheus gazes upon the image of his own dispersion to which he also remains blind. In seeing, although not comprehending his demise, he, as it were, always steps beyond death. It is as if Orpheus's work, described in the gaze of Orpheus, were the vision of a torn figure in one place and yet also in the place of Eurydice, no place. In his work, he would be at once Orpheus and yet no-one, neither one figure nor another, an affirmation of infinite groundlessness. There is thus always a decentring in the work, as in the "il" of the neutral narrative voice, rather than an ultimate moment of revelation.

The space of literature is about a plurality; the work is not the expression of a single, personal achievement. Innumerable writers and characters are described in *The Space of Literature* and *The Book to Come* where the borders between the real and the imaginary are always displaced. Spectres of names figure in this space of literature: James, Woolf, Homer, Melville, Ulysses, Ahab, Broch, Virgil, Mallarmé and others. These are the proper names of those who are also anonymous like the facelessness of Eurydice. Thus Broch who writes on Virgil applies himself to "the exercise of a vigilant thought" (*BC* 122/*LV* 179) and in Adolphe, Benjamin Constant deals with that which has been hidden from him "constantly" (*BC* 184/*LV* 273). The narrative voice might be said to be the celebration of the passage of many figures, and also of none. Doubled by the impersonal voice, it is as if they were there and yet missing. Thus the work cannot be circumscribed once and for all within a structure or history. In a discussion of Mallarmé's Book and the Orphic explanation of the Earth, Blanchot writes about the "space" of literature (*BC* 237–8/*LV* 349),[20] although insisting more in subsequent readings of Mallarmé on an affirmation of play, on fragmentation and the "'*senseless game of writing*'" (see especially *IC* 422/*EI* 620). Under the heading "'Made, being' ['Fait, étant']" Blanchot writes: "The book is without author, because it is written starting from the speaking disappearance of the author" (*BC* 229/*LV* 334).

Orpheus's dispersion is paramount in Blanchot's notion of the work in *The Space of Literature*. In this text, there is an absence in the work which can be read not simply in terms of the author's nostalgic and hazardous search for unity, but as that which defies any simultaneity of the work. In this reading, the gaze of Orpheus is the groundlessness which marks an excess; the work is always traversed by this supplementary gesture and inscribed in the unknown.[21] Thus the non-totalization of the space of literature is not so much about the perilous project of realising the work which would say everything, but about the transgression of this work and an affirmative notion of play emphasised by Derrida. The emptiness which pervades the work cannot simply be seen in terms of the pursuit or loss of a centre. The work describing the limit encounter of Orpheus and Eurydice, indeed Orpheus and Orpheus, writer and character, shows the undoing of its boundaries. What is evident is the dispersed and mobile "il" of neutral narrative voice belonging neither simply to one figure nor another. Indeed, in the detour of writing, Blanchot is already turning around, absent. This reading shows that Blanchot's conception of the work can be considered to exceed a restricted economy. In discussing Nietzsche and a "non-dialectical experience of language" (*IC* 154/*EI* 231)[22] in "Nietzsche and Fragmentary Writing," Blanchot writes: "To interpret: the infinite: the world. The world? A text? The text: the movement of writing in its neutrality" (*IC* 168/*EI* 252). A neutral narrative voice is always already apparent in Blanchot's space of literature whose figures are an affirmation of infinite dispersion.

ENDNOTES

[1] The third and final section of Maurice Blanchot's *The Infinite Conversation* takes its title "The Absence of the Book (the neutral, the fragmentary)" from the last text in it, "L'Absence de livre." In that text, Blanchot uses the term *absence d'œuvre*, the "absence of (the) work," as well as *désœuvrement*, translated by "worklessness or unworking." Michel Foucault also published the important text "La folie, l'absence d'œuvre" as an appendix to *Histoire de la folie à l'âge classique* (Paris: Gallimard, 1972), 575–82. Blanchot writes: "To write is to produce the absence of the work (worklessness)" (*IC* 424/*EI* 622). (I have modified the English translations throughout.) On this major issue, see among other texts, Paul Davies, "The Work and the Absence of the Work", in *Maurice Blanchot: The Demand of Writing*, ed. Carolyn Bailey Gill (London: Routledge, 1996), 91–107; Gerald L. Bruns, *Maurice Blanchot: The Refusal of Philosophy* (Baltimore: Johns Hopkins University Press, 1997), 145–72; Leslie Hill, *Blanchot: Extreme Contemporary* (London: Routledge, 1997), 103–20.

[2] The title of this text is translated in *The Infinite Conversation* as "Narrative Voice (the 'he,' the neutral)" *IC* 379/*EI* 556.

[3] Alexandre Kojève, *Introduction to the Reading of Hegel* [1947], ed. Alan Bloom, trans. James H. Nichols, Jr. (New York: Basic Books, 1969). Blanchot refers to Kojève's text in "Literature and the Right to Death" (*WF* 314, 323/*PF* 305, 312).

4 *WF* 343/*PF* 330; see also *WF* 316–21/*PF* 307–11. Hegel writes: "the life of Spirit is not the life that shrinks from death and keeps itself untouched by devastation, but rather the life that endures and maintains itself in it." G.W.F. Hegel, *Phenomenology of Spirit*, trans. A.V. Miller, with an analysis of the text and foreword by J.N. Findlay (Oxford: Oxford University Press, 1977), 19; *Phänomenologie des Geistes, Werke in 20 Bänden* (Frankfurt am Main: Suhrkamp, 1969–71), 3: 36.

5 Jacques Derrida, *Writing and Difference*, trans. Alan Bass (London: Routledge, 1978), 369, hereafter *WrD*/ *L'Écriture et la différence* (Paris: Seuil, 1967), 427, hereafter EcD. See also "Force and signification", *WrD* 1–35/*EcD* 9–49 and in particular F. Nietzsche, *The Birth of Tragedy* and *The Case of Wagner*, trans. Walter Kaufmann (New York: Vintage, 1967)/ *Die Geburt der Tragödie, Werke,* I, ed. Karl Schlechta (München: Carl Hanser, 1969).

6 Derrida, *WrD* 369–70/*EcD* 426–8.

7 See Derrida's discussion of Blanchot's narrative voice in "Survivre," *Parages* (Paris: Galilée, 1986), 149–52/"Living On", *Deconstruction and Criticism* (New York: Seabury, 1979), 104–7.

8 The elaborate framing of the story of *The Turn of the Screw* (1898) highlights the act of narration. It is interesting to note also that the various characters often occupy each other's place, adopt each other's perspective and to a certain extent one is substituted for the other. It is as if the narrative voice showed the characters enacting a series of repetitious and somewhat unreal moves. *The Novels and Tales of Henry James*, New York Edition (New York: Charles Scribner's Sons, 1908), 12: 145–309.

9 See also the fourth section of *The Space of Literature*, "The Work and Death's Space", *SL* 85–159/*EL* 99–211.

10 "La rencontre de l'imaginaire" also has the sense of the encounter of the imaginary kind, the imaginary encounter. On the image, see in particular *BC* 91–2/ *LV* 136–8; *SL* 32–4/*EL* 25–8; "Vast as the Night", *IC* 318–25/*EI* 465–77.

11 See *BC* 5–7/*LV* 12–4. The *récit* is an event, an exceptional event, or the approach to one, as opposed to the light-hearted fiction of the novel, yet the difference cannot be so clearly established. This is also evident when Blanchot refers to Plato's *Gorgias* and the *récit* of the Last Judgement.

12 Blanchot returns, from a different perspective, to this question of seeing, vision and light with reference to Emmanuel Levinas; see "Knowledge of the Unknown" *IC* 57/*EI* 82; and "Speaking is Not Seeing" *IC* 31/*EI* 43.

13 On this text, see in particular Levinas, "Le Regard du poète", *Sur Maurice Blanchot* (Montpellier: Fata Morgana, 1975), 7–25; Chantal Michel, *Maurice Blanchot et le déplacement d'Orphée* (Paris: Librairie Nizet, 1997); Walter A. Strauss, *Descent and Return: The Orphic Theme in Modern Literature* (Cambridge: Harvard University Press, 1971). See also Blanchot's text "Ne te retourne pas", *Digraphe* "Roger Laporte," 18/19 (1979): 159–63.

14 The myth states that the poet and musician Orpheus could bring his dead wife Eurydice back to the upper world from hell, on condition that he not look behind

him until they reached the sunlight. However he turned around and she was lost. Orpheus was finally torn apart. Robert Graves, *The Greek Myths* (Harmondsworth: Penguin, 1974), 1: 111–5.

[15] On "undecidability" see in particular Derrida, "The Double Session", *Dissemination*, trans. Barbara Johnson (London: Athlone, 1981), 173–285/*La Dissémination* (Paris: Seuil, 1972), 199–317.

[16] See Georges Bataille, "Hegel, Death and Sacrifice," *The Bataille Reader*, ed. Fred Botting and Scott Wilson (Oxford: Blackwell, 1997), 279–95; first published in *Deucalion*, 5 (1955), 21–43.

[17] Bataille, *Inner Experience* [1954], trans. Leslie Anne Boldt (New York: SUNY Press, 1988); *Œuvres complètes, L'Expérience intérieure* (Paris: Gallimard, 1973 [1943 and 1954]), 5: 129. On Bataille, see in particular the first two sections of "The Limit-Experience" *IC* 202–17/*EI* 300–22; and the section "The Negative Community" in *UC* 1–26/*CI* 9–47.

[18] After writing that the life of Spirit maintains itself in death, Hegel states that Spirit "wins its truth only when, in utter dismemberment [*in der absoluten Zerrissenheit,* 'in absolute tearing'], it finds itself." *Phenomenology of Spirit*, 19/ *Phänomenologie des Geistes*, 36.

[19] See also Denis Hollier, "De l'au-delà de Hegel à l'absence de Nietzsche", *Bataille*, sous la direction de Philippe Sollers (Paris: U.G.E., 1973), 75–96; and, in the same volume, "Discussion", 97–105.

[20] In a number of passages, Blanchot draws on Heidegger's interpretations of poetry, but he also distinguishes his own readings from them. For example, Blanchot insists on the relationships among words and the space which they presuppose, however he considers that Heidegger emphasises certain fundamental words tied to the history of Being, *BC* 235, 265–6 n.9/*LV* 345 n.1. For a discussion of Blanchot's reading of Mallarmé, see Paul de Man, "Impersonality in the Criticism of Maurice Blanchot", *Blindness and Insight: Essays in the Rhetoric of Contemporary Criticism* (Minneapolis: University of Minnesota Press, 1983), 60–78.

[21] On the supplement, see in particular Derrida, *Of Grammatology*, trans. G.C. Spivak (Baltimore: John Hopkins University Press, 1976)/*De la grammatologie* (Paris: Minuit, 1967).

[22] Blanchot states that he wrote these pages in the margins of a number of writings, including several texts in Derrida's *Writing and Difference* (*IC* 452 n.16/*EI* 255).

"THE ABSOLUTELY DARK MOMENT OF THE PLOT"
Blanchot's Abraham

Chris Danta

> *To the arbitrariness within oneself there*
> *corresponds the accidental outside oneself.*
> Søren Kierkegaard, *Either/Or*

> *The poet borrows all his materials other than images.*
> Novalis, "On Goethe"

[1] "NOBODY HERE DESIRES TO BIND THEMSELVES TO A STORY"

ALL WRITING, ACCORDING TO THE TITLE OF MARGARET ATWOOD'S RECENT
book on the subject, is a *Negotiating with the Dead*. For Atwood: "All
writers must go from *now* to *once upon a time* … all must descend to
where the stories are kept; all must be careful not to be captured and held
immobile by the past."[1] Here, she has in mind that myth of the pursuit of
poetic inspiration that endlessly inspired Maurice Blanchot: the descent
of the poet-songster Orpheus into the Underworld to recover his dead
wife Eurydice.[2] But, as Atwood quickly qualifies, the descent can only be
half – even if perhaps the most interesting half – of the story. For there
can be no story – no negotiating with the dead – without a return to the
present that reinstates the divide between life and death as impermeable.
Atwood continues: "The dead may guard the treasure, but it's useless
treasure unless it can be brought back into the land of the living and
allowed to enter time once more – which means to enter the realm of the
audience, the realm of the readers, the realm of change."[3] Orpheus' fateful
turn expresses not just an insouciant, transgressive desire for his beloved.
It also communicates a refusal to be held immobile by the past or to be
transfixed by his loss. It circumscribes the fragile enterprise of writing
by reinstating the basis of all storytelling: the return to the present, the
reascent to the earth's surface to be once more amongst others.

The title of this chapter – "the absolutely dark moment of the plot [*le moment absolument sombre de cette intrigue*]" – is one of the ways Blanchot figures the enigmatic return to the present that takes place within his own narratives. This phrase appears in the final paragraph of Blanchot's 1951 *récit*, *When the Time Comes*. As the narrator of this story formulates it, the "absolutely dark moment of the plot" is "the point at which [the plot] keeps returning to the present [*retourne constamment au présent*], at which I can no longer either forget or remember, at which human events, around a center as unstable and immobile as myself, indefinitely construct their return" (*WTC* 260/*AMV* 165). It is the point at which the narrative ceases to be a function of an ideal, fictive or subjective sense of time and instead returns to the present so as to "crush" time in its subjective, fictive or ideal dimensions. As such, it is intimately bound up with the problem of the end of the story. Blanchot's narrative finishes up, somewhat typically, by reflecting upon the problem of its own end. The narrator remarks how "the passion for the end [*la passion de la fin*]" must express itself "eternally" in the present moment: "even if I had to write this eternally [*éternellement*], I would write it in order to obliterate eternity [*pour effacer l'éternel*]: Now, the end" (*WTC* 260/*AMV* 166). In returning to the present, eternity is indeed obliterated. But subjectivity is also elided or neutralised. Subjectivity disappears into the grammatical black hole opened up by the violent collision of the end of the story with the present moment: "Now, the end [*Maintenant, la fin*]."

The speculative question I derive from Blanchot's *récit* is as follows: what is the relation between narrative subjectivity and the end of the story? Claudia, one of the three protagonists in *When the Time Comes*, declares to the narrator at one point in the text: "Nobody here desires to bind themselves to a story [*Personne ici ne désire se lier à une histoire*]" (*WTC* 239/*AMV* 108, trans. mod.). This sentence makes a deep impression on the narrator. He notes: "I thought I saw a light spring from it, I had touched a spot of surprising brightness [*un point d'étonnante clarté*]" (*WTC* 239/*AMV* 108). The "absolutely dark moment of the plot" is, in some sense, the obverse of this "spot of surprising brightness." It is the moment in the narrative in which the reluctance to be bound to a story no longer emanates from the subject, but rather becomes the ethereal rule of narrative itself. It is the point at which the story gains expression without having to bind itself to anybody, that is, without taking place as a function of subjective will or intentionality. Blanchot's *récit*, *The Madness of the Day* (1949/73), ends with an apparent refusal to tell a story: "A story [*récit*]? No. No stories [*pas de récit*], never again" (*MD* 199). But, here, the narrator's refusal to be bound to a story – the very theme and content of the narrative – is no longer entirely subjective in its origin. It no longer comes from a subject who is capable of beginning to tell a story: the narrator, that is, *qua* narrator. Rather, it comes from the end of the story as this elides or erases narrative subjectivity so as to bring about a return to the present and an end to the narrative.

Whether it is expressed positively as possession or negatively as refusal, desire comes to circulate in the narratives cited so far independently of the subjects who first give it expression. The passage of narrative thus comes to be expressed as the passage of desire towards a point of objectivity or externality. Orpheus refuses to accept the premature death of his wife (by snakebite). By going to the Underworld, he tries to reduce the distance between them to nothing. But desire proves to be both irrepressible and irreducible and so he turns and loses Eurydice for a second and final time. His gaze consecrates the distance between them as ever more objective or sensible. As Blanchot notes in *The Infinite Conversation*: "The desire that carries Orpheus forward ... is not an impetus able to clear the interval and pass over absence, even the absence of death" (*IC* 188). Desire betrays Orpheus because it never lets itself become the sole possession of a sole subject. Blanchot writes, again in *The Infinite Conversation*: "Desire is separation itself become that which attracts: an interval become *sensible*, an absence that turns back into presence" (*IC* 188). The significance of the end of the story is that it converts the anthropomorphising desire that circulates between subjects (precisely in terms of possession and refusal) into desire in a pure state: "an interval become *sensible*, an absence that turns back into presence." The interdiction of the gods proves to be productive to the extent that it *allows* desire to exceed the bounds of narrative subjectivity. As Ovid writes with great pathos in his now canonical account of the myth: "What was there [for Eurydice] to complain of, but that she had been loved?"[4] As Orpheus turns against the will of the gods, his desire exceeds the bounds of (his) subjectivity, and enables the other (whether Eurydice or ourselves) to experience desire in a pure state, that is, to be loved by him.

[2] "A DEVASTATING STORY": BLANCHOT ON GENESIS 22

There is perhaps no better place to begin investigating how the end of the story transfigures narrative identity in Blanchot than with his striking reprisal in *When the Time Comes* of a well-known story involving both a binding and an unbinding: the trial of Abraham in Genesis 22. In

Genesis 22, Abraham goes at God's request to Mount Moriah to sacrifice his beloved son, Isaac – only for the human sacrifice to be called off at the last minute by the Angel of the Lord and a ram substituted for the son (Gen. 22:13).[5] Genesis 22 is known in Jewish thought as the *Akedah* or the "binding" in reference to Abraham binding Isaac to the altar in Gen. 22:9. In *When the Time Comes*, Blanchot takes up the story after the climactic moment of the ram's substitution – that is to say, after Isaac's unbinding from the alter. In quasi-midrashic fashion, Blanchot imagines Abraham being confronted on the return home to Beersheba by a mirage of the near-death of his son. He writes:

> When Abraham came back from the country of Moria, he was not accompanied by his child but by the image of a ram [*l'image d'un bélier*] and it was with a ram that he had to live from then on. Others saw the son in Isaac, but they didn't know what had happened on the mountain, but he saw the ram in his son, because he had made a ram for himself out of his child. A devastating story [*Histoire accablante*]. (*WTC* 253/*AMV* 147)[6]

In Blanchot's passage, the image of the ram marks the impossibility of Isaac's death, Isaac's death as it falls – like Gregor transformed into a gigantic insect in Kafka's story *The Metamorphosis* – back into existence. In this sense, it is human death become a mirage. Abraham makes a ram out of his son – produces this mirage – by allowing Isaac to become almost interchangeable with the ram that eventually occupies the place of death in the story. The image of the ram taking Isaac's place on the return to Beersheba thus refolds into the narrative passage of time the thought of Isaac's death as a narrative possibility. No one else can see this because no one else has seen what happened on Mount Moriah. The image thus makes visible – but in a still privative or imaginary way – what otherwise falls outside the register of sight at the end of Genesis 22. This is Isaac's material death as it continues to be a condition of the narrative beyond the moment of the substitution.

Two related readings of Genesis 22 – the one as prominent as the other is obscure – precede and orient Blanchot's own reflections on the story. The first is Søren Kierkegaard's famous 1843 "Dialectical Lyric," *Fear and Trembling*. The other is Franz Kafka's cryptic, posthumous parable, "Abraham," which cobbles together various notebook entries and letters to friends Kafka produced between 1917 and 1921 in response to reading Kierkegaard and, in particular, *Fear and Trembling*.[7] Despite Blanchot being a prodigious and attentive reader of Kierkegaard (the opening review in *Faux Pas* [1943] is of "Kierkegaard's *Journals*"), his account of Genesis 22 emerges more or less directly and more or less unproblematically from his engagement with Kafka and with Kafka's Abraham. Indeed, apart from the passage in *When the Time Comes*, Blanchot only comments on Abraham in essays on Kafka: first in the 1949 essay, "Kafka and Literature"; and then in the 1952 essay, "Kafka and the Work's Demand."

Blanchot is drawn to Kafka's reading of the *Akedah* by the way it displaces the existential melodrama of *Fear and Trembling*. Constituting the narrative of Kierkegaard's text is the decision to downplay the significance of the ram's substitution at the end of the story. "If the one who is to act wants to judge himself by the result," Kierkegaard writes, "he will never begin."[8] "Heroism is not determined by the end(ing) but rather by beginnings."[9] For Kierkegaard, we all know how the story ends; the point is rather to return to the beginning and to reconsider how Abraham heroically overcame "the pain of the trial" in order to become the prototypical "knight of faith."[10] For his part, Kafka disparages this reification of Abraham.[11] He writes to Max Brod in 1918: "[Kierkegaard] doesn't see the ordinary man . . . and paints this monstrous Abraham in the clouds." In a 1921 letter to Robert Klopstock, Kafka paints an utterly unheroic Abraham who "certainly would never have gotten to be patriarch or even an old clothes dealer."[12] In this letter, Kafka even goes so far as to imagine Abraham being prevented from carrying out the sacrifice by the fact of not yet having a son to sacrifice: "It was different for these other Abrahams, who stood in the houses they were building and suddenly had to go up on Mount Moriah; it is possible they didn't even [*noch nicht*] have a son, yet already [*schon*] had to sacrifice him."[13]

This image of Abraham having already to sacrifice a son who does not yet exist fascinates Blanchot; indeed, so much so that he appropriates it in order to figure the paradoxical situation of the writer. For Blanchot, the writer experiences the end of the story not as the triumph of the hero's will (as in Kierkegaard), but as the translation of the "pain of the trial" into imaginary suffering (as in Kafka). By privileging the end of the story over the beginning, Blanchot reverses Kierkegaard's existentialism and upholds Genesis 22 as a narrative very much concerned with the problem of the imaginary and thus with the act of literature. In other words, he figures Abraham's dilemma in Genesis 22 to be that of the writer. As he argues in "Kafka and the Work's Demand," while comparing Kierkegaard's and Kafka's relation to the *Akedah*: "For Kafka, the ordeal [*l'épreuve*] is all the graver [*plus lourde*] because of everything that makes it weigh lightly [*légère*] upon him. (What would the testing [*l'épreuve*] of Abraham be if, having no son, he were nonetheless required to sacrifice this son? He couldn't be taken seriously; he could only be laughed at. That laughter is the form of Kafka's pain)" (*SL* 61/*EL* 69).[14]

[3] MIDRASH DEGREE ZERO

The question being raised by the epiphenomenon of the image of the ram in Blanchot's passage is of how to conceptualise the space of Isaac's near-death *ex post facto*. According to the Jewish sources, this is a space not just of "fear and trembling" (that is, of Abraham's or of Isaac's experience of the trial), but also literally of death (that is, of Sarah's experience of trial). The account of Sarah's death immediately follows the Offering of Isaac. In Genesis 23:1–2, we read: "Sarah lived to be a hundred and twenty-seven years old. She died in Kiryat Arba (that is, Hebron) in the land of Canaan and Abraham went to mourn Sarah and to weep for her." The Rabbis in *Genesis Rabbah* use the narrative proximity of Sarah's death to Isaac's sacrifice to draw the following inference: "From where did [Abraham] come? From Mount Moriah, for Sarah died of that pain."[15]

What does it mean to connect Sarah's death to the *Akedah*? It is perhaps to reconnect the experience of death in the story to the experience of a human death. According to Hebrews 11:19: "Abraham reasoned [in Gen. 22] that God could raise the dead, and figuratively speaking, he did receive Isaac back from death." On this New Testament reading of the story, Abraham's gift of death remains firmly a matter between Abraham and God. But in the Midrash I have just cited, Sarah realises the entirely human death, which Abraham disavows in Genesis 22 by holding to the Christian belief in God's power to resurrect Isaac. That is to say, she takes the place of the ram that has already taken the place of Isaac's death. To connect Sarah's death to the *Akedah* is to re-establish – to re-inscribe in/through/on the body – an economy of mourning and consolation that Abraham can be thought to have suppressed in order to carry out the sacrificial decree. In this sense, Sarah's corpse comes to embody the narrative possibility, eventually elided in Genesis 22, of Isaac's material death. Here, Sarah dies for Isaac. This second substitution in turn goes towards re-covering the lost *mater*iality of Isaac's death and works to undo the ideality of Abraham's sacrificial act by forcing him, in mourning the death of his wife, also to mourn the death of his son. Of course, impossibly: because this death does not take place as such – at least, not in the present.

The rabbinical appeal to Sarah's corpse in Genesis 23 produces a way of reading Genesis 22 otherwise than in terms of the heroic sense of subjectivity required to begin on the trial. In this regard, it opposes the Kierkegaardian reading of the sacrifice. For Kierkegaard, mastering the pain of the trial means interiorising the threat of Isaac's accidental death. But to rethink the *Akedah* in relation to Sarah's death in Genesis 23, as the Rabbis do, is precisely to rethink the dialectic of the sacrifice and the pain of the trial in terms of the role the contingent plays in the story. If Isaac is the indispensable condition for the beginning of the story (Gen. 22:2: "Take your son, your only son, Isaac, whom you love"), then the ram is the indispensable condition for the end of the story. The "absolutely dark moment of the plot," as I am describing it, occurs at the point at which the condition for the end of the story interferes with the condition for the beginning so as to assume priority over it. As the image of the ram obscures Isaac on the way home from the country of Moriah, narrative is shown to take place no longer in terms of the movement of heroic subjectivity, but rather in terms of the narrative accident that displaces the telos of heroic subjectivity. This is the pain of the trial as it refuses to be contained by Abraham's sacrificial actions – as it still offers a way to account for the contingent fact of Sarah's death.

By linking Sarah's death directly to the *Akedah*, the Rabbis begin to think the material presence of death in the *Akedah*: death as it precisely invokes the mater and the mother figure as it in turn allows for mourning. Connecting Sarah's death to Isaac's sacrifice in this way makes it possible to read the substitution of the ram as otherwise than figurative. Here, Isaac's sacrifice becomes identified with a *type* of death which paradoxically gains significance by refusing to stand in meaningful relation with anything outside it. Sarah's death re-presents the non-eventuation of the sacrifice as producing an experience of materiality outside all living experience – that is, the experience of the corpse. My claim is that this is the intended effect of the image of the ram in Blanchot's *récit*. The image confronts Abraham with that which it was impossible for him to confront during the sacrifice. This is the thought of the corpse: the materiality of the other's death as it neither coincides nor coheres with the ideality of the sacrifice.

[4] "THE THOUGHT THAT IDEALISM HAS, FINALLY, NO
  GUARANTEE OTHER THAN A CORPSE": BLANCHOT ON THE
  IMAGE AND THE CORPSE

An appendix essay to *The Space of Literature*, "The Two Versions of the Imaginary [*Les Deux Versions de l'imaginaire*]" (1952), composed around the time of *When the Time Comes*, proves pivotal in formulating this link between the image and the corpse. Blanchot there proposes two versions of the imaginary. The first concerns the production of ideal meaning; the second the obscure materiality of which this production is the telltale sign. Blanchot writes:

> The image can, when it wakens or when we awaken it, represent the object to us in a luminous *formal* aura; but it is nonetheless with *substance* [*fond*: depth, matter, background, end, extremity] that the image is allied – with the fundamental materiality, the still undetermined absence of form, the world oscillating between adjective and substantive before foundering in the formless prolixity of indeterminacy. Hence the passivity proper to the image – a passivity which makes us suffer the image even when we ourselves appeal to it, and makes its fugitive transparency stem from the obscurity of fate [*l'obscurité du destin*] returned to its essence, which is to be a shade. (*SL* 255/*EL* 342)

As this passage indicates, Blanchot only treats the first version of the imaginary cursorily; it is with the second that he is truly concerned. According to the first version, the image helps us grasp something formally or ideally. The image holds the thing or situation at a temporal distance in order for it to be comprehended within a system of meaning or truth. In the temporal gap that separates the image from the thing represented, death functions productively to convert the material, the substantial into the ideal. Put in somewhat Hegelian terms, the image is thus the life-giving negation of the thing: prolix matter negated into meaning.

"We might bear in mind," Blanchot writes in "Two Versions of the Imaginary," "the thought that idealism has, finally, no guarantee other than a corpse [*n'ait . . . d'autre garant qu'un cadavre*]" (*SL* 258/*EL* 347).[16] According to the second version of the imaginary, the version Blanchot privileges as the precondition of the first, the image resembles the corpse, which in turn bears a resemblance to nothing. The corpse shares with the image a propensity to suspend the relation to place. "Death suspends the relation to place . . . the place is missing, the corpse is not in its place. Where is it? It is not here, and yet it is nowhere else. Nowhere? But then nowhere is here" (*SL* 256/*EL* 344). The corpse suspends the relation to place precisely by over-determining (its) place: by transforming the here and now – the present – into nowhere. "The corpse is here, but here in turn becomes a corpse: it becomes 'here below [*ici-bas*]' in absolute terms, for there is not yet any 'above [*là haut*]' to be exalted" (*SL* 256/*EL* 344).

Here, death does not (re)present a productive transformation whereby, according to the first version of the imaginary, meaning always escapes into another meaning. Rather, death figures as a bleak substitution – of the known and the living for the dead and unknown, of the here and now for the no(w)here.

A second characteristic the image shares with the corpse is the propensity for self-resemblance. For Blanchot, while "no man alive, in fact, bears any resemblance yet," the corpse shows itself to be "similarity par excellence" (*SL* 258/*EL* 347).

> The corpse appears in the strangeness of its solitude as that which has disdainfully withdrawn from us. Then the feeling of a relation between humans is destroyed, and our mourning, the care we take of the dead and all the prerogatives of our former passions, since they no longer know their direction, fall back upon us, return toward us. It is striking that at this very moment, when the cadaverous presence is the presence of the unknown before us, the mourned deceased begins to resemble *himself* . . . The cadaver is its own image [*sa propre image*]. It no longer entertains any relation with this world, where it still appears, except that of an image, an obscure possibility, a shadow ever present behind the living form which now, far from separating itself from this form, transforms it entirely into shadow. (*SL* 257–8/*EL* 346–7)

In Blanchot's schema, the image also addresses us from the inhuman place at which the relation with the living other is lost and true mourning becomes impossible. This address in turn breaches our sense of interiority, that is, the sense in which we might identify ourselves purely by way of deep interiority.

> The image speaks to us, and seems to speak intimately to us of ourselves. But the term "intimately [*intimement*]" does not suffice. Let us say rather that the image intimately designates the level where personal intimacy [*l'intimité de la personne*] is destroyed and that it indicates in this movement the menacing proximity of a vague and empty outside [*d'un dehors vague et vide*], the deep, the sordid basis upon which it continues to affirm things in their disappearance. Thus it speaks to us, à propos of each thing, of less than this thing, but of us. And, speaking of us, it speaks to us of less than us, of that less than nothing that subsists [*demeure*] when there is nothing. (*SL* 254/*EL* 341)

The image, like the corpse, is "not the same thing at a distance [*éloignée*] but the thing as distance [*comme éloignement*], present in its absence" (*SL* 255–6/*EL* 343). It is substitution as it stops us from projecting the differential of ourselves – our productive or lively lack of self-resemblance

– onto the object or situation being represented. The image is in this sense objectivity as it utterly refuses subjective manipulation. It is substitution that is no longer differential (and deferential) but absolute – substitution whereby one thing merely supplants another: the blow of substitution.

Blanchot asks: "What happens, for example, when one lives an event as an image?" He answers in a way that bears directly upon the passage in *When The Time Comes* I am seeking to interpret:

> To live an event as an image is not to see an image of this event, nor is it to attribute to the event the gratuitous character of the imaginary. The event really takes place [*a lieu vraiment*] – and yet does it "really'" take place? The occurrence commands us, as we would command the image. That is, it releases us, from it and from ourselves. It keeps us outside; it makes of this outside a presence where "I" does not recognise "itself" [*"Je" ne "se" reconnaît pas*]. This movement implies infinite degrees. (*SL* 262/*EL* 353)

That Abraham comes to live the event of Genesis 22 as an image does not mean that the event becomes imaginary. The event really takes place; really has a place. But the place – in which the Lord provides in place of (Moriah) – only provokes a sense of placelessness. The retroactive effect of the image is to divest Abraham of his commanding presence in the event, of his ability to distinguish between his son (the unique and irreplaceable condition for the beginning of the story) and the ram (the unique and irreplaceable condition for the end of the story). The passing of the event carries him outside himself – into the space of the outside, which is dedicated "not to the resurrection embodied in conceptual thought [that is, the ideality of the sacrifice, the hope of Isaac's return], but to the unthinkable singularity that precedes the concept as its simultaneous condition of possibility and impossibility."[17] The unthinkable singularity conditioning the possibility and the impossibility of conceptual thought is the event horizon that resides outside the dialectic of (the) sacrifice. This is not the ideality of Isaac's death, which always remains thinkable or calculable within the dialectic of the sacrifice. It is rather Isaac's death as it can be linked to Sarah's corpse – death as it attaches itself to the incalculable and material response of the other to the sacrifice, death as it remains involved with the substitution at the end of the story. The contingency that cannot be accounted for or sublated here is the sense of death that attaches itself to the outside perspective. Abraham begins to experience this perspective – this non-productive relation to death – in the persistence of the image of the ram, that is, as he remains unable to reverse the effect of the substitution and becomes aware of the terrifying incommensurability opening up between his fated act and his character.

In supplanting Isaac's identity on the return to Beersheba, the image of the ram reverses the traditional meaningfulness of the story, transforming it from *histoire* [story, history] into *histoire accablante*: story/history which overwhelms history. The power of the image, as Blanchot here invokes it, is the power to reverse the first version of the imaginary into the second, to interrupt or un-work the possibility of meaningful or idealised temporal slippage upon which the first version is based. Whence: "Here, *meaning* does not escape into another [*un autre*] meaning, but into the *other* [*l'autre*] of all meaning" (*SL* 263/*EL* 354). According to the second version of the imaginary, the statement to which the corpse attests in its self-resemblance – namely, that "man is made in his image [*L'homme est fait à son image*]" – must first be understood as "*Man is unmade according to his image* [*l'homme est défait selon son image*]" (*SL* 260/*EL* 350, original emphasis). This is because where there is complete self-resemblance, there is no longer any man. For Blanchot, literature begins with the recognition of this anachronistic reversal of absolute subjectivity – the illusion of the purely spiritual act, Kierkegaard's Abraham – into absolute objectivity and passivity. It begins, that is to say, when one recognises the ideal leap of faith to be predicated, paradoxically, upon the temporal and material contiguity of Sarah's corpse to that leap.

For Blanchot, literature begins with the phenomenal passivity one experiences before the corpse. Literature, he writes in "Literature and the Right to Death," wants "Lazarus in the tomb and not Lazarus brought back into the daylight, the one who already smells bad" (*WF* 327). On June 4, 1966, René Magritte wrote to Michel Foucault of his decision to replace the figures in Manet's painting *Le Balcon* (1868) with coffins: "Why did I see coffins where Manet saw pale figures? . . . *Perspective: Le Balcon de Manet* [1950] implies its own answer: The image, my painting reveals where the décor of the 'Balcony' is suitable for placing coffins."[18] Similarly, the myth of Orpheus and Eurydice presents to Blanchot as a story of the creative act because of the way it substitutes the corpse for the pale figure. The image Orpheus must use in his song to recover Eurydice is inevitably the image – the sense of self-resemblance – she projects as a corpse. As Blanchot notes in *The Writing of the Disaster*: "The mortal leap of the writer without which he would not write is necessarily an illusion to the extent that, in order really to be accomplished, it must not take place" (*WD* 64). For Blanchot, Orpheus' great activity – of going to the underworld by the power of his own will – is an illusion and thus a passivity predicated on the double sense of the corpse and the imaginary. Orpheus' heroic journey to the underworld figures the journey of interiority, the absolute idealism of which must nonetheless be disavowed at the surface of the earth: that is, before the unimpeachable reality of the corpse. In this sense, Orpheus makes his *salto mortale* only by failing to leave Eurydice's side, by confirming the experience of incommensurable exteriority before her corpse to be the anachronistic precondition for his art. The artist is fated to begin with the after-image, the end of the story as it nonetheless produces the illusion of the heroic beginning. The artist, the writer is alone before the corpse rather than God – moreover, only in order to acknowledge the priority of the *socius*.

The passivity proper to the experience of the corpse is that proper to literature itself: "a passivity which makes us suffer the image even when we ourselves appeal to it, and makes its fugitive transparency stem from the obscurity of fate returned to its essence, which is to be a shade" (*SL* 255/*EL* 342). In Blanchot's account of Genesis 22, Abraham suffers the image – as Orpheus suffers the loss of Eurydice – as the obscurity of his fate returned to its essence. This is his sacrificial act as it begins to resemble itself, detach itself from the question of his character and preclude him (or anyone else, for that matter) from identifying with it or gaining a sense of identity from it. As Blanchot writes in *When the Time Comes*: "To bind oneself [*Se lier*] to a reflection – who would consent to that? But to bind oneself [*se lier*] to what has no name and no face and to give that endless, wandering resemblance the depth of a mortal instant, to lock oneself up with it and thrust it along with oneself to the place where all resemblance yields and is shattered – that is what passion wants" (*WTC* 258/*AMV* 161). To live an event as an image – to bind oneself passionately to its reflection – is to experience the event as it has become a corpse and the blow of substitution. Read in these terms, Genesis 22 presents not just the making of Abraham's character, as Kierkegaard argues, but also as Kafka and Blanchot attest, the unmaking of it. This movement – from the pure activity of faith to the pure passivity of suffering the image – implies infinite degrees.

[5] THE INSTANT OF MY DEATH

The treatment of Genesis 22 in *When the Time Comes* perhaps calls to mind a "devastating story" bound up with Blanchot's own fate: namely, "The Instant of my Death" (1994). This *récit* recounts the near-death by firing squad of a young man we are encouraged to identify as the young Blanchot. We now know that Blanchot himself was almost summarily executed in the summer of 1944 when the Vlassov army passed by his family home in Quain, Saône-et-Loire.[19] In the story, a feeling of incommensurable lightness accompanies the failure of the protagonist's death to take place as expected. This feeling of lightness overturns the initial assumption of the event as an entirely private experience – "The young man said, 'At least have my family go inside'" (*ID* 5) – and enables others (including the protagonist's own self as another) to identify with the event's passing: that is, to live the event as an image.

Blanchot writes:

> There remained [*Demeurait*], however, at the moment when the shooting was no longer still to come the feeling of lightness [*le sentiment de légèreté*] that I would not know how to translate: freed from life? the infinite opening up [*l'infini qui s'ouvre*]? Neither happiness, nor unhappiness. Nor the absence of fear [*crainte*] and perhaps already the step beyond [*le pas au-delà*]. I know, I imagine that this unanalysable feeling changed what there remained for him of existence. As if the death outside of him could only henceforth [*désormais*] collide with the death inside him. "I am alive. No, you [*tu*] are dead." (*ID* 8–9)

For Blanchot, the neutralisation of the existential relation contained in the image is accompanied by the awakening to suffering outside the self: "No doubt what then began for the young man was the torment of injustice" (*ID* 7). What conditions this awakening – this tormented fall back into existence – is the imagination of the corpse ("No, you are dead") that immediately empties the affirmation of absolute subjectivity ("I am alive") of all sense of absolution. In this unmaking of the first version of the imaginary by the second, the "I" becomes without a self, without existence, without. As Derrida noted in his speech at Blanchot's cremation (on Monday, 24 February 2003), "A Witness Forever": "'I am alive. No, you are dead,' these two voices compete for or share speech in us. And conversely: I am dead. No, you are alive."[20]

In "Reading Kafka," Blanchot reflects upon literature's astonishing capacity to generate a state of permanent *peripeteia*:

> If each word [*terme*], each image, each story [*récit*] can signify its opposite – and the opposite of that as well – then we must seek the cause of that in the transcendence of death that makes it attractive, unreal, and impossible, and that deprives us of the only truly absolute ending, without depriving us of its mirage. Death dominates us, but it dominates us by its impossibility. (*WF* 9/*PF* 17)

In *When the Time Comes*, Blanchot uses the trial of Genesis 22 to show how literary narrative "deprives us of the only truly absolute ending, without depriving us of its mirage." When Abraham confronts the mirage of his son's near-death on the return home from Moriah, he not only confronts the traumatic kernel of his purely private religious act but also the condition of narrative itself. As he returns to the present, if only to obliterate the eternality of his act, he experiences "the transcendence of death that makes it attractive, unreal, and impossible." This is the image of the end of the story as it displaces the existentiality of the beginning: the ram as it obscures the beloved son. In this moment, death dominates him, but by its impossibility. This impossibility in turn takes the form of a story, a *récit*, in which "Once upon a time" becomes "Now, the end" and in which "I am alive" becomes "No, you are dead."

[6] "WRITE." – "FOR WHOM?" – "WRITE FOR THE DEAD . . ."

Kierkegaard – who published *Repetition* along with *Fear and Trembling* on 16 October 1843 – intended to include two versions of "An old saying" as epigraphs to *Fear and Trembling*. The first was directly inspired by Herder and read as follows:

> "Write." – "For whom?" – "Write for the dead, for those in the past whom you love." – "Will they read me?" – "Yes, for they come back as posterity." (An old saying)

The second was to be the same dialogue, slightly but crucially altered.

> "Write." – "For whom?" – "Write for the dead, for those in the past whom you love." – "Will they read me?" – "No!" (An old saying slightly altered)[21]

With this defiant "No!" the writer gives up the desire to monumentalise himself through the act of writing. The return to the present at the same time paradoxically disconnects him from all sense of historical continuity – indeed, even from the instant of his own death. The paradox finally to emerge here is that writing is a negotiating with the dead, which takes place nowhere else but here and now. Orpheus must reascend to the surface because, in a sense, he has never left it. His descent has been (into the) imaginary. He is still before Eurydice's corpse as this in turn signifies death's irreversibility.

The section of *The Gay Science* in which Nietzsche introduces the notion of the eternal return (§341) is entitled, "*The greatest weight* [*Das grösste Schwergewicht*]." In it, Nietzsche posits the thought of the eternal return as a paradoxical way to escape living as a man of *ressentiment*:

> If this thought [of eternal return] gained possession of you, it would change you as you are or perhaps crush you. The question in each and every thing, "Do you desire this once more and innumerable times more?" would lie upon your actions like the greatest weight. Or how well disposed would you have to become to yourself and to life to crave nothing more fervently than this ultimate eternal confirmation and seal?[22]

Blanchot's fiction – with the same desire to escape the problem of *ressentiment* – nonetheless figures "this ultimate eternal confirmation and seal" not as a great weight upon existence but as an incommensurable lightness – a moment without existence, an experience of the image and of the imaginary.

ENDNOTES

[1] Margaret Atwood, *Negotiating with the Dead: A Writer on Writing* (London: Virago, 2003), 160.

[2] In a letter to Evelyn London, Blanchot approves of the story of Orpheus as an interpretive lens for his works of fiction: "*le sujet . . . me semble très justifié:* L'Arrêt de mort, Celui qui ne m'accompagnait pas, Au moment voulu *et aussi d'une manière plus désespérante (peut-être, mais peut-être non)* Le Dernier Homme *ou* L'Attente l'oubli *sont portés par ce mouvement* [the subject seems to me very justified: *Death Sentence, The One Who Was Standing Apart From Me, When the Time Comes* and in a more provoking way (perhaps, but perhaps not) *The Last Man, Awaiting Oblivion* are carried by this movement]." Cited in Gary D. Mole, "Blanchot's *Au moment voulu* and the Silence of Abraham", *Australian Journal of French Studies*, 32:1 (1995), 58, my translation.

[3] Atwood, *Negotiating with the Dead*, 160.

[4] See *The Metamorphoses of Ovid*, trans. Mary M. Innes (Harmondsworth: Penguin, 1955), Bk. X, ll. 60–1.

[5] All references are to The Holy Bible, New International Version (Grand Rapids, Michigan: Zondervan Publishing House, 1984).

[6] There is not space here to read this passage in relation to Blanchot's *récit* as a whole. For good discussions of Abraham in *When the Time Comes* see Mole, "Blanchot's *Au moment voulu* and the Silence of Abraham"; and Larysa Mykyta, "Blanchot's *Au moment voulu*: Women as the eternally recurring figure of writing", *boundary 2*, 2.2 (Winter 1982), 77–95.

[7] Franz Kafka, *Parables and Paradoxes*, ed. Nahum N. Glatzer, in German and English (New York: Schocken Books, 1961 [1935]).

[8] Søren Kierkegaard, *Fear and Trembling / Repetition*, ed. and trans. Howard V. Hong and Edna H. Hong (Princeton, NJ: Princeton University Press, 1983 [1843]), 63.

[9] Sylviane Agacinski, *Aparté: Deaths and Conceptions of Søren Kierkegaard*, trans. Kevin Newmark (Tallahassee: Florida State University Press, 1988), 91.

[10] Kierkegaard, *Fear and Trembling / Repetition*, 53.

[11] Agacinski takes up this problem in her essay "We Are Not Sublime: Love, Sacrifice, Abraham and Ourselves", in *Kierkegaard: A Critical Reader*, ed. Jonathan Rée and Jane Chamberlain, (Oxford: Blackwell, 1998). She writes: "We tremble before the man of faith just as he trembled before his God. Abraham encountered the mystery of God, but we only encounter the mystery of Abraham" (144).

[12] Kafka, *Parables and Paradoxes*, 42.

[13] Kafka, *Parables and Paradoxes*, 43.

[14] What else is laughter, one might ask, but a form of imaginary pain? When Sarah overhears God promising her and Abraham a son in Genesis 18:12, she "laughed to herself as she thought: 'After I am worn out [that is, barren] and my is master old, will I now have this pleasure?'" In Hebrew, the name Isaac means "he laughs."

[15] *Genesis Rabbah: The Judaic Commentary to the Book of Genesis*, trans. Jacob Neusner (Atlanta: Scholars Press, 1985), 58:5.

[16] "The Two Versions of the Imaginary" responds in part to Levinas' polemic against the image in "Reality and its Shadow," first published in Sartre's journal, *Les Temps modernes*, in 1948. See Emmanuel Levinas, *Collected Philosophical Papers*, trans. Alphonso Lingis (Boston: Martinus Nijhoff, 1987).

[17] Leslie Hill, *Blanchot: Extreme Contemporary* (London: Routledge, 1997), 112.

[18] Michel Foucault, *This is not a Pipe*, trans. James Harkness (Berkeley: University of California Press, 1982), 56.

[19] See *Nowhere Without No: In Memory of Maurice Blanchot*, ed. Kevin Hart (Sydney: Vagabond, 2003), 7, 21–2. In "A Witness Forever," Derrida testifies to receiving a package from Blanchot with *L'Instant de ma mort* and a letter that begins: "July 20 [1994], fifty years ago I experienced the happiness of being almost shot. Twenty-five years ago, we set foot on the moon" (41). See also *ID* 52.

[20] Derrida, "A Witness Forever", 47.

[21] Kierkegaard, *Fear and Trembling / Repetition*, 244.

[22] Friedrich Nietzsche, *The Gay Science*, trans. Walter Kaufmann (New York: Vintage Books, 1974), 274.

MIDNIGHT, OR THE INERTIA OF BEING

Eleanor Kaufman

THERE IS HARDLY A MORE CONSISTENT THINKER THAN MAURICE BLANCHOT. His work is disarming in its weave of fiction and philosophy, in its timeless anonymity, its undoing of the dialectic, and the affirmation of worklessness and the community of those who have nothing in common. Though in a sense elusive, this work is also infinitely substitutable. Almost any paragraph of Blanchot's is quintessentially Blanchotian. It is daunting, then, if not impossible, to suggest and delineate a fissure that runs through Blanchot's œuvre, a fissure between the liminal, atemporal, fleeting instant and the more weighty inertia of presentness, the inertia of being. It is this fissure that also marks a profound yet barely palpable divide between the thought of Blanchot and Deleuze, especially with regard to the realms of temporality and ontology. While Blanchot's notion of Midnight resonates most strongly with a Deleuzian insistence on temporal becoming (as opposed to present being), it also gestures to a state that is beyond becoming in that it is too unworkable, too inert. It is my claim that this inertia, rather than marking a lesser or pathological state, may point to a new path for ontology.

Midnight would seem to be always to come, or always just past. It is never purely present, but another time composed of the interplay of past and future, the time of infinite becoming. Deleuze would call this time of becoming Aion, as opposed to the static being of present time, or Chronos. Indeed, Deleuze evokes Blanchot's "personal and present death" (the death the self chooses to die) as opposed to his "impersonal and infinitive death" (the other death that chooses you, where this is no longer a self to choose) in the process of elaborating how the atemporal time of Aion is, like the other death, at odds with an immobile presentness.[1] In this regard, Midnight's out-of-timeliness marks a strong convergence between Deleuzian and Blanchotian formulations of an atemporal temporality, a state of becoming as opposed to being that conjoins past and future but is outside of present, static, chronological time. It would seem, too, that Deleuze and Blanchot coincide in their mutual eschewal of the dialectic insofar as it stands in for a present and positive ontology (or at least in so far as Deleuze eschews the present and Blanchot the positive). If there is a difference at stake between Blanchot and Deleuze, it is a difference that centers on ontology's movements, or lack thereof. If Deleuze redeems being by perceiving its hidden potential for movement, Blanchot affirms being by perceiving its disarming potential for inertia.

It is hard to be, really, in the presence of inertia. Inertia is deceptive in that it might appear to be going somewhere (I am working to clean up the house and move out of here), while at the same time quietly asserting itself in its active inaction. Deleuze writes of American literature that the "becoming is geographical. There is no equivalent in France. The French are too human, too historical, too concerned with the future and the past. . . . To flee is not exactly to travel, or even to move. . . . Flights can happen on the spot, in motionless travel."[2] It is interesting to note that, among their mobile contemporaries, Deleuze and Blanchot stand out as two great twentieth-century French thinkers who did not travel, did not move. Yet, if there is a difference to be distilled between these two thinkers, and even within Blanchot's corpus, it is to be found around the issue of movement. What is always at issue for Deleuze is a movement of thought, which is a movement of becoming, even if one does not travel, even if one stands still. In this regard, though both Blanchot and Deleuze shun the dialectic, there is nevertheless a hidden dialectic punctuated by the uneasy relation between movement and stillness: even if there would seem to be a stoppage of physical movement, there is still the potential for a movement of thought.

On the one hand, Blanchot is quite close to Deleuze, though in what follows I will seek to locate a distinct space of difference. In the vein of Deleuze, it would seem that all of Blanchot's work hinges on the enunciation of a type of textual movement. This is a movement of circularity and repetition that characterizes both Blanchot's critical work and his fiction and that is articulated with particular clarity in *The Space of Literature*. The movement of Blanchot's thought is one of excessive repetition; yet this repetition is always slightly displaced – it is not repetition in the strictest sense but rather a movement that doubles back upon itself in a circular fashion. A series of sentences from a three-page span of *The Space of Literature* illustrates this circular movement:

> To write *is* to surrender to the fascination of time's absence. The
> time of time's absence has no present, no presence. ... The time
> of time's absence *is* not dialectical.... The reversal which, in time's
> absence, points us constantly back to the presence of absence. ...
> The dead present *is* the impossibility of making any presence real ...
> Here fascination reigns. ... and fascination *is* passion for the image.
> ... Fascination *is* solitude's gaze. ... To write *is* to enter into the
> affirmation of the solitude in which fascination threatens. (*SL* 30–3)

Blanchot explicates in a definitional way a series of terms that are related yet
metonymically displaced. Here, this chain of displacements circles around
the term "fascination," though almost all of Blanchot's sentences could
be mapped in a similar fashion onto other sentences which they repeat
and enhance through the same circular movement of displaced repetition.
This formal movement indeed mirrors the content of Blanchot's statements, for, like "the time of time's absence," it would appear not to be
dialectical, to have no presence as such, no temporality as such, just a
reign of fascination. Blanchot's writing, his phrasing, is at one with the
theme of movement that does not move, that reverberates as a central
tenet of Blanchot's thought, and resonates also so clearly with Deleuze.

Certainly Blanchot's insistence, at the level of the verb, on the
ontological in the form of the "is," is of a piece with the slightly displaced
repetition of his writing style. His incessant repetition of the verb "to be,"
usually in the form of the word "is" (emphasized in the quote above), is
simultaneously a stylistic and a theoretical motif in his writing, one of the
many points where the form and the content of his work merge. Blanchot
frequently relates a certain idea of being, one encapsulated by the words "it
is," to his notion of literature or the work of art. He writes that "the work
– the work of art, the literary work – is neither finished nor unfinished; it
is" (*SL* 22). Also, "the poem – literature – seems to be linked to a spoken
word which cannot be interrupted because it does not speak; it is" (*SL* 37).
This "is-ness," this ontology of the work of art, is also its impossibility, for
its supreme moment of becoming is also its dissolution:

> But this exigency, which makes the work declare being in the unique
> moment of rupture – "those very words: *it is*," the point which the
> work brilliantly illuminates even while receiving its consuming burst
> of light – we must also comprehend and feel that this point renders
> the work impossible, because it never permits arrival at the work. It
> is a region anterior to the beginning where nothing is made of being,
> and in which nothing is accomplished. It is the depth of being's inertia
> [*désœuvrement*]. (*SL* 46)

On the one hand, this "is" marks the juncture of being and becoming, that point where being becomes nothingness. Such a juncture is also the space of Blanchot's text. Marked by the recurrent "is" of being, Blanchot's writing propels this "is" along in a circular and repetitive movement that is the mark of becoming. This is a type of movement that never really attains a goal or even a concrete expression of thought. If anything, the movement works to obscure thought, but in this act it illustrates thought of another order, an even more exterior form of thought. Yet, on the other hand, is "the depth of being's inertia," being's seeming unworking, not also beckoning to an ontology of its own, even while resisting such a fixedness of being? Is this, moreover, the slight difference between the "it is" and the "there is" (*es gibt, il y a*)? While both express an ontological encounter, the *il y a*, with all its Heideggerian and Levinasian inflections, would evoke a being towards something, an ontological state where some form of movement is at issue, whereas the "it is" is what stops movement, is much more emphatically inert, all that there is.

This interpretative bifurcation is nowhere better emblematized than in the Blanchotian figure of Midnight. For all its fleetingness, Midnight's ever receding presence nevertheless suggests an ontology of the present that is to some extent at odds with the tenor of Blanchot's œuvre. Midnight, which Blanchot discusses in *The Space of Literature* in his chapter on Mallarmé's *Igitur*, serves as a figure for the circular movement of Blanchot's thought. Midnight marks both the repetitiveness and the perpetual displacement of time. Midnight indeed recurs every day, comes back around in a circular motion – actually the motion of a double circle – but it is never the same midnight as the day before. Some midnights are more officially commemorated than others, such as the midnight which is New Year's Eve, and these midnights signal the passing of a greater expanse of time, recalling as they do the previous year's midnight instead of the previous day's. But in all its forms, midnight is a unique entity that punctuates the repetitiveness, the doubling back, and the circularity of time. In this regard, it serves as a mise-en-abyme for the movement of Blanchot's thought, which is characterized by the same patterns. Blanchot himself comments on the import of the circular nature of thought: "Whenever thought is caught in a circle, this is because it has touched upon something original, its point of departure beyond which it cannot move except to return" (*SL* 93).[3]

Midnight thus bears witness to the convergence of being and becoming that is registered in Blanchot's use of "is." Midnight is, in a sense, always in the process of becoming. It is something that, except for a fleeting instant, is either about to happen or already just past. As Blanchot writes, "Midnight is precisely the hour which has never yet come, which never comes, the pure, ungraspable future, the hour eternally past" (*SL* 116). This evocation of Midnight is remarkably similar to Deleuze's depiction of Aion, the time of the event, in *The Logic of Sense*: "the event in turn, in its impassibility and impenetrability, has no present. It rather retreats and advances in two directions at once, being the perpetual object of a double question: What is going to happen? What has just happened? The agonizing aspect of the pure event is that it is always and at the same time something which has just happened and something about to happen; never something which is happening."[4] The instant of Midnight's being is the momentary present of pure nothingness. Midnight is not the marker of anything tangible; there is nothing out there but darkness and night; yet, because of this daily moment of nothingness, time is made to repeat its continual circle of becoming. Midnight itself never really "is"; it is an absent presence, one that is only registered as presence because of the movement of its becoming. In this, it would seem to be the pure parallel of Blanchot's writing.

Yet alongside this incessant becoming lurks a strange persistence of being, for the nothingness of midnight inaugurates and mediates the movement of time and in this respect enables time's presence to be measured. This presence that comes from absence leads to an affirmation that is not counterbalanced by negation. Blanchot explicates this in his reading of Mallarmé, and once again gestures to a hidden ontology:

> One can say that Mallarmé saw this nothing in action; he experienced the activity of absence. In absence he grasped a presence, a strength still persisting, as if in nothingness there were a strange power of affirmation. . . . It is in unreality itself that the poet encounters the resistance of a muffled presence. It is unreality from which he cannot free himself; it is in unreality that, disengaged from beings, he meets with the mystery of "those very words: *it is.*" And this is not because in the unreal something subsists . . . but because when there is nothing, it is this nothing itself which can no longer be negated. It affirms, keeps on affirming, and it states nothingness as being, the inertia of being [*le désœuvrement de l'être*]. (*SL* 109–10)

In this passage, Blanchot is at his most Deleuzian in that he repeatedly emphasizes the power of affirmation over negation, the affirmation of nothingness. Yet here, and in strange resonance with Sartre, this affirmed nothingness is also being in its most pure and elusive state.[5] This being is signaled by the "mystery" of "it is." However, this being is also something beyond movement, beyond an ever fleeting march and retraction of time. It is precisely, once again, "the inertia of being." And yet, how is this inertia also an affirmation of nothingness? For isn't inertia in some sense a surplus of presence, a plenitude of stuckness, and in this sense not entirely nothing?

This inertia of being is dramatized throughout Blanchot's fiction, which, if such a narrative-defying *œuvre* can be categorized according to any one narrative rubric, is constantly restaging a scenario where people are stuck in living spaces – houses, apartments, infernal institutions, hotel rooms. Often they just walk in and stay put, as in *Aminadab* and *When the Time Comes*. Sometimes we don't entirely know how they got there, as in the strange concentrationary institution of "The Idyll" or the elongated hotel room of *L'Attente l'oubli* (*Awaiting Oblivion*). But in almost every case, the most striking thing is that they don't or don't want to or cannot leave, even when it seems like that wouldn't be the hardest thing to do (reminiscent of Buñuel's *The Exterminating Angel*). It is never clear why the narrator of *When the Time Comes* appears unannounced one day at the apartment of his friend Judith and her friend Claudia, whom he has not met before, and just stays there, barely acknowledging that there is a world outside. In one of the rare moments where there is any mention of a space outside the apartment, the narrator rather paradoxically maintains that he could just walk out the door and join this outside world: "If it hadn't been so great, the deception would have been final. I would have left. I, too, would have gone into the front hall, and from there rejoined the tranquil flow of the rue de la Victoire and gone down towards the Opéra, which I liked at that hour, and I would have been happy" (*WTC* 21).[6] Yet, like the dinner party guests in *The Exterminating Angel* who remain unable simply to cross the threshold and leave the space of the imprisoning house, Blanchot's narrator remains stuck behind the immaterial boundary of the space of the apartment, too immobile to leave despite his perception that he might happily do so.

It seems that what makes the characters and situations in Blanchot's *récits* so disarming is that they don't leave when they might, that they are driven by a relentless yet almost lighthearted inertia. On this count alone, it is not surprising that Blanchot's fiction is sometimes evoked alongside the likes of Beckett or Melville's "Bartleby," for who can surpass these writers in portraying such incredible stuckness so calmly? What is disarming in these writers is that the customary weight of such profound immobility also has such a lightness, even though, as in Bartleby's case, it may be deadly. One might even say there is a mobility or affirmation or becoming to this stuckness. But does that mean it can then be located in the atemporal time of Deleuze's Aion, of the past-future disjunction? While to some degree it does partake of the temporality of Aion, this stuckness conjures more nearly an arrested, endless present over and above a convergence of past and future. Such an endless present marks a dwelling in being, a sticking with being, far beyond the ordinary. In other words, great stuckness seems to be, if anything, an excess of being – pure, immobile, profound being. For usually being is not this stuck and not this pure. Usually being is grounded in a narrative, in a task at hand, in something that makes it unstuck and undead. If Midnight is always arriving and always past, yet never exactly there, Blanchot's characters are on the contrary minimally arriving and never leaving, and always entirely there, so much so that they might paradoxically seem not to be, because their thereness is hard to fathom. Like Bartleby, who moves in to his boss's office and refuses to vacate the premises, this intensity of not leaving is its own form of aggressive passivity.

It is easy to comprehend movement. Globalization and cosmopolitanism and travel and exile may be subjected to and incorporated into a range of critical positions, but on a fundamental level, they are not challenging to understand. One might debate the stakes and goals and nexuses of power behind such movements on the global scale, but the fact that movement happens, and that movement is basically a good thing even if it is the product of bad forces, would seem to be the unstated assumption behind the logic of globalization. But what about people who fall outside this framework? (There is, to be sure, a whole ecological world – trees, rocks, etc. – that falls outside this framework, but since it doesn't bother most people that a tree or a rock, as opposed to a human being, would be stuck and not moving, I will leave aside this line of speculation.[7]) People who don't move, whether willfully or not, form the least examined aspect of cosmopolitan discourse. Though much attention may be given to the question of the local, it is generally not at the level of the phenomenology of what it means to inhabit the local, for anyone trying to analyze or write about that realm is almost necessarily and by definition not in it.

We are trained not to look for immobility, or if we find it not to stare at it in the face. If someone never leaves their house or crosses their state line, it seems like a lesser way of being, at least from the world of the mobile intelligentsia. But could it be that what such a form presents is not so much a state to be pitied but a state that is too challenging to look at because it represents a fullness of being that we are not accustomed to encountering, at least we in the classes of the largely mobile community of scholars? Deleuze writes of Herzog's films that they comprise two forms, the Small and the Large (just as he argues that Melville's fiction portrays the greatly good and the greatly evil).[8] He notes:

> in both cases – the sublimation of the large form and the enfeeblement of the small form – Herzog is a metaphysician. He is the most metaphysical of cinema directors. . . . When Bruno asks the question: "Where do objects go when they no longer have any use?" we might reply that they normally go in the dustbin, but that reply would be inadequate, since the question is metaphysical. Bergson asked the same question and replied metaphysically: that which has ceased to be useful simply begins to *be*. And when Herzog remarks that "*he who walks is defenceless*," we might say that the walker lacks any strength in comparison with cars and aeroplanes. But, there again, the remark was metaphysical. "Absolutely defenceless" is the definition which Bruno gave of himself. The walker is defenceless because he is he who is beginning to be, and never finishes being small.[9]

What I wish to suggest is that there is yet another bifurcation apart from that between the big and the small, or between the past and the future. It is that very weightiness of an endless present, that state that Deleuze describes as "beginning to be," that is the unthought and underside of the big/small and past/future disjunctions. It is not so much the oscillation between the small and the large that is crucial, but the fact that at either extreme one is more proximate to a realm of pure being. In this regard, the crucial split is not between the opposing terms of becoming (becoming smaller, becoming larger), but between the *movement of becoming* they both invoke and the *realm of being* that is their (utopian or dystopian) limit.

This bifurcation between becoming and being resides at the spatial margins of Thomas Carl Wall's beautiful chapter on Blanchot in *Radical Passivity: Levinas, Blanchot, and Agamben*. In his reading, which is focused in particular on Blanchot's *L'Arrêt de mort* (*Death Sentence*), Wall emphasizes at several junctures how there is only a disjunction of past and future, but no present in the time-space of Blanchot's *récits*. He writes: "Not a plural text, *L'Arrêt de mort* is a text emptied of all presence and, what is more, it violently empties time of all presence. Put more simply and more abruptly, *L'Arrêt de mort* destroys time. The past – the things that happened to the narrator in 1938 – are not offered to the reader, to the present, but instead offered to a futurity whose coming our reading already echoes. The *récit* is absolutely indifferent to 'my time,' 'my death.' It skips over the present moment."[10] These sentences touch at the heart of Blanchot's thought, for surely if anything it is a thought that upends any chronological or ordinary notions of time and space. If for Wall the death of J. in *L'Arrêt de mort* defies chronological time ("That death does not complete the movement of dying disturbs the often too facilely understood notion of human finitude: the equation of death with rest and peace. Far from setting a limit to dying, death magnifies its incompletion, placing it, as it were, under glass. Like the time of writing and of the image, it never achieves the present moment"),[11] then the narrator's strange non-inhabitation of his apartments is equally defiant of spatial presentness.

Wall analyzes the extraordinary example of the narrator's drive to simultaneously rent or sublet several apartments at once as a way of deflecting his presentness in his space, of being proximate to himself rather than present to himself. Wall writes the following in his gloss of Blanchot:

> For example, one day I may return home with a strange desire to move to another apartment and, after a few weeks, I may do just that. But then I may wish to move to yet another apartment, and then yet another, and another, and so on and so on – until I am no longer able to "return" "home." I may even, like the narrator in *L'Arrêt de mort*, maintain three or four flats at the same time. What can compel someone to maintain several apartments at once, since he or she cannot inhabit them all simultaneously? I may give in to this mad impulse because in any one of my apartments I could enjoy my absence from it as well, and at the same time. . . . By virtue of taking pleasure in the possibility of his flight from room to room, the narrator encloses himself in himself and he enjoys the separation of subjectivity. The enjoyment is precisely that each "here" is also an "elsewhere." It is not the presence of this room in its actual particularity that contents him, but his savoring of its proximity to each other room he rents out. That which he enjoys is not present, is not consumed or used up, not even partially.[12]

Here, Wall succinctly touches on the core of Blanchot's otherworldly sense of spatiality, especially the spaces of apartments and houses. The inhabiting of several apartments simultaneously so as to better appreciate the proximity of habitation and non-habitation, to perceive oneself in the non-habitation of one's space, and thus outside oneself, beyond oneself, to achieve through disjunction a continuity of perception – this Blanchotian motif is, once again, not only echoed throughout Blanchot's œuvre, but also in strong resonance with the work of Deleuze. Yet, do these emptyings of the present of space and time also foreclose an equally

Blanchotian motif, one that addresses – albeit in a fashion so similar that it might not seem really to be distinct – the opposite temporal and spatial dimension, that of staying inexorably put in one space and time?

Wall touches on this dimension when he writes about the question of a pure possibility of history. Here, he comments on the fact that in *L'Arrêt de mort*, the narrator notes that the larger political events of the late 1930s dominated every aspect of life, yet strangely in the aftermath of the war, it was those seemingly trifling and mundane aspects of daily life that lingered with him more than the large scale historical events that he participated in working as a journalist:

> While the events of the war years are dead, these inconsequential happenings have managed to live on and remain undead and unrecorded by virtue of their insignificance.... They are what the journalist did not write about at the time because they were inessential events, of secondary importance, mere everyday life. They were already supplementary to the time of the coming war. . . . But in a certain sense, these everyday events are purely historic. They are history purged of historic events, or, the everyday as the pure possibility of history.[13]

It seems that Wall's formulation of "history purged of historic events," or "the everyday *as* the pure possibility of history" is subtly at odds with his non-localizable and non-present notion of Blanchotian time and space. Indeed, what makes for pure history is the fact of a strange stability of locale and present daily life in the midst of such worldly upheaval. How is such a being in the mundane present to be represented against the more omnipresent sense looming in the late 1930s of an ominous futurity, and the retrospective vantage point that would necessarily situate this time within what would be its dominant (wartime) context? To remember above all the aspects of daily life would seem to be a blasphemous form of narrating history. While the two might blend together – the dailyness of the present and the more grandiose future anterior of the event – they must also and even more emphatically be at odds.

I wish to turn briefly to another work of fiction, written in the early 1950s just before Moroccan independence, that is focused so intently on the daily lives of the inhabitants of a small rural village that it was accused of being negligent of the larger and more dominant world events and therefore improperly historical. This work is Mouloud Mammeri's *La Colline oubliée*, which details the intricate social dynamics of an Arabo-Berber village in the Atlas mountains of Morocco during World War Two. What is most striking is that this narrative refuses to engage with the war – a war that takes the men away from the small village and brings back only some of them – except in the most perfunctory of ways. Instead the villagers are preoccupied primarily with a local case of potential wife repudiation.

In one of the novel's early passages, when news of the imminent outbreak of World War Two has just reached the small village of Tasga where the story is set, the narrator describes a sense of listlessness in the village, an anxious waiting for something to happen, whatever the results of the awaited event – where even the outbreak of war seems to be more desirable than nothing at all. The narrator characterizes this state of waiting as an unnamable malady: "Indeed for a long time our city suffered from a strange, imperceptible malady. It was everywhere and nowhere; it seemed to disappear for several months, then it would rise up abruptly, terribly, as if to seize the short respite it had left us. We tried all remedies; nothing worked, and even worse no one knew exactly what caused the ailment."[14] According to Mammeri's critics, the imperceptible and unnamable malady described in this passage should be designated in a more absolute fashion, and given the name of colonialism.[15] However, the most challenging part of the narrative is that it is precisely this sense of the absolute that is being put into question. Whether it be named colonialism or World War II, it seems that Mammeri is at least putting forth the possibility of there not being a recognizable change in the community at Tasga, and this whether or not World War II breaks out, whether or not Morocco gains its independence. It is this possibility of there not being a noticeable difference, or there not being an absolute standard for decidability, that is the real point of crisis. As Blanchot writes in *The Writing of the Disaster*, "I will not say that the disaster is absolute; on the contrary, it disorients the absolute" (*WD* 4). It is this sense of disorientation, one brought on by an excessive, even obscene focus on the everyday, that Mammeri captures most forcefully in this first novel.[16]

This might be reformulated in the words of Ann Smock who glosses Blanchot's notion of disaster in the following fashion in her introduction: "That there should be no difference (no difference as difference is ordinarily understood) between disaster and none at all: this is the disaster."[17] It seems that the community in question retains a state of quiet explosiveness whether or not many of its central members are present, and whatever the outcome of the larger political events. The fact that the community of Tasga itself contains its own possibility for dissolution is, more than anything, the unpronounceable disaster.

To return, then, to Wall's reading of the pure history of the everyday that emerges alongside the overdetermined events of World War II, at issue once again is the repressed question of being, and being static. Wall writes eloquently of "the time of radical divergence of past from future" and how "this discontinuity or radical uncertainty insinuates itself into continuous time," indeed "this void-time is the very hollowing out of time that makes continuity possible in the first place."[18] I would concur, following Deleuze and the German mathematician Dedekind, that this radical disjunction is indeed what makes the thought of continuity possible.[19] And one need not go any further than this, when all is said and done. Yet again, when all is said and done, I would claim that to think the pure history of the everyday in the face of larger events, to think staying in one apartment all the time rather than inhabiting several simultaneously – to really think these things is to venture to a different and perhaps more vexed domain that is not squarely the atemporal domain of the past-future disjunctive synthesis. For this vexed domain is not of the order of becoming; rather, it is unbecoming, and unbecoming so deeply stuck that it verges on being itself.[20]

This cannot be far from what Sartre evokes by the notion of the *in-itself* in *Being and Nothingness* and the *practico-inert* in *The Critique of Dialectical Reason*, terms that Sartre subjugates to the more properly political and dynamic notions of the *for-itself* and *praxis* respectively.[21] These debased terms are challenging because they fall short of the proper, just as it is improper to live in a small rented apartment for forty years and not leave it or fix it or buy property or work at a job or go anywhere or straighten up the avalanche of accumulated papers. This would seem to be the irredeemable marker of a life gone awry. Yet, I would propose that this is the outpost or limit of the Blanchotian universe, which is first and foremost that disarming atemporal and aspatial terrain that Wall and others so forcefully describe. But that Blanchotian terrain, marked as it is by a disjunction of past and future, the ability for the narrator to distance himself from himself by renting multiple apartments, is both striving towards and conditioned by that other singularity where there is only one apartment that is never left, only one time that is endlessly present, only one death and one night and one midnight that shimmer behind the doubleness of Blanchot's two nights, Blanchot's two deaths.

If the desire to be proximate to oneself by inhabiting multiple spaces is one of *becoming*, then how different is it really from the *being* still of the Bartlebys who inhabit with exclusivity their home or their office? Perhaps they are just two sides of the same operation in that the ones who remain in one place are also proximate to the space across the street, just by staying put where they are. Surely in this way becoming and being access the same thing. But to strive for proximity is nonetheless different from *being* proximate, even if the difference seems indiscernible. Blanchot must be credited, in addition to his Orpheus-like striving and losing, for also being, in his silent retreat, beyond that striving, maybe not superior to it, but nonetheless dwelling in a realm of being that is beyond, not because it is immune from becoming, but because it has wholly incorporated, wholly become, becoming. To perceive this distinction, not sustainable and even against the very fiber of Blanchot's thought, is nonetheless to perceive that the one trapped in becoming aspires to the utopia of being while the one in that latter ethereal realm can only speak of it unsentimentally as a prison to be someday escaped. But the perception is to see that maybe becoming will never reach its utopia of being, and being will never leave the dystopia to which it long ago arrived. Is the perception of this enough to sustain serenely the force of it, which would seem also to be shattering?

By way of conclusion, I would like to consider this question of the difference or indifference between becoming and being as it is simultaneously evoked and foreclosed by two critics attuned, very much in the fashion of Wall's *Radical Passivity*, to the phenomenology of passivity and inertia. In *What Is There To Say?*, Ann Smock describes with characteristic finesse the suspension of the fissure I have been at pains to outline between becoming and being. She poses it in terms of a choice at stake in Melville's *Billy Budd*, the choice to speak or to kill, which is also one that, for Smock, links Melville and Blanchot, and later on Louis-René des Forêts: "Blanchot has scarcely stated the bleak choice – either speak or kill – when he adds that speech founds this very alternative. To choose speech (when the sole choice is between speech and murder) turns out not to consist in choosing so much as in maintaining the wavering, undecided movement of the either-or. … What concerns me, in other words, is an opposition abruptly neutralized. When human beings draw near to one another, the difference is sometimes suddenly suspended between the impatience and the inertia in them."[22] This notion of choice which is also an infinite suspension of choice or difference is the recurrent Blanchotian motif of Smock's study. Yet it also raises the question of whether it then might be possible to choose to not suspend, to let the suspension go, so that it is no longer a matter of suspension between impatience and inertia, but just inertia itself. Is this possible, and does it look any different?

Smock herself gives an example of what this might look like, one taken from des Forêts's story "Un Malade en forêt." Here, a stranded South African pilot who will betray himself if he speaks, because his English will betray him to the Germans, becomes so ill that it is not clear if he will remember the prohibition against speaking. Playing dead so that he won't have to speak, he turns out, to the surprise of his comrades, actually to be dead. As Smock glosses the occurrence:

> Indeed, there is something striking in the still body of the dead RAF pilot – in the indisputable presence, lying flat on a stretcher in the sun by the side of the road, of the verdict that rules any such verdict out. The South African's motionless form can just fleetingly be felt to embody the insignificance of the gravest sentence – the one that decides, once and for all, but not anything. One feels in this motionless person the gravity that is proper to the perfectly inconsequential alone.[23]

There are so many words in these lines that indicate weightiness, stillness, gravity, inertia: "something striking in the still body," "in the indisputable presence," of the "motionless form," "lying flat," "the gravest sentence," "the gravity that is proper," "in this motionless person." Unmoored slightly from their context – one that emphasizes suspension and hanging – these words point to something beside suspension, to an inertia that is here the inertia of deadness caught by surprise. Such a surprised deadness is paradoxically all the more alive for the very fact of the startle it produces, for the fact that it catches the comrades and the reader off-guard, but off-guard in a way that, as Smock indicates, precludes any verdict being reached. If we linger not so much on the absent verdict but on the present inertia, then it would appear that obliquely, quietly, alongside the choice that is not a choice, there is also a parousia of inertia so full it must announce its own singular ontology in the very process of seeming to undermine it. My claim, then, is that standing beside, indeed enabling, the suspension of difference that Smock reads in Blanchot and Melville and des Forêts is an unsuspended ontology of inertia.

This very phrase is echoed in another critical essay that focuses on a certain languid strain of American literature, and more specifically on a "Hawthornesque lassitude" that is transmitted even while being questioned and rejected by Melville and James. In "Postponing Politics in Hawthorne's *Scarlet Letter*," Christopher Diffee situates *The Scarlet Letter* as a nodal point in a trajectory of lethargic writing. If this lethargy comes to infect the likes of Melville and James (and one can certainly see the resonances, as Diffee points out, not only in "Bartleby" but also in James's "The Altar of the Dead" and "The Beast in the Jungle"), they interestingly distance themselves from it to locate it all the more squarely with Hawthorne alone. As Diffee writes, citing Melville, "Melville charges Hawthorne with being neither harmless nor profound but in having 'too largely developed' his undevelopment, hence not veiling what he did not do and so appearing to be 'a sequestered, harmless man, from whom any deep and weighty thing would be [sic] hardly be anticipated.'"[24] If Hawthorne eschews weightiness, or, according to Diffee's gloss of James on Hawthorne, "Hawthorne's essence is itself inessential,"[25] there is a paradoxical momentousness to the very lack of weightiness, to the inessential itself. As with Smock, this paradox permeates Diffee's very text. In discussing James on Hawthorne, he writes:

> James' final word about Hawthorne's imagination is to pronounce it essentially sterile and arid, a passivity so withdrawn as to become a ghostly absence. . . . Reluctant to "produce himself," even hesitation fails to end but lingers on – in observation, expectation, contemplation – reproducing in parenthetical aside what falters as sense. The oddity of Hawthorne emerges not through a positive assertion – as if there could be an ontology of inaction – but when one is put in the awkward situation of realizing a fondness for absence "on almost any occasion."[26]

Once again, there is a torrent of terms indicating a plentitude of stillness and absence: "essentially sterile," "a passivity so withdrawn as to *become*," "even hesitation fails to end but *lingers on*" (my italics). Given this, it seems incongruous that Diffee characterizes Hawthorne's oddity as not emerging through positive assertion. To be sure, this lack of positive assertion accurately captures a certain essence of Hawthorne's (and Melville's and James's and Blanchot's) œuvre, but it also belies the full-blown absoluteness of a passivity that lingers to the point of becoming an essence in its own right. It seems odd, then, that Diffee would place "an ontology of inaction" in a twisted conditional – "as if" there could be one (but surely there is not) – for it seems that such an ontology of inaction is precisely what Diffee's reading – and Smock's and Wall's – captures but does not claim as such, preferring not to maintain any sort of pure being when it can be credited to something else. But isn't the emphatic preferring not, as in the case of Bartleby, so antithetical to the presumed passivity that the passivity is itself ontologized into action?

All the more striking in Diffee's analysis is the network of texts that he reads, the attenuated inertia at the heart of the classics of the American canon. Blanchot (and all the more so des Forêts) might seem like an esoteric and obscure writer, even within the French tradition, and the questions of radical passivity, of being and becoming, to which his œuvre gives rise, might seem peculiarly French and not universalizable questions. However, if one perceives that this inertia of being is also at the heart of the national literature that would seem to be the most movement-focused (portraying endless road trips and mobility), then it might lead one to conclude that perhaps such movement, such infinite becoming, is equally the mask for the inertia that is so entrenched as to become invisible. The ones who have no choice but to inhabit this inertia fully are the unwitting and disrespected guideposts to an ontology that is so present as to seem pathological, or not to seem at all.

ENDNOTES

[1] Gilles Deleuze, *The Logic of Sense*, trans. Mark Lester with Charles Stivale (New York: Columbia University Press, 1990), 222.

[2] Gilles Deleuze and Claire Parnet, *Dialogues*, trans. Hugh Tomlinson and Barbara Habberjam (New York: Columbia University Press, 1987), 37.

[3] Interestingly and somewhat divergently, Deleuze links cyclical time to the less favored and present-inflected Chronos: "Thus the time of the present is always a limited but infinite time; infinite because cyclical, animating a physical eternal return as the return of the Same, and a moral eternal wisdom as the wisdom of the Cause." *The Logic of Sense*, 61.

[4] *The Logic of Sense*, 63.

[5] Though *The Space of Literature* certainly represents a reaction to the engaged humanism of Sartre's *"What is Literature?,"* it is much less at odds with Sartre's philosophical studies or with his early short stories collected in *The Wall* than it might seem. See *'What is Literature?' and Other Essays* (Cambridge: Harvard University Press, 1988) and *The Wall*, trans. Lloyd Alexander (New York: New Directions, 1948). See also note 21.

[6] The narrator indeed refers openly to his extraordinary immobility: "my steps were the steps of immobility" (*WTC* 4); "there could be nothing of me there but this endless immobility" (*WTC* 6).

[7] For a discussion of the immobility or potential mobility of natural objects from a legal standpoint, see Christopher D. Stone, *Should Trees Have Standing?: And Other Essays on Law, Morals, and the Environment* (Dobbs Ferry, N.Y.: Oceana Publications, 1996).

[8] See Gilles Deleuze, *Essays Critical and Clinical*, trans. Daniel W. Smith and Michael A. Greco (London: Verso, 1998).

[9] Gilles Deleuze, *Cinema 1: The Movement-Image*, trans. Hugh Tomlinson and Barbara Habberjam (Minneapolis: University of Minnesota Press, 1986), 185.

[10] Thomas Carl Wall, *Radical Passivity: Levinas, Blanchot, and Agamben* (Albany: SUNY Press, 1999), 88.

[11] *Radical Passivity*, 95.

[12] *Radical Passivity*, 79–80.

[13] *Radical Passivity*, 83–4.

[14] Mouloud Mammeri, *La Colline oubliée* (Paris: Plon, 1952), 26, my translation.

[15] See Mildred Mortimer, *Mouloud Mammeri, écrivain algérien* (Sherbrooke, Québec: Naaman, 1982), 14.

[16] Such an oblique portrayal of the disaster, in this case the Algerian war, through an eerie defamiliarization of the everyday, is the achievement of Mohammed Dib's *Who Remembers the Sea*, trans. Louis Tremaine (Boulder, CO: Lynne Rienner Publishers, Inc., 1985).

[17] Ann Smock, "Translator's Remarks" in *WD*, ix.

[18] *Radical Passivity*, 95.

[19] See Richard Dedekind, "Continuity and Irrational Numbers" in *Essays on the Theory of Numbers*, trans. Wooster Woodruff Beman (Chicago: Open Court, 1909).

[20] For a meditation on unbecoming, see John Paul Ricco, *The Logic of the Lure* (Chicago: University of Chicago Press, 2002).

[21] See Jean-Paul Sartre, *Being and Nothingness*, trans. Hazel Barnes (London: Routledge, 1989) and *Critique of Dialectical Reason*, trans. Alan Sheridan-Smith (London: NLB, 1976). For a redemptive discussion of the *in-itself* and the *practico-inert* as concepts that enable a theory of the inhuman and the incorporeal *avant la lettre*, see my "Solid Dialectic in Sartre and Deleuze", *Polygraph* 14 (2002), 79–91 and my "'To Cut Too Deeply and Not Enough': Violence and the Incorporeal", in *Theology and the Political: The New Debate*, ed. Creston Davis, John Milbank, and Slavoj Žižek (Durham: Duke University Press, 2005).

[22] Ann Smock, *What Is There To Say?* (Lincoln: University of Nebraska Press, 2003), viii–ix.

[23] *What Is There To Say?*, 84.

[24] Christopher Diffee, "Postponing Politics in Hawthorne's *Scarlet Letter*," *MLN* 111.5 (1996), 835–71 (837).

[25] Diffee, 840.

[26] Diffee, 839.

LITERATURE OF INDISTINCTION
Blanchot and Caproni

Paolo Bartoloni

> *Quelque chose lui est arrivé, et il ne peut dire que ce soit vrai,*
> *ni le contraire. Plus tard, il pensa que l'événement consistait*
> *dans cette manière de n'être ni vrai ni faux.*
>
> Maurice Blanchot, *L'Attente l'oubli*

FACE-TO-FACE

ON THE MANUSCRIPT OF THE POEM "LE PAROLE" (THE WORDS, 1977), the Italian poet Giorgio Caproni wrote a note: "In 1946 [I said that] the words dissolve the object, but only in 1953 Blanchot launched his motto 'the name empties the thing' [*il nome vanifica la cosa*]."[1] Caproni, one of the most acclaimed Italian poets of the twentieth century, kept a close eye on the work of Maurice Blanchot. Thanks to his command of French and the outstanding cultural enterprises of the journal *Botteghe Oscure*, whose issues featured original works of important yet barely known international intellectuals, in the years 1951–58 Caproni read, amongst others, Blanchot's "Le Retour," "Le Calme," "Comme un jour de neige," "L'Attente" and "La Bête de Lascaux."[2] There is no evidence that Blanchot and Caproni ever met, or that Blanchot read Caproni (although individual poems were translated into French much earlier, volumes of Caproni's works in French translation appeared only in the '80s), and yet their writing enacts an uncanny correspondence, which is not so much an affinity as a natural availability to be "face-to-face." They stare at each other through their poetic language, which is also the product of a series of philosophical preoccupations that they shared with their time. More specifically, it was the reflection on language, subjectivity and temporality mediated through the work of Hegel and Heidegger that appears to take centre stage in Blanchot's and Caproni's work. If Hegel led them to think the relation between sign and thing, Heidegger might have prompted them to look beyond this relation at the space in which sign and thing are exposed to each other and, astonished and silent – indistinct – open up. This essay is an attempt to trace this coming "face-to-face" of Blanchot and Caproni through a reading of Blanchot's *L'Attente l'oubli*, Caproni's *Il muro della terra*, and the interface between these writings and Hegel's and Heidegger's thought.

THE SOUND OF PRESENCES

Maurice Blanchot published *L'Attente l'oubli* in 1962, seven years after *L'Espace littéraire* and twenty-one years after the first version of *Thomas l'obscur*. Giorgio Caproni wrote *Il muro della terra* (*The Wall of the Earth*) between 1964 and 1975. This collection of poems marked a poetic as well as literary watershed, splitting Caproni's work into two major and distinct sections. The historical context in which *Il muro della terra* and *L'Attente l'oubli* were conceived is instructive, if only for the relation that literature and philosophy seemed to enjoy at that particular time in European writing. This relation is typified not only by the willingness of poets and novelists to engage with philosophical issues as part of the creative process, but also by the overt stylistic fusion of two discourses that had for many years been deemed separate. Blanchot's work is emblematic of this stylistic encounter in which literature and philosophy melt into each other with linguistic as well as poetic ease. And yet, this apparently happy meeting is the public visage of a much more problematic and painful review of language, knowledge and subjectivity. It is in this sense that the writing of Blanchot demonstrates the simultaneous occurrence of linguistic flow and inscrutability. Blanchot's is a language that speaks the impossibility of expression and, in doing so, exists in the space of its own negativity.

L'Attente l'oubli is set in a hotel room in an undefined location at an undefined time. Two characters, a man and a woman, speak to each other, or rather they are seen and heard speaking to each other since the narrative is ostensibly constructed to include the reader, but only as spectator and listener. Later in the narrative, the reader is made to realize that the woman has gone to the man's room after the two, until then strangers, had exchanged glances through their respective windows. There are several instructive things to be learned from this simple narrative structure. The hotel room is an enclosed space, containing and circumscribing the narrative. It is this small and compact space, somewhat reminiscent of meditative monastic cells, into which the gaze and hearing is drawn. Clearly, the expectation is that of witnessing a series of *tableaux vivants* or actions frozen on the page for the benefit of the onlooker. The narrative structure of Blanchot's *L'Attente l'oubli* appears to be crafted specifically for this purpose by providing a well defined architectural space in which a series of existential and metaphysical events can be ordered, stored, crystallised so as to be observed and heard. It is the idea of the meditative mental space so central to medieval thought; a space deemed necessary for recollection and invention. Further, it is unobstructed and uncluttered with day-to-day events, empty and quiet, purified of the contamination of quotidianity. Blanchot's hotel room is the quintessential example of the literary and philosophical exilic zone: solitary and elemental. Nothing can be heard besides the voices of the two protagonists, and nothing can be perceived other than their floating thoughts searching for a language that would ground them in some sort of oral and aural existence. And yet, Blanchot's mental picture lacks visual continuity to the extent that the viewer is confronted by intermittent images whose visibility invariably gives way to moments of darkness and invisibility. We see but also do not see. The visual segmentation so typical of *L'Attente l'oubli* generates a mental dizziness and an iconographic short circuit whereby vision soon loses its bearings, becoming engulfed by disorientation and confusion. What is not affected is hearing. But the language we hear is the cause of our visual collapse and the reason for our sense of loss, of being disoriented in a peculiar landscape where representation and communication have vanished.

> He was looking at her furtively. Perhaps she was speaking, but on her face, no expression of good will with respect to what she was saying, no agreement to speak, a barely living affirmation, a scarcely speaking suffering.
>
> He would have liked to have the right to say to her: "Stop speaking, if you want me to hear you." But at present, even saying nothing, she could no longer keep silent.[3]

The language spoken by the woman says nothing in its uninterrupted saying. It has lost all sense of communication and representational imagery. It merely floats around the room as pure sounds that can be heard but not understood. The English translation is only partially correct when translating "entendre" as "hear." The verb "entendre" implies understanding and the successful outcome of communication. In Blanchot's narrative, the character hears but does not understand what he hears to the extent that he questions whether the woman is actually speaking, "Peut-être parlait-elle" (perhaps she was speaking). The problem is that words and expression, language and images, do not relate, do not match. As words flow from the woman, her facial expression does not change. In other words, she does not make visible the language she uses through her body. Image and language are separated, fractured. This is language as such, a language that speaks *in* itself and not through something outside of itself. The idea that communication could arise from the suppression of this disorienting noise, in silence, comes to the man as he wishes for the woman to stop uttering sounds without meaning. But this possibility is soon obliterated by a further explanation. It is perhaps that she has forgotten how language works:

> He understood quite well that she had possibly forgotten everything. That didn't bother him. He wondered if he didn't want to take possession of what she knew, more by forgetting than by remembering. But forgetting... It was necessary that he, too, enter into forgetting.[4]

REMEMBERING AND FORGETTING

The extraordinary thing that takes place here is that in the apparent aphasia of the woman the man perceives an unquantifiable form of knowledge that he wishes to possess. In this nothing of language the man glimpses something that his knowledge lacks and desires. The sentences that follow are instructive. The entrance into this knowledge clothed by nothingness – the surface of knowledge – might be achieved by two, different routes that conventional semantics treats as opposite: "remembering" or "forgetting." But in this instance, "forgetting" and "remembering" are close; they share a common trait. They both imply a journey, and the journey is in both instances a reversal, a journey of return. And yet, in the case of "forgetting" the journey takes place by accessing a totally new dimension in which the recovery of the origin must start from nothing. "Remembering" is based on the visualisation *of* and meditation *on* an acquired knowledge, of a recovery of known and stored principles and notions. "Forgetting," on the other hand, depends on the erasure of such principles and notions, on unlearning the foundations of epistemological conditions for the benefit of a new experience. "Forgetting" means obliterating. As such, it is the entrance into the domain of oblivion and the acceptance of knowing nothing: "Mais l'oubli... Il lui fallait entrer, lui aussi, dans l'oubli."

Oblivion is the banishment of the known and it is ushered in by the will to forget and by a conscious determination to exclude the known. Forgetting, like remembering, cannot originate in the unconscious. If remembering is a careful elaboration of images and notions, forgetting is the studious deleting of such images and notions attained by pouring onto these very images and notions a layer of contrivances whose effect is to disorient and confuse the already known. In the case of language, the language *through* which we speak can be disoriented by piling over it sentence after sentence whose communicative and representational value is unclear. The result is still a language that speaks in sentences whose grammar and syntax are clear and correct, but whose meanings have crossed the threshold of indistinction. The man in Blanchot's *L'Attente l'oubli* is determined to connect with the woman by "speaking nothing": "But I will say nothing; be aware of this. What I say is nothing."[5]

A LIT DARKNESS

In the section "Bisogno di guida" (In need of a guide) of *Il muro della terra* we find the short poem "Istanza del medesimo" (Instance of the similar): "What should I ask for./ Leave me to my darkness./ Only this. That I may see."[6] In *Il muro della terra*, as in many of Caproni's other collections of poems, the journey is a central image. It is not by accident that one of the three short poems introducing *Il muro della terra*, "Falsa indicazione" (False directions), revolves around the movement in space: "'Border,' the sign said./ I looked for the Customs. Not there./ I saw no trace/ of a foreign land/ behind the fence."[7] The "I" of Caproni's poetry embarks on a journey to what he expects to be a foreign land. Travelling to the unknown, which is either deep inside, buried underneath layer upon layer – which have been scanned in alternation through metaphysical or psychoanalytical lenses – or high up, into stratospheric distances, is a classical literary trope. What dramatically changes in Caproni's poetry is the intelligibility of the unknown, whose existence is tightly interwoven with the known. The borders are sign-posted and yet the lands which they separate appear identical. A guide is required to travel into this novel terrain which has all the semblance of the old, and yet is new. It is precisely the acute awareness of this novelty clothed in the familiar, an apparent visibility which, however, cannot be correctly understood if read through the usual instrument of learning, that puzzles but also reinforces the subject's desire to be left in a lit darkness, where vision (*vedere*, to see) is paired with its own impossibility (*buio*, darkness). Watching nothing equates with speaking nothing and both inhabit the area of indistinction where knowing is coupled with not-knowing and being with not-being. It is in this sense that poems like "Ritorno" (Return) and "Esperienza" (Experience) in the section titled "Feuilleton" must be read. Their apparently nonsensical discourse, based on a set of antinomic oppositions which simultaneously say and refute what has been said, is determined by a language that has chosen an epistemological route on which visibility and intelligibility are traded for indistinguishability. Clearly, this is a language that inhabits the space of indistinction and potentiality in which myriads of possible meanings and images are intertwined and tightly connected to the extent that no clear image or meaning can be disentangled. What can this language of disorientation (*spaesamento*) and "nothingness" tell us? Further, what kind of episteme can it bequeath us? Let us read the two poems. "Ritorno":

> I returned there
> where I had never been.
> Nothing, from how it was not, has changed.
> On the table (the checkered
> cloth), half filled
> I found the glass
> never filled. Everything
> is still as
> I have never left it.[8]

And "Esperienza":

> All the places I have seen,
> I have visited,
> now I know – I am certain of it:
> I have never been there.[9]

The mirroring assertions and refutations that mark the pace of the two poems, the careful fracturing of meaning through *enjambements*, are typical of a language that searches in vain for its own face. This is a poetry that dares to watch a mirror that does not reflect, where not even the self of poetry can recover its own features. This negation of visibility and refraction is made even more compelling by the actual presence of poetry and the actual presence of the self, both of which are actually *there* where they have never been. As such, this is not a discourse that annihilates and negates presence or cognition. It is rather a discourse that locates presence and cognition in a space in which they must be re-discovered and re-learned from regaining the "superficial" language of the origin by discarding the language of referentiality. What I am stressing here is that the area of indistinction that a language which speaks nothing realises is a tangible and experiential zone; a potentiality which ceases to be hypothetical in order to be. A further question thus arises that must be asked in conjunction with the two preceding ones: what kind of *habitus* – in Bourdieu's sense of the word, as a cultural and ethical mindset – can a potentiality as such be?

VIEILLE PAROLE

An answer is found in the passage from *L'Attente l'oubli* that I quoted as the epigraph to this essay:

> Something happened to him, and he can say neither that it was true, nor the contrary. Later, he thought that the event consisted in this manner of being neither true nor false.[10]

The word "événement" (event) must be stressed here, for it emphasises the taking place of something concrete, a liveable experience that can be investigated and articulated. But this experience belongs in the interstices between truth and falsehood, and as such in the course of a process of cognition in which the impossibility of an evaluation is the fundamental trait of the process's existence and the only possible *habitus* of Blanchot's characters. The ineffability of a potential truth or of its opposite decrees its indistinguishability and ultimately its irrelevance. What remains to be explored and lived is the only possible ontological space which lies in-between truth and falsehood and in-between their respective effability and ineffability and their visibility and invisibility. This is the zone of indistinction. It is here that language can be itself without being forced to speak and where it can roam at ease without losing itself in mere wandering: "An utterance that must be repeated before it has been heard, a traceless murmur that he follows, wandering nowhere, residing everywhere, the necessity of letting it go. It is always the ancient word [*la vieille parole*] that wants to be here again without speaking."[11]

The messianic project that one finds in Benjamin's reflection on language and his interest in reconnecting with the original language – *die reine Sprache* – is present in Blanchot's work as well, *la vieille parole*. Both Blanchot and Benjamin speak and retrace in their writing the linguistic split that has characterized the Western understanding of language throughout the centuries, and can be traced back to the Fall from grace in the Garden of Eden. The Fall determined the passage from the *in language* before the Fall to the *through language* after the Fall, and the irredeemable fracture between the original language and the many derivative languages that were born as a consequence of this fracture. Benjamin and Blanchot, together with many other writers and philosophers of the twentieth century, engage with this fracture and attempt to understand and articulate its meaning by inhabiting the only possible and available vantage point. This is the fracture itself, where *in language* and *through language* intermingle and disappear into each other. It is the will to be in indistinction that invites the characters in Blanchot's *L'Attente l'oubli* to look for the "the poverty in language,"[12] and that encourages them to "remain ignorant of what one knows, only that."[13]

"ELEUSIS"

In 1796 the young Hegel wrote a poem entitled "Eleusis" and dedicated it to Hölderlin. This poem on the Eleusinian mystery speaks of the impossibility of stating the ineffable, of proffering the "sacred": "and in vain," writes Hegel, "strive/ the scholars, their curiosity greater than their love/ of wisdom (the seekers possesses this love and/ they disdain you) – to master it they dig for words [*graben sie nach Worten*],/ in which your lofty meaning might be engraved [*In die Dein hoher Sinn gepräget*]!"[14] The only possible way to apprehend the secret of the "sacred initiations" is to remain silent or to "speak the language of angels" (*Spräch er mit Engelzungen*), "to experience the poverty of words" (*fühlt' der Worte Armut*). In this poem the young Hegel reiterates the Platonic idea of words as mere simulacra – "only dust and ashes do they seize" – and the primacy of pure thought, the silence residing in the poverty of words. But the poem does something even more interesting, especially in relation to our present discussion: it appears to offer Blanchot the original platform on which to found his own project of language. Between Blanchot's "pauvreté dans le langage" and Hegel's "the poverty of words" there is clearly a striking proximity. Indeed, this is a proximity of thought on which a whole philosophical and poetic experience hinges. Blanchot's could well be a "translation" of Hegel's poem, but only if by translation we mean that process that rewinds the work, that breaks its death-mask. In the case of Blanchot we are not confronted with the translation of a given text, Hegel's "Eleusis," but rather with the translation of a philosophical condition; in other words with the "property" Hegel, whose *imago* reaches us through the unconcealment of this very "property" mediated by and in language. But is Blanchot's translation faithful? Does *L'Attente l'oubli* say the same thing as "Eleusis"? About one hundred and fifty years separate Hegel's and Blanchot's texts, and many more separate them from the ancient Greek *ur-texts* on being and language from which both *L'Attente l'oubli* and "Eleusis" originate. But more poignantly, and definitely more problematically, the space in-between "Eleusis" and *L'Attente l'oubli* is occupied by Hegel's *Phenomenology of Spirit*. It is well known that the philosophical position articulated by the young Hegel in "Eleusis" is dramatically reviewed and changed by the Hegel of the *Phenomenology*. For the latter, the truth arrived at through "silence" and "the poverty of language," the sense-certainty, is void ("most abstract and poorest truth"),[15] unless it is mediated by language. It is language that provides truth with a universal meaning and a concrete anchoring which, although plunging the object of utterability into negativity, preserves this object as a property and a universal truth. According to Hegel, language crystallizes truth by bringing to the fore of cognition not so much the singularity of truth (its very thingness) as its universality as opposed or compared to other universalities. It is in this sense that Hegel's dialectic sacrifices the particularity of things in favour of their properties. In effect, Hegel's language is a language that says the object by negating it, by removing the tangibility of the object from view and from knowledge. What we know through Hegelian language is not the object as such, it is not its singularity, it is not its "who." Language speaks the truth by removing it. It is this significant contradiction that characterizes Western thought and indeed generates it.

ALETHEIA

If the Hegel of the *Phenomenology* is the philosopher of the *logos* and the dialectic, Heidegger is the philosopher who lent the Hegelian *logos* a fuller and more definite ontology, in turn changing the inherent negativity of Hegelian thought into a factual presence. One must recognise that for Heidegger the true meaning of Dasein is far more than the commonly assumed "being-there." In a letter to Jean Beaufret dated 23 November 1945, Heidegger writes: "For me *Da-sein* does not so much signify here I am, so much as, if I may express myself in what is perhaps impossible French, *être-le-là*. And *le-là* is precisely *Aletheia*: unveiling-disclosure."[16] *Aletheia* is one of the foundational terms of Heideggerian philosophy, a word that the German philosopher returns to time and time again in order to question, problematize and translate. He enters the word and attempts to live it, use it, think it as the ancient Greek philosophers did. This is what translation means for Heidegger. For him translation is not just a mere transposition from one language to another, a simple exchange of word – this for that. It is rather the integration of a whole language and culture, a whole mode of thinking (in his case ancient Greek thinking), into another language and culture (German). This is not just offering hospitality to something foreign; it is more like allowing the foreign to penetrate the familiar, and perhaps to introduce violence to the familiar, to change it forcefully. This is nowhere more apparent than in the essay that Heidegger devotes to discussing Anaximander's saying; an essay that he wrote in 1946, just one year after writing the letter to Beaufret. Anaximander's saying is considered the oldest fragment of Western philosophy, indeed the very basis of Western philosophy. It is assumed that it is from this saying that the following conceptualisations of "being" and "language" have developed, first and foremost through the interpretation that Plato and Aristotle gave of this saying. It is not possible here to provide a detailed discussion of Heidegger's dense analysis of Anaximander's saying. What is of considerable importance for our discussion is first to relate the notion of *aletheia* to Anaximander's saying, and second to see how Heidegger's thinking of it connects with his overall philosophical project, as well as the links between this project and Hegel's reflection on language.

Aletheia is not a word actually used in Anaximander's saying. The central role that aletheia acquires in Heidegger's thinking of the saying, to the extent that it becomes the central key to its understanding and translation, originates form Heidegger's very unique understanding of translation. Heidegger is convinced that the saying, the actual words said by Anaximander, produced an "aura" which contains a broader meaning. The potential discovery of this apparently invisible trace can only be founded on a careful and rigorous etymological analysis of the semantic and semiotic content of what is left of Anaximander's saying. The two words that Heidegger focuses on to approach a recovery of the lost "whole" are *eon* and *eonta*. According to Heidegger, it is from these two original words that "the fundamental words of the early thinking are said."[17] Amongst these fundamental words are *logos* and *Aletheia*. "Only by means of *En* [the one]," writes Heidegger, "which is to be thought back in the realm of the fundamental words, do *eon* and *einai* [to be] become the explicit words for what is present. Only from out of the destiny of being, the destiny of the *En*, does the modern age, after essential upheavals, enter the epoch of the monadology of substance, which completes itself in the phenomenology of the Spirit."[18] Here the connection is made between ancient Greek philosophy and Hegel, *qua* modern philosophy. By way of translation, Heidegger does two things: he first bestows on language the power of bringing forward the essence of what is thought in language, and second he exposes the essence of Anaximander by way of his very language. It follows that "being" is that which constitutes itself as "the unconcealed" through language. It is this Dasein, this "being-there in language" that Heidegger calls the authentic being, the truthful being, the *aletheia*. Language is at one and the same time that which conceals being by placing it before the world and also that which unconceals being by throwing it into the world. But if the language of concealment is the language that names and that shows, the Hegelian "This" (*Dieses*), then the language of unconcealment is that which devours the very "This" by annulling it in the process of absorbing it. Paradoxically, it is by articulating language and by turning it into grammar that humans enter the world and partake of it. Therefore, and if one follows this idea to the letter, participation means removing the very singularity of whatever we participate in and with. Participation, communality, being in the world come from sacrificing the very thing that participates, that becomes part of a community, that is in and with the community. In saying "This," the natural language which is responsible for naming things also creates an impassable barrier between the subject and the object, which will continue to confront each other as two irrevocable and invariable singularities. It is by removing the singularity of the object through speaking it that the other can be reached, can be experienced, yet no longer as singularity but as negativity.

THE STORY

Let us go back now to the Hegel of "Eleusis" and the Blanchot of *L'Attente l'oubli* and compare them not only to each other but also to the Hegel of the *Phenomenology* and the Heidegger who propounds this reading of *aletheia*. It should be clearer now that the apparent contradiction between the young Hegel and the mature Hegel is not a contradiction at all. It is rather an evolution of the same line of thought, an ideal continuation in which the consistent study of language and being is taken to its conclusion. For the mature Hegel, as for the young Hegel, the "sacred initiations" – the essence and singularity of truth – cannot be rescued by language, or be brought to light and visibility in language. What changes, though, in the passage from "Eleusis" to the *Phenomenology* is that the impossibility of speaking the essence is not circumvented in silence or in the "poverty of words" but is actually spoken by language itself. The difference between the young and the mature Hegel is, as Agamben has clearly seen, that while for the young Hegel the mystery is guarded by silence, for the Hegel of the *Phenomenology* it is language that guards the mystery: "The Eleusinian mystery of the *Phenomenology* is," writes Agamben in *Language and Death*, "thus the same mystery of the poem *Eleusis*; but now language has captured in itself the power of silence, and that which appeared earlier as unspeakable 'profundity' can be guarded (in its negative capacity) in the very heart of the word."[19]

The simple fact that Blanchot writes is a testimony to the fact that he too believed that the "unspeakable 'profundity' can be guarded in the very heart of the word." And yet, when he speaks of silence, his positioning silence so closely to the "poverty of language" demands attention and a certain degree of caution. Let us quote again Blanchot's passage, with the addition this time of a further section:

> His desire to hear her well had long since given way to a need for silence whose indifferent background would have been formed by everything that she had said. But only hearing could nourish this silence. They both searched for poverty in language. On this point, they agreed. For her there were always too many words and one word too many, as well as overly rich words that spoke excessively. Although she was apparently not very learned, she always seemed to prefer abstract words, which evoked nothing. Wasn't she trying, and he along with her, to create for herself at the heart of this story a shelter so as to protect herself from something that the story also helped attract?[20]

It is true that Blanchot writes about silence, but this is a silence that resounds with words and their demand to be heard. Therefore, it is not the mute silence of the Eleusinian mystery, the no-sound effected by closing one's mouth and stopping the flow of words, together with their deadly instantiation of a mere simulacrum. But by the same token it is not the preservation of a "property" either. This "indifferent," indistinct, humming of words, whose interpenetration has rendered them expressionless, does not represent anything, neither the "property" nor the negativity of the object. Its preservation, its *salvare* – if it is a preservation at all – is the preservation of its own becoming of language in-between sense-certainty and universality. As such, this indifferent language guards more than the negativity of truth; it guards both the negativity and the presence of truth by simultaneously incorporating and con-fusing negativity and presence. The language of indistinction, being the becoming and the potential, is also an auratic fragment, whose abandonment (*abbandono*) of representation and presentation carries their echoes, their haloes, within itself. This language is not silence and it is not expression – "For her there were always too many words and one word too many, as well as overly rich words that spoke excessively. Although she was apparently not very learned, she always seemed to prefer abstract words, which evoked nothing." It is obviously not representation, unless by representation one means the Hegelian guarding of negativity. Indeed, at times Blanchot's *L'Attente l'oubli* is nothing more than a Hegelian parable about language and death, language and its commensurability with the void. And yet this tale about the "nothingness" of language tells another story: "Wasn't she trying, and he along with her, to create for herself at the heart of *this story* a shelter so as to protect herself from something that the *story* also helped attract?" Is there somebody telling a story, and to whom, and for what purpose? Clearly, the woman tells a story that the man sets about transcribing. Yet the story that she tells is "unrepresentable" because, as in the Eleusinian mystery, its essence, its secrets, are unsayable: "He picked up the sheets of paper and wrote, 'It is her voice that is entrusted to you, not what she says. What she says, the secrets that you collect and transcribe so as to give them their due, you must lead them gently, in spite of their attempt to seduce, toward the silence that you first drew out of them.'"[21] Let us suspend for a moment the reference to the voice and draw attention not only to the inherent silence of the "secret" but also, more importantly, to the fact that in listening – or, perhaps, merely hearing – the man weaves a story himself and both stories, the woman's and the man's, are ultimately encapsulated within another story. This is why "the story" provides shelter from what "the story" attracts. If words empty the essence of things – "it is a hotel room no different from those he has always lived in, the kind he likes, in a modest hotel. But as soon as he wants to describe it, it is empty, and the words that he uses apply only to emptiness"[22] – they also point at them: "Yet with what interest she watches him when he says to her: here is the bed, there a table, over where you are, an armchair."[23] But if the Hegelian negativity of language is so fundamental to Blanchot's story, more important is the way in which Blanchot eschews the negativity that embraces him and his language by letting it be. It is the act of saying the thing of language, its quiddity – which is also the transcription into written language of the voice – that allows Blanchot to produce a language that is both negative and positive and a language that is firmly ensconced in the instant (*nell'istante*). Temporally speaking, the instant is that which makes itself as it undoes itself and, like the language of indistinction, is the temporal cipher of the abandonment of the self. It is no accident that Blanchot's language, the language of indistinction, is also the language of instantiation.

I suggest that we approach the notion of abandoning the self by way of the Italian "*partire da sé*" (leaving from oneself). *Partire da sé* incorporates and includes two apparently opposite and irreconcilable ideas; it can mean constructing something from the self or leaving the self behind. In the first instance, there is a firm connection to and grasping of the self. The self is the grounding and supervising presence. In the second instance there is the taking leave from the self, the shedding of a shell. The link between these two diametrically opposed meanings is provided by the verb *partire* (to leave). In both instances we confront a departure and an abandonment, which is perhaps temporary on the one hand, and definite on the other. But what interests us here, irrespective of the outcome, is that the departure and the abandonment imply and subsume an unveiling and a disclosure. They imply the Heideggerian *aletheia*. And it is precisely in the Heideggerian notion of *aletheia* that the distinction between the two meanings of *partire da sé* become indistinguishable. Moreover, it is in *aletheia* that *partire da sé* draws language and being into an indissoluble knot. If, on the one hand, language is the original home of human beings, the shelter that protects and decrees (*decreta*) our communality, language is also the very tool through which we risk exposure and unconcealment. In the words of Heidegger, *aletheia* is the sheltering which discloses. And in the words of Blanchot, language is the shelter that protects the woman "from something that the story also helped attract." It is because of language that we face the world, and it is also because of language that we enter the world. It is the language of expression that allows us to share universal truths, but this very language also negates our singularity. What remains to be thought, though, is the process that brings about the state of unconcealment, and the passage from singularity to community and from voice to saying.

Language, the word, empties the object and relegates it to negativity. It pushes it aside, out of sight, and replaces it with the representation of its property. This is either the representation of something through a symbol or the presentation of a pure negativity that, although absent, speaks to us through the medium of language. The latter is precisely Heidegger's understanding of language expressed by way of translation. In the essay "Anaximander's Saying" we read these words: "does the word's literal translation pay heed to what in the saying comes to language?"[24] In this rhetorical question – Heidegger's preferred route to reflection – Heidegger not only illustrates what he believes to be the principal task of translation, that is, the process that he himself implements in discussing Anaximander's saying; but he also comes to express clearly and explicitly the coming to language of the "thing," its disclosure – unconcealment – in language. But what is put into language is not the actual thing but rather a mediation. It is the task of translation to rewind language to arrive at that moment of the thing. It is in this sense that for Heidegger translation is the processing of language whose function is to illuminate what lies behind language. Representation and presentation can also be thought of as cohabiting, and not only and exclusively as irreconcilable opposites. Language represents by presenting the symbol of negativity, by presenting an emptiness behind which lies the "thing" of representation. Can we now understand better the Heideggerian sheltering property of language? Language shelters, in Agamben's words *custodisce* (guards), the singularity of the thing by not disclosing it. This is the great ambiguity of language, and also its great power and its *meravigliosa poesia* (wonderful poetry).

EMPTINESS

It was on 16 May 1970 that Giorgio Caproni put the last touches to his poems "Senza Esclamativi" (Without Exclamatives):

> How high pain is.
> Love is such a beast.
> Emptiness of the words
> that dig into emptiness empty
> monuments of emptiness. Emptiness
> of the grain that already attained
> (in the sun) the height of the heart.[25]

How is it possible that Caproni, this passionate lover of language, can impress the mark of emptiness and void on the object of his love? "Vuoto" (emptiness) resounds ominously throughout "Senza Esclamativi," its syncopated rhythm and battering anaphora, the strategically placed *enjambements* haunt us to the extent that nothing remains besides the sense of emptiness and void. And yet this is not a simple emptiness and, more importantly, it is not an emptiness devoid of presence. It is rather "Vuoto/ del grano che già raggiunse/ (nel sole) l'altezza del cuore." It is the shelter behind which an illuminating image rests and vibrates. It says "emptiness" but in representing and presenting this "emptiness" it partakes of and shares with the reader the essential experience of the thing itself.

Caproni is the poet of small things, of glasses and table-cloths, of wine and taverns. Italo Calvino was very much aware of Caproni's fondness for day-to-day objects. But he also warns us that these objects, this apparently quotidian reality with its strong textures and vivid colours, are not to be trusted.[26] Calvino refers to them as "emblems," Caproni would have called them words. As we saw at the beginning of the chapter, Caproni made a point to stress – with a hint of irony – that he anticipated Blanchot when in 1946 he stated that "words dissolve the object." Besides the slight competitiveness in claiming the ownership of an idea, it is clear that Caproni recognizes and acknowledges a poetic correspondence which is not so much based on the privileging of "things" as on their dissolution through language. Or better still, on the celebration of poetic language as the shelter of things. It is to language that Caproni offers his unconditional trust and this trust is based on nothing other than language's property of emptying its referent. It is in this sense that Caproni turns the apparent inadequacy of language inside out, founding his entire poetic project not on the alleged incapacity of language, but on the very power of this supposed incapacity. As in Benjamin, Caproni's language is a fragment, or, more precisely, a halo through which one can actually *see* the empty presence of the object. In March 1977, seven years after "Senza Esclamativi," Caproni returned with restored clarity to present his poetic word. Here is the poem "Le Parole," published in the collection *Il franco cacciatore* (the frank hunter): "Words. That's right./ They dissolve the object [*l'oggetto*]/ like the fog with trees/ the river: the ferry [*il traghetto*]."[27] Two verses of two lines separated by a blank space with a rhyme that calls up the object by unifying it in the house of language ("oggetto – traghetto"). But it is precisely because of the power of language, its supreme sheltering and guarding prowess – emphasized here by the rhetorical construction of the rhyme – that the object disappears behind the fog and the horizon. It is not that the object is not there, it is only that we cannot see it any longer. Or is it perhaps that we can see it better? But only if we accept seeing its emptiness through the prism of language. The simplicity of this poem is staggering, no less than its magisterial construction. See the engineer of words at work. Caproni breaks the syntax and the flow of language by assembling the words paratactically – obviously remembering the lesson of the other great Italian poet of small things, Giovanni Pascoli and his *Myricae* – simultaneously stressing their individuality and their being together, not only with other words, but also, and more importantly, with the silence of the blank space, and with words' resounding emptiness. There is no continuity, not even a discontinuity marked by *enjambements*, as in "Senza Esclamativi." There are instead walls of silence and emptiness, that undifferentiated silence that the characters in Blanchot's *L'Attente l'oubli* hear resonating and humming in their hotel room. What resonates is nothing other than the object as it disappears, as it departs, carried away on its vessel-shelter: "oggetto – traghetto."

SONO SENZA PAROLE

The word protects by clothing (and sheltering) our being with an aura of existence and purposefulness and by providing an image of what we are in the world. Being left wanting for words is a traumatic experience. There is a common expression in the Italian language which is used to express *sgomento* (anguish) as well as an extraordinary sense of vulnerability but also futility: *sono senza parole* (literally: I am without words). In this very short and colloquial saying, whose real meaning is no longer reflected upon, is the powerfully compacted sense of non-existence and the feeling of total loss. And this loss is first of all the loss of subjectivity. *Sono senza parole* means, in effect, "I do not exist," "I am transparent." This being translucent, surfaceless, is the real negativity of being and its irreducible emptiness. To be "without words" means to exist in the impossibility of self-manifestation and disclosure. It is neither the state of concealment nor that of unconcealment. It is rather the state of nothingness. The saying *sono senza parole* takes us out of the world. It is interesting that this saying and its considerable philosophical implications are used not only as a way of sharing the experience of pain, but also as a way of comforting those who suffered the pain. It is as if the pain of the other is met, and thus partly dissipated, by our voluntary departure from existence. The loss is counterbalanced by another loss. Following what we have discussed so far, the loss of language equates with the loss of subjectivity. Our being without words is our non-being. In this sense *sono senza parole* is synonymous with *sono senza me* (I am without me). What is also instructive is that the exit from being is enacted by a linguistic expression. So if it is true that we enter the world with language, it is also true that we exit it with language. Would it be possible, then, to interpret silence as the pause of subjectivity and the waiting of language? In other words, could silence be the resounding halo through which subjectivity *is* waiting to be again? Is this halo that Blanchot and Caproni make visible in their work?

ENDNOTES

This chapter is taken from a work in progress titled *About the Cultures of Translation, Exile and Writing* which is forthcoming with Purdue University Press. I would like to thank John Gatt-Rutter and Tony Stephens for their precious comments and suggestions.

[1] Giorgio Caproni, *L'opera in versi*, ed. Luca Zuliani (Milano: Mondadori, 1998), 1596, my trans. "Nel 1946 [dissi] che le parole dissolvono l'oggetto, però fu solo nel '53 che Blanchot lanciò il suo motto 'il nome vanifica le cose'."

[2] All these texts cited are held in the former library of Giorgio Caproni, Biblioteca dell'Orologio, Rome, Italy.

[3] *AwO* 3–4/*AO* 12. "Il la regardait à la dérobée. Peut-être parlait-elle, mais sur son visage nulle bienveillance à l'égard de ce qu'elle disait, nul consentement à parler, une affirmation à peine vivante, une souffrance à peine parlante. Il aurait voulu avoir le droit de lui dire: 'Cesse de parler, si tu veux que je t'entende.' Mais elle ne pouvait plus se taire à présent, même ne disant rien."

[4] *AwO* 4/*AO* 12. "Il se rendait bien compte qu'elle avait peut-être tout oublié. Cela ne le gênait pas. Il se demandait s'il ne désirait pas s'emparer de ce qu'elle savait, plus par l'oubli que par le souvenir. Mais l'oubli… Il lui fallait entrer, lui aussi, dans l'oubli."

[5] *AwO* 4/*AO* 13. "Mais je ne dirai rien, sachez-le. Ce que je dis n'est rien."

[6] Giorgio Caproni, *The Wall of the Earth*, trans. Pasquale Verdicchio (Montreal: Guernica, 1992), 48/ *L'opera*, 324. "Cosa volete ch'io chieda./ Lasciatemi nel mio buio./ Solo questo. Ch'io veda."

[7] Caproni, *The Wall*, 18/*L'opera*, 282. "'Confine', diceva il cartello./ Cercai la dogana. Non c'era./ Non vidi, dietro il cancello,/ ombra di terra straniera."

[8] Caproni, *The Wall*, 81/*L'opera*, 374. "Sono tornato là/ dove non ero mai stato./ Nulla, da come non fu, è mutato./ Sul tavolo (sull'incerato/ a quadretti) ammezzato/ ho ritrovato il bicchiere/ mai riempito. Tutto/ è ancora rimasto quale/ mai l'avevo lasciato."

[9] Caproni, *The Wall*, 88/ *L'opera*, 382. "Tutti i luoghi che ho visto,/ che ho visitato,/ ora so – ne son certo:/ non ci sono mai stato."

[10] *AwO* 4/*AO* 13. "Quelque chose lui est arrivé, et il ne peut dire que ce soit vrai, ni le contraire. Plus tard, il pensa que l'événement consistait dans cette manière de n'être ni vrai ni faux."

[11] *AwO* 4/*AO* 13. "Parole qu'il faut répéter avant de l'avoir entendue, rumeur sans trace qu'il suit, nulle part-errante, partout-séjournante, nécessité de la laisser aller. C'est toujours la vieille parole qui veut être là à nouveau sans parler."

[12] *AwO* 8/*AO* 19. "pauvreté dans le langage."

[13] *AwO* 6/*AO* 16. "ignorer ce qu'on sait, seulement cela."

[14] G.W.F. Hegel, *Werke in zwanzig Bänden*, vol. 1, *Frühe Schriften*, ed. Eva Moldenhauer and Karl Markus Michel (Frankfurt: Suhrkamp, 1971), 231. English translation in Giorgio Agamben, *Language and Death: The Place of Negativity*, trans. Karen Pinkus (Minneapolis: University of Minnesota Press, 1991), 6–9.

[15] Hegel, *Phenomenology of Spirit*, trans. A.V. Miller (Oxford: Oxford University Press, 1977), 58.

[16] Martin Heidegger, *Lettre à Monsieur Beaufret*, in *Lettre sur l'humanisme*, trans. Roger Munier (Paris: Éditions Montaigne, 1964), 182. English translation in Agamben, *Language and Death*, 4.

[17] Heidegger, *Off the Beaten Track*, trans. Julian Young and Kenneth Haynes (Cambridge: Cambridge University Press, 2002), 263.

[18] Heidegger, *Off the Beaten Track*, 265.

[19] Agamben, *Language and Death*, 13–4.

[20] *AwO* 8/*AO* 19. "Le désir qu'il avait de bien l'entendre avait depuis longtemps fait place à un besoin de silence dont tout ce qu'elle avait dit aurait formé le fond indifférent. Mais seule l'entente pouvait nourrir ce silence. Ils cherchaient l'un et l'autre la pauvreté dans le langage. Sur ce point, ils s'accordaient. Toujours, pour elle, il y avait trop de mots et un mot de trop, de plus des mots trop riches et qui parlaient avec excès. Bien qu'elle fût apparemment peu savante, elle semblait toujours préférer les mots abstraits, qui n'évoquaient rien. Est-ce qu'elle n'essayait pas, et lui avec elle, de se former au sein de cette histoire un abri pour se protéger de quelque chose que l'histoire aussi contribuait à attirer?"

[21] *AwO* 3/*AO* 11. "Il reprit les feuillets et écrivit: 'C'est la voix qui t'est confiée, et non pas ce qu'elle dit. Ce qu'elle dit, les secrets que tu recueilles et que tu transcris pour les faire valoir, tu dois les ramener doucement, malgré leur tentative de séduction, vers le silence que tu as d'abord puisé en eux.'"

[22] *AwO* 7/*AO* 17. "c'est une chambre d'hôtel, comme il en a toujours habité, comme il les aime, un hôtel de moyenne catégorie. Mais, dès qu'il veut la décrire, elle est vide, et les mots dont il se sert ne recouvrent que le vide."

[23] *AwO* 7/*AO* 18. "Pourtant avec quel intérêt elle le surveille, quand il lui dit: ici le lit, là une table, là où vous êtes un fauteuil."

[24] Heidegger, *Off the Beaten Track*, 267.

[25] Caproni, *The Wall*, 58/*L'opera*, 339. "Com'è alto il dolore./ L'amore com'è bestia./ Vuoto delle parole/ che scavano nel vuoto vuoti/ monumenti di vuoto. Vuoto/ del grano che già raggiunse/ (nel sole) l'altezza del cuore."

[26] See also the discussion of this point in my *Interstitial Writing: Calvino, Caproni, Sereni and Svevo* (Leicester: Troubador, 2003), xii.

[27] Caproni, *L'opera*, 460. "Le parole. Già./ Dissolvono l'oggetto./ Come la nebbia gli alberi,/ il fiume: il traghetto" (my trans.).

WHITE WORK

Elizabeth Presa

PLASTER IS MIXED AS A POWDER WITH WATER, POURED INTO MOULDS AS A slurry or modelled with the hands as a paste before it warms, thickens and sets. It expands as it heats, then shrinks and cools. As it solidifies drops of clear water weep from its surface. In its final state plaster remains soft enough to carve with simple metal tools and abrasives.

Plaster possesses extraordinary forensic properties to reproduce and imitate form, surfaces and textures. Life casts and death masks are used to preserve the image of the living and the dead. These casts replicate the features as well as the finest details of the face and body, including the pores, lines, scars and hair follicles of the skin. Plaster casts also preserve the various stages of clay sculpture before casting into bronze or carving in marble. Plaster is a medium of empathy and mimesis.

But plaster also possesses the most poetic of qualities in its delicacy and subtlety. When poured it shrouds and veils forms in an opaque liquidity. It mutes the dissonances between shapes, conceals imperfections, melds and elides surfaces and planes. It coats, clings and adheres. In intense light plaster appears as an opaque and impenetrable surface, yet at certain liminal moments, such as at dawn and dusk, plaster glows as though illuminated from within. At these times the articulation of surface detail and shadow subsides, giving way to a faint and even whiteness.

Plaster breathes. It respires, becomes damp to the touch absorbing and re-absorbing moisture in the atmosphere yet becomes crisp, parched and brittle when the humidity drops. It calcifies, fossilizes, and vitrifies.

The lime in plaster burns and peels the skin. But the lime also purifies and bleaches, distils sediment in liquid, and draws out impurities and residues. Water-based colour forms a chemical reaction with fresh plaster, which holds pigment as a deep skin of crystalline carbonate lime. In a fresco the image, as colour, is embodied, absorbed and held within the thickness of the plaster.

The ancient Greeks made plaster so exquisite in quality that it was equivalent to an artificial marble. It could be polished, Vitruvius tells us, till it would reflect the beholders face as in a mirror. And fine translucent sheets of polished plaster were used as windows in their temples. Water from the rivers, lakes, ponds, lagoons and bays was mixed with dry plaster. Thus, the once living water was stilled, set and frozen within a white calcification.

As a sculptor I have experimented for many years with the forensic and poetic qualities of plaster and have been intrigued by historical accounts of how others have used this medium. Rainer Maria Rilke's beautiful writing on Auguste Rodin's casting and working practices has been like a secret scripture for my own work. And when I started reading Maurice Blanchot some years ago, I could not help but be struck by his interest in images of casting and sculpting as well as by the apparent connections between his writing and that of Rilke. These connections were particularly evident in Blanchot's conceptualisation of textuality where the metaphor of the text as cast or death mask connects to an understanding of reading as a form of resuscitation or resurrection. Indeed, these links between the two writers prompted work I made for an installation entitled "Peel,"[1] as well as a current project which links skin patterns of jellyfish with the death mask of an unknown woman who drowned in the Seine, known as *L'Inconnue de la Seine.*[2] Both Rilke and Blanchot wrote about her death mask.[3] This essay, therefore, is prompted by my own interest in the materialization of textual metaphor through sculpture. It is an investigation of possible connections between the studio processes of Rodin, as observed and written about by Rilke, and Blanchot's understanding of textuality.

On display and in the reserve of the Rodin Museum in Paris are many of Rodin's plaster sculptures. They are often partial figures, fragments of bodies including arms, hands and feet, works without dates, without titles and without histories of enlargement, bronze casting or carving. They were not exhibited, seldom photographed or commented upon by visitors to the studio and critics. They were the unknown works of Rodin, the white works of plaster. Traditionally in sculpture, plaster marks an interval, a temporary and intermediary site between the living plasticity of the clay and the frozen permanence of the bronze cast or marble carving. Yet the processes that Rodin employed in making and remaking the works in plaster, including dipping them in liquid plaster, was his way of resuscitating and breathing new life and meaning into the remnants and the fragments that had belonged to his other sculptures. The liquid plaster had the effect of concealing discrepancies in proportion and the identity of sexual parts, and allowed even violent gestures to appear imprisoned within the form itself. It created a sense of the image withdrawing or turning back into the form, beneath an opaque veil.

The direct observation of the making of these unknown works had a profound influence on Rilke, who at the age of twenty-eight worked for some months as Rodin's private secretary. Two years after Rodin's death, Rilke wrote: "these fragmentary posthumous works are permanently assured of a link with their surviving *œuvre*."[4] These posthumous works were the collected remains, the "acres of fragments" from the major commissions and other exhibited works.

In a letter to his wife Clara, herself a student of Rodin, Rilke provides a description of a large pavilion of plaster casts in Rodin's garden at Meudon:

> It is a tremendously great and strange sight, this vast white hall with all its dazzling figures looking out from the many high glass doors like the denizens of an aquarium... You see, even before you have entered, that all these hundreds of lives are *one* life, – vibrations of one force and one will.[5]

The luminosity of the figures framed within the glass enclosure suggested some strange aquatic accretion comprised of hundreds of smaller organisms. This impression must have been most compelling at those times of the day, when in subdued light, plaster gives the appearance of emitting a glow. This glow has the effect of dissolving all surface detail and incident into a unified form. Such moments would have magnified the illusion of a singular though multifaceted organism contained behind the glass of the pavilion. Rilke recorded seeing some of the enormous glass-windows filled entirely with the fragments from the *Porte de l'Enfer*, Rodin's interpretation of Dante's *Inferno*. These works, submerged within the light of their environment, were the embodiment of dissolved suffering and unhappiness, as though plaster itself materialised all the images of fateful destiny, despair, death and suicide.

For Rilke the whole scene was "indescribable":

> Acres of fragments lie there, one beside the other. Nudes the size of my hand and no bigger, but only bits, scarcely one of them whole: often only a piece of arm, a piece of leg just as they go together, and the portion of the body which belongs to them. Here the torso of one figure with the head of another stuck onto it, with the arm of a third.[6]

This scene must have looked like some haunting collection of calligraphy, a raw and primal alphabet comprised of body parts whose syntax, lexicon, grammar and rules were still being negotiated. The particular poignancy of this scene would not have been lost on a young poet struggling to find the originary elements of a language which could form the structure of his work. Here was the sculptural equivalent to language laid bare, stripped of all convention, ornament and artifice. But it was a language that could be held, grasped, stuck together, made to speak in its own way according to its own laws -- a language of infinite generation and regeneration, that would endure all the grafting, shaping, wounding, breaking, scratching and carving performed by the sculptor. And the sea of whiteness laid out across the studio floor must have reminded the poet of his obligation to the page, the white ground of his work.

Throughout his monograph on Rodin, Rilke made frequent reference to these works, to their materiality and to their mystery:

> Here beside me is another work, a quiet face to which belongs a hand expressive of suffering, and the plaster has that transparent whiteness . . . and now I find myself among objects all of which are new and nameless . . . they keep no count of time. (*R* 67)

He described another work as: "A small thing whose name you have forgotten, made out of a white shining embrace which holds together like a knot" (*R* 50). What was "nameless" and what was "forgotten" in language nevertheless emerges in a stark materiality. This failure of language, its aphasia or poverty, stood in contrast to the apparent fluidity and eloquence of the small sculptures.

From his detailed observations of Rodin's studio practice, Rilke saw that what lay at the origin of the sculptors' achievement was a commitment to the observation of objects and processes located in the everyday. He identified a form of perception, a way of seeing, that enabled Rodin to treat the living and the dead, the organic and inorganic, as a singular substance, entity and "surface":

> There is only one single surface which suffers a thousand changes and transformations. It was possible to think of the whole world for a moment under this conception, so that it became simple, and was placed as a task in the hands of a man who so thought of it. For the endowment of an object with life of its own does not depend on great ideas but upon whether such ideas can create a metier, a daily labour, something that remains with one to the end. (*R* 49)

Through his efforts to understand what the sculptor had done and how he had succeeded in finding a daily process of working, Rilke came to understand what he himself had to do as a young poet and how he had to proceed as a maker of poems: "I must follow him, Rodin… Somehow I too must get down to the making of things; not plastic, written things, *but realities* springing from some handcraft."[7]

In exploring the possibilities for literature, Blanchot enters into dialogue with several writers including Rilke.[8] What Blanchot comes to term "the space of literature" is this ontological investigation of the experience from which art comes. Indeed, he describes Rilke's poetry as "the lyrical theory of the poetic act" ("The Disappearance of Literature", *BR* 139). Given Blanchot's fascination with the origins of art and his use of metaphors of death, dying and resurrection in his fictional as well as critical works, it is perhaps not surprising that he would be influenced by Rilke's accounts of the sculptor's studio. And one would imagine that Rilke's descriptions of the plaster fragments and processes of dipping and casting found particular resonance with Blanchot's sensibility. Indeed, Blanchot makes reference to both the forensic and poetic qualities of plaster in *Death Sentence* and in *Thomas the Obscure*. Furthermore, one could argue for deeper, underlying connections between Blanchot's aesthetic and understanding of textuality, and Rilke's descriptions of Rodin's sculpture, particularly the works in plaster. Perhaps the most fundamental connection is that writing, like plaster, has the capacity to take on a shape, to hold and set events in time with an exacting attention to the detail and texture of things. Writing allows time to coagulate around objects, spaces and events, setting them within the white opacity of the page.

Death Sentence embodies something of this congruence between writing and the process of plaster casting. The narrator in *Death Sentence* describes casting as "a process which is strange when it is carried out on living people, sometimes dangerous, surprising…" and there the sentence concludes with three dots leaving the reader to ponder what exactly Blanchot had in mind (*SHR* 183). The cast, whether as a plaster death mask or as a form of words in a text, becomes a simulacrum of the events it seeks to record. Impressions and sequences of events are captured and set as images within the work, just as the images of the two women in *Death Sentence* are set within the plaster casts. Furthermore, as J. Hillis Miller argues in *Versions of Pygmalion*, the cast of the story can be given an extended life through holding the text in our hands and reading. This act of reading is likened to a form of prosopopoeia, like Pygmalion giving life to the ivory sculpture.[9] Thus events that take place in time are cast in words, and then resuscitated or brought back to life through the act of reading.

An enactment of this process occurs in *Death Sentence*, with the "very beautiful" plaster cast of J's hand made by a sculptor who is later referred to as X. The narrator comments that he cannot describe J's hands "although at this very moment I have them under my eyes and they are alive."

> Their lines seemed to me altogether unusual – cross hatched, entangled, without the slightest apparent unity. . . . Moreover, these lines grew blurred sometimes, then vanished except for one deep central furrow . . . that line did not become distinct except at the moment when all the others were eclipsed; then the palm of her hand was absolutely white and smooth, a real ivory palm, while the rest of the time the hatchings and wrinkles made it seem almost old. (*SHR* 137)

Here the hands themselves become the face or the image of the text. The "blurring" and "vanishing" cross hatchings and wrinkles are like a biological calligraphy, a text of the skin susceptible to disease and wounding.

In his essay entitled "Reading" Blanchot privileges the isolation and resistance of sculpture over the book. He writes:

> The plastic work of art has a certain advantage over the verbal work of art in that it renders more manifest the exclusive void within which the work apparently wants to remain, far from everyone's gaze. (*SHR* 430)

Blanchot sees the act of reading as the book writing itself, writing itself "this time without the writer as intermediary" (*SHR* 431). The book unburdens itself of the "sometimes terrible, always dangerous" weight of the author. He writes:

> Reading endows the book with the kind of sudden existence that the statue "seems" to take from the chisel alone: the isolation that hides it from eyes that see it, the proud remoteness, the orphan wisdom that drives off the sculptor just as much as it does the look that tries to sculpt it again. (*SHR* 431)

Here is Blanchot's desire for the book as a work. As a work it must stand isolated – a thing in the world but not of the world – with its own laws and structure, its own cold hardness and self assuredness that will allow it to resist the gaze of anyone even the writer who tries to undo or tamper with what has already been set in place.

Blanchot's description of Rodin's *Balzac* as a work "without gaze, a closed and sleeping thing, absorbed in itself to such a degree that it disappears" (*SHR* 431), closely echoes Rilke, who in a note from 17 November 1900 writes:

> A sculpture which shares the same atmosphere with the viewer, must be better at "looking away." This means: it must be totally occupied with itself. This, too, Rodin has achieved to perfection: No viewer (not even the most conceited) will be able to claim that a bust by Rodin, say *Rochefort* or *Falguière*, let alone the inspired *Balzac*, has looked at him! (*R* 73)

And a few weeks later on 2 December 1900 he writes:

> There are sculptures which carry the environment in which they are imagined, or out of which they are raised, *within* themselves, they have absorbed it and they radiate it. The room in which a statue stands is its foreign land – it has its environment *within* itself, and its eye and the expression of its face relate to that environment concealed and folded within its shape. (*R* 74)

Here Rilke is describing the way Rodin's sculptures exist in perfect continuity within their own space, their own "foreign land."

It is as if Blanchot has this in mind when he characterizes the space of sculpture as:

> This decisive separation, which sculpture takes as its element and which sets out another, rebellious space in the centre of space – sets out a space that is at once hidden, visible, and shielded, perhaps immutable, perhaps without repose – this protected violence, before which we always feel out of place. (*SHR* 430)

This is a space of "complete self absorption" (*SHR* 430) that resists the gaze of the viewer as much as it frees the work from the maker. There is an absolute distance. The work is always facing the other way, back to an empty site. It stands isolated from its environment, from the viewer and the maker, within its own space, its own "foreign land." Again one could think of Rilke's account of the unruly space in those ancient sculptures in whose hieratic gestures "the restlessness of living surfaces was contained like water within the walls of a vessel" (*R* 14). However violent and turbulent the movement contained within a sculpture, and from wherever it comes, "it must return to the marble," Rilke writes, "the vast circle must be closed, that circle of solitude within which a work of art exists" (*R* 15).

Blanchot pursues the comparison between sculpture and the book by reference to burial, which is not so much an archaeological reference as an allusion to death and resurrection.

> The statue that is unearthed and displayed for everyone's admiration does not expect anything, does not receive anything, seems rather to have been torn from its place. But isn't it true that the book that has been exhumed, the manuscript that is taken out of a jar and enters the broad daylight of reading, is born all over again. (*SHR* 430)

The literary text in Blanchot's understanding requires the act of reading to come into existence. The burial of a sculpture, sometimes for centuries, creates a rich patination on the work of bronze or stone, the result of its coming into contact with the chemicals in the soil. Burial also preserves the work, protecting it from violence and harm. But whereas sculpture endures as in hibernation and thus emerges sacrosanct in its form and meaning, the written text diminishes in appearance and suffers indecipherability and illegibility. Its marks, notations, alphabets and syntactical structures and hence its meaning must be revealed, resuscitated and brought into living language.

The intersecting themes of burial and exhumation are referenced in *Thomas the Obscure*. Blanchot describes Thomas digging, for the seventh time, a hole in the earth. With his bare hands he moves aside the soft earth to fit his own shape. But as he does so the hole offers a resistance as if already filled by not so much a corpse of a man as an assemblage of gestures, hands and limbs. Blanchot writes:

> And while he was digging it, the hole, as if it had been filled by dozens of hands, then by arms and finally by the whole body offered a resistance to his work which soon became insurmountable. The tomb was full of a being whose absence was absorbed. An immovable corpse was lodged there, finding in this absence of shape the perfect shape of its presence. (*SHR* 73)

This grave, like the six dug previously, serves as a mould of Thomas's body, as, Blanchot writes, it is "exactly his size, his shape, his thickness." But the grave is already filled with Thomas's precise form, though this form is less the shape of an individual man than the assemblage of many parts of men. This recalls Rodin's practice of assembling numerous fragments of his figures to form a singular, but unknown and unnameable organism. Rilke writes:

> A hand laid on the shoulder or limb of another body is no longer part of the body to which it properly belongs: something new has been

formed from it and the object it touches or hold, something . . . which is nameless and belongs to no one. (*R* 19)

As Thomas struggles to bury himself within this shape filling the grave, he finds a body a "thousand times harder that the soil." The mould of his grave is already cast, just as the graves of the dead of Pompeii, who, buried in darkness for centuries, had the negative form of their incinerated bodies filled with liquid plaster. During the excavation of this ancient city, plaster poured into cavities solidified all the strange combinations of hands, gestures, knotted limbs and contorted bodies that had, until then, existed only in their absence.[10]

The description of Thomas's grave "filled by dozens of hands, then by arms" is suggestive of the many plaster hands and limbs kept amassed in drawers and on shelves in Rodin's studio. Rilke described these hands as independent from the body, yet alive with their own identity and history. He wrote of:

Criminal hands weighted by heredity. Hands that are tired and have lost all desire, lying like some sick beast crouched in a corner, knowing no one can help them . . . Hands have their own history, indeed their own civilization. (*R* 19)

It is as though all human suffering, grief and loss could be contained within a set vocabulary of forms, and that a part of a body, even the smallest part, had a capacity for representation equal to, if not greater than, the entire body. Similar images of an accumulation of body parts and gestures occur in Rilke's description of *The Burghers of Calais*, for in Rodin's memory:

There rose up gestures, gestures of renunciation, of farewell, of relinquishment. Endless gestures... It was as if a hundred heroic figures rose up within his memory... And he accepted the whole hundred and made of them six. He formed them nude, each by itself, in all the communicativeness of their shivering bodies. (*R* 36)

Blanchot describes Thomas buried, suffocated and "soaked in an icy medium... that resembles plaster" – an intermediate zone, "a prison where he was confined in impenetrable silence and darkness." Thomas, though suffocated, "managed to breath again" (*SHR* 74) and comes forward to walk beneath the pale light of an indifferent sun and falling stars. He is the "opaque corpse . . . becoming ever more dense, and, more silent than silence" (*SHR* 77) who walks past other dead, "breathing them, licking them, coating himself with their bodies" (*SHR* 78). This so closely resembles Rodin's desire to hold his work in an intermediate state and his process for doing so by re-casting and coating his figures in liquid plaster. This coating had the effect of veiling, muting and silencing the features of the sculpture. It provided a new surface to be inscribed, etched and scratched, gouged with a knife and remarked with graphite, and it also served to conceal the strangeness of chance combinations of body parts, the co-joined heads, sexes and limbs. In Rodin's hands this process held the image in abeyance allowing for the addition and subtraction of detail. That which withdraws beneath the plaster shows itself only as a subtle play of shadow creeping over the surface. Rodin's process of dipping portraits into liquid plaster served to withdraw and conceal the nakedness of the face, to hold the image in an interval, in order to turn it back into a more powerful presence.

In dipping his many idiosyncratic combinations of figurative fragments in plaster, in making features disappear then reappear through gouging and scratching back into the plaster, Rodin was making shadow the determinant of form. Plaster by its nature invites the revelation of form through the slow movement of shadow over its surface. This suggests a parallel with Blanchot's account of literature as a form of turning back:

> When in the depth of night, when everything has disappeared, disappearance becomes the density of the shadow that makes flesh more present, and makes this presence more heavy and more strange, without name and without form; a presence one cannot then call living or dead, but out of which everything equivocal about desire draws its truth. (*IC* 188)

Here one might think of Rodin's insistence that sculpture involve the lump and the hollow. Eye sockets and the mouths become sites where shadows form and slowly thicken. The strange vegetable-like anatomy reveals itself in the contours of darkness creeping over the white opaque surfaces. There shadow thickens about the portals framed by limbs, mouths, and folds of flesh and cloth.

And finally, Blanchot's description of Anne's embodiment in *Thomas the Obscure* bears a close resemblance to Rilke's accounts of sculpture. Anne's hardened body which "no longer cried out beneath the blows . . . made itself, at the price of its beauty, the equivalent of a statue" (*SHR* 104). As though composed of fragments, her body sustains infinite change and mutation. Blanchot describes Anne against a wall, her body having entered a pure void,

> [her] thighs and belly united to a nothingness with neither sex nor

sexual parts, hands convulsively squeezing an absence of hands, face drinking in what was neither breath nor mouth, she had transformed herself into another body . . . there too was body without head, head without body. (SHR 93)

Anne's body melds with that of Thomas. In her liquefied and "melted" form she is a *mélange* of sticky bodily fluids and vapours:

Her words became moist, even her weakest movements glued her against him, while within her swelled up the pocket of humours from which perhaps, at the proper moment, draw extreme power of adhesion. (*SHR* 81)

She was, Blanchot writes, "flesh being grafted." Like Rodin's unknown works of co-joined body parts, sexes and assembled fragments held together in a fresh skin of plaster, Anne merges with the body of the narrator:

She saw me with my eyes which she exchanged for her own, with my face which was practically her face, with my head which sat easily on *her* shoulders. She was already joining herself to me . . . she melted in me. (*SHR* 117)

As though herself a work of sculpture rather than of nature, Anne is described as:

A false figure emerged from the shadows, acquiring through a useless meticulousness a greater and greater precision and a more artificial one. (*SHR 87*)

Through a futile but meticulous accumulation of detail, she acquires through artifice, the semblance of a living woman. Anne, who has suffered a thousand changes and transformations, becomes a work, a thing, a simple thing, or in Rilke's words:

Something that came into existence blindly, through the fierce throes of work, bearing upon it the marks of exposed and threatened life, still warm with it – to take its place amongst the other things, assume their indifference, their quiet dignity, and looked on as it were, from a distance and from its own permanence with melancholy consent. (*R* 47)

Anne emerges as a "thing," in the world but not of the world. Disembodied, pithed and emptied, she is devoid of a sense of proprioception. With a "greater and greater precision and a more artificial one," she emerges, adapting her gait, posture, pose and form through an exact and detailed attention. She emerges as a veiled, blanched, melancholy presence, a presence held in reserve. Her materiality is no longer that of the modelled clay and mud of the earth, but that of a white porous and opaque vitrification bathed in light and shadow. In this sense Anne, like the two women in *Death Sentence*, is a literary equivalent to the white works of Rodin, whose aesthetic, Blanchot had so completely digested and transformed. Thus, writing desires to be the plaster cast, "that thing" that remains:

> And now that thing is over there, you have uncovered it, you have looked at it, and you have looked into the face of something that will be alive for all eternity, for your eternity and for mine! Yes, I know it. I know it. I've known it all along. (*SHR* 185)

And in reverse and in reflection it is through the writings of Maurice Blanchot that I now know – perhaps sculptors have known it all along – that giving a face to language requires silence and the tactful touch of distance.

ENDNOTES

[1] An exhibition held at Éditions Galilée, Paris, January 2004. The exhibition was based on Jacques Derrida's text, *Chaque fois unique, la fin du monde* (Galilée, 2003), and was enacted as a work of mourning. See www.elizabethpresa.com/peel.html. See also the front cover of the present volume.

[2] An installation entitled "Moon Water" which comprised of photos of the moon over the Seine in Paris, and the plaster and gauze moulds made of hundreds of jelly-fish (medusas). The plaster was used to make visible the variety of lines and patterns of skin of the normally translucent sea creatures. ("He had studied Paracelsus fairly seriously and devoted himself to conducting experiments that were sometimes outrageous and sometimes childish . . . he was, it seems to me, a great deal more reliable in his diagnosis than most", *DS* 136.) The photos and moulds bring together a nocturnal scene between two hemispheres; between the sky and the water, and the river and the sea. The alchemist and astrologer Paracelsus believed that the moon impregnates the substance of water with a noxious influence, and that water, which has been exposed to lunar rays for a long time, remains poisoned water. He wrote that "the moon gives to those whom it influences a taste for water from the Styx."

The plaster moulds become vessels of white opaque skin – small sepulchres for the delicate remains of creatures that once swarmed in the moonlight. Each takes on the lunar roundness of a face – an inversion and disfigurement that exposes with the hard resistance of eyes without protection, what is softest and most uncovered. See www.elizabethpresa.com/moonwater.html

³ Rilke wrote about the death mask of "L'Inconnue de la Seine," the name given to the death mask made of a young girl found drowned in the Seine at the quai du Louvre in the late nineteenth century. During the first decades of the twentieth century copies of a young woman's death mask were widely sold in France and in Germany and hung on the walls of many houses. In Rilke's *The Notebooks of Malte Laurids Brigge* the young narrator passed the mask everyday. "The mouleur, whose shop I passed everyday, has hung two masks behind his door. The face of the young drowned woman, which they took a cast of in the morgue, because it was beautiful, because it smiled, because smiled so deceptively, as if it knew." Rilke, *The Notebooks of Malte Laurids Brigge*, trans. Stephen Mitchell (New York: Random House, 1982), 76. Rilke also writes of her in the third of the *Duino Elegies*.

Blanchot kept a cast of the famous death mask of "L'Inconnue de la Seine" in the room he used most often at his small house at Èze, where he lived from 1947. He describes it as "une adolescente aux yeux clos, mais vivante par un sourire si délié, si fortuné . . . qu'on eût pu croire qu'elle s'était noyée dans un instant d'extrême bonheur [an adolescent with closed eyes, but enlivened by a smile, so relaxed, so rich . . . that one may be lead to believe that she died in a moment of extreme happiness]." Maurice Blanchot, *Une voix venue d'ailleurs* (Paris: Gallimard, 2002), 15. (*A Voice From Elsewhere*, trans. Charlotte Mandell, SUNY Press, forthcoming.) I thank Christophe Bident for drawing my attention to this passage.

⁴ Rainer Maria Rilke, "The Rodin Book", *Rodin and Other Prose Pieces* (London: Quartet Encounters, 1986), 71. This volume hereafter cited parenthetically as *R*.

⁵ Rilke, *Selected Letters 1902–1926* (London: Quartet Encounters, 1988), 5.

⁶ Rilke, *Selected Letters 1902–1926*, 5.

⁷ Rilke, Letter of 10 August 1903 to Lou Andreas–Salomé, *Selected Letters 1902–1926*, 36.

⁸ See for example "The Essential Solitude" in *SHR* and "Artaud (1956)", in *BR*.

⁹ J. Hillis Miller, *Versions of Pygmalion* (Cambridge, Mass.: Harvard University Press, 1990), 186–7.

¹⁰ Jean Genet offers the following description, published in 1958, of Giacometti's plaster and bronze figures: "His statues seem to belong to a former time, to have been discovered after time and night- which worked on them with intelligence – had corroded them to give them that both sweet and hard feeling of eternity that passes. Or rather, they emerge from an oven, remnants of a terrible roasting. Giacometti tells me that he once had the idea of molding a statue and burying it. . . . Would burying it be to offer it to the dead?" Jean Genet, "The Studio of Alberto Giacometti", in *Fragments of the Artwork*, trans. Charlotte Mandell (Stanford: Stanford University Press, 2003), 53.

CONTRIBUTORS

PAOLO BARTOLONI teaches Italian and comparative literature at the University of Sydney. He is the author of *Interstitial Writing: Calvino, Caproni, Sereni and Svevo* (2003), the editor of *Re-Claiming Diversity: Essays on Comparative Literature* (1996) and co-editor of *Intellectuals and Publics: Essays on Cultural Theory and Practice* (1997). His new book, *About the Cultures of Exile, Translation and Writing*, will be published by Purdue University Press in 2006.

CHRISTOPHE BIDENT teaches at Université Paris 7 – Denis Diderot. He is the author of numerous articles and three books: *Maurice Blanchot, partenaire invisible. Essai biographique* (1998); *Bernard-Marie Koltès, Généalogies* (2000); and *Reconnaissances – Antelme, Blanchot, Deleuze* (2003). He co-scripted the film *Maurice Blanchot* (1998), produced by Hugo Santiago.

CHRIS DANTA completed a PhD at Monash University, Melbourne, on the figuring of Abraham in Kierkegaard, Kafka and Blanchot. He now teaches and works as a research assistant in the School of English at the University of New South Wales.

CHRISTOPHER FYNSK is professor of Comparative Literature and Director of the Centre for Modern Thought at the University of Aberdeen, Scotland. He is the author of *Heidegger: Thought and Historicity* (1986), *Language and Relation* (1996), *Infant Figures* (2000), and *The Claim of Language: A Case for the Humanities* (2004).

KEVIN HART is Notre Dame Professor of English at the University of Notre Dame where he is also Concurrent Professor of Philosophy. He is the author of *The Trespass of the Sign: Deconstruction, Theology, and Philosophy* (1989), *A. D. Hope* (1992), *Samuel Johnson and the Culture of Property* (1999), *Postmodernism* (2004) and *The Dark Gaze: Maurice Blanchot and the Sacred* (2004). He is the editor of *The Oxford Book of Australian Religious Verse* (1994) and *Counter-Experiences: Reading*

Jean-Luc Marion (2006), and the co-editor of *The Power of Contestation: Perspectives on Maurice Blanchot* (2004) and *Derrida and Religion: Other Testaments* (2004) and *The Experience of God* (2005). He is the author of seven volumes of poetry, the most recent being *Flame Tree: Selected Poems* (2002).

LESLIE HILL is Professor in the Department of French Studies at the University of Warwick, and the author of *Beckett's Fiction: In Different Words* (1990), *Marguerite Duras: Apocalyptic Desires* (1993), *Blanchot: Extreme Contemporary* (1997), and *Bataille, Klossowski, Blanchot: Writing at the Limit* (2001). He is currently working on a study of fragmentary writing in Blanchot.

MICHAEL HOLLAND is a Fellow of St Hugh's College, Oxford. He is the editor of *The Blanchot Reader* (1995) and the author of a number of articles on Blanchot. He is currently preparing a book on Blanchot's fiction. A study of two plays by Eugène Ionesco appeared in 2005. He is a founding editor of *Paragraph: A Journal of Critical Theory*. A special issue of the journal, devoted to Blanchot, co-edited by Michael Holland and Leslie Hill, is forthcoming in 2007.

ELEANOR KAUFMAN is Assistant Professor of Comparative Literature and French at the University of California, Los Angeles. She is author of *The Delirium of Praise: Bataille, Blanchot, Deleuze, Foucault, and Klossowski* (2001) and co-editor of *Deleuze and Guattari: New Mappings in Politics, Philosophy, and Culture* (1998).

HECTOR KOLLIAS received his PhD in Philosophy and Literature from the University of Warwick for a study of German Romanticism and deconstruction, and currently lectures in French at King's College, London. His main research interests lie in the relation between philosophy and literature, as inaugurated by German Romanticism and continued in continental thought of the 20th century. He is also working on the interaction between psychoanalysis and queer theory, and is currently writing a book-length study of French queer writers and theorists in an attempt to 'reclaim' the psychoanalytic notion of perversion for queer theory. He is the author of forthcoming articles on Jean Genet and Jean-Luc Nancy.

BRIAN NELSON is Professor of French Studies at Monash University, Melbourne, and editor of the *Australian Journal of French Studies*. His publications include *Zola and the Bourgeosie* and, as editor, *Naturalism in the European Novel: New Critical Perspectives* and *Forms of Commitment: Intellectuals in Contemporary France.* He has translated and edited Zola's *The Ladies' Paradise* (*Au Bonheur des Dames*), *Pot Luck* (*Pot-Bouille*) and *The Kill* (*La Curée*) for Oxford World's Classics. His current projects include *The Cambridge Companion to Emile Zola.*

ELIZABETH PRESA is the Head of the Centre For Ideas at the Victorian College of the Arts, Melbourne. She is a sculptor and installation artist who has exhibited in Asia, France and the United States. In 2002 she was artist-in-residence at Nanyang Academy of Fine Arts, Singapore, and the recipient of the Power Institute scholarship for a six-month residency at the Cité Internationale des Arts, Paris. In January 2004 Éditions Galilée, Paris, presented an exhibition of her work focusing on *Chaque fois unique, la fin du monde* by Jacques Derrida.

ROBERT SAVAGE works in the Centre for Comparative Literature and Cultural Studies, Monash University, Australia. He has published on German Critical Theory and modern Australian poetry.

CAROLINE SHEAFFER-JONES teaches in the School of Modern Language Studies at the University of New South Wales. Her main research interests are critical theory and the works of twentieth-century francophone writers, including Blanchot, Camus, Carrier, Cocteau and Kofman.

ALAIN TOUMAYAN is Associate Professor in the Department of Romance Languages and Literatures and Director of the Program in Literature and Philosophy, University of Notre Dame. He has published three books and various articles on 19th and 20th-century subjects. His most recent book is *Encountering the Other: The Artwork and the Problem of Difference in Blanchot and Levinas* (2004). His current research project looks at the figuration of otherness in Balzac, Flaubert, Baudelaire, and Maupassant. He is also working on Levinas' concept of responsibility in relation to the doctrine of "the responsibility to protect."

DIMITRIS VARDOULAKIS teaches at the Victorian College of the Arts and at Monash University. His articles have appeared in Greek and in English, recently in *Walter Benjamin and History* (2005). Translations into Greek include Alasdair Gray's *Poor Things* (2001) and Peter Lyssiotis's *The Bird, The Belltower* (2005). He is co-editor of the journal *Colloquy* and has guest-edited with Andrew Benjamin a special issue of *Angelaki* journal on "The Politics of Place" (2004).

INDEX